THE CARIBBEAN POSTCOLONIAL

The Caribbean Postcolonial

Social Equality, Post-Nationalism, and Cultural Hybridity

Shalini Puri

palgrave
macmillan

First published 2004 by
PALGRAVE MACMILLAN™
175 Fifth Avenue, New York, N.Y. 10010 and
Houndmills, Basingstoke, Hampshire, England RG21 6XS
Companies and representatives throughout the world.

PALGRAVE MACMILLAN is the global academic imprint of the Palgrave Macmillan division of St. Martin's Press, LLC and of Palgrave Macmillan Ltd. Macmillan® is a registered trademark in the United States, United Kingdom and other countries. Palgrave is a registered trademark in the European Union and other countries.

ISBN 978–1–4039–6182–2

Library of Congress information on this book is available from the Library of Congress.
A catalogue record for this book is available from the British Library.

Design by Newgen Imaging Systems (P) Ltd., Chennai, India.

First edition: January, 2004
10 9 8 7 6 5 4 3 2 1

Printed in the United States of America.

Transferred to Digital Printing in 2008

for my teachers,
in gratitude

and

for Leela Sofía,
who each day shows me
the dancing word

Contents

Permissions

First and foremost, I would like to thank the numerous calypsonians and composers who permitted me to quote their work: Errol Ballantyne (Bally), Leroy Calliste (Black Stalin), Barnet Henry, Franz Lambkin (Delamo), Hollis Liverpool (Mighty Chalkdust), and Andrew Marcano (Lord Superior).

I am grateful to Louis Regis, Keith Warner, and Donald Hill for sharing their experience with me as I sought permissions. Thanks are due to the Copyright Organisation of Trinidad and Tobago and The Performing Right Society in England for helping me locate members. Every effort was made to contact composers and performers before quoting their work.

Warmest thanks to Pascal Meccariello for permitting me to use his art installation entitled "Window onto Paradise" on the cover of my book, and to Camille King for taking the photograph.

I am grateful to Ramabai Espinet for giving me permission to quote her story "Barred: Trinidad 1987." Thanks to New Beacon Press for permission to quote Erna Brodber's novel *Myal*; to Monthly Review Press for permission to quote from José Martí's "Our America"; to South Bank Centre and Yale University Press for permission to quote Oswald de Andrade's "Anthropohagite Manifesto" from their *Art in Latin America: The Modern Era, 1820–1980.* (The manifesto originally appeared in *Revista de Antropofagia* n. 1, May 1928 in São Paulo.) To Farrar, Strauss, and Giroux, thanks for granting me permission to quote from Derek Walcott's poem "A Far Cry from Africa," which was featured in *Collected Poems 1948–1984*, Walcott's play *Pantomime*, and his Nobel-Prize lecture, *The Antilles: Fragments of Epic Memory.* Thanks to Oxford University Press for allowing me to quote excerpts of "Calypso" and "Pebbles" from Kamau Brathwaite's *The Arrivants: A New World Trilogy.* Complete bibliographic citations for all these texts appear in the Works Cited at the end of the book.

Parts of chapter six and substantial sections of chapter seven have previously appeared in *Cultural Critique* 36 (Spring 1997) under the title "Race, Rape, and Representation: Indo-Caribbean Women and Cultural Nationalism." Brief parts of chapters one, two, and seven were included in my essay "Canonized Hybridities, Resistant Hybridities: Chutney-Soca, Carnival, and the Politics of Nationalism" in Belinda Edmondson, ed., *Caribbean Romances: The Politics of Regional Representation* (University Press of Virginia, 1999). An early version of chapter five appeared in *ARIEL: A Review of International Literature in English* 24.3 (July 1993) under the title "An 'Other' Realism: Erna Brodber's *Myal*."

I am grateful to the Richard D. and Mary Jane Edwards Endowed Publication Fund for helping to defray the cost of permissions.

Acknowledgments

This project began in 1990, when cultural hybridity was just emerging as the *episteme regnant* of Postcolonial Studies. I was fortunate to have an able and dedicated doctoral committee, consisting of Professors Biodun Jeyifo, Debra Castillo, Walter Cohen, and Satya Mohanty, who have continued to be well-wishers and interlocutors. I am especially grateful to B.J. for his suggestions on my book manuscript, which had become a very different creature from the dissertation he read.

My continuing daily collaboration with Carlos Cañuelas also stretches back to those days as a graduate student. There is no convention of acknowledgment that permits me to register adequately the extent of his involvement, insight, and support in this project, or the joyful context in which it unfolded.

I am grateful to Fiona Cheong for her subtle and uncompromising reading of my manuscript. Nothing escapes her eyes. I thank her for her counsel—conceptual, artistic, strategic—and for delighting my daughter while I worked. She has defined friendship for me.

To Kajri Jain, deep thanks for the daunting reach of her insights, and for the modesty, humor, and affection with which they were delivered.

To Nancy Glazener I owe more than I can say. Her readings of my work unfailingly refreshed my thinking, epitomizing in miniature all that a brilliant reader outside one's field of specialization can offer. She was an indefatigable reader, whose comments combind generosity and rigor—and rivaled my manuscript in length! Her friendship was an added gift.

Chapter three, in particular, first began as a result of Nancy's pushing me to account for the immense popularity of discourses of hybridity. My thinking about chapter three also benefited greatly from exchanges with Luiza Moreira, Janet Lyon, Gerard Aching, Kathryn Flannery, Carlos Cañuelas, and Kajri Jain.

Special thanks also to Susan Andrade for many stimulating readings and warm conversations.

For their collegial goodwill and friendship, encouragement, and insightful readings of drafts of several chapters, I am grateful to Jonathan Arac, Dave Bartholomae, Eric Clarke, Cathy DenTandt, Kathryn Flannery, Olakunle George, Shuchi Kapila, Mark Kemp, Jim Knapp, Geeta Kothari, Colin MacCabe, Laura Murray, Mimi Sheller, and Mariolina Salvatori. For his calm good humor and the interest he took in the project, thanks to Paul Foster.

I worked out many of the ideas in this book in dialogue with my students in my graduate seminars on Caribbean Literature and Postcolonial Discourse. I am especially grateful to Patricia Saunders for the vibrancy and texture of our conversations about Trinidad over the years.

My work in Trinidad benefited from the insights of several colleagues. For clarifications, criticisms, and conversations, I am indebted to Sara Abraham, Peter Hanoomansingh, Indira Maharaj, Prabhu Mohapatra, Tejaswini Niranjana, Takashi Osugi, Carol Prorok, Rhoda Reddock, Gordon Rohlehr, Burton Sankeralli, Kevin Yelvington, and the often explosive exchanges with participants in the Conference on the Indian Diaspora held in Trinidad in August 1995.

My initial fieldwork in Trinidad, which was decisive for the directions that chapters 6 and 7 took, was enabled by a graduate student grant from Cornell University. I was also the appreciative recipient of University of Pittsburgh's Faculty of Arts and Sciences Faculty Research Grants, Hewlett International Grant, and Center for Latin American Studies Faculty Grant, as well as a postdoctoral fellowship from the Center for the Humanities of Oregon State University at Corvallis.

My editor Kristi Long's extraordinary efficiency, flexibility, and encouragement was a boon. It was a pleasure to work with her and later with Farideh Koohi-Kamali, Roee Raz, Melissa Nosal, and Sonia Wilson at Palgrave. I am grateful also to the anonymous readers of my manuscript for their suggestions. Mary Seneviratne and April Sikorski provided efficient and imaginative research assistance. Salomé Skvirsky worked on the index with characteristic energy, thoroughness, and insight.

Finally, there are those whose gifts to this book are of a different order altogether: Carlos, again; my parents Amrita and Arjun Puri; and my brother Abhay Puri. Their love, encouragement, and faith in my abilities never wavered. My daughter Leela Sofía demanded weeks out of my work schedule, but in her inimitable way, refreshed them and gave them back.

I have been extraordinarily fortunate in my friends, family, and colleagues. But I finished my book in the shadow of a loss. Two people, ideal readers whom I had always assumed would read this, did not live to see its completion: Christopher Raleigh and Jan Friese. I remember them with this book.

Introduction

The Caribbean Postcolonial treats the Caribbean as both an instance and an interrogation of postcoloniality. Its central project is to consider the range of ways in which different discourses of cultural hybridity have functioned as strategies for constructing, deconstructing, and reconfiguring trans/national imaginaries. So doing involves examining how theories of hybridity move between the space of political representation and the space of aesthetic representation. At the heart of the book, then, is an attempt to understand the ways in which cultural forms participate in politics.

My guiding political questions in this study, as well as my provisional answers, are enabled by marxist cultural theory. What is the relationship between cultural hybridity and social equality? Is one possible without the other? Can they reinforce each other or do they compete with each other? What are the material interests to which particular discourses of hybrid identity are attached? According to what logics are particular hybridities consecrated and others disavowed? Are there more and less egalitarian critiques of so-called pure identities? What might a hybridity that threatens the domestic and/or international status quo look like? How might it redraw existing lines of class, race, and gender power? What are the terms on which elements of the nation are included in or excluded from the national narrative, and what are the possibilities for reconfiguring those terms? As the feminist philosopher Nancy Fraser puts it, a transformative rather than merely affirmative notion of difference would require a combination of socialism and deconstruction (32), the former emphasizing a deep restructuring of relations of production, a blurring of group differentiation, and a remedying of some forms of misrecognition; the latter emphasizing a deep restructuring of relations of recognition and a destabilization of group differentiation (27). The crucial point is that "cultural differences can be freely elaborated and democratically mediated only on the basis of social equality" (186).

At the core of my work is the belief that we need to connect a poetics of hybridity to a politics of equality. In this study, "equality" is a necessarily open-ended term, the meanings, reach, and sites of which may continually expand through social struggles. In the course of the book I consider several examples of hybrid identities—creole, *jíbaro, mestizo*, mulatto, dougla—each of which inflects "equality" differently. Part I of this book addresses the directly sociopolitical mobilizations of such terms. However, these identities are also focal points for aesthetic and cultural imaginings (which in turn have political imports). Thus, our understanding of particular articulations of hybridity can only be deepened by considering them in relation to genre, form, performance, and the everyday practices in which they are embedded. Part II of the book is devoted to these specifically aesthetic and cultural questions.

The Caribbean, first site of European colonization, yields productive insights into these questions.[1] In several ways, it can test many of the generalized claims we make about cultural hybridity. First, the Caribbean has some of the earliest and richest elaborations of cultural hybridity. The sheer number and nuance of the Caribbean's accounts of hybridity, its diverse sources, modalities, and consequences, are unparalleled in any other region of the world. As an archipelago whose culture was forged in the crucible of colonialism and slavery from what Derek Walcott has called a "shipwreck of fragments," discourses of hybridity have been central to the Caribbean's political culture. For the Caribbean has had to negotiate its identities in relation to Native America; to Africa and Asia, from where most of its surviving inhabitants came; to Europe, from where its colonizing settlers came; and to the United States of America, its imperial neighbor. The Caribbean can justly claim to have some of the world's earliest global cities. In addition, Caribbean nations have had to position themselves politically in relation to the New World, the Third World, the socialist bloc, and one another. Some of the most innovative poetics of hybridity—from Creole poetics, to mulatto aesthetics, to magic and marvelous realism—have emerged from the region.

Yet Latin America and the Caribbean (particularly the non-Anglophone Caribbean) have been marginalized from the canon of a Postcolonial Studies still dominated by the English Crown and still often conceived in terms of East/West binaries. The Caribbean, of course, is a "Western" neo/colony and can deepen our understanding of a hybridity conceived neither in exclusively East/West, nor even in North/South terms. To the extent that the Caribbean has entered into postcolonial discussions of hybridity, it has often been in the form of *proof* of metropolitan claims for cultural hybridity, or a figure for them. (Thus James Clifford declares: "We are Caribbeans in our urban archipelagoes."[2]) But Caribbean discourses of hybridity do not only prefigure or confirm our current concerns; they also have important *cautionary* lessons to teach us. There is indeed something of the arrogance of Columbus's claims to Discovery in our own metropolitan relationship to hybridity discourse, for the latter has flourished, and been theorized and contested by the "natives" for at least a hundred years, yet our own breathless rhetoric often celebrates it as the New World of Theory or the promise of El Dorado.[3] Thus, in contrast to the approach that somewhat appropriatively generalizes from the experience of "the" Caribbean to a global condition, I have taken the approach of further *specifying* Caribbean elaborations of hybridity. For it seems to me we are better served by terms such as *mestizaje*, creolization, douglarization, *jibarismo*, and the like—not because any one of them constitutes a perfected discourse, model, or explanation, but because the multiplicity of terms itself helps keep visible the specificities and histories of each term. In contrast, the umbrella term "hybridity" enacts a dehistoricizing conflation. (Ironically, hybridity itself may be on its way to subsumption under the still broader term "globalization," the newer discourse with claims to master-narrativity.) In fact, with its array of conflicting discourses of hybridity, the Caribbean example suggests we should be wary of any generalization about cultural hybridity. It is in part from a desire to study the immense diversity of actually existing hybridities rather than ideal types of hybridity that I have chosen to make the Caribbean the site of my case studies. I have thus tried to be faithful to the marxist injunction to, in Fredric Jameson's famous phrasing, "Always historicize!" (*The Political Unconscious* 9).

Few theoretical terms have achieved cultural hybridity's energetic endorsement from across the political spectrum. That cultural hybridity has done so invites attention to the malleability of the term—a malleability that I believe should preclude absolutist endorsements or condemnations of the term. Undoubtedly, one source of the increasing appeal over the last fifteen years of the rhetoric of cultural hybridity lies in its refusal of racist purisms. Beyond that common denominator, however, the discursive genealogies and implications of discourses of cultural hybridity are more complex than current celebrations of it admit. Robert Young's historical study, *Colonial Desire: Hybridity in Theory, Culture and Race*, an illuminating account of the role hybridity played in nineteenth-century literary and cultural discourses of "Englishness" (such as Matthew Arnold's), scientific racial/racist discourse (such as Gobineau's), and debates over the monogenist or polygenist origins of mankind, demonstrates that neither "cultural hybridity" nor the older theories of race in opposition to which cultural hybridity is often mobilized is as essential or fixed as we have retrospectively constructed them to be (27). Moreover, racial purism was not the only narrative resource of racism; racial hybridity was also one. Thus, Young cautions us to remember that when we invoke the concept of cultural hybridity, "we are utilizing the vocabulary of the Victorian extreme Right as much as the notion of an organic process of the grafting of diversity into singularity" (10). Whereas the proliferation of the plural in cultural criticism today ("musics," "englishes," "peoples," etc.) marks an anti-essentialist and liberal relativist impulse, Young reminds us that in the nineteenth century the use of the plural "civilizations" often represented not a liberal cultural relativism, but a polygenist emphasis on the absoluteness of racial and cultural difference (49).[4] Moreover, both the history of discourses of racial hybridity (rooted in anxiety about the production of miscegenated children) and the metaphorical application of the term to describe culture mean that "hybridity as a cultural description will always carry with it an implicit politics of heterosexuality, which may be a further reason for contesting its contemporary pre-eminence" (Young 25).[5] Similarly, Lola Young warns of the risks attending the term's slide from the context of animal husbandry to interracial human sexual activity to human cultural and artistic endeavor (157). And Pnina Werbner notes the paradox that "hybridity is celebrated as powerfully interruptive and yet theorized as commonplace and pervasive"; it is both routine and transgressive (1). In liberal multicultural discourse cultural hybridity has long offered a way of advancing culturalist notions of difference as inclusion or nonconflictual diversity; it functions there as an assimilationist discourse at a time when "separate" ethnic identities and inequalities threaten to become unmanageable. But far from resolving the crisis of multicultural societies, particular hybrid identities have been intimately connected with modes of both domination and resistance. In contemporary corporate discourse, the cultural hybridity symbolized by the "global village" provides an enabling discourse for the aggressive economic expansion of capital, the terms and terminology of which are increasingly marking not just the discourse of Economics, Business, and Communication in the academy, but also the discourse of the Humanities and Cultural Theory—arguably compromising their potential as a "critical" discourse.

My point is not that the long and often unsavory history of the idea of hybridity prohibits its appropriation by other agendas but that it should alert us to the *precariousness* of such appropriations. Throughout, I show that the political economy of cultural hybridity entails both progressive and conservative filiations and alliances. It is therefore toward not only the inclusions but also the exclusions of these discourses that I direct my attention.

My attempt at historicizing our understanding of cultural hybridity takes the form of a conjuncturalist methodology. This permits me to draw attention to the historical specificities of different discourses, specificities which reveal a variety that can be absorbed into any absolutist claim only through drastic simplification and reduction. As Ella Shohat has pointed out in her essay "Notes on the 'Post-colonial,'"

> A celebration of syncretism and hybridity per se, if not articulated in conjunction with questions of hegemony and neo-colonial power relations, runs the risk of appearing to sanctify the *fait accompli* of colonial violence. . . . As a descriptive catch-all term, hybridity per se fails to discriminate between the diverse modalities of hybridity, for example, forced assimilation, internalized self-rejection, political cooptation, social conformism, cultural mimicry, and creative transcendence. (109–110)

Shohat's insight is important not only for its delineation of the different epistemologies of cultural hybridity, but also for their relationship to political economy. In my investigation of cultural hybridity in both the Caribbean and the contemporary metropolitan academy, I have tried to resist framing cultural hybridity as exclusively or perhaps even primarily an epistemological category, and have attempted to read the diverse epistemologies themselves in conjunctural terms.[6]

For cultural hybridity does not only contain internal epistemological contradictions and differences; epistemologically *similar* discourses of hybridity may be harnessed to quite different political projects (from bourgeois nationalism and dependent capitalism to socialism or fascism). It is therefore important to read particular discourses of hybridity not only in themselves, but also in relation to other available cultural discourses at the time. Thus, for example, the meanings of creolization lie not only in texts about creolization, but in historical intertexts of both racist-purist and racist-hybridist beliefs, discourses of négritude, and so on. Similarly, the functions of *mestizaje* become clearer in relation to discourses of *insularismo*, *indigenismo*, *cubanidad*, *negrismo*, and *socialismo*. Furthermore, discourses of hybridity are conjuncturally framed by particular alignments of economic, military, and ideological forces that bear on both the projects and the pragmatic possibilities of the discourses. A conjunctural approach, then, allows us to study the shifting functions, effects, and possibilities of the *same* discourse at different conjunctures, thereby resisting two temptations: that of reducing its epistemological and utopian value to its historically realized political effects, and that of inflating its epistemological possibilities in disregard of the horizon of political possibility. Finally, a conjunctural analysis of hybridity requires us to seriously engage the contemporaneous *local* contestations and critiques of cultural hybridity. These critiques have circulated widely in the Caribbean and Latin America, yet because they have not been studied adequately in the mainstream of metropolitan Postcolonial Studies, their insights have been lost to the latter. A conjunctural reading thus asks that we read the historical moment in question, rather than raid it for material that fits current needs and models.

For example, the purist discourse characteristic of so many nationalist and imperialist projects that metropolitan theories of hybridity have been devoted to overturning has simply not been available to Caribbean nationalisms. (This is, of course, a very different proposition from saying that racist discourse has not been available to Caribbean nationalisms.) Instead, invocations of cultural hybridity have been crucial to Caribbean nationalisms. Caribbean history can thus help explain what current mobilizations of discourses of cultural hybridity to deconstruct homogenizing and/or racist nationalisms cannot: the tremendous appeal of cultural hybridity to so many nation-building projects, and indeed to several racist and classist discourses as well as egalitarian ones. Caribbean discourses thus undo the generalized claim that hybridity and the nation-state are opposed to one another and enable a broader questioning of invocations of a "global village" and the death of the nation-state.

By investigating a range of nationalist mobilizations of discourses of cultural hybridity, I will argue for both the prematurity of declarations of the demise of the nation-state and the error of many accounts that press cultural hybridity into the service of a post-nationalist agenda. In the vehemently post-nationalist academy I inhabit, it is perhaps necessary to clarify that my attention to the nation and my interest in differentiating amongst different nationalisms do not stem from a reactionary desire to reinstall the nation-state or nationalism as privileged categories of cultural analysis. Rather, I believe that transnationalist agendas, which I share, are poorly served by denying the continuing, though discernibly declining, power of the nation-state. I thus draw a distinction between *post*-nationalist and *trans*nationalist scholarship. Transnationalism is devoted to studying aspects of human experience and societies that cannot be contained within the boundaries of a nation-state. As a lens of analysis, it includes in its purview transnational nationalisms, transnational antinationalisms, and strategic internationalisms. In contrast, post-nationalism, which I reject, declares the nation effectively dead as a political and analytic category.[7]

Some examples may help explain why the latter stance is mistaken. Consider Kikwit, Zaire: A city of half a million. No radio or television; electricity for only two hours a day. When the Ebola virus breaks out in

1995, medical students use battery-powered megaphones to dispense basic hygiene advice to people in the city and countryside. This in an age of so-called instant global communication.[8] Or take the case of Cuba: Devastated by a tropical storm in March 1993, Cuba receives minimal international aid. For years there is neither direct mail nor direct flights between the United States and Cuba. In 1992, the United States of America's "Cuban Democracy Act" extends the U.S. blockade of Cuba to include food and medicines, punishing third countries for trading with Cuba. Ninety miles from a center of capitalist power, Cuba's remoteness is not a physical or geographical one, but an ideological one. While Zaire belongs to the peripheries of world capitalism, the forces of global capitalism would make Cuba the "village" pariah.

Although the increasing power and reach of transnational corporations (whose budgets indeed often outstrip those of many nation-states), the transnational mobility of financial capital, and the leaps in communications technology are undoubtedly reshaping the world, their distribution remains highly unequal along axes of both class and nation.[9] For example, the international mobility of finance capital for the most part occurs between selected national locations and global cities. For example, in the early 1990s, developing countries received only about 31 percent of the total global stock of Direct Foreign Investment, most of which was distributed amongst just ten countries. Africa received a mere 1.7 percent of the world total, Latin America and the Caribbean 9.8 percent, West Asia 0.8 percent, and East, Southeast, and South Asia 18.8 percent.[10] At the end of the 1980s, the entire Third World's share of international bank-lending was a mere 11 percent, the bulk of which went to the "Asian tigers" (Kiely 11). Moreover, transnational corporations still tend to have their headquarters, center their research activities, and pay taxes in First World nation-states; IBM, after all, does not have its headquarters in Antigua or Burkina Faso. The corporations themselves are overwhelmingly owned by nationals in their home-base country (Mann 117). Moreover, pay-scales and minimum wages tend to be national, a key factor in transnationalist corporate and national governments' *cooperation* in the setting up of Export Processing Zones. Garment workers in most Caribbean countries, for instance, are paid about $1 per hour compared to $11 an hour to their American counterparts, whose cost of living is not substantially different (Klak 8).

Finally, notwithstanding the increasing mobility of capital, the nation-state continues to be a force to contend with in the circulation of *labor* across national borders. Despite the increasing mobility of people across national borders, it is worth remembering that only about 2.5 percent of the world's population migrates across national boundaries.[11] Contrary to those who invoke the appearance of "the Third World in the belly of the First" as a sign of the demise of nation-state, center, and periphery, I suggest that those migrations to the First World testify to the continuation, and possibly the intensification, of national inequalities—inequalities that only a tiny fraction of the world's population can attempt to mitigate by migration. To declare these migrations evidence, therefore, of the transcendence of the nation-state risks abandoning altogether the urgent task of social and economic reconstruction of peripheral nations.[12]

Notwithstanding the rhetoric of the "global village," then, for most of the planet's population, the struggle is for basic food, potable water, and basic communications. Seventy percent of children in the Third World suffer malnutrition; 82,000 children starve to death each day. Nearly one-third of the four billion people in the developing world do not have access to clean drinking water.[13] Although the telephone is a 100-year-old technology, over half of the world's population has never made a phone call. Tokyo has more mobile phones than does the entire continent of Africa; in Jamaica in 1990, there were only four phones per 100 people.[14] Only 4 percent of the global supply of computers is owned by people in the Third World.[15] In 1990, First World nation-states consumed about 50 percent of the world's energy resources, compared to one-sixth in the Third World.[16] These are stark statistics—and they pin us to the realization that if one truly looks at the globe as a whole, dirt roads are still more the norm than the information superhighway that cultural theorists travel. Moreover, the evidence suggests that the nation-state has historically been and continues to be a necessary condition for the transnationalization of capital. To the extent that tensions exist between transnationalism and nationalism, they are not always or necessarily disabling to either; in other words, there are constant and mutual accommodations being made between globalization and the nation-state, transnationalism and nationalism.[17]

If the nation-state continues to be one axis mediating social and economic power, then the question of the continued inequality amongst nation–states becomes a matter of continued relevance. Whilst the core–periphery model developed by the Dependency School (associated most closely with Andre Gunder Frank and Walter Rodney) has been criticized justly for emphasizing (inter)national over class inequalities, it can help us make partial sense of the foregoing data. (In the partiality of its explanation of inequality it is not unlike theories of race, gender, class, and sexuality. The disproportionate delegitimation of one partial explanation—the core–periphery model's—suggests that there may be ideological and cultural logics of disavowal at work that are independent of the internal theoretical limitations of the model.)

The core–periphery model cautions us that, contrary to the recent celebrations of placelessness in cultural theory, place and location matter. Manuel Castells describes the new globalization's reinscription of center–periphery hierarchies thus:

> While its effects reach out to the whole planet, *its actual operation and structure concern only segments of economic structures, countries, and regions, in proportions that vary according to the particular position of a country or region in the international division of labor*... Thus, while the informational economy shapes the entire planet, and in this sense it is indeed global, most people in the planet do not work for or buy from the informational/global economy. (Castells 1996: 102–103, emphasis in the original. Qtd. in Kiely 9)[18]

The foregoing discussion should make manifest what the ubiquitous phrase "global village" occludes. First, contrary to the myth of a global village, space is not being collapsed; it is being reorganized. Second, this reorganization continues to be hierarchical. The Third World's emergent intimacy with the cultural products of the West does not betoken equality with the West. The phrase "global village," then, projects a false notion of inclusive community and international equality. (And villages, too, have their outcasts.) Third, the term "global village" represses the pivotal point of conjunction and mediation between the global and the local: the nation-state. Fourth, the phrase "global village" draws together many unequal "villages" into a single "village" *through the discursive trope of hybridity.* It is through the hybrid singularization "global village" that the ongoing travesty of social inequality is repressed—by the academic Left and Right alike. (In this sense, the term is not unlike the tired metaphor of the melting pot.) For while affirming a hybrid global village is already an explicit part of the discourse of the economic Right, what is less recognized is that this hybrid village forms a part of the political unconscious of much cultural and academic discourse on the Left.[19] As I will show in chapter one, it may be significant that the most energetic declarations of nationlessness come from the strongest nation-states. If, as Homi Bhabha suggests in "DissemiNation," the anxiously repetitive self-assertions of the nation-state reveal its weakness, then, conversely, perhaps one could argue that compulsive declarations of the death of the nation-state might in fact signal its strength and well-being.

My investigation of nationalist projects does not stem from a rejection of transnational alliances, but rather reconsiders whether nationalist projects are necessarily opposed to such alliances or can be an enabling precondition for them. If the latter is the case, as I believe, then the struggle for the construction of egalitarian national communities and identities can, should, and perhaps even must, accompany the struggle for egalitarian local and global communities and identities. Since both nationalist and transnationalist forces shape the cusp moment we inhabit, two questions need to be articulated together: First, how does the national impede and/or assist transnational organizing? And second, how do transnational forces help constitute the national?[20] My own transnational interests will be evident in my comparatist cross-Caribbean treatment of cultural hybridity.

Following Benedict Anderson, I hold that nationalism is better understood not as an ideology like fascism or liberalism, but rather as a "framework" for political activity, and a structure of feeling (Anderson compares it to kinship, religion, and gender).[21] Understood thus, it becomes clearer that there is a potentially infinite variety of ways of imagining the nation—although some of that variety may be curtailed by Anderson's emphasis that nationalism is a movement aimed at gaining control of a state. If, as Anderson argues, nations are distinguished by their styles of imagining, it follows that they are sites where cultural energies, desires, and longings are and can be mobilized. As Jeff Goodwin points out, the consolidated nation-state made it possible to extensively remake social arrangements in fundamental ways, making it attractive not only for reactionary agendas but also for progressive ones (14): "the actions of foreign as well as domestic states help to make cognitively plausible and morally justifiable certain sorts of collective grievances, emotions, identities, ideologies, and associational activities (but not others)" (13–14).[22] In a brilliant elaboration of Anderson's analogy between nationalism and gender, Eve Kosofsky Sedgwick similarly points out the impasse of liberal analysis' "always accurate but spectacularly unanalytic diagnosis" of nationalism's Others, for though such study has helped Others achieve visibility within national narratives, "the trope of the Other in relation to nationalism must almost *a priori* fail to do justice to the complex activity, creativity, and engagement of those whom *it* figures simply as relegated objects—their activity, creativity, and engagement with and on behalf of, among other things, that protean fabric of public discourse that does also figure their own relegation" (239). In short, singularizing talk of "*the* nation" and "*the* state" seems to have displaced empirical, historical, and theoretical inquiry into the varied, divergent, and contradictory practices of nations and states. Sedgwick's essay sketches directions for a more subtle account of the relationships between nationalism and its Others.

Whereas some contemporary cultural theory has usefully addressed the ways in which corporations and the market are not monolithic in their aims or effects, but may shape and express significant and diverse popular desires and longings, Goodwin's argument points to the need for the same insight in relation to both the state and studies of the state. This is particularly urgent in several Third World contexts of dependent capitalism, where, according to John Kraniauskas, "the historical absence of local centers of capital accumulation, strong civil societies and national markets" leads to a "*political*, state-centered (rather than commodity-centered) dialectic of cultural modernity" where social relations with the nation-state (the political) predominate over social relations with the market (the economic) (248). To return to the problematic of cultural hybridity, studying hybridity in relation to national narratives, politics, and economies enables us to address the insufficiently theorized question of how hybridity is structured by institutional frameworks and policies (Coombes and Brah 2; García Canclini *Consumers and Citizens*), including those of both nation-state and free market.

None of my claims suggests that the nation or the state is the *only* agent shaping collective identities or projects; instead, they permit the possibility of addressing precisely the gaps between those cognitive frames recognized by the state and those that are not. It is, after all, in part through the exercise of state power that certain issues and identities are framed as local. Furthermore, it should be clear that if I insist on the analytical value of the category "national culture," I insist equally that national culture should be thought of not as a site of shared consensus but as the site of unequally shared debates and contestations.

Antonio Gramsci's formulation of "the national-popular" is useful for such a project, drawing attention to the fact that the word "popular" is historically related to the nation-state, for it was during the rise of the nation-states during the Enlightenment that "the people" first came to be invoked (García Canclini, *Hybrid Cultures* 147). Moreover, the word "popular" was *problematically* related to the nation-state—on the one hand required to legitimize a secular and democratic government, and on the other hand "the bearer of that which reason wants to abolish: superstition, ignorance, and turbulence" (García Canclini, *Hybrid Cultures* 147); furthermore, invoking the popular has been a key strategy of nationalist appropriation of popular struggles and of the romanticization of the Volk. This ambivalent reading of the popular has thus been a problem in both capitalist and marxist nation-states and in marxist cultural theory.[23] However, the term "national-popular" has the conceptual strengths of acknowledging civil society as a significant site of struggle and avoiding class reductionism by recognizing struggles common to more than one class (Forgacs 189). I investigate Caribbean instances of the "national-popular," then, not because I assume a ready, *a priori*, or singular relationship between the national and the popular, but because the term offers a way of examining the historical strains, alliances, and articulations between those forces. I enter this discussion, therefore, keen to hold the political valences of both terms open—not to assume the nation is necessarily repressive and not to assume that the people/popular are necessarily progressive. For while history bursts with examples of a repressive relationship between the nation and the popular, fully grasping the contradictions in their relationship requires that we not foreclose the possibility of utopian articulations between the national and the popular—or, for that matter, the transnational and the popular.

The Caribbean offers an instance where imagining "the people" has been a project fraught with particular difficulty. The region includes what are surely some of the world's most fragile nation-states, often marked by repressive, if weak, governments, neocolonial dependency, cyclical and mass migrations of population, environmental degradation, saturation by an international tourist culture, and economies that concentrate wealth in the hands of a tiny elite. Its history of colonial subjection and postcolonial dependency has made national sovereignty and regional self-determination hard to sustain. Nonetheless, against deconstructions of "the people" as a fabricated identity, I defend the idea of imagining "the people" in democratic and egalitarian ways as a political *achievement* worth struggling for.[24] Such negotiations might involve reconceiving the relationship of different elements within and amongst nations, and struggles by disenfranchised groups over law, policy, allocation of resources, and cultural representation, that is, intervening in the relationship between elements of the nation and the state. The Caribbean's cultural, economic, and geopolitical coordinates make it both urgent and difficult to imagine Caribbean community identity. How much more so to imagine it as a community of equals.

With the foregoing set of considerations in mind, chapter one addresses several significant metropolitan and Caribbean theories of hybridity (Bhabha, Gilroy, Anzaldúa, the Créolistes, and Grosfoguel and Negrón-Muntaner's) in order to explore the mutual imbrication of post-nationalist ideology and critiques of Enlightenment epistemology. It argues against transforming hybridity from a highly differentiated field of historical and rhetorical practices with very different political agendas, interests, and consequences into an abstract principle of interruption of pure origins. Our assessments of particular discourses of cultural hybridity need to be alert for not only the presence of critiques of purism but also the *absence* of critiques of inequality. Finally, through symptomatic readings of the repressions and slips of the texts under consideration, chapter one demonstrates the existence of what I call a "national unconscious," by which mechanism the nation-state continues to operate as a cultural category and structure of feeling in the work of avowedly post-nationalist theories.

Chapter two challenges post-nationalist claims for hybridity by demonstrating both the centrality and the immense ideological range of discourses of hybridity in nationalist projects in the Caribbean. It includes in its purview comparative and conjunctural readings of *mestizaje*, creolization, *jibarismo*, cannibalism, and *antillanité* as they appear in the works of such late nineteenth- and twentieth-century figures as José Martí and José Vasconcelos, Kamau Brathwaite and Derek Walcott, Oswald de Andrade and Wilson Harris, and Édouard Glissant.

In an attempt to account for the immense hold cultural hybridity has on our imaginations, chapter three shifts the ground of the argument from a critique of the political economy of discourses of cultural hybridity to an investigation of their aesthetics and erotics, exploring aesthetic desire and pleasure in relation to political lacks and utopian imaginings. I argue there that several of the preceding accounts of hybridity, including the academic theories, are better understood as manifestos. This generic reclassification facilitates greater attention to both their poetics and their programmatic and utopian desires, since the literary genre of the manifesto is one significant site where the meanings of equality have been contested. I read the strategies of the manifestos in terms of what Glissant calls "forced poetics," and consider Glissant's own *Caribbean Discourse* as a productive example of a manifesto for hybridity that displays a forced poetics. The emphasis of the chapter thus lies not on the truth-claims of the texts in question but on the extent to which their performances successfully reconcile utopian politics, strategic practice, and rhetorical affect.

Chapter four takes up contemporary hybridity theory's tendency to privilege popular resistance and transgression and to delegitimize more specifically oppositional agency. Working in critical dialogue with James Scott's conception of cultural practices as "dress rehearsals" for openly declared public political opposition, I demonstrate that the performative rehearsals of hybridity, resistance, and transgression in Derek Walcott's play *Pantomime* (1978), far from being antagonistic to political opposition, function as enabling conditions for it.

Chapter five studies *Myal*, the second novel of the Jamaican novelist Erna Brodber, for the careful modulation of its claims for a mulatto poetics and for the ways in which it tutors us to develop an ethical reading practice. Reading the novel's deployment of the nonrational subjectivities of spirit possession that refuse both the Reason of realism and the antirealism of postmodernism, this chapter is concerned with reframing debates in Postcolonial Studies over the global reception of Caribbean and Latin American marvelous and magic realisms.

Chapters six and seven are companion pieces intended to be read together. Picking up a thread developed in chapter two in relation to Brathwaite's and Walcott's discourse, they explore the hybridities arising from the convergent bonded voyages of Africans and Indians across the oceans and the twin servitudes of slavery and indentureship. These are hybridities marginalized in Postcolonial Studies, Africana Studies, and Indian Diaspora Studies alike, for much of the work done under the rubric "Africana Studies" has ignored the Indian presence in the Caribbean and its relation to the African diaspora; equally, the bulk of the work done under the rubric "Indian Diaspora" has tended to construct a purist and conservative Indian culture, affirming racist, bourgeois, and patriarchal Indian interests, and erasing solidarities between Afro- and Indo-diasporic populations. Chapters six and seven respond to these absences in both postcolonial nationalisms and disciplinary formations such as African and Indian Diaspora Studies, absences structured in part by the continuing legacies of neocolonialism and imperial discourse.

These last two chapters of the book focus on the lived everyday experience of hybridity as it intersects with regulation by the state in a context of ethnic competition in Trinidad. In particular, I focus on the place of the dougla, the mixed descendant of African and Indian, in negotiations over national and cultural identity, and I distinguish between "creole" and "dougla" hybridities on the basis of the different national and political projects they might serve in the present moment.

Framing my discussion of contemporary relations between Indo- and Afro-Trinidadians with nineteenth-century colonial discourse and independence-era calypsos, in chapter six I develop a relational reading of the historically Afro-Creole practice of Carnival and the historically Indo-Caribbean observance of Hosay (the commemoration of the martyrdom of the grandsons of the Prophet Muhammad). For whereas Carnival has been hailed as a major national festival of the Caribbean, my reading of colonial legislation and reports and Ismith Khan's novel *The Jumbie Bird* points to an active *de*-nationalizing of Hosay. I also understand the prominence of racial and gender stereotypes in race politics today as deriving from colonial discourse and calypso's use of stereotype as a formal aesthetic device.

Chapter seven takes up the gendered constructions and contestations of Indo-Caribbean nationalism by analyzing the Indo-Caribbean feminist writer Ramabai Espinet's short story "Barred: Trinidad 1987" (1991) and the controversies that erupted in the 1990s around the Indo-Caribbean woman singer Drupatee Ramgoonai and the hybrid musical form chutney-soca. It concludes with what could be considered a meta-manifesto urging the elaboration of dougla poetics and identities. Drawing on the original meaning of the word "dougla" as bastard or illegitimate, on calypsos and soca-chutney that deploy a dougla poetics in contestatory ways, and on the narratives of gender in texts such as Espinet's, I argue that in present-day Trinidad a "dougla poetics" might be developed to figure egalitarian hybrid identities delegitimized or disallowed by dominant cultural nationalist discourses.

I hope that my close readings of aesthetic texts will demonstrate that the alternatives to present discourses of hybridity do not return us to purism. The risks of purist conceptions of nations or communities are readily apparent in the wake of our shameful histories of holocaust, ethnic cleansing, and genocide. My sense of the urgency of this book arises from the belief that the social risks of weak models of cultural hybridity, though less obvious, are no less real.

Part I

Critique and Methodology

Chapter 1

Theorizing Hybridity: The Post-Nationalist Moment

The philosophical burden of the concept of cultural hybridity in the postmodern academy has been to correct purist, essentialist, and organicist conceptions of culture. More specifically, postmodern theories of cultural hybridity have been mobilized to critique Enlightenment epistemology and institutions, particularly the nation-state and modern conceptions of a stable unitary subject.[1] It is in this context that border-crossing, nomadism, travel, homelessness, and nationlessness have emerged as important tropes for cultural liberation. Thus, for example, animating much of Homi Bhabha's work is the tension between the heterogeneous people and the homogenizing nation (*Location of Culture* 29, 145–146, 164). Similarly, Paul Gilroy's *The Black Atlantic: Modernity and Double Consciousness* constitutes an energetic critique of the nationalism and statism of British Cultural Studies, and advances the Black Atlantic as an alternative unit of analysis (15–16). And Gloria Anzaldúa's *Borderlands/La Frontera* explores the complex and multiple marginal identities that emerge along the U.S.–Mexico border and contributes to the emergence of the field of "Border Studies." All these substantially different cases invoke tropes of hybridity as evidence of the undermining or transcendence of the nation-state. In other words, they draw a clear connection between cultural hybridity and post-nationalism.

This chapter subjects that connection to scrutiny. In particular, it identifies the moves by which various practices of cultural hybridity are abstracted into a *principle* of hybridity. Moreover, it demonstrates not only that post-nationalist theories of hybridity implicitly privilege metropolitan centers as the objects and sites of political action (a point that has been amply and acutely made already), but also that in this privileging surfaces what I will call a "national unconscious."[2]

After exploring these dynamics in the relatively well-known work of Homi Bhabha, Paul Gilroy, and Gloria Anzaldúa, I will consider two Caribbean texts that complicate any impulse to reduce the metropolitan emphases of theorists of hybridity to functions of their metropolitan location: "Éloge de la Créolité" ("In Praise of Creoleness") by the French Caribbean Créolistes Jean Bernabé, Patrick Chamoiseau, and Raphaël Confiant; and *Puerto Rican Jam: Rethinking Colonialism and Nationalism*, an anthology edited by Ramón Grosfoguel and Frances Negrón-Muntaner. My purpose is to critique these dominant understandings of hybridity for the sake of proposing a more productive framework for approaching hybrid identities.

The tendency to abstract hybridity into an epistemological principle is clearly evident in Cultural Studies' selective appropriations of Benedict Anderson's *Imagined Communities: Reflections on the Origin and Spread of Nationalism.* According to Anderson, "[c]ommunities are to be distinguished not by their falsity or genuineness, but by the style in which they are imagined" (15). Anderson's emphasis on subjectivity, his interest in styles of imagining, and his bracketing of the question of empirical truth make his work particularly appealing for Cultural Studies. However, many appropriations of Anderson ignore the fact that Anderson's "imagined community" does not simply privilege the fictionality of national narratives, but posits a tension between fact and fiction: "the nation is imagined as a community because, *regardless of the actual inequality and exploitation that may prevail in each*, the nation is always conceived as a deep, horizontal comradeship" (16, emphasis added). What many critics ignore is the language of political economy that enters Anderson's work through the phrase "actual inequality and exploitation." This elision epitomizes in miniature a common formalist move by which the critique of nationalist rhetoric and its totalizing epistemology often displaces the question of actual social inequality within and between nation-states.[3]

A brief passage from "Mexican Migration and the Social Space of Postmodernism," Roger Rouse's otherwise insightful anthropological study of work and economies along the U.S.–Mexican border, is representative of the tendency in several theories of hybridity to treat any nationalist structure of feeling as an anachronistic hankering after the epistemological comfort of modernity: "We live in a confusing world, a world of criss-crossed economies, intersecting systems of meaning, and fragmented identities. Suddenly, the comforting modern imagery of nation-states and national languages, of coherent communities and consistent subjectivities, of dominant centers and distant margins no longer seems adequate" (8). The emphases on the fragment, unstable signification, the refusal of coherence and consistency, and the valorization of the local as ways of refusing "universal" knowledges all participate in postmodernism's critique of Enlightenment epistemology; and it is by means of this critique that nationalism is reframed as a modernist nostalgia for certainty in a postmodern world.

Similarly, Homi Bhabha's attention to cultural minorities and their socioeconomic and cultural marginality becomes somehow interchangeable with an epistemological commitment to disrupting universalizing knowledges: "The 'difference' of cultural knowledge that 'adds to' but does not 'add up' is the enemy of the *implicit* generalization of knowledge or the implicit homogenization of experience" (163). In turn, hybridity via cultural difference is defined as "the perplexity of the living as it interrupts the representation of the fullness of life; it is an instance of iteration, in the minority discourse, of the time of the arbitrary sign—'the minus in the origin'—through which all forms of cultural meaning are open to translation because their enunciation resists totalization" ("DissemiNation" 314; see also *The Location of Culture* 162). Hybridity is now associated with a "structure of undecidability" (312), a formal principle of interruption of origins and destabilization of centers that Bhabha will uncover again and again.[4] For him, moreover, the discursive contradiction inherent in the nation "makes untenable any supremacist, or nationalist claims to cultural mastery" (150). But untenable in what register? For while cultural hybridity may point to potentially destabilizing contradictions in purist and homogenizing narratives of the nation, these contradictions in logic do not necessarily disable the nation or render it untenable in practice—even at the level of rhetoric, far less at the level of political economy.

What is occluded by awarding primacy to semiotic interruption in the following passage: "The people are not *simply* historical events or parts of a patriotic body politic. They are also a *complex* rhetorical strategy of social reference where the claim to be representative provokes a crisis within the process of signification and discursive address" (145, emphasis added)? Bhabha's preference is for "the dangerous tryst with the 'untranslatable'—rather than arriving at ready-made names" (227). Thus:

> My interest lies *only* in that movement of meaning that occurs in the writing of cultures articulated in difference. . . . The effect of such "secondariness" is not *merely* to change the "object" of analysis—to focus, for instance, on race rather than gender or native knowledges rather than metropolitan myths; nor to invert the axis of political discrimination by installing the excluded term at the center. The analytic of cultural difference intervenes to transform the scenario of

> articulation—not *simply* to disturb the rationale of discrimination. ("DissemiNation" 312, emphasis added; see also *The Location of Culture* 162)

What is the weight of those words "merely" and "simply"? What do they emphasize and what do they brush aside? Invocations of "the people" indeed embody complex rhetorical strategies that merit attention, but what does it mean to sweep aside the "simplicity" of historical events as unworthy of scholarly attention, in order to make room for the more "complex" emphasis on rhetoric? Bhabha's valorization of a formal deconstruction of narrative authority displaces any exploration of the continuing effects of power and inequality as well as any work to construct an opposition to that inequality. These he dismisses as "merely" changing the object of analysis. Inadequate also, according to the above passage, is the desire to "invert the axis of political discrimination by installing the excluded term at the center." The South African battle against apartheid, movements for women's suffrage, the Ejército Nacional de Liberación's struggles for Indian rights within the Mexican nation, colonial invocations of imperial laws to restrain crippling imperial practices, quests for national independence by emergent postcolonial nation-states, and a host of struggles by colonized peoples to turn to their advantage those modern institutions of the law, constitutional equality, and nation-state: this vast range of complex political activity would be dismissed by Bhabha as deluded and deficient. Would the 1857 Indian Mutiny have merited Bhabha's attention had the Mutiny not seen confusion over what was signified by the mysterious circulating chapatis (202–204)? Had that ambivalent code not opened up "a new, hybrid space of cultural difference in the negotiation of colonial power/relations" (204), had the chapatis "merely" enabled a politically successful Revolt that might have transformed a hundred years of colonial rule, would the Mutiny still have been worth studying? Bhabha's preoccupation with a Derridean dismantling of oppositions blinds him to precisely such sites of struggle, yet, ironically, his rigid separation of the material and the symbolic, complex rhetorical and simple political maneuvers, tends to reverse, then reinscribe, those very oppositions.[5]

Moreover, once Bhabha has set up cultural hybridity as that which makes nationalist claims untenable, it seems he must valorize margins as disruptions of the nation. But when postcolonials and minorities are *defined* as disruptions of the national narrative, deemed significant only insofar as they interrupt the center, what these people actually say or do become quite irrelevant. As Ania Loomba has pointed out, their resistance is cast as the effect of the contradictions within dominant discourse, rather than any active agency on their part (Loomba 91). Furthermore, Bhabha cannot tell us very much about how different marginalized groups negotiate their relationship not to the center, but to one another; nor can he address the consequences of their making one choice rather than another. Instead, colonized or minority subjects can only point to the limits of the center from the margins of his essays.

Whilst, unlike Bhabha, the Chicana feminist and queer theorist/poet/activist Gloria Anzaldúa in *Borderlands/La Frontera* makes minority subjects her focus, in her desire for pluralist inclusion and nonexclusive forms of affiliation and identity, she, too, conflates different forms of cultural hybridity, marginality, and border-crossing:

> A borderland is a vague and undetermined place created by the emotional residue of an unnatural boundary.... The prohibited and forbidden are its inhabitants. Los atravesados live here: the squint-eyed, the perverse, the queer, the troublesome, the mongrel, the mulato, the half-breed, the half dead; in short, those who cross over, pass over, or go through the confines of the "normal." (3; see also 62–63)

However, the general trajectory of Anzaldúa's work is to theorize the specific pluralities of the U.S.–Mexico border. Her vision is of borderlands that can sustain many different names as well as mark their ironies: *mestiza*, *chicana*, *latina*, *tejana*, *mexicano de este lado*, *mexicano de otro lado*, *raza* (62).

Yet despite this multiplication of names, I believe that, as in many discourses of hybridity, an implicit, unacknowledged, and untheorized elevation of one hybrid identity occurs—in this case, that of the *mestiza*. When Anzaldúa asserts "I identified as 'Raza' before I ever identified as 'mexicana' or 'Chicana'" (62), she grants "raza" a certain priority; similarly, her claim that her "chicana identity is grounded in the Indian woman's history of resistance" (21) privileges the Indian component of her identity. Part 5 of the book, although in sections it appears to deliberately use the full range of nominative possibility, leaves us with the sentence: "we, the *mestizas* and *mestizos*, will remain" (64). Similarly, Part 7 of the book, named after the *mestiza*, prophesies: "*En unas pocas centurias*, the future will belong to the mestiza" (80). In its combination of nineteenth-century scientific discourse about race and romantic mysticism (77, 85), the language about the *mestiza* in these instances closely recalls that of José Vasconcelos in *La Raza Cósmica* (*The Cosmic Race*), an influential text that Anzaldúa invokes in her elaboration of the "La conciencia de la mestiza: Towards a New Consciousness" (77).

What is at stake in this privileging? What national locations, what histories, do these terms foreground and why? Clearly, the *mestiza* and the historico-mythical figure of La Malinche provide a resonant vocabulary for Anzaldúa to express the tensions between her ethnic and sexual identities and to figure the double victimage of Native Americans by Hispanics and Anglos alike (21–25, 78). The choice to work with the figure of the *mestiza* thus attempts a feminist reclamation of La Malinche, as accounts such as Norma Alarcón's point out.[6] It is also precisely to the extent that *mestiza* operates in Anzaldúa's work as a racial–biological–mystical category (77) that it is privileged, for these categories offer a visionary transcendence of history that the "merely" political/historical, in Anzaldúa's view, cannot. In contrast, "chicana" encodes a cultural hybridity that is explicitly politicized and traceable to specific historical struggles of organized agricultural labor on this side of the border, with their own barely uttered stories of gender inequality.[7] The choice, then, to foreground the *mestiza* over the arguably historically more present and accessible hybridity "chicana" is not without consequence. It locates the privileged source of identity on the other side of the present-day U.S.–Mexico border. Thus, the term "mestiza consciousness" does not quite confront precisely how the *mestiza* identity *borders* with the United States; it displaces attention away from those aspects of U.S. culture the *mestiza*/ chicana participates in.

Although the refusal to recognize national borders in much liberal and leftist post-nationalist discourse undoubtedly stems in part from a genuinely utopian declaration of solidarity with the nation's Others, the strategic wisdom of that refusal is questionable. For it absolves one of considering the power and privilege that might accrue to one's own national location.[8] A more productive transnationalism that could both attend to the politics of location and de-essentialize it would ask: "How do I, even as a dissident, participate in nationally mediated structures of power and oppression?" Anzaldúa's pronouncement that "being Mexican is a state of soul, not of mind, not of citizenship" (62), which upholds a mystical Mexico over a political one, claims a victory over the national/rational scar that is the U.S.–Mexico border (3), but it precludes asking the complicated question of whether and in what situations holding U.S. citizenship can place one in a relationship of national privilege with respect to undocumented workers or migrant workers within Mexico, even while one may be subject to oppression on the basis of class, gender, race, and sexual orientation in the United States. Lost from view in Anzaldúa's analysis are the different kinds and purposes of border-crossing—by undocumented migrant workers and five-star tourists, by death squads and multinational corporations.[9] Similarly, Paul Gilroy's suggestive metaphor of the ship as a site of transnational identities needs to be elaborated further so that we can distinguish between the cultural hybridities and border-crossings represented by, say, slave-ships, U.S. warships, luxury cruise ships, and Haitian rafts. Only the failure to consider such issues can explain why border-crossing is so often cast as intrinsically subversive. This may be why Bhabha remarks so often upon the "empowering condition of hybridity" (227) but remains resoundingly silent about situations in which cultural hybridity may be disempowering.

That the fundamental political concerns described here can recede from view is the result of the theoretical construction of hybridity as a principle of difference abstracted from historical specificities. Refusing certain forms of hybridity and border-crossing may have less to do with a modernist nostalgia for secure origins than with struggles for physical survival and political liberation. Against the self-issued invitation to cross borders, against the desire for identification, intimacy, and complete access, the hard lesson that the declared but undisclosed secrets of Rigoberta Menchú's *testimonio* teach us, even as the text reaches out for transnational aid, is that there are terrains where the reader- or theorist-in-solidarity is not welcome. So, too, Jamaica Kincaid's *A Small Place* unceremoniously tells us to stay home. Perhaps there are harder lessons for theorists to learn than participating imaginatively in the borderlands and seeking welcome there.

It should be clear that my argument for attending to the political economy of nationalisms does not privilege "fact" over "fiction," or replace "rhetoric" with "materiality." Rather, it asks that we be more attentive to the interpenetrations, accommodations, and negotiations of the material and the symbolic as well as to the range of hybrid identities. For in failing to distinguish between different discursive interpellations of nationalism and citizenship, we shrug off as epistemologically unchallenging or uninteresting the differences between one form of nationalism and another—differences that can mean the difference between life and death for tens of thousands of people. This is to fall prey to the worst kind of formalism—the worst, not just because it ignores "content," but because it does not even take into account the variety of forms.

Moreover, addressing the tensions between the poetics and politics, the economics and epistemologies, of particular hybridities would enable us to address ways in which the colonized might be able to seize the structures and institutions of modernity, including the nation, and hybridize them. Such acts of hybridization are conspicuously absent from contemporary theorizations of hybridity. Given

Bhabha's interest in hybridity, for example, it is indeed surprising that he does not explore instances in which the colonized might transform the nation; instead, his initial challenge to imperial Britain slips into skepticism toward all nations and national projects.[10] But might we not read the anxious condemnation by the United States of Third World nationalisms such as Grenada's and Cuba's as a sign of the threat these "marginal" nationalisms pose to the center? Must colonized nationalisms simply replicate First World nationalisms or could they *mimic* them, in Bhabha's sense of the term?

It is precisely these questions that Mary Louise Pratt takes on in *Imperial Eyes: Travel Writing and Transculturation* through her conceptions of "autoethnography" and the "contact zone," which refer to discursive and geographical sites of hybridization wherein the colonized "selectively collaborate" with and hybridize the codes and epistemes of the colonizers (7). Pratt's approach permits us to read the interventions of the colonized in the nation-state as modes of hybridization and to treat their interventions not simply as naiveté, but rather as considered conjunctural strategies of translation and negotiation to gain political intelligibility. Her reading of Guaman Poma de Ayala's 1613 letter to King Philip III of Spain (2–4), for example, puts to work in a politically nuanced way post-structuralist insights about compromised and complicitous forms of resistance. Particularly now, with nation-states weakened by global capitalism, one could argue that they are no longer as well positioned to fulfill their totalizing or totalitarian desires and are therefore more manipulable. In a similar argumentative vein, John Kraniauskas notes the analytic advantage of recognizing how "the cultural hybridity of modern Latin American nations illuminates 'the oblique powers that are involved in the mixing of liberal institutions and authoritarian habits, social democratic governments with paternalist regimes'" (García Canclini 14, qtd. in Kraniauskas 246). What Bhabha might find self-contradictory in a nation's practices or ideologies might from other perspectives appear as evidence of its hybridization—whether that hybridization served repressive or progressive purposes.

Common to the dominant articulations of cultural hybridity I have described earlier is a move in which the critique of totalizing knowledges and totalitarian nationalisms is unaccompanied by any comparable critique of a totalizing capitalism. Rather, as Alok Yadav observes, the "'recognition' of present realities [specifically, the powerful effects of global capitalism] is posited as a kind of superior insight, self-consciousness, and political maturity which typically serve to distinguish 'us' from other parts of the world" (200). Ironically, then, the post-nationalist denunciation of nationalism itself has the structure of a xenophobic nationalism; moreover, it is a structure not far removed from that colonial discourse which constructs the Third World as pathological.[11]

And yet, despite Bhabha's strictures against a nation understood as undifferentiatedly malign, he regretfully recognizes the absence from *Nation and Narration* of "those who have not yet found their nation: amongst them Palestinians and Black South Africans" (7). I do not for a moment question the sincerity of Bhabha's sympathetic reference; it is the inconsistency of the lament that I find remarkable. For, as I have shown, his identification of nationalism with violent homogenization leaves little room for progressive or oppositional nationalisms. His *sentimental* support of Palestinian and Black South African nationalisms, then, cannot be explained in the terms of his *theory* of cultural hybridity; it appears instead as the political unconscious or sentimental excess of his argument.[12]

In this curious way, the nation whose importance is denied or repressed at the level of post-nationalist argument significantly resurfaces in post-nationalist theories of hybridity—sometimes as object of desire, sometimes as structuring absence. Without making claims for the general applicability of Fredric Jameson's controversial account of First and Third World allegories in "Third World Literature," in the specific cases I address in this chapter, I have found very suggestive his observation that national allegorical structures are not so much "absent from first-world cultural texts as they are *unconscious*" (79). It is such an unconscious nationalism that characterizes the aforementioned "us" versus "them" formula. Similarly, in some of the strongest, most vehement and politically engaged antinationalist writing, one nonetheless sees references to, for example, "the Egyptian feminist A," or "the Indian historian B," "the Cuban exile," or "the Senegalese filmmaker." It is worth putting some pressure on these moments to examine what exactly the adjectives "Egyptian," "Indian," "Cuban," or "Senegalese" describe. Do they mark a political, legal, or cultural identity? To what extent does the nation-state mediate these identities? I tend to agree with the now-common observation that hyphenated identities increasingly suggest a break rather than a connection amongst different cultural, legal, and political identities. But does "Cuban" in the example I cite above refer to the state, the nation, or the nation-state? Is the Egyptian feminist's relationship to the nation and/or state one of unqualified opposition? In what ways does "India" shape the conceptions, approaches, and so forth of an "Indian school of historiography?" What is the conceptual, institutional, or commercial purchase of terms like "Egyptian" or "Indian" or "Jamaican" in a post-nationalist academy? Are these usages simply unreflective residues of a previous era's mode of inquiry or do they betray the continuing operation of the category of the nation-state even in those discourses that most vigorously denounce it? In answering these questions, I have found John Borneman's distinction between nationalism and nationness helpful (*Belonging in the Two Berlins* 28–30, 339). Borneman's argument would suggest that the national markers make reference not so much to nationalism (understood, following Ernest Gellner, as a "willed adherence to a community"), but to what he calls "the praxis of belonging," that is, the ways in which everyday practices and subjective meanings are shaped by national culture, ideologies, and state policies.

It is especially interesting to see this national unconscious surface in the work of Paul Gilroy, which in other respects avoids many of the pitfalls of Bhabha's and Anzaldúa's work on cultural hybridity.[13] For although like Bhabha, Gilroy faults purists such as Afrocentrists and correctly traces that purism to their cultural *nationalism*, unlike Bhabha, Gilroy develops a clearly historicized model of transnationalism rooted in the specificities of the transatlantic slave-trade triangulated by Europe, Africa, and the Americas. Moreover, Gilroy's continued investment in modernity, to which the Black Atlantic stands in a relationship of critical participation, and his explicitly political investment in narratives of equality and collective emancipation, distinguish his project from Bhabha's. Moreover, Gilroy explicitly recognizes the historical instances and possibilities of co-opting and stabilizing open, hybrid cultural forms and identities (31). As examples of this restabilization of destabilizing hybrid constructs, he cites the nationalist rewriting of hip-hop as an exclusively African-American form (107) and nationalist refusals to acknowledge the intellectual exchange between black and white thinkers—refusals the book is devoted to challenging. Above all, then, Gilroy takes an explicitly interventionist stance in adjudicating between competing constructions of blackness. His work, therefore, is not predominantly concerned with the relationships of Others to a White British Self; it is also committed to sorting through the implications *for minorities* of different mobilizations of minority identity.

Yet Gilroy, too, makes a double movement between denying the nation-state—as when he claims that the new arts have created a "new topography of loyalty and identity in which the structures and presuppositions of the nation state have been left behind because they are seen to be outmoded" (16)—and unintentionally reinscribing that nation-state. For his own project is inescapably shaped by his negotiations between blackness and *Britishness*. Moreover, this negotiation cannot be read as proof of Gilroy's claim about the oppressive power of the nation-state *per se*, since it is the national imaginary of *black America* that is crucial to his construction of a dissenting black Britishness: "The Caribbean, Africa, Latin America, *and above all black America* contributed to our lived sense of a racial self" (109, emphasis added). Although the significance of this sentence could be minimized by reading it as a simple statement of autobiographical fact, the general claims of the book as a whole support it. Without a doubt, "black America" is a complex and internally divided term, African-Americans standing in a relationship of marginality to America. But what is it about *America* that enables *its* minority articulations to achieve global reach? For in point of fact, majority and minority expressions from the Caribbean, Africa, and Latin America recede from Gilroy's account of the Black Atlantic, while America is repeatedly prioritized. What this signals is that even in an avowedly post-nationalist text, visibility and invisibility are partially determined along national axes.

Similarly, upon reading the essay "Diaspora, Utopia, and the Critique of Capitalism," where Gilroy refers to the "dependency of the British music scene" and its "strictly subordinate place" (343), one might well ask: subordinate in relation to what? Most likely not the Caribbean or Africa. It is the United States that seems to become the implied norm in relation to which the British music industry is subordinate. But what of, say, Caribbean music industries? In this regard, Gilroy begins: "Whatever the effect of the reggae film *The Harder They Come* in the Caribbean, in Britain..." (347), and then devotes the essay to reggae in Britain, confining the Caribbean reception and impact of the film to a single subordinate clause. It is precisely this subordination that can become problematic. Gilroy continues: "The Caribbean was becoming an increasingly important subcultural *resource* once white British youth began to break free of their dependency on American images" (348, emphasis added). Though there is nothing wrong with this example *a priori*, when it is read as part of a consistent displacement of Caribbean struggles against dependency, we must begin to ask whether it is a *structural* displacement. When critical cultural theory speaking in the name of the Black Atlantic repeats the subordination of the Caribbean, it must surely give us pause. Like Bhabha's work, Gilroy's study tends to frame transatlantic hybridity as a resource for metropolitan minority reconstruction rather than also as a way of organizing analyses of struggles for peripheral reconstruction.[14]

I am suggesting, then, that the widespread marginalization of Africa and the Caribbean in much transatlanticist and hybridity-theory is not simply an unfortunate coincidence, but can be traced to a theoretical and methodological weakness: the repression of the nation-state as a key axis of power and production, a repression that makes it impossible for the theories in question to comment upon the absence of certain nations in their accounts. I submit that rather than revealing the unequal crossings of national borders symptomatically, we need to be able to theorize those borders directly. Such an approach could bring Africa and the Caribbean back into transatlantic visibility. We would benefit, moreover, from a genuinely comparatist rather than identitarian approach to transatlantic hybridity. For exploring the *discrepant* histories of and within Africa and the Caribbean (as well as the discrepant studies of them) would engage transatlantic discontinuities as fully as continuities, and would thereby build on Gilroy's insight that black history is a history of discontinuity—a discontinuity that his generalizations often absorb back into a transatlantic continuity under the sign of a globalized U.S./British culture.[15]

The dominant articulations of cultural hybridity that I have outlined here are not simply a product of the geographical location of their theorists in the metropolitan First World, as I will show through my reading of *Puerto Rican Jam* (1997) and "Éloge de la Créolité" (1989), texts that are instructive for the ways in which they both reinforce and complicate the foregoing metropolitan accounts of hybridity.[16] Unlike the foregoing diasporic postcolonial and minority metropolitan theorists, the Créolistes are based in the French Caribbean; and, while several of the contributors to *Puerto Rican Jam* do live and work in the United States or move between the United States and Puerto Rico, their theories address political events, proposals, and articulations of identity in relation to the island of Puerto Rico. However, I suggest that because Martinique, Guadeloupe, and Puerto Rico are not independent nations, but nations without states—part of France and the United States respectively—these texts share some of the minoritarian strategies of Bhabha, Gilroy, and Anzaldúa.[17] In contrast to a tendency within Postcolonial Studies to dismiss political independence as "merely formal," bringing only an illusory self-determination in a neocolonial globe, I suggest that the Créolistes' and *Puerto Rican Jam*'s conceptions of hybridity are significantly different from those cultural nationalist formulations that do take recourse to political nationalism. They express a different relationship of nation to state, most specifically in their splitting cultural from political nationalisms. As I will demonstrate, while *Puerto Rican Jam* claims to be postnationalist, in fact it stakes a claim to the United States; and while the Créolistes have in personal practice historically supported independence and are affiliated with particular political parties (Burton, "The Idea of Difference"), their delinking of culture and economy undermines their goal, forcing them back into a post-nationalist logic and the orbit of France. Both texts reveal themselves to be significantly structured by imperialist nationalisms. The cases of Puerto Rico, Martinique, and Guadeloupe also caution against naming the present conjuncture as "postcolonial," since the nations in question are neither postcolonial nor even necessarily neocolonial, but rather, in many respects, classically colonial; they are thus pertinent to understanding the experience of much of the Dutch Antilles (Aruba, Bonaire, and Curaçao, in particular) as well as that of Native America and Palestine.

The editors of *Puerto Rican Jam*, Grosfoguel and Negrón-Muntaner, urge Puerto Ricans to form an "ethnonation" within the United States; Grosfoguel explicitly argues against political independence, advancing instead the proposal of "radical statehood" in which Puerto Rico would become the fifty-first state of the United States. His method is to undo the traditional opposition between colonialism and nationalism. It is the consistent critique of pro-independence nationalisms that unites the otherwise wide-ranging group of essays in the anthology and draws them into the service of Grosfoguel's radical statehood project.[18] Recognizing the inevitability of U.S. hegemony over Puerto Rico regardless of the latter's official legal status, Grosfoguel argues for statehood on pragmatist and populist grounds. Beginning with a call to reorganize Puerto Rico's political parties so that they are not organized around the status alternatives (currently independence, statehood, and commonwealth) (74), he nonetheless proceeds to provide a "political–economic–ecological–sexual program" for radical statehood (70), with the goal of taking statehood back from the Right. His initial move is to advocate statehood in place of an idealistic notion of freedom, on the *pragmatic* grounds that winning the maximum possible concessions from the colonial state and expanding the social democratic rights already recognized (70, 17) would enable a "milder form of oppression." However, this tactic gives way to an attack on *ethical* grounds of the independence movement, which Grosfoguel characterizes as elite, white, Catholic, Hispanophile, male, sexist, and homophobic.[19] Although the Créolistes differ from *Puerto Rican Jam* in that in principle they oppose integration into France and invoke sovereignty as a step toward a Caribbean confederation, as I will show, this invocation is both brief and abstract, and is undercut by some of their metaphors. Thus they share a broader post-nationalist *logic* that delinks cultural and political autonomy.

In the Créolistes' work, the delinking of cultural and political autonomy occurs by privileging the Creole language as the most important site and vehicle for the regeneration of a vibrant culture.

(Indeed, it is over the status they accord Creole that they break with their intellectual ancestor Édouard Glissant, theorist of *antillanité*, whom I discuss in chapter two.) The Créoliste critique of History and the tyranny of Europe's written Word leads them to privilege the Oral as the medium that holds the truth of a Caribbean experience that exceeds official narratives: Thus, they proclaim: "we are Words behind Writing" (896). Their capitalizations signal particular historical phenomena being recast as abstract principles in ways reminiscent of Bhabha's. Furthermore, in the context of Guadeloupe and Martinique, the insistence on Creole is problematic not only because it freezes linguistic contact in a particular historical moment, which contradicts their claim of Créolité as "open specificity" and generates the nostalgia and folklorism that haunt their work, but also because the linguistic survival of Creole cannot be achieved through linguistic means alone; it needs to be developed in conjunction with a project for social, political, and economic regeneration. The Créolistes seem to throw in their lot with the secret codes and trickster strategies of Creole, without recognizing that these modes of resistance cannot lead very far without simultaneous support from socioeconomic measures. The structure of "Praise" points also to, first, the separation in their analysis of politics and culture, and, second, the subordination of politics to culture: Their relegation of "Creole and Politics" to a one-page appendix captures their somewhat perfunctory treatment of politics; it is further reinforced by their claim that "for the moment, full knowledge of Creoleness will be reserved for Art" (893, capitalized in the original; see also 896), and exacerbated by their failure to specify when that "moment" passes.[20]

Underwriting the elevation of cultural politics in the work of both "Praise" and *Puerto Rican Jam* is a somewhat romantic notion of the epistemic privilege and progressiveness of "the people." In an oddly essentializing movement, "Praise" tends to assume that "the people" inherently possess a *counter*culture; in fact, claim the Créolistes: "Creole orality, even repressed in its aesthetic expression, contains a "*whole* system of countervalues, a counterculture" (895, emphasis added). Thus, although in principle they oppose any form of purism, they nonetheless do not see Creole and French cultures as *mutually* infiltrating. Chamoiseau's insistence in his novel *Texaco* on the physical contiguity of squatter and imperial city, in which the squatters traverse and infiltrate the imperial space, thus does not admit as easily to the lines of contact that run in the opposite direction. In their desire to revalue Creole culture, then, the Créolistes understate the ways in which it is scarred by colonial history. In the contradiction between their recognizing that there is no physical "outside" to which one can retreat to mount an attack and their claiming an intact Creole culture, we see a familiar move by which hybridity discourse often smuggles back the concept and value of authenticity.

Similarly, *Puerto Rican Jam* insistently construes popular refusal of independence as a sign of popular wisdom. Yet given its faith in popular judgment, it is inconsistent that the invocation of the 1993 status referendum (279) ignores the implications of the fact that, although only 4 percent of voters opted for independence, the majority voted for options other than statehood. Nor does the anthology explain why the most conservative versions of political nationalism historically gained the widest mass support in Puerto Rico or why the authorial collective seeks to expand feminist and gay rights to which there is mass popular resistance. Neither *Puerto Rican Jam* nor "Praise," then, takes on the full consequences of the fact that that popular culture is itself infiltrated, compromised, and responsive to changing political pressures.

In practice, their populism involves enshrining a particular segment of the people as the embodiment of popular wisdom. Thus, for example, Chamoiseau's novel *Texaco* is often critical of the long-heroized figure of Caribbean separatist resistance, the maroon, and celebrates as folk heroes, instead, plantation slaves and urban squatters (whom he sometimes refers to as urban maroons). In fact, in *Texaco*, the relationship between Creole and French is mirrored by the relationship of the titular squatters' slum to the capital city of Fort-de-France. The Créolistes' emphasis on the traffic between slum and city, or the daily negotiations between plantation slaves and masters, privileges a poetics of infiltration rather than separation. Reversing imperial and entrepreneurial images of the slums as living parasitically off the city, the Créolistes assert not only the superior vision of the marginal, but the dependency of the center on the margin. As with Anzaldúa's borderlands, the nagging irony remains that in recognizing that the city is dependent upon the slum (and by extension, perhaps, that France is dependent upon Martinique), they implicitly concede that the slum *sustains* the city; the margin *reinforces* the center. Or, at the very least, any epistemic disruption of the center that the margins might effect is at odds with the economic consolidation they enable. In *Puerto Rican Jam*, the equivalent metaphor becomes that of *jaibería*, the *jaiba* or crab becoming a figure for "oblique advancement," "subversive complicity," "collective practices of nonconfrontation and evasion," "the feminization of resistance" (30–33)—all versions of the long-standing Afro-Caribbean trope of the trickster—which are invoked to replace what they see as a virile, masculine, heroic, nationalist conception of resistance. In the case of *Puerto Rican Jam*'s intervention in the often tense relations between island Puerto Ricans and the diasporic mainland

Puerto Ricans, who are estimated to constitute between one-third and one-half of the total population, somehow the hybrid diasporic Puerto Rican becomes the most authentic Puerto Rican subject, the supreme example of internal rather than external resistance, a case in point of tactics of oblique advancement. The island of Puerto Rico is meanwhile constructed as the site of an exclusivist purism.[21]

The problem that both *Puerto Rican Jam* and the Créolistes are grappling with, one they share with Bhabha, Gilroy, and Anzaldúa, is how to imagine resistance to a hegemonic state from within. A poetics and politics of infiltration becomes their solution to the absence of a separate physical space. A revealing alternative formulation is Derek Walcott's in *The Antilles: Fragments of Epic Memory*, in which the Caribbean's assimilation of U.S. influence is figured as Florida's neocolonial penetration of the Caribbean. In contrast, the Créolistes figure assimilation as the *engulfment* of the Caribbean. The former evokes the subordinate exteriority of the Caribbean to metropolitan/continental power, the latter the subordinate interiority of Creole to continental/metropolitan (French) power. Walcott, drawing on his experience of the politically independent Caribbean nation-states of Saint Lucia and Trinidad, makes no explicit mention of a state, but he nonetheless can assume the existence of separate Caribbean states; the Créolistes and *Puerto Rican Jam* cannot, and their solutions are structured by that fact.

Like many other celebrations of cultural hybridity, "Praise" and *Puerto Rican Jam* tend to construct misleadingly simple oppositions, which their own articulations of hybridity (embodied in the urban squatter and diasporic Puerto Rican respectively) then transcend or deconstruct. As John Hutynk has said: "Hybridity-talk, creole, and so on, seem to imply a bogus notion of the prior and the pure—pre-hybrid cultures" (119). It is only through a drastic simplification of maroon societies, for example, that they can be held up as signs of an impossible and outdated purism, for as Richard and Sally Price remind us, "these maroon communities were, in fact, the most thoroughly (and earliest fully) 'creolized' of 'New World communities'" (130).[22] *Puerto Rican Jam*, in obscuring the dynamic diversity of the Puerto Rican island, replicates the Créolistes' treatment of the maroons. Its entirely legitimate desire to revalue the large diasporic Puerto Rican population unfortunately depends upon the simultaneous devaluation of the island population as purist. It holds out the immense possibilities of Puerto Rican coalitions with other minority populations in the United States, but glosses over the possibilities of pan-Caribbean and pan-Latin American or feminist coalitions on the island. Similarly, it is silent about the diversity and dynamic cultural hybridity on the island that has arisen from the presence and cultural practices of Dominicans, Cubans, and migrants from the lesser Antilles, to name but a few groups. Agustín Lao's essay refers to the "constrained freedom of New York" (181), but makes no room for a similarly "constrained freedom" in Puerto Rico. Similarly, Manuel Guzmán's essay on "sexiles" dramatizes the homophobia of the island and the relief of New York. But what of the fact that San Juan is widely regarded as the gay capital of the Caribbean? And how do the claims one makes for American progressivism change if one considers not only New York but also, say, Paradise, Pennsylvania, or rural Alabama, where the prospects of a public gay identity are distinctly less promising? New York misleads as a synecdoche for the United States, just as the frozen image of the most reactionary of *jibarista* nationalisms misleads as a synecdoche for contemporary Puerto Rican nationalism. It is, in fact, such silences and simplifications that enable the construction of urban diasporic Puerto Ricans as the privileged subjects of change rather than, more modestly and accurately, also and equally subjects of change.

Grosfoguel readily concedes the political imperialism of the United States, claiming to seek statehood as a means of minimizing damage from that imperialism, but his claim that Guadeloupe's status as a DOM led to an "enriching transformation" (74) (a claim the Créolistes would vigorously contest) points in a different direction. I want to suggest that the political maps that *Puerto Rican Jam* and "Praise" draw are organized not only by political and economic imperialism but by cultural imperialism. For *Puerto Rican Jam* and "Praise" share with their imperial rulers, at best, indifference to Third World political struggles and, at worst, deep skepticism toward them.

The content of the appendix to "Praise" is revealing in this regard. In the first paragraph the Créolistes distance themselves from economistic marxisms and narrow nationalisms, citing as unfortunate examples "many countries in the Third World and Eastern Europe" (904). That such unfortunate examples in fact abound I have no hesitation in admitting. But the Créolistes provide not one instance of either antidemocratic Western states or democratic Caribbean and Third World states. Notwithstanding their claim to the contrary, then, their hope for a Caribbean confederation and a "multipartisan, multiunionist, and pluralist regime" (904) appears to be imagined in a Western European mode. Although the Créolistes invoke a pan-Caribbean federation and claim solidarity with both the Caribbean islands and South America, their invocation is rendered somewhat abstract by the meagerness of historical and cultural detail. "As Creoles, we are as close, if not closer, anthropologically speaking, to the people of the Seychelles, of

Mauritius, or the Reunion, than we are to the Puerto Ricans or the Cubans" (894). Significantly, it is creoleness as mediated by France (Seychelles, Mauritius, Reunion) that is privileged through this elaboration. Thus, the Créolistes' global gaze is perhaps more circumscribed by French ideology and colonial history than they admit. The Prices contend that even the Créolistes' conception of the Creole language is marred by Francocentrism, and charge them with accommodationism:

> In contrast to most literary critics, who accept the Créolistes' self-definition as intellectual rebels (see, for example, Burton, "Idea"; Scarboro, "Shift"), we would argue that much of the ideology of the Créolité movement, from its emphasis on the role of French (as opposed to African languages) in the development of Creole to its championing of ethnic diversity, fits comfortably within its historical moment. Indeed, we believe that, in terms of cultural politics, the kinds of specificities championed by the Créolistes are in step with a rapidly modernizing Martinique in which people are, with considerable coaching from France, adjusting to their new place within a greater Europe. (135; see also 138)

At the very least, the fact that Chamoiseau's work is routinely hailed as enriching the French language testifies to the pressures of co-optation that threaten infiltrationist politics.

Whereas a creeping Francocentrism appears in Créolité, visible in its choice of national references, and its neglect of the rest of the Caribbean, which undermines in practice the pan-Caribbeanism it proclaims in theory, *Puerto Rican Jam* displays an unapologetic affiliation with the United States and an explicit and unapologetic casting aside of pan-Caribbeanist politics. Grosfoguel shares the Créolistes' skepticism about socialist projects and their faith that the Western liberal welfare state is the best guarantor of democratic rights. His essay dismisses the independence movement as elitist and "aristocratic" (69); it holds out the spectres of Latin American *caudillismo* and dictatorship, clumping together as examples Cuba, Haiti, and the Dominican Republic. Grenada, Nicaragua, and Jamaica share but one sentence in which they function as examples of unpragmatic attempts at self-determination. It is in this interpretive context that for Grosfoguel the only viable democratic tradition becomes that of the United States. Indeed, *Puerto Rican Jam*'s revisionary history combines detailed speech about the progressive measures and effects of the colonial state with silence about comparably progressive *independentista* measures. Although the *independentista* movement is far from free of sexism, it has spearheaded many of the major pro-feminist initiatives on the island; yet the anthology details only the openings for feminist organizing provided by U.S. colonization. Similarly, the editors combine energetic speech on the subject of *independentista* violence with silence on the antidemocratic actions of the U.S. state—actions which have included mass surveillance, disappearances, statistically staggering police abuse of New York Puerto Ricans in U.S. jails, imprisonment of pro-independence Puerto Rican activists for terms that made them the longest-held political prisoners in the Western hemisphere, the mass sterilization of a third of all Puerto Rican women of childbearing age in the 1970s, the use of Puerto Ricans as cannon-fodder in the Vietnam War, U.S. proposals to take over the Rainforest, and the literal blasting to pieces of several Puerto Rican islands by the U.S. Navy. Allusions to such U.S. atrocities may be a staple of *independentista* rhetoric, but what is demanded then is not to sweep them under the carpet, but to seriously evaluate their implications for the radical statehood platform. Moreover, *Puerto Rican Jam*'s vociferous awareness of the risks of a purely formal political independence is not matched by any accompanying awareness of the risks of a purely formal political equality within the United States. Indeed, their platform is essentially a multiculturalist version of the African American civil rights platform, whose gains have been circumscribed at best.

It is in this context of speech and silence that Agustín Lao's essay's invocation of "Our Ame-Rica: A Federation of Diasporas" parodically alludes to José Martí's "Nuestra América." It, too, refuses Martí's oppositional pro-independence stance and anti-imperialist hemispheric politics in favor of the model of resistance from within. The deliberately bilingual and linguistically hybrid "Our Ame-Rica" is stripped of its Spanish orthography, thereby erasing the written accent but enhancing the spoken Spanish accent; it plays with the promise of wealth in this Ame-*rica*, for *rica* means rich and evokes contrast to the implied scarcity that independence would bring. In its grammatical shift from the masculine "Puerto Rico" to the feminine "Ame-Rica" it enacts at the level of form and grammar the "feminization of resistance" for which Grosfoguel calls. Similarly, Manuel Guzmán's celebration of the political possibilities offered by the drag performances at the New York Latino gay club "La Escuelita" refers to their " 'Made in the USA' marginality" (223), a moving phrase that evokes a Latino sweatshop worker faced with a racist state. But then he refers to their "Third World origins—*the romanticized memories, the carcass, of a Latin American spirit left behind*" (223). The parody of Martí, the exclusive focus on diasporic Latinos in the United States, and the image of Latin America as a carcass, together promise less the cutting edge of a critical multiculturalism than the blunt contempt of mainstream America for Latin America. Both *Puerto Rican Jam* and "Praise," then, are more deeply marked than they admit by the dominant ideologies of the metropolitan states they claim to critique.

Moreover, they share with most of the other theorists of hybridity whose work I have dwelt upon the tendency to present hybridity as the synthetic transcendence of tyrannical and reductive binary oppositions. Focusing on resistance and heterogeneity "within" rather than on opposition "between" becomes a key move enabling the delinking of cultural and political nationalisms. It is also the means by which the thesis of cultural imperialism is transformed from a critique of the ideological machinery of inequality into a defense of purism, essentialism, or nativism.[23] Furthermore, those who argue for the political and analytic relevance of the term "cultural imperialism" may not desire refuge from modernity but a share in shaping the forms that modernity will take. At stake are not pure origins but egalitarian futures. If many studies invoking cultural imperialism models have been guilty of theorizing inequality largely in East/West terms, so too have many studies of cultural hybridity erred in theorizing hybridity in largely East/West terms, neglecting the relations of power in more "local" processes of hybridization. Both approaches thus occlude local inequalities and both should theorize local and global forms of inequality together—precisely because local and global forms of domination so often reinforce one another. For example, critics of the cultural imperialism model argue that Coke or blue jeans in Sri Lanka do not remain foreign cultural products, but are incorporated into local systems of meaning and become cultural hybrids. Perhaps so. But what these critics ignore is that they may also be incorporated into local structures of privilege and inequality. Thus, an empirical study of, say, consumer practices in India would likely reveal new articulations of the "traditional" local practice of dowry with post-deregulation consumerism.

The trend in Postcolonial and Cultural Studies that treats opposition as epistemologically reductive seems to me to entail some grave errors and misrepresentations. It charges oppositional politics with purism, essentialism, and mystified binaristic notions of Self and Other which, once deconstructed, can be transcended. Identifying ambivalence and the inevitably contradictory consequences of particular social practices seems currently to absolve us of *weighing* those consequences and making a choice. Moreover, the present move delegitimizing opposition conflates political opposition (more appropriately thought of, perhaps, in terms of "conflict") with logical opposition in language (the object of Deconstruction's critique). As Benita Parry insists in her critique of Bhabha, "the notion of conflict... certainly does infer [*sic*] antagonism, but contra Bhabha, does not posit simplistically a unitary and closed structure to the adversarial forces" (6). Moreover, contrary to the way in which theorists like Anzaldúa, Bhabha, and Benítez-Rojo frame binary oppositions, binaries are neither the source of social inequality (since there are unequal societies that do not subscribe to binaristic thinking and more egalitarian ones that do) nor the exclusive provenance of the West. It is only by misunderstanding opposition as a static, rationalist relationship between monolithic, abstracted forces that so much contemporary theory can condemn it wholesale. Political opposition is better thought of as a contingent, conjunctural, and critical action people take after weighing the complexities and contradictions of their particular circumstances. It need not entail simplification of those complexities, nor does it have to essentialize them; one can take an oppositional stance on the basis of a more rather than a less complex argument, or on the basis of a critique of essentialism. That one might be wrong in one's judgment is entirely possible but hardly unique to that stance.

Given *Puerto Rican Jam*'s mobilization of the rhetoric of anti-purism, diaspora, and post-nationalism, it is tempting to consider it a manifesto for post-nationalist hybridity. Certainly, it claims to be one: "Capitalist transnationalization has made nation-states' structures obsolete in attempting to control economic processes within their borders" (8). But as I have argued elsewhere, this notion of transnationalization does not explain why migrants believe their prospects for economic opportunity change so drastically by crossing a national border. Moreover, to concede to *Puerto Rican Jam*'s post-nationalist self-definition would require us to ignore that its delegitimation of nation-states is selective: while it delegitimizes Puerto Rico's claims to becoming an independent nation-state, it in fact seeks to take up a place in the most powerful nation-state in the world.

Too often, the "resistance within" model focuses on "the Third World in the belly of the First" by casting aside the Third World in the belly of the *Third*. The problem is not that diasporic or minority experience in the First World is the object of study; the problem arises when such study simultaneously invokes, stands in for, and replaces the study of minority and subaltern experience in the Third World. An appropriative First World national unconscious again raises its head. Although the rhetoric of "the Third World in the belly of the First" can be traced back to the (substantially different concerns of) the model of "internal colonialism," post-nationalist discourse has exacerbated the consequences of such substitution, contributing to what Gayatri Spivak calls "sanctioned ignorance."[24] For such discourse ignores the ways in which the dissident, oppressed, and minority subject's experience is filtered through a national location which, I would argue, constitutes both a project (or an avenue for political mobilization) and a limit. It is a project in the sense Spivak identifies: "There is no way that the 'radical' or the 'ethnicist' can take a position against civil rights, the Equal Rights Amendment, or great transformative opinions such as *Roe v. Wade.* One way or another, we cannot not want to inhabit this great rational abstraction."[25] On the other hand, national location is a limit in the sense that it makes the black Caribbean migrant the object of racism, exploitation, and oppression, the Other of dominant culture (in a way, for example, that a black Jamaican and Hindu Indian may not be in their nations of origin even though they may face extreme forms of oppression there along other axes). The stakes of substituting First World for Third World contexts are further raised when scholarship speaks not in the name of "Britain" or "The United States," but in the name of transnationalism and "the global," for such studies too often not only posit an equivalence between minorities in the First World and majorities in the Third World, they also generalize on the basis of those minorities accessible to the metropolitan states in question. Charges of the appropriation of experience cut the other way, too, for intellectuals of several American minority groups see Postcolonial Studies as appropriating and marginalizing their experience of oppression.[26] Both sets of charges, it seems to me, are responses to the logic of substitution that characterizes much post-nationalist discourse. They will continue to be made—and our disciplines made to serve dominant institutional convenience—as long as the commonalities between minorities in the First World and subalterns and elites in the Third World are taken as axiomatic rather than themselves made the objects of investigation. It would be more productive to undertake genuinely comparative studies of both minorities and minoritized populations in the First and Third Worlds. Such comparatist study is essential to specify the precise grounds of alliances, differences, and possibilities of coalition across differences.

If discourses of hybridity are not to become simply an intellectual version of "we are the world"—equally well-intentioned, equally inaccurate, and equally damaging—it should recontextualize migrancy, which it now accords a privileged epistemological and political vantage point. Moreover, while Cultural Studies historically has been skeptical—and with good reason—of Area Studies programs dominated by the positivist and empiricist methodologies of the social sciences, grounding our theories of hybridity in various Area Studies programs is one way to keep areas of the globe other than the metropolitan cities of the United States, France, and Britain visible on our political and intellectual maps, and to acquire a literacy in diverse subaltern histories, including but not confined to the multiple subaltern diasporas across the globe. It should be clear that the "areas" of "Area Studies" are not pre-given, but rather themselves the objects of reflection, articulation, and debate—as Paul Gilroy's mapping of a "black atlantic" and Gloria Anzaldúa's mapping of Border Studies or the articulation of "South Asian" identities in the United States indicate. Finally, as we approach these areas, it is crucial to remember that, whether posed by hybridists or essentialists, the simplifying alternative "hybridity or essentialism?" misleads. The real question has never been "hybridity or not?" but rather "which hybridity?"

Chapter 2

Theorizing Hybridity: Caribbean Nationalisms

> There are no people there in the true sense of the word, with a character and purpose of their own.
>
> —James Anthony Froude

> A fragile reality (the experience of Caribbeanness, woven together from one side of the Caribbean to the other) negatively twisted together in its urgency (Caribbeanness as a dream, forever denied, often deferred, yet a strange, stubborn presence in our responses).
>
> This reality is there in essence: dense (inscribed in fact) but threatened (not inscribed in consciousness).
>
> This dream is vital, but not obvious.
>
> —Édouard Glissant

> The unity is submarine.
>
> —Edward Kamau Brathwaite

Let me begin this chapter with a bold claim: the very vision of the Caribbean as a place of historical possibility turns on the question of hybridity. There has been vigorous debate from both within and without the Caribbean as to whether the Caribbean can yield a modernity at all, and if so, a modernity monstrous or marvelous. At the heart of these debates lie assumptions about the status and value of hybridity. For colonialists like James Anthony Froude, the cultural hybridity of the Caribbean offered a discursive means by which to delegitimize the West Indian colonies as potentially sovereign nation-states, a delegitimation that became particularly urgent for the colonial powers after the Haitian Revolution in 1804 inaugurated the world's first black republic. Froude's declaration in *The English in the West Indies Or, the Bow of Ulysses* (1888) that the Caribbean had "no people in the true sense of the word" served to rationalize his advocacy of continued British rule over the West Indies. His insistence on the failure of an imagined community in the West Indies, as for example in his infamous declaration that the "African and the Asiatic will not mix," depended on ignoring the substantial colonial legislation in his time that was intended precisely to *halt* processes of cultural hybridization that were generating a cross-ethnic imagined community at the popular level. Moreover, his writing relied on an imperial fantasy (albeit a rhetorically successful one) of a homogeneous and unified imperial Britain, and elided the divisions, tensions, and hybridizations between the sparring constituents of the "United Kingdom." In a vein comparably dismissive of the Caribbean, Charles de Gaulle is reputed to have said on a visit to Martinique: "Between Europe and America I see only specks of dust."

The genealogies of debates between colonialists and nationalists on the subject of hybridity can be traced back to constructions of Caliban and the (ig)noble savage. The various literary articulations on the subject closely parallel positions within the scientific racist debates of the nineteenth century.[1] For Froude, as for Prospero, the Caribbean/Caliban is the devil "on whose nature/Nurture will never stick" (*The Tempest* IV.i: 188–189), in other words, a primitive Other who cannot be hybridized at all, an ignoble savage. In variations on this theme, there are those who assert that the Caribbean can be hybridized, but its hybridity can achieve no more than pathetic mimicry. This is the role some nationalists have attributed to Shakespeare's Ariel, forever destined to remain an apprentice—a cultural model whose economic equivalent is underdevelopment. One version of the mimicry formulation sees Caribbean hybridity as a composite that cannot be synthesized into anything new; such is the infertile and essentially dysfunctional hybridity that postcolonial skeptics like V.S. Naipaul see, leading him to declare, echoing Froude in his own act of colonial mimicry, that "[h]istory is built around achievement and creation; and nothing was created in the West Indies" (*The Middle Passage* 29).

On the other hand lies the spectrum of thinkers who claim the Caribbean's hybridity enables a path toward a productive modernity. For them discourses of hybridity have offered a rhetorical clearing-space for assertions of Caribbean (and Latin American) national and regional identities. Refuting colonialist delegitimations of distinct New World identities has been a requirement for the assertion of Caribbean and Latin American nationalist identities. Thus, for example, José Martí, in "Nuestra América" (1891) describing the moment at which a merely imitative, composite hybridity begins to turn into an authentic and synthetic hybridity rooted (to use his organicist metaphor) in the Americas, says: "Nations stand up and greet one another. 'What are we?' is the mutual question, and little by little they furnish answers" (91). Similarly, José Vasconcelos in *La Raza Cósmica* (1925), another key formulation of *mestizaje* in postrevolutionary Mexico, addresses a central anxiety about identity, referring to "the question the *mestizo* has often asked himself: Is my contribution to culture comparable to that of the relatively pure races that have made history upto our days?" (4). As late as 1971, in Cuba's own post-revolutionary socialist nation-building phase, the Cuban intellectual Roberto Fernández Retamar structures his essay "Caliban" as a response to the skeptical question of a European journalist: "Does a Latin-American culture exist?" These questions about identity all turn to the rhetoric of hybridity to provide affirmative answers and link the diverse elements of the Caribbean. The interrogative structure of Martí's, Vasconcelos's, and Fernández Retamar's meditations clears the space for them to valorize hybridity to refute colonial skepticism—all in key moments of nation building.

Discourses of hybridity in the Caribbean perform several functions. They elaborate a syncretic New World identity, distinct from that of its "Mother Cultures"; in doing so, they provide a basis for national and regional legitimacy. Second, they offer a way of balancing and/or displacing discourses of equality, which has led to their importance in many instances for securing bourgeois nationalist hegemony. Third, discourses of hybridity have been implicated in managing racial politics—either by promoting cultural over racial hybridity or by producing racial mixes acceptable to the élite. For all these reasons, post-colonial nationalisms in the Caribbean have canonized nonthreatening hybridities such as those embodied at particular times by the callaloo, the creole, and the mestizo.

In the realm of the arts, it is no accident that the Haitian communist writer Jacques Stephen Alexis, the Cuban communist novelist Alejo Carpentier, the Colombian novelist Gabriel García Márquez, the Martinican writer Édouard Glissant, and the Guyanese writer Wilson Harris invoke marvelous and magic realism. For the sense of abundance, energy, and miraculous possibility, in conjunction with a focus on cultural hybridity, makes marvelous or magic realism a nationalist resource in the hands of artists like Alexis and Carpentier.[2] Similarly, Fernando Ortiz' and Ángel Rama's elaborations of *transculturación*, Oswald de Andrade's "Anthropophagite Manifesto," Derek Walcott's "mulatto aesthetics," Wilson Harris's "cross-cultural imagination," and Édouard Glissant's *antillanité* all claim hybridity as a route to a dynamic and viable modernity. In both the national–political culture and the cultural politics/aesthetics of the Caribbean, notwithstanding the many differences in the directions of nationalist projects, then, cultural hybridity has been a central preoccupation.

Given the claims I have made for the connection between hybridity and nationalisms, it might appear logical to turn to the example of Haiti and the triumph of the Haitian Revolution in 1804—not only because Haiti was the world's first black Republic, and the second New World nation-state, whose independence preceded the Spanish Caribbean's by a hundred years and the Anglophone Caribbean's by about one hundred and sixty years, but also because of Haiti's symbolic significance for subsequent Caribbean nationalist projects. Indeed, C.L.R. James held that it was with the Haitian Revolution that West Indians first became aware of themselves as a people ("From Touissant L'Ouverture to Fidel Castro" 296). Kamau Brathwaite, too, has noted the Haitian Revolution as one of three events decisive for the development of a Creole concept of nation.[3] Yet Haiti is the one Caribbean nation where hybridity has not been an integral part of nation-building discourse. The reasons for this lie in Haiti's unique history and demographic politics: Haiti is one of the Caribbean's most racially homogeneous societies; it had one of the Caribbean's smallest white elites, and was the only Caribbean nation where after independence there was no substantial internal control of power by a white elite. One hundred years later, it was thus a populist rhetoric of *blackness* that was so skillfully manipulated against a mulatto elite in the long years of Duvalier repression. In fact, as Michael Dash has observed, Haiti is the only Caribbean nation to have seen a fully developed indigenism or nativism (*The Other America* 73). Hybridity was not, then, part of the popular vocabulary for the democratizing impulses of the revolution.

Yet, one could argue nonetheless that the discursive emphasis on blackness was a muted expression of the *lived experience* of hybridity in the years of the Revolution. For "blackness" in the revolutionary era (unlike in the crass opportunism of the Duvalier regime) itself functioned as an index of political hybridity and political emancipation, referring not to any particular race, but to the citizens of the new Republic.[4] Moreover, as the title of James's classic account of the Haitian Revolution, *The Black Jacobins*, foregrounds, the Haitian Revolution was a hybrid political project of modernization, in which the rhetoric of French political thought was to be mapped on to and combined with the inherited economic and racial institutions of a plantation society—a project quite distinct from simple imitation or mimicry. Although the Haitian Revolution has sometimes been read by writers such as Aimé Césaire as an act of *marronnage* (i.e. an indigenist turning inward that cut off contact with the wider world), it was in fact driven by a modernizing impulse consistent with that of creolization. Michael Dash concurs with C.L.R. James's reading of the Haitian Revolution in this light:

> By focusing on state formation as an alternative revolutionary strategy, James was already shifting attention away from resistance as marronnage (that is, the creation of isolated communities, united by shared defiance of a dominant force) to the importance of the state—a state that would try to restructure relations shaped by the plantation or colonialism and produce a new self-consciousness through the creolizing power of the state. (Dash, *The Other America* 15)[5]

Thus, though the Haitian Revolution did not mobilize *discourses* of hybridity in any obvious way, it *was* a hybridizing force. Contrary to many contemporary metropolitan accounts of hybridity, then, Caribbean history reveals that the state need not be opposed to or threatened by hybridity, but may claim to emerge from it and, indeed, be an agent of hybridization.

This recognition of the creolizing power of the state, combined with different demographic dynamics elsewhere in the Caribbean, makes for the prominence of hybridity in Caribbean political nationalisms. It is, in other words, no accident that in the Caribbean and Latin America the rise of discourses of hybridity and the rise of (proto)nationalisms coincide. The link in the Caribbean between nationalism and hybridity can explain the seventy-year lag between a foundational text of *mestizaje*, José Martí's "Nuestra América," written in 1891, and comparable Anglophone discussions of creolization, which took place in the 1960s—for these were the periods of independence movements in each context.

However, whatever the nationalist ideology to which these discourses were appended, the hybrid national subject was rarely imagined differently from the unitary Enlightenment subject. The rhetoric of hybridity's crucial role in forging political opposition between nationalists and colonialists, then, entailed no necessary epistemological break with prior modes. A close reading of the speeches of Eric Williams, the first prime minister of independent Trinidad and Tobago, reveals the extent to which hybridity discourses may share many of the same assumptions as colonialist discourse. Froude's production of an ethnically and culturally homogeneous Britain as a model of nationhood clearly informs Eric Williams's account below:

> There can be no Mother India for those whose ancestors came from India.... There can be no Mother Africa for those of African origin, and the Trinidad and Tobago society is living a lie and heading for trouble if it seeks to create the impression or to allow others to act under the

> delusion that Trinidad and Tobago is an African society. There can be no Mother England and no dual loyalties; no person can be allowed to get the best of both worlds, and to enjoy the privileges of citizenship in Trinidad and Tobago whilst expecting to retain United Kingdom citizenship. There can be no Mother China, even if one could agree as to which China is the mother; and there can be no Mother Syria or Mother Lebanon. A nation, like an individual, can have only one mother. The only Mother we recognize is Trinidad and Tobago, and Mother cannot discriminate between her children. (281)

Notwithstanding its invocation of a hybrid Trinidad, this passage insists on the need for a fairly traditionally imagined unitary national subject with a singular allegiance, even as the sternly disciplining tone testifies to popular desires for non-unitary or nonexclusivist identifications. In a manner that supports Bhabha's arguments, William's admonitions clearly reveal the dangerous proximity of diversity and division. So, too, does the metaphor of the callaloo, which, like that of the American melting pot and the more recent language of multiculturalism, attempts to manage difference by projecting an image of nonconflictual diversity.[6] Jamaica's motto "Out of many, one people," Guyana's "One people, one nation, one destiny," Trinidad's "Together we aspire, together we achieve" and Haiti's "Unity is strength" (Stewart 151–152), all bear out Bhabha's claims about the nation's anxious "double time" that continually refers to an achieved unity in an attempt to produce it (*Location of Culture* 154–155). Haunting all of these assertions is a recognition of the fragility of the "we" of the race- and class-divided nations. Yet what Bhabha does not recognize is the grounding paradox of many Caribbean nations: that while discourses of hybridity can disable the nation, they are also an enabling condition for it. If Williams is to legitimize a Trinidadian nation, he must produce it as both hybrid *and* homogeneous.

Williams's discourse is representative of Caribbean national discourses in several regards. Racial and nationalist discourses in the Caribbean frequently offer contradictory instances of tearing apart and stitching together "the people," and discourses of hybridity offer a crucial means of managing those contradictory tendencies. Having validated a hybrid Trinidadian national identity, Williams goes on to seal off that hybridity and encase it in the familiar organicist metaphor of the nation-as-family. The hybrid Trinidadian national subject necessary for the foundational legitimacy of the nation thus turns quickly into a stabilized, unitary subject with exclusive affiliations.

Although hybridity offers Williams a vocabulary for unifying Trinidad by producing a hybrid identity that is different from the identities in the ancestral lands of its inhabitants, it is important to note that it is a cultural hybridity, not a racial one. The tendency to play up cultural hybridity as a way of playing down racial hybridity is a recurrent move of many foundational Caribbean nationalist invocations of cultural hybridity. As I elaborate in chapters six and seven, Trinidadian nationalist (and regional) politics have resorted to tearing apart the fabric of "the people" along racial lines, developing opposed bourgeois-nationalist Afro-Creole and Indian political parties. For this reason, although Williams requires cultural hybridity for his national project, he cannot afford racial hybridity; the races must be kept distinguishable and apart. The rhetoric of cultural hybridity in Trinidadian national politics, then, has been linked to state "divide and rule" racial policies.

Yet the examples of Eric Williams and the national mottoes above also demonstrate that, far from threatening the nation-state, discourses of hybridity can also provide the rhetorical *glue* to a nation-state that threatens to fall apart. The rhetoric of hybridity has served as one important idiom of populism. According to John Beverley, it is the contradictory pressures of exploitation and populism that necessitate a "wobbl[ing] between bourgeois nationalism and a marxist analysis and vision of liberation."[7] Populism offers a mode of "non-class integration" (143) of the masses with whom the national bourgeoisie needs to ally itself against oligarchy and foreign domination (147). Although this alliance requires some accommodations to the masses, it need entail no fundamental shift in the relations of production. For as Frantz Fanon foresaw, to the national bourgeoisie "nationalization quite simply means the transfer into native hands of those unfair advantages which are the legacy of the colonial period" (*The Wretched of the Earth* 152). History has certainly borne out Fanon's warning, showing that the "foreign domination" theories of the dependency school can be continuous with the project of national capitalism fully as much as with socialism. In most Caribbean nation-states, where the national bourgeoisie has not the resources to become a productive bourgeoisie, even as the national bourgeoisie commits the nation to neocolonial dependence, it must invoke the populist anticolonial struggle through which it came to power. The populist appeal of hybridity discourse should serve as a reminder that whilst discourses of hybridity may reveal epistemological contradictions in nationalist discourse, these contradictions can be rhetorically overcome. In fact, I have been arguing that the rhetoric of hybridity has been a crucial instrument in *managing* those contradictions. Hybridity might reveal the nation is a lie, but it can also enable the lie to function. Not disruption, but consolidation of the nation-state, then, has been one historical function of discourses of hybridity in the Caribbean.

Also common to the political slogans and images I have outlined (such as "all o' we is one" and the callaloo) is the fact that in them the rhetoric of hybridity displaces the issue of social equality between and within groups. Still more striking is the fact that this displacement is common to both hegemonic nationalist discourses and many oppositional discourses of hybridity. In this displacement of equality, then, lies an unexpected congruity between dominant and oppositional discourse.

Hybridity and hegemony have thus been crucially linked in the Caribbean, the former providing a vehicle for both populist nonclass integration of the masses and more utopian desires—from popular desires for communities permitting multiple affiliations to images of trans-ethnic solidarity and regional feminisms, many of which draw on the idiom of hybridity. If the rhetoric of cultural hybridity has offered the ruling classes a means of stabilizing the status quo through various strategies for displacing a politics of equality, its role in achieving hegemony has also offered oppositional constituencies the opportunity to seize upon the slippages, contradictions, and accommodations of ruling-class rhetoric. In short, the lag between communities imagined as equal and realities of exploitation and inequality, the duplicity of populism, the gap between what Mary Layoun calls the grammar and the rhetoric of the nation (411)—these discrepancies form the terrain of discourses of hybridity. This is the area where narratives of hybridity articulate the relationship of nation to state, of culture to economics and politics.

Mestizaje and creolization have been the two most widely influential sets of articulations of these relationships in the Caribbean. I address some major examples of *mestizaje* discourse to lend historical depth to our understanding of contemporary discussions of hybridity and to heighten our awareness of the subtle and significant differences in inflection of different variants of these discourses. To keep in sight the heterogeneity of the political impulses and projects of these variants, I have chosen to think of creolization and *mestizaje* as *discursive complexes.* As a cultural theorist, I am particularly interested in the ways in which discourses of creolization mobilize the category of culture to negotiate that of class—whether to demonstrate the irreducibility of cultural identities to class ones, or to provide an area of symbolic resolutions for class conflicts, or to function as a rehearsal or bridge to the resolution of those problems.

Mestizaje is the earliest fully elaborated discursive complex of hybridity in Latin America and the Caribbean, and remains the reigning official liberal ideology. In its strictest sense *mestizaje* refers to the mixing of Native American and Spaniard, locating the contemporary identity of Mexico, in particular, in the complexly mythologized relationship of the royal Aztec La Malinche (renamed Doña Marina by the Spaniards) with the Spanish conquistador Cortez, with whom she bore a son. *Mestizaje* thus imagines Mexicans as the mixed descendants of Indians and Spaniards. More broadly, *mestizaje* (*métissage*, in the French Caribbean) has come to refer to cultural and racial mixing of any kind, and is often used synonymously with black/white mixing—a substitution that, as we will see, is not without significance.

Trenchant Latin American critiques of the discursive complex *mestizaje* have long existed; more recently, the emergent field of Afro-Hispanic Studies has also contributed its critiques of *mestizaje*. However, Postcolonial Studies, owing in part to its Anglophone bias, has not registered the presence of these vibrant critiques, all of which are acutely aware that inclusion in the national imaginary by no means assures inclusion as equal—a point that the Peruvian marxist *indigenista* José Mariátegui addressed in relation to land rights and, more recently, Doris Sommer addressed in relation to the mobilization of the genre of the romance by foundational national fictions. At the heart of the critiques to which I have referred lies the question of how *mestizaje* positions Blacks and/or Indians.[8] If, as Doris Sommer has argued, in the case of Mexico, promoting a mestizo identity as the national identity sanctioned the mixing of Native American and Spaniard, but repressed from the national imaginary the black population of the nation, then how much more grave is this repression in the case of the Spanish Caribbean, whose Native American populations were are all but decimated within a few years of Columbus's arrival, but whose large, living Afro-Caribbean populations go unnamed in the dominant official discourse of cultural hybridity.[9] *Negrismo, Negritud*, and *Indigenismo* historically developed as contestatory alternatives to *mestizaje*. The more recent critiques of *mestizaje* emerging from Afro-Hispanist Studies, however, have tended to homogenize the different orientations and different conjunctural politics of the discursive complex of *mestizaje*.[10] Richard Jackson, for example, has made a rather hyperbolic association between *mestizaje* and "ethnic lynching."[11] I should hardly need to point out that invocations of blackness or refusals of "Westernization" in the Caribbean have by themselves been no guarantee of progressive racial politics, far less progressive gender or sexual politics. Thus, in the 1920s and 1930s, Haitian indigenism and the black nationalist *Les Griots* movement tended toward fascism (Dash, *The Other America* 73–76); the neo-Indianism of the Brazilian modernist *Verde-Amarelo* and *Anta* groups in the 1920s and 1930s was closely associated with the rise of fascism and the institution of the fascist *Estado Novo*; in mainstream Dominican discourse "*indio*" is the preferred term for Afro-Dominicans, establishing a racial distance from "*negro*," a term reserved for the demonized Haitians.[12] To those who attack *mestizaje*'s rhetoric of hybridity on grounds that it is no more than a euphemism for racial assimilation or suicide of blacks or Indians, it is worth remembering that an identical rhetorical function may be performed by invoking "pure" race discourses, whether those of Indianness or blackness.

Considering the slipperiness of *mestizaje*, then, both absolutist celebrations and absolutist rejections of it miss the point. Jorge Klor de Alva is quite right to consider the conceptual and political slipperiness paradigmatic of *mestizaje*: "The chameleonic nature of *mestizaje*—Western in the presence of Europeans, indigenous in the native villages, and Indian-like in contemporary United States barrios—is its crucial characteristic" (Klor de Alva 253). In a sense, this chapter attempts to survey the shifting *terrains* of *mestizaje* that color the chameleon. The differences within the discursive complex become easily apparent if we read them conjuncturally, that is, in relation to material and discursive issues at the time. For instance, what domestic and international struggles did the discourse participate in? Was it oppositional or hegemonic? Was it involved in elaborating an emergent nationalist project or was it the official discourse of consolidation? Did it focus on class and/or ethnic difference? (Most discourses of *mestizaje*, as well as critiques of it, tend to splinter according to which of these terms they emphasize.) How did conceptualizing hybridity as a primarily racial or a primarily cultural category serve the political agendas of each text? These questions taken together enable us to understand the temporal, regional, and individual differences in discourses of *mestizaje*; they are crucial to understanding how the same terms, "*mestizo*," "indian," and "black," functioned quite differently in different articulations of *mestizaje*.

Such differences can be addressed by examining two of the foundational texts of *mestizaje*: José Martí's "Nuestra América" (1891) and José Vasconcelos's *La Raza Cósmica* (*The Cosmic Race*) (1925). Although I will read their work for its epistemological and political implications, any conjunctural analysis must also recognize that the enormous influence of Martí's and Vasconcelos's conceptions of *mestizaje* is at many levels quite independent of the content and epistemology of their writing, having more to do with the political influence of the historical figures of Martí and Vasconcelos, and the symbolic importance of Cuban Independence. At the level of epistemology, Martí and Vasconcelos represent the opposing poles of *mestizaje* discourse; in relation to their work one could go on to position Simon Bolívar (Venezuela), Antenor Firmin (Haiti), Arturo Uslar Pietri (Venezuela), Cassiano Ricardo (Brazil), Gilberto Freyre (Brazil), Roberto Fernández Retamar (Cuba), and Brau and the Jibaristas (Puerto Rico), to name only a few.

Both Martí and Vasconcelos were active in the national politics of their time—and it is pertinent to our discussion of the conceptual elasticity of *mestizaje* that Martí should be claimed by nationalists from across the political spectrum. Martí was an influential member of the Cuban Revolutionary Party, writing from within—and against—a Cuban independence movement that was markedly conservative on the racial issue; his thought derives from the antislavery branch of *independentista* thought. Vasconcelos for his part wrote *The Cosmic Race* in the phase of intense nation-building that followed the Mexican Revolution. By his time, *mestizaje* was poised to become official state ideology. He was for many years Minister of Education in Mexico, in which capacity he was a key architect of Mexican educational and cultural policies; he also ran unsuccessfully for president. *Mestizaje* also makes clear the transnational structuration of nationalist discourse, for the writings of both men were framed by the ascendant threat of their imperialist neighbor, the United States of America, whose expansionist designs had threatened both Cuba and Mexico. Their notions of *mestizaje* were thus deeply concerned with asserting a regional identity that could provide a viable alternative to U.S.-satellite status.

Fighting for independence from Spain and cognizant of "the difference in origins, methods, and interests between the two halves of the continent" (93), Martí is explicitly concerned with developing a form of government appropriate to the hybrid reality of the Americas, so as to chart a path between the twin tyrannies of Spanish and U.S. domination. In this spirit, he rejects the "imported book" (87), declaring:

> To know one's country and govern it with that knowledge is the only way to free it from tyranny. The European university must bow to the American university. The history of America from the Incas to the present, must be taught in clear detail and to the letter, even if the archons of Greece are overlooked. Our Greece must take priority over the Greece which is not ours. We need it more. Nationalist statesmen must replace foreign statesmen. Let the world be grafted onto our republics, but the trunk must be our own. (88)

The rhetoric of *mestizaje* provides Martí ways of insisting on the moral superiority of a "*mestizo* America" figured as being in racial harmony—in implied contrast to a racially divided and segregated United States; it also provides an attempt at racial unity necessary to win the battle against Spain and the United States. Thus, Martí declares: "the native halfbreed [*mestizo*] has conquered the exotic Creole" (87). He claims that a cross-racial "soul, equal and eternal, emanates from bodies of various shapes and colors" (94). Most provocatively: "There can be no racial animosity because there are no races" (93–94).[13]

Martí's claim of racial transcendence is beyond doubt false. Indeed, elsewhere in the essay, he himself betrays the residual discursive pull of racial types. In a move similar to Eric Williams's, the discourse of *cubanidad* found its way around the racial question by focusing on cultural (rather than racial) fusion so as to avert the risks of a potentially conflictual cultural pluralism; it claimed a cultural mainstream or a unified national culture that had successfully incorporated both African and Spanish elements. In fact, as Kutzinski points out, "Afro-Cubanism was the product of a predominantly white local intellegentsia" (155); the idea of cultural synthesis encodes a strategic avoidance of race (157). This subsumption of the race question under the national question is a much-noted feature of Cuban nationalist discourse. More subtly, it is certainly the case that the primary agency in "Nuestra América" seems reserved for elite white and mulatto Christians who would "rescue the Indian" and "make a place for the competent Negro" (91; see also 88). However, these remarks do at least make it ethically incumbent upon those with greater political power to make progressive political changes.

Moreover, although Martí's naming of the *mestizo* rather than the Afro-Cuban is often seen as typical of *mestizaje*'s elision of blacks, Martí was by no means silent on the subject of black Cubans. His position on Afro-Cubans emerges more clearly in his "My Race" (1893) and "Manifesto of Montecristi: The Cuban Revolutionary Party in Cuba" (1895). In the latter, against conservative elements of the CRP, he simultaneously eulogizes and enlists Afro-Cubans in the Independence struggle, praising (albeit in the problematic inherited language of racial types) their kindred spirits, laborious culture, free man's fervor, amiable character, integrity and intelligence (394–395). His valorization of Afro-Cubans serves both his strategic interests in the war against Spain and his interest in portraying an integrationist Cuba as a counterpoint to a segregationist United States. Cuba's first war of independence (1868–78) failed partly because of insufficient participation of black Cubans, and abolition had been a key issue in the long-term battle for Cuban independence. Thus, Martí's practical recognition was comparable to that of Lincoln's in the American

Civil War where it became clear that if the North was to win the War it would need the support of African Americans. Perhaps rather than dismissing Martí's *mestizaje* out of hand as no more than political opportunism, it would be more accurate to say that his liberal humanism and romantic idealism converged with practical necessity. A conjunctural reading of Martí's emphasis on *mestizaje* could also understand it not only in the context of the Cuban nation where there were more Blacks than Indians, but also in the context of an anti-imperialist-Latin Americanism, which sought to claim a cultural fusion and harmony that was morally superior to the U.S. genocide of Indians.[14]

The balance of political ideology and strategic necessity is quite different in José Vasconcelos's *The Cosmic Race*. A substantially different relationship between *mestizaje* and blackness emerges there. *The Cosmic Race* is a treatise on the creation of a fifth race, the cosmic race, "fashioned out of the treasures of all the previous ones" that meet in the Americas (40). Although couched in the language of mysticism and spirituality, as the title indicates, Vasconcelos's thought is in fact far more preoccupied with biological or racial hybridity than Martí's. For Vasconcelos, it is the *racial* hybridity of Latin America that becomes the enabling premise for his assertion of a regional political identity and mission. Vasconcelos, whose meditation on *mestizaje* is also haunted by the spectre of U.S. imperialism, casts the United States as the land that anachronistically continued to seek racial purity: "The Yankees will end up building the last great empire of a single race, the final empire of White supremacy" (20), but the future belongs to Latin America. "The one wants exclusive dominion by the Whites, while the other is shaping a new race, a synthetic race that aspires to engulf and to express everything human in forms of constant improvement" (19). It is the synthetic quality of Latin American society that gives it its mission. Like Martí, Vasconcelos turns to hybridity to distinguish Latin America from both Spain and the United States: "If Latin America were just another Spain, *to the same extent that the United States is another England*" (21, emphasis added) then the situation would be quite different. Racial hybridity serves to legitimize the identity of Latin America as distinct from Europe; asserting the former's historical preeminence over the United States requires that Vasconcelos represent the United States as homogeneous. There is thus in Vasconcelos a deliberate neglect of U.S. contemporaneous discourses of hybridity and more progressive responses to ethnic heterogeneity—from the melting pot to Emma Lazarus's "The New Colossus" (1883) to Whitman's "Song of Myself" (1855), which casts the United States as a "nation of many nations" to Randolph Bourne's "Trans-National America" (1916), to name a few. In fact, Vasconcelos's own discourse holds in tension the *same* poles as U.S. discourse: liberal inclusion and virulent racism, liberal humanism and Manifest Destiny.

While Vasconcelos somewhat magnanimously grants that the "mestizo, the Indian, and even the black are superior to the white in countless numbers of ways" (32), his version of *mestizaje* in many respects approximates nineteenth-century discourse of races and their proper places.[15] Throughout Vasconcelos's essay, the mystical discourse is underpinned by scientific discourses about race—eugenics, Mendelianism, geographical determinism—which shape the text's relationship to non-White peoples. *Mestizaje* becomes for Vasconcelos a means of racial improvement through the "voluntary extinction" or "absorption" of the "lower types" by the "higher types," a process through which the "black could be redeemed"; it is an "aesthetic eugenics" through which "a selection of taste would take effect, much more efficiently than the brutal Darwinist selection" (32). Passages such as this contradict the common claim that Vasconcelos did a political about-face in his politics after his defeat in the presidential elections, for the elements of his subsequent conservatism are present in *The Cosmic Race*. It seems that Vasconcelos's version of *mestizaje* is closer than Martí's to the project of *emblanquimiento* (whitening) that Afro-Hispanists critique in general as *mestizaje*. Indeed, George Yúdice's comparison between "*mestizo* normativity" and "Anglo conformity" in the context of the United States applies well to Vasconcelos (xxxviii).

Moreover, unlike Martí, Vasconcelos is silent on the subject of equal political and economic rights for the different races. Although his silence on this subject is rendered less conspicuous by the spiritual and mystical tones of his writing, a distinctly imperialistic imagery, drawn from the vocabulary of colonization and discovery, nonetheless stains his accounts of the spirit:

> The people that Hispanic America is forming in a somewhat disorderly manner, yet free of spirit and with intense longings on account of the vast unexplored regions, can still repeat the feats of the Castilian and Portuguese conquerors. The Hispanic race, in general, still has ahead of it this mission of discovering new regions of the spirit, now that all lands have already been explored.
>
> Only the Iberian part of the continent possesses the spiritual factors, the race, the territory necessary for the great enterprise of initiating the new universal era of Humanity.... The only thing lacking is for true love to organize and set in march the law of History (38)

Notwithstanding the mystical overlay, the material politics of this project are chilling. The passage seeks to carve out an imperial identity for Mexico, in what I think we could reasonably term Vasconcelos's version of the doctrine of Manifest Destiny and (Latin) American exceptionalism. Racial hybridity is his rhetorical/conceptual aid in this enterprise. This is a very different version of *mestizaje*, a very different regional identity, from that which Martí elaborates. What emerges from Vasconcelos's work is admiration for the Spanish expansionist project, an expansionism Vasconcelos seeks to *extend* to the spiritual sphere. Furthermore, it is telling that despite all the eulogizing of the "cosmic" race according to this passage, it is neither the cosmic race nor the *mestizo* race that will lead Latin America in its mission—but the "Hispanic" race. Vasconcelos's greater hispanophilism as compared to Martí's can be explained partly by the former's ideological affinity with Spain's political project, and partly by the fact that, unlike for Martí, there was no war with Spain on the horizon. Since Spain was no longer competing for Mexico, it could be acknowledged admiringly in a way that the United States could not.[16]

Toward the end of *The Cosmic Race*, when Vasconcelos shares his architectural vision for the Palace of Public Education, the role of various national cultures in the future Mexico emerges still more tellingly. I consider the passage a metonym for the tension between racial inclusion and exclusion that characterizes Vasconcelos's work:

> On the panels at the four corners of the first patio, I had them carve allegories representing Spain, Mexico, Greece, and India, the four particular civilizations that have most to contribute to the formation of Latin America. Immediately below these four allegories, four stone statues should have been raised, representing the four great contemporary races: The white, the red, the black, and the yellow, to indicate that America is home to all and needs all of them. (40)

A complex relationship emerges here amongst nation, race, and culture. The passage recognizes the physical presence of the four races, each of whom Latin America needs.[17] The order in which they are presented—white, red, black, yellow—offers a clue as to the hierarchy of inclusion. If it seems unusual that the Chinese occupy in Vasconcelos's model a position lower than the blacks, Vasconcelos's preoccupation with restricting Chinese immigration to Latin America can explain the anomaly; his fear was that rapid Chinese reproduction would color, so to speak, his great experiment in the racial laboratory of Latin America. His repeated praise of Indian and Hindu culture (which had no significant representatives in Mexico at the time) also becomes suspect in light of his silence about that other Asian classical civilization: China. Indeed, his invocation of Indian cultural wealth may enable his silence on Chinese cultural wealth, a silence that is also driven by his opposition to Chinese immigration.[18]

Yet while Vasconcelos recognizes the physical presence of all the races, he does not recognize the *cultural* presence of all the races, unlike Martí, who recognized black Cubans as a significant cultural and political presence. The civilizational re/sources for Latin America that Vasconcelos acknowledges are Spain, Mexico, Greece, and India (again, the order may be significant). Of Africa he makes no mention. The silence on the subject of the cultural contributions of Africa and China confirms the import of Vasconcelos's language of racial improvement, suggesting that the physically present African and Chinese would be absorbed into a superior civilization. This is in marked contrast to Martí's vision, which emphasizes political and economic integration of the races as equals rather than their elimination through absorption.

In this context, then, Vasconcelos's precarious distinction between a United States that seeks to "subjugate" and his own mission that seeks to "civilize" (105) fails to persuade. Both Vasconcelos's invocations of the Hispanic race and his consistent prioritization of a Spanish culture under whose aegis the "civilization" would presumably take place make the distinction suspect. History should make us wary of any claims to "civilize"; and Vasconcelos's work, with its recurrent invocation of racial and cultural hierarchy and racial essences, is no exception for being from the previously colonized or Third World. Rather, it stands as a warning of the risks of Third World official nationalisms. His discourse is clearly anti-purist (although it is by no means anti-essentialist), but its anti-purism serves a regional imperial project. It is an important reminder that the rhetoric of hybridity can be both a defense against racism and a weapon in its advancement.[19]

The thirty-five-year gap between Martí's and Vasconcelos's texts may also attest to a shift in the nineteenth- and twentieth-century functions of *mestizaje.* Jorge Klor de Alva's summary below of the key claims of official twentieth-century Latin American narratives of *mestizaje* captures the moment *after mestizaje*'s shift from oppositional to hegemonic cultural construct has been achieved. In that latter moment, we may say of *mestizaje* in Latin America (though not to the same extent the Caribbean islands, including Cuba):

> (1) it is the felicitous product of the coming together of various "races"; (2) drawing from all of these, it became the essence of American reality; and (3) it is the unique expression of a synthesis that (through a revealing contradiction) culminates with Christianity, the Spanish language, and the embrace of the West. This paradoxical final point alludes to the common but problematic application of the concept

> of *mestizaje* as both a euphemism for the overwhelming presence of Western influences and as an excuse for eliding/dismissing that which is indigenous. (250)

This summary helps explain the attractiveness of *mestizaje* to official bourgeois nationalisms.

In the twentieth-century Latin American context, the political functioning of the term *mestizaje/mestizo* becomes more readily apparent when it is placed in relation to the term "*indio.*" The rhetoric of *mestizaje*, under the national leadership of a culturally hybrid *criollo/mestizo* elite, "sought to weaken local 'Indian' identities (and increase the criollo economic base) by disestablishing indigenous corporate communities (and lands), hoping that as a byproduct anti-criollo sentiments would disappear with the indigenous villages" (Klor de Alva 247). *Mestizaje* thus had both cultural and economic consequences for Indians. At the level of intercultural mediation, *mestizaje* tended to idealize a mythic cultural past of Native Americans even as it condescended to the culture of their present, seeking to assimilate or Westernize it.[20] At the level of mediations between economics and culture, *mestizaje* made the familiar move of alternating between symbolic exaltation and material deprivation, a move identified and condemned by José Carlos Mariátegui in his 1928 essays "The Problem of the Indian" and "The Problem of Land." There Mariátegui alerts his audience to the elisions of class and landownership in Peruvian *mestizaje* discourse and insists that the issue of the place of Native Americans in the nation-state could not be resolved through administrative, legal, ethnic, moral, educational, or ecclesiastical means (24). In short, he recognizes the inadequacy of attempts at the *cultural* renovation or rehabilitation of "the Indian" unless they were firmly backed by far-reaching anti-feudal *economic* measures, notably radical land reform. Thus, he bitingly dismisses the tactics of official Peruvian ideologies of *mestizaje* at the time: "We are not satisfied to assert the Indian's right to education, culture, progress, love, and heaven. We begin by categorically asserting his right to land" (31). A critique such as Mariátegui's objects not to the modernizing aspect of *mestizaje*, which clearly seeks to integrate Indians into a national mainstream, but to the unequal inclusion of the Indians in that mainstream. In contrast, more recent critiques, like Stutzman's about Indians and the Afro-Hispanists' about Blacks, argue for the right to difference of minoritized ethnic groups, that is, their right to define their identities outside of parameters set by the nation-state. The interventions that these discourses make is different: to put it in Nancy Fraser's terms, one seeks equality, the other difference.

Mariátegui may be faulted for a certain economic reductionism which says, in effect, that the state's business is to take care of the economics and to let the ethnic identities take care of themselves. Yet his writing is marred by none of the cultural condescension or sentimentalism toward Indians that so many liberal proponents of *mestizaje* exhibit. This may derive in part from Mariátegui's socialist commitment to some elements of pre-Columbian culture, notably the collective ownership of land. Moreover, both Mariátegui's anti-essentialism and his insistence that the discourse of cultural value is not in and of itself enough are useful correctives to liberal discourses of hybridity.

Many of the key features and variables of *mestizaje* are repeated in other national discourses of hybridity in the Spanish-speaking Caribbean. Though Puerto Rico's discourse of *jibarismo* does not have the same continental sweep as *mestizaje*, remaining a national rather than a pan-American discourse, it is characterized by a similar tension between equality and difference and a similar ideological shift over time. The symbol of the *jíbaro* or poor, rural, white peasant nationalized a culturally hybrid but whitened Creole identity, symbolically erasing the troubled issues of slavery, black and white racial mixing, and the material claims of blacks and mulattoes upon the nation.[21] While *jibarismo* valorized a marginal group, it was a group that was culturally conservative and politically inactive—in sharp contrast to other marginalized sectors such as an emerging militant organized working-class and women's movement, and those articulating politicized Afro–Puerto Rican racial identities. Once again, sanctioning nonthreatening hybridities was accompanied by disallowing threatening ones.

Yet just as *mestizaje* was not a monolithic discourse, neither was *jibarismo*. Lillian Guerra warns against monolithic readings of *jibarismo*, distinguishing nineteenth- from twentieth-century versions of *jibarismo*, elite from popular manipulations of it. In particular, she traces a shift from nineteenth-century elite *jibarista* reformist alliances with the popular classes (for example, Brau and Zeno Guandía) toward a twentieth-century elite construction of the *jíbaro* as an idealized Other whose material conditions the *jibarista* elite showed no interest in improving. Like *mestizaje*, moreover, *jibarismo* was also profoundly shaped by the contested relationship of Puerto Rico to the United States, a relationship that continues to form the horizon of public political discourse today.

Lillian Guerra's study of *jibarismo* acutely identifies the contradictory impulses of the ethos:

> Complicitous in the political and economic domination of the island by foreigners, the island elite found that their interests as a class increasingly

> depended upon the continued imperial presence of the United States; but at the same time, they sensed that their values, customs, and sense of identity were inevitably being compromised by their collaboration.... By strategically inserting themselves in the margins through a particular stream of nationalist discourse, these intellectuals sought to project an image of their class as less culpable in the fomentation of colonialism and more victimized by its extremes. (46–47)

Jibarismo thus offered a way of managing the tensions between the *economic* and *cultural* identities of the national elite by symbolically privileging the latter. While constructing a Creole identity was crucial to resisting American colonialism, constructing a whitened or white creole identity entailed its own racism and hostility to organized labor politics. It may therefore be significant that the *jíbaro* went on to become the emblem of the Partido Popular Democrático, a party which, after initially advocating independence from the United States, went on to advocate "Commonwealth" status for Puerto Rico. In the PPD's appropriation, a hybrid and autonomous cultural identity is delinked from access to an independent political state.[22] In the 1950s, as the pro-Commonwealth party, it shifted from an earlier interest in developing a national bourgeoisie to implementing "Operation Bootstrap" or "industrialization by invitation." In this instance, then, a Creole hybrid poetics was appended to the antiegalitarian economic policies of dependent capitalism. That linkage was possible in part because of the ability of the symbol to gloss over or stabilize the contradictions in populist bourgeois nationalism, suturing together conflicting class and cultural identities.[23]

Although separated from early articulations of *mestizaje* by nearly three quarters of a century, the discursive complex of creolization shares the influence, conceptual slipperiness, and many of the discursive maneuvers and nationalist goals of the *mestizaje* complex—this notwithstanding the fact that, unlike *mestizaje*, creolization emerged in the Anglophone Caribbean first as an academic discourse from the disciplines of sociology and history.[24] I will consider some academic and some artistic examples of discourses of creolization.

In *Contradictory Omens: Cultural Diversity and Integration in the Caribbean* (1974), the Barbadian poet, historian, and cultural theorist Edward Kamau Brathwaite places creolization at the center of the Caribbean experience. He traces the etymology of the word "creole" to the Spanish verb *criar* (to create, imagine, found, or settle) and *colon* (a colonist, a founder, a settler). *Criollo* refers to "a committed settler, one identified with the area of settlement, one native to the settlement though not ancestrally indigenous to it" (10).[25] "Creolization," then, comes to mean the indigenization of the nonnative-American population of the Caribbean; it includes both "acculturation" and "interculturation," and thus offers a key resource for refuting diffusionist theories of culture.

Like *mestizaje*, creolization is a concept riven by internal fissures. The version of creolization that treats it as a process of homogenization or unification is often preferred by official nationalists and members of the elite and bourgeoisie, who find in it a way around explicit acknowledgment of class antagonisms; it is also often favored by artists whose own work embodies a hybrid creole aesthetic in which aesthetic unity is achieved before social unity and is offered as a bridge toward that unity. On the other hand, there are those who treat creolization more as a process of contention. These tend to be members of the non-Party Left, critics of the state, and leftist cultural theorists, all of whom foreground class narratives (which are necessarily racialized in the Caribbean); they emphasize the conflictual *process* rather than the product of cultural transformation. For instance, the noted Jamaican sociologist M.G. Smith, who argues that the Caribbean consists of plural rather than creole societies, pointing to the "graduated hierarchy of European and African elements," notes a painful paradox that both belies nationalist claims and reinforces them: "The common culture, without which West Indian nationalism cannot develop the dynamic to create a West Indian nation, may by its very nature and composition preclude the nationalism that invokes it. This is merely another way of saying that the Creole culture which West Indians share is the basis of their division" (5–6). Both versions of creolization, then, invoke or recognize a nation; the question is whether creolization is considered a nation-building force or a nation-dividing force. The fault lines along which the concept of creolization splinters are those of unification/disintegration; consensus/contention; class identity/cultural identity, equality/difference, material equality/symbolic value. Moreover, a central preoccupation of creolization from the start has been how to establish an Afro-Creole culture as the norm rather than as a deviation from a European standard. As such, the discursive complex has concerned itself with cultural status and value, intervening in such areas as education, syllabi, linguistics, the literary canon, and standards of beauty.

The sociologist Nigel Bolland's powerful critique of the creole-society thesis illuminates the trade-offs made by some of these interventions. Faulting the creolization model for its flawed conception of culture as an aggregate of individuals and its undialectical understanding of the relations of antagonistic forces (67), he points out: "The creole-society thesis does not enable us to see how or why the system of domination in the colonies changed from *status* inequalities during slavery to *class* inequalities after legal emancipation, as a consequence of both the social dynamics within the colonies and the colonies' relations with the metropoles" (73). In other words, early academic discussions of creolization sometimes deploy the category of culture in such a way that they focus on status inequalities to the exclusion of class inequalities, and in this regard risk repeating the gestures Mariátegui critiqued in Peruvian *mestizaje*.

For instance, trying to distinguish the centripetal from the centrifugal force of creolization, Orlando Patterson distinguishes between "segmentary" and "synthetic" creolization thus: Segmentary creolization permits the development of distinct Euro-West Indian and Afro-West Indian creole cultures; synthetic creolization shares some aspects of segmentary creolization:

> [t]he political, economic, educational, and legal institutions of synthetic Creole are, essentially, slightly modified versions of Euro-West Indian segmentary Creole; whereas its language, theater, music, dance, art, and literature are actively drawn from Afro-West Indian segmentary Creole sources. (Patterson, "Context and Choice in Ethnic Allegiance: A Theoretical Framework and Caribbean Case Study" 319, qtd. in Bolland 63)

What Patterson does is to set up culture as a domain of relative autonomy, a domain where unequal relations of power are not as debilitating as in the domain of economics and politics narrowly understood. This move is common in academic, political nationalist, and cultural nationalist discourses. Partha Chatterjee, for example, notes a similar division between economics and culture in Indian nationalist discourse—with the difference that in the discourse he critiques "culture" is privatized and drawn back into the realm of the home. Paul Gilroy has argued that because of the historical experience of slavery, African-American and Afro-Caribbean cultures have placed their emancipatory hopes not in the workplace but in the realm of aesthetic expression. Patterson's and Gilroy's approaches hint that it is Caribbean expressive culture (narrowly conceived) rather than its political and public institutions that carry the "essence" of a Caribbeanness from which future utopias might spring. In other words, for them, it is culture that houses a resistant non-colonial Afro-Caribbean subjectivity. This belief, not disciplinary predisposition alone, might explain the common tendency of cultural theorists of the Caribbean to focus on cultural resistance to the neglect of other forms of political resistance.[26]

I suggest, then, that the key to both the appeal and the limits of creolization may lie in the difference to which Bolland alludes between status and class inequalities, and the ability of creolization and other discourses of hybridity to blur that difference. This difference may also explain the relative success of creolization as a model for poetic practice and the relative weakness of creolization as a social theory of the material organization of society.

I will situate the work of two writers in relation to Bolland's claim: Edward Kamau Brathwaite and Derek Walcott. Their essays, to which I will restrict myself in this chapter for the sake of generic continuity, span the 1970s to the present and inflect the cultural politics of creolization in significantly different ways. In their practice of selective inclusion, both reveal surprising overlaps with dominant nationalist discourses.

Kamau Brathwaite's *Contradictory Omens* describes creolization thus:

> Started as a result of slavery and therefore in the first instance involving black and white, European and African, in a fixed superiority/inferiority relationship, it tended first to the culturation of white and black to the new Caribbean environment; and, at the same time, because of the terms and conditions of slavery, to the acculturation of black to white norms. There was at the same time, however, significant interculturation going on between these two elements. (11)

At its strongest, Brathwaite's writing displays this passage's careful class-based analysis of the unequal terms of interculturation.[27] However, there is a tension in Brathwaite's work between the transformational tenets of creolization and the cultural primacy and prioritization he accords Africa.[28] Although, as I will show in chapter three, the tension between these two impulses results in some innovative poetic practice, it remains a problem in Brathwaite's nonfictional writing not because it results in a contradiction—the title of his essay acknowledges such contradiction—but because it remains an *under-theorized* contradiction. Even Brathwaite's poetry cannot overcome some of these problems. He is legitimately concerned there, at the levels of form, theme, and content, with the cultural rehabilitation, acknowledgment, and celebration of African-derived components of Creole culture. But he rarely makes celebratory note of non-African-derived cultural practices (particularly European ones)—in some ways throwing the creolizing impulse into question.[29] We may read this absence as the trace of an unnamed and legitimate class critique that Brathwaite's version of creolization cannot explicitly theorize. As Gordon Lewis observes: "Brathwaite's very system of classification—dealing separately with European, Euro-Creole, Afro-Creole and West Indian segments—implicitly recognizes the sharp and often mutually irreconcilable character of the groups" (322). Yet Brathwaite rejects Smith's plural society model, calling it a "colonial rather than a creole contribution" (qtd. in Bolland 60).

It comes as something of a surprise, then, that Brathwaite himself goes on to invoke the pluralism model when he talks about the East Indian or Indo-Caribbean presence in the Caribbean. In Brathwaite's treatment of East Indians, both his class and cultural analysis falter. For Brathwaite's is a hybridity that encompasses only those parts of the Caribbean population that are black, white, or the mixed descendants of black and white. The term "creole," even as it is used today in the Anglophone Caribbean, does not include people of East Indian or Chinese descent, groups that together constitute about 20 percent of its population; in Guyana and Trinidad people of East Indian descent are the largest ethnic group. Using creolization as a figure for Caribbean hybridity thus has its own complex legacy of exclusion.

Brathwaite's formulation allows us to glimpse this exclusion: he refers to "the arrival of East Indian and other immigrants" and to the fact that these "other elements had to adjust themselves to the existing creole synthesis and the new landscape." The arrival of these elements, he points out, effected a shift from a creole to a plural society (11). But describing the East Indians who arrived in the Caribbean as "immigrants," rather than as indentured laborers who replaced slave labor after the abolition of slavery, blocks an understanding of their position of social subordination, from which they negotiated their Caribbeanization. In other words, Brathwaite is more careful in his analysis of the effects on interculturation of the "terms and conditions of slavery" than he is in his analysis of indentured labor that was also subordinated to white colonial power and its institutions. Moreover, in his reference to East Indians, Brathwaite does not make the useful distinction between acculturation and interculturation which he makes in regard to the black/white creolization process. In fact, implicit in his discussion of Indians in Trinidad are three contradictory and/or under-specified claims: that Indians are simply "assimilated" into the Creole society, that they are creolized (although they do not thereby become Creoles), and that with their advent the Caribbean became a "plural" society.[30]

It is important to read in Brathwaite's analysis both the strength of his insight, made in relation to Creoles, that Caribbean hybridity is the result of accommodation and transformation between unequal social elements, and the analytic danger of losing sight of those inequalities, which his discussion of East Indians reveals. Faced with the delegitimation of black culture, Brathwaite's impulse is to insist on the Caribbean's cultural continuities with Africa. Thus, his imaginative discursive repositioning of his native island of Barbados (known as Little England on account of its Anglophilia) as being geographically closest to Africa, and his poetic invocation of the harmattan whose breath extends to the Caribbean, poetically articulate this reclamation. Yet in solving that problem, Brathwaite inadvertently exacerbates the erasure that has dogged Indo-Caribbeans since their arrival.

Derek Walcott's project, too, is shaped by forces to which Brathwaite was subject, but his aesthetic treatment of creolization in *The Antilles: Fragments of Epic Memory* is inflected differently for at least three reasons. First, unlike Brathwaite, Walcott maintained a somewhat skeptical and critical distance from black nationalist cultural and political projects of national reconstruction.[31] Second, whereas Brathwaite's creolization tends to emphasize the Afro-Creole, Walcott emphasizes a multiracial, multicultural creolization. In this regard, Walcott and C.L.R. James are similar, for in both their work creolized European aesthetics and signifying systems are powerful presences, both affirmative and constraining.[32] Third, as a relatively recent text, *The Antilles*, Walcott's 1992 Nobel Prize acceptance address, offers us insight into our more recent postindependence moment. Given the present neocolonial subordination of Caribbean nation-states, *The Antilles* cannot be read as an instance of a theory of hybridity in a period of nationalist emergence or consolidation; rather, one might read in it the stresses of a modernist writer grappling with a postmodern moment. In 1992, then, Derek Walcott, frames the alternatives to (neo)colonialism differently from Brathwaite, organizing his narrative of class and status in the Caribbean nation also somewhat differently. Political questions of power and inequality are prominent in his treatment of the hybridization arising out of globalization and an *inter*national economy of tourism, but recede from his discussion of hybridity with*in* the nation-state.

The structuring opposition in Walcott's narrative is the opposition between the traveler and the native. The terms of Walcott's opposition between traveler and native—indifference versus love, motion versus stasis—enable Walcott to deal differently with international and domestic cultural hybridity. Walcott asserts: "A traveler cannot love, since love is stasis and travel is motion. If he returns to what he loved in a landscape and stays there, he is no longer a traveler but in stasis and concentration, a lover of that particular part of the earth a *native*" (24, emphasis added). Walcott's distinction between traveler and native is not in any meaningful sense an essentialist one; it is a strategic response to a geopolitics in which colonial travel narratives and tourism disproportionately and damagingly shape our understanding of the Caribbean; in such a context it is unsurprising that he invokes the "native" as a means of asserting popular self-determination by the nation. The opposition "traveler versus native" does, however, gloss over Walcott's own position as a *traveling native.* It is precisely as a traveling native that Walcott takes up his position in a global economy, as the internationally canonized national writer from the Caribbean. His own address, made at his acceptance in Sweden of the Nobel Prize, therefore circulates in an international economy, where it exists in a tense relationship with the other texts to which he alludes: the tourist brochure, the colonialist/anthropological narrative, and the texts of other Caribbean writers. Indeed, the nationalist opposition between traveler and native is a particularly vexed one in the Caribbean context, in which, for example, impoverished natives have traveled in large numbers to the metropoles as labor, and there has been a tradition of "natives" who have traveled to the colonial metropolis and there elaborated Caribbean nationalist projects—figures such as Fanon, Césaire, C.L.R. James, and Martí, for example. The question to which I will return is: what work does the figure of the native perform?

Walcott's critique of the border-crossing represented by tourists—"rootless" travelers—takes the form of an attack on the pastiche of tourist aesthetics. He claims:

> In our tourist brochures the Caribbean is a blue pool into which the republic dangles the extended foot of Florida as inflated rubber islands bob and drinks with umbrellas float toward her on a raft.... this is the seasonal erosion of their [the islands'] identity, that high-pitched repetition of images of service that cannot distinguish one island from the other.... What is the earthly paradise for our visitors? Two weeks without rain and a mahogany tan, and at sunset local troubadours in straw hats and floral shirts singing "Yellow Bird" and "Banana Boat Song" to death. (31–32)

Charles de Gaulle returns to the Caribbean as a tourist, now mildly interested in the Caribbean to the extent that it consists of sunlit specks of dust. Walcott vividly evokes tourism's indifferently homogenizing hybridity that is so threatening to Caribbean national identities. It is a particularly neocolonial hybridity that draws the Caribbean islands into the economic and epistemological sphere of the neocolonizing United States, metonymically represented in his text by Florida's penetration into the Caribbean sea.

If Walcott refuses purist aesthetics, he also rejects the impure but dehistoricizing pastiche of tourist aesthetics, locating both with respect to power. Of purists, he says, they "look on such ceremonies (the hybridized and fragmented Caribbean cultural practices) as grammarians look on a dialect, as cities look on provinces, and empires on their colonies.... In other words, the way the Caribbean is still looked at, illegitimate, rootless, mongrelized" (5–6). Walcott's rebuttal of Froude—and de Gaulle—consists of articulating the value and beauty of the impure. Refusing both Froude's cultural purism and neocolonial hybridity, Walcott nonetheless celebrates hybridity as the basis for distinctively Caribbean national identities: "Tonally the individual voice is a dialect; it shapes its own accent, its own vocabulary and melody in defiance of an imperial concept of language, the language of Ozymandias, libraries and dictionaries, law courts and critics, and churches, universities, political dogma, the diction of institutions. Poetry is an island that breaks away from the main" (10). Hybridity here becomes a creative centrifugal force resisting the inertia of institutions. Significant here is that Walcott's formulation shifts hybridity to a matter of epistemological import, offering a glimpse of the value of what we might call peripheral vision. Breaking away from the main is a means of wresting political and cultural autonomy from the centers of power. In light of his critique of tourism, and of the Caribbean islands' being satellites of the United States ("islands floating *towards* Florida"), his claim that "[p]oetry is an island that *breaks away* from the main" represents both a project of economic delinking from the mainland and a project of linguistic and epistemological delinking from institutionalized or dominant language.[33] What the metaphor accomplishes is to locate his poetics of hybridity within an *alternatively imagined political economy.* It neither brackets politics and economics, nor acquiesces to their present form, nor makes any epistemological accommodation to them in the name of necessity. Unlike Bhabha's and Anzaldúa's conceptions of hybridity that bracket economics and reject the nation-state, Walcott's celebration of hybridity is accompanied by a nationalist refusal of subordinate incorporation into the global economy. Hence his statement that the Caribbean's "proportions are not to be measured by the traveler or the exile, but by its own citizenry and architecture" (23).

Why then does his powerful conjunctive scrutiny of epistemology and economics together disappear from his discussion of the Caribbean nation? The national "citizenry" Walcott produces to oppose an international cultural and political imperialism, the collectivity he marks when he speaks of "our history," achieve their stability only through a discursive displacement of issues of power and inequality in Walcott's representation of hybridity *within* the postcolonial Caribbean nation-states. In fact, the slippage between the more politicized word "citizen" and the more poeticized—and dehistoricizing—word "native" underwrites his selective attention to power. His highly poeticized construction of the native in terms of stasis, rootedness in the earth, and love, sets the stage for his erasure of the dynamics of power. "Break a vase," he says, "and the *love* that reassembles the fragment is stronger than that love that took its symmetry for granted when it was whole.... It is such a love that reassembles our African and our Asiatic fragments" (8–9, emphasis added). Within the nation-state, the language of political economy is replaced by the language of sentiment.

How does one read this substitution? National consciousness or community identification of any sort necessarily involves sentiment, for communities are rarely formed on the basis of the rational or abstract recognition of shared needs or interests alone; rather, they invariably involve a felt emotional need. Indeed, Walcott's essay may be considered just such an act of love. The potential problem with Walcott's passage lies not in its sentimentality *per se*, but in the way that the sentiment becomes a ruse for silence on inequitable relations of power. Read thus, Walcott's narrative bears out warnings that a dependency school analysis of "foreign domination" may be consistent with bourgeois nationalism. Walcott's treatment of hybridity within Caribbean nation-states thus appears to be an aesthetically accomplished reinscription of official Caribbean national mottoes such as Jamaica's "Out of many, one" and Trinidad's "All o' we is one." The metaphor of the vase shattered and reassembled is a variation on the metaphor of the nation-as-mosaic; moreover, like the mosaic, the vase suggests a coexistence of fragments rather than any more radical hybridization; the national vision of hybridity is, then, a more traditional composite. Like those official mottoes and metaphors, Walcott attempts to forge a unity without attending to the unequal terms of inclusion in the national imaginary or the unequal access to the resources of the state; it posits in advance a unity and equality that has yet to be achieved. Similarly, Walcott asserts: "They [the remembered customs] survived the Middle Passage and the *Fatel Rozack*, the ship that carried the first indentured Indians from the port of Madras to the canefields of Felicity, that carried the chained Cromwellian convict and the Sephardic Jew, the Chinese grocer and the Lebanese merchant selling cloth samples on his bicycle" (11–12). The syntactic equivalence that Walcott inscribes here of these different subnational groups sutures over their economic and cultural inequalities. Moreover, conspicuously absent from this list is the privileged French Creole class, which represents not the small business to which Walcott pays homage, but the node between national and international capital. The point I am making is that Walcott's strategy for organizing difference within the nation amounts to a liberal multiculturalist project of inclusion, which leaves the relations of production and class structure within the nation essentially untouched. The peaceful syntactic coexistence of East Indian and African in Walcott's sentence belies Trinidad's postcolonial history of intense economic and cultural competition between the two groups. Also unanswered is the question of how the additive seriality of self-enclosed entities relates to some more interactive and dynamic process of hybridization.

Walcott's construction of East Indians illustrates this point. His celebratory inclusion in *The Antilles* of the Indo-Trinidadian performance of the the Hindu epic *Ramleela* is an important gesture at including Indo-Trinidadian cultural practices in the national imaginary. However, he performs this inclusion by celebrating the Ramleela as sheer "exuberance," a "celebration of a real presence," "faith," devotees' ritual renewal through sacrifice (rather than amateur actors' performance). Through metaphors of stunning beauty, Walcott imagines Indo-Caribbeans not as intruders or latecomers, but as naturally belonging in the landscape, like Trinidad's scarlet ibises. But in the process, the Ramleela becomes the sign of a naturalized and spontaneous Indo-Trinidadian culture; and Indo-Trinidadians become sentimentalized natives rather than struggling citizens implicated in political contestations. His strategy for including Indo-Trinidadians in the national imaginary, then, ignores the fact that performances and funding of the Ramleela are embedded in a politics of intercultural *antagonism*, orchestrated in part by the conservative Indian bourgeois-nationalist party. The Ramleela, then, is not timeless celebration but a site of cultural struggle.[34] Both Brathwaite's and Walcott's references to Indians obscure the dynamics of negotiations for power *between and within subordinate groups*. While in Brathwaite's analysis Indians are marginal to the formative synthetic mainstream of a Creole society, in Walcott's they gain a poeticized inclusion. In other words, Walcott intervenes in the status of Indo-Caribbeans in much the same way that Brathwaite does for Afro-Caribbeans, and Walcott's interventions, too, are limited by his separation of status from class inequalities. If the epistemological possibilities that Walcott opens up at the international level are forced back into relatively traditional multiculturalist conceptions of hybridity at the national level, it is in part because Walcott does not admit the relationship of cultural practices to class or to the state's role in mediating class relations. He represses discussion of the cultural means through which nations or potential nations attempt to gain control of state and economy.

Caribbean and Latin American literary deployments of cannibalism, a capacious and tenacious metaphor for hybridity, have affinities with both *mestizaje* and creolization in their understanding of the relations between culture and politics. Although for obvious reasons the metaphor has not been the provenance of official state discourse but of a cultural avant-garde, its proponents and logic have certainly been closely associated with particular political ideologies, from communism to fascism to universalism.

The Brazilian modernist Oswald de Andrade was the earliest influential proponent of cultural cannibalism as a metaphor and model for Brazilian national culture. His "Anthropophagite Manifesto," published in 1928 in the inaugural journal of *Revista de Antropofagia* (*Cannibal Review*), like several elaborations of *mestizaje* and *jibarismo*, aims to articulate an original Brazilian culture in the context of dependent capitalism and uneven development. From the first lines of the manifesto—"Only anthropophagy unites us. Socially. Economically. Philosophically. The world's only law" (312)—to its exhortation "Down with all the importers of the canned conscience" (312) to Oswald's advocacy in his 1924 "Manifesto da Poesia Pau-Brasil" ("Manifesto of Brazil-wood Poetry") of "poetry for export," the language of economics is inescapable at both the literal and metaphorical levels. Oswald's manifestos oppose both Brazil's neocolonial economic dependence on imports and its cultural dependence (i.e., the importation and imitation of European culture).

"Tupy or not tupy, that is the question" (312) remarks Oswald with characteristic parodic wit. Inspired by the Tupy Indian custom of cannibalizing defeated enemies to absorb their strengths, the manifesto constructs Brazil as the Tupy devouring Europe, thereby reversing the relations of economic power between Europe and Brazil and placing Europe and European technology at the service of Brazil. In a reversal of the neocolonial relationship, cannibalism metaphorically transforms Europe into one of the raw materials for a Brazilian manufactured culture.[35] The metaphor of Tupy cannibalism also reverses Brazil's *cultural* dependence on Europe, figuring Brazilian culture as synthetic, original, and prior to European culture and hence, by definition, not imitative. (Indeed, the manifesto itself cannibalizes Francis Picabia's "Dada Cannibal Manifesto," Shakespeare's *Hamlet*, and Freud's conceptions of totem, taboo, and the unconscious.) Moreover, Carahiba Brazil, far from being the cultural apprentice of Europe, is recast as the prior model of European Revolutions:

> We want the Carahiba Revolution. Bigger than the French Revolution. The unification of all successful rebellions led by man. Without us, Europe would not even have its meagre Declaration of the Rights of Man... Montaigne. Natural Man. Rousseau. From the French Revolution to Romanticism, to the Bolshevik Revolution to the Surrealist revolution and the technical barbarity of Keyserling. We continue our path. (312)

This formulation enables Oswald to hold out the Tupy's primitive communism, matriarchy, limited labor, and alternative to bourgeois reason and morality as the prefiguration of other utopias,[36] even as it sharply reminds us that the profits from colonization were amongst the enabling conditions for the expansion of democratic rights in Europe. At the cultural level, then, Oswald offers a celebratory primitivism that reverses the European negative valuation of cannibalism and the Jesuit repression of the custom. In contrast to a colonial project predicated on that Jesuit repression, Oswald restores cannibalism to a position of historic centrality, satirically breaking with the missionary calendrical time of B.C. and A.D., dating his manifesto instead "the year 374 after the swallowing of the Bishop of Sardinia" (313). The manifesto, then, simultaneously uses cannibalism as a metaphor for the violence of all social relations ("only anthropophagy unites us") and uses it as a metaphor for a postbourgeois utopia that can transcend capitalism having incorporated its technologies and productive abilities.

Although the manifesto's celebration of force and irrationality forebodes a fascism comparable to that of the Italian futurists, Oswald's manifesto in fact was written in response to and against the work of the fascist-oriented groups *Verde-Amarelo* (Green-Yellow) and *Anta* (whose work, incidentally, was influenced by Vasconcelos); Oswald himself would later join the Communist party. Randall Johnson has noted two crucial differences between Oswald and his counterparts, the fascist modernists: first, Oswald's anthropophagy entailed a deliberate cosmopolitanism, which, although it suggested a hegemonic or elite program for cultural reconstruction as Prado Bellei has noted, had none of the xenophobia of the *Verde-Amarelista* nationalisms. Second, the different positioning of the Indian is key to the differences between the two orientations, for while Oswald's manifesto celebrates a synthetic Indianness figured through cannibalism, the *Amarelista*'s celebrates the Indian as immanence or essence. Rejecting the images of cannibalism and the noble savage, the *Amarelistas* instead claimed that the Europeans had absorbed the Indians' qualities. Johnson observes: "Rather than having the colonizer absorb the qualities of the defeated foe, Oswald valorizes the cannibalization of the colonizer by the Indian" (49). As with *mestizaje*, then, manipulating the figure of the Indian is a crucial move in both these discourses of national and cultural identity, and as with various versions of *mestizaje*, making the Indian metonymically stand in for the colonized here does little to better the material conditions of surviving Indians—benefiting instead a cultural elite—or to make visible the place of black Brazilians in this cannibalistic feast. Still, at the very least, in Oswald's work the figure of the Indian is mobilized to imagine a revolutionary utopian future.

A counterpoint to Oswald's elaboration of cannibalism is that of the Guyanese novelist and essayist Wilson Harris, who eschews fascism and communism alike, remaining markedly aloof from all forms of nationalist politics. That Harris's particular deployment of cannibalism as a figure for Caribbean hybridity has never achieved the currency and circulation of Oswald de Andrade's 1928 "Anthropophagite Manifesto" can, to be sure, be traced in large part to the fact that Harris's meditations on cannibalism are neither sustained nor gathered in a single text, but, rather, are scattered through his *oeuvre*. However, the lack of fit between Harris's notions of hybridity and nationalist ones may well provide a deeper reason for his marginalization from a Caribbean literary canon shaped largely by nationalist concerns. Indeed, in this chapter, he stands as the lone modernist unmoved by nationalist considerations.

Inspired by anthropological narratives of Carib cannibalism, Harris observes: "The Carib flute was hollowed from the bone of an enemy in time of war. Flesh was plucked and consumed and in the process secrets were digested. Spectres arose from, or reposed in, the flute" ("A Note on the Genesis of *The Guyana Quartet*" 9). Harris's imagination of the Carib ritual shares with Oswald's a critique of reason, but does not lead him to primitiv*ism*. Whereas for Walcott the transcendence of History and the achievement of a hybrid whole can be achieved through an act of aesthetic and sentimental *will*, for Harris, it is the "*involuntary* association" between "privileged and afflicted cultures" ("Creoleness: The Crossroads of a Civilization?" 239, 241) that provides access to a Jungian collective unconscious. In other words, involuntary association becomes the route to a regenerative "creolization of the chasm" (241) by forms of consciousness that are not reducible to the ego.[37]

Whilst for Oswald the metaphor of the Brazilian Self devouring the European Other figures a reversal of relations of economic, political, and epistemic power, a "*permanent* transformation of taboo into totem" (312, emphasis added), for Harris cannibalism enables a more metaphysical transformation. Harris's account provides the security of neither reversal nor permanence. For him, the Other is not definitively destroyed, subdued, or incorporated. Whilst the incorporation of the Other is a source of strength for the Self, that strength is never secure or securing; rather, the spectre of the Other remains an *unsettling* presence for the Self. This epistemology of unsettling becomes the cornerstone of Harris's aesthetic project—which he also imagines in cannibalistic terms: to create a "fiction that seeks to consume its own biases through many resurrections of paradoxical imagination"

("A Note on the Genesis of *The Guyana Quartet*" 9). The philosophical insistence that, as Paget Henry puts it, "fulfillment is the opposite of consolidation" (Henry 101) is what ultimately makes Harris's work unassimilable to a nationalist project. Harris's project, then, requires not the breaking away or asserting of boundaries which Walcott seeks, but a *reduction* of distance, a dissolution or transgression of psychic and cultural boundaries. Like the metaphor of the bone-flute, Walcott's metaphor of breaking away involves an aesthetic of the fragment; however, in Walcott's case, the images of the separation of the colony from the empire, and the pieces of the broken vase, are accompanied by a move to consolidate these fragmentary identities. Whereas traditional anticolonial nationalisms require the consolidation of identities and the presence of clearly demarcated boundaries, Harris is interested in precisely the disruption of such certainties.

Moreover, Harris's cannibalism is less politically oppositional, tapping not the conflict between the Self and the Other, but the *desire* of the Self for the Other. Rather than pitting Europe and the Americas in political opposition to each other, Harris's conception of cannibalism provides a route through "the complex labyrinth of the family of humankind" ("Creoleness" 237–238) to unify a divided humanity. The bone-flute becomes an evocative image of the beauty that can emerge even from acts of extreme violence. As such, the metaphor of the bone-flute resonates cross-culturally with several archetypal myths in which music enables the transformation and transcendence of catastrophe. Thus, in Harris's Carib bone-flute we hear echoes of Ovid and Philomela. Harris's is ultimately a universalist vision that reworks cannibalism as a metaphor for intuitive reconnection, thus recasting conflict as reconciliation.[38]

It is perhaps significant for his nonnationalist purposes that he decenters the colonial encounter, choosing not to focus on the Carib encounter with Europeans, but on Carib encounters with other Indian tribes such as the Arawaks. This de-emphasis is repeated when he asserts that "*All cultures* are subject to the ravages of unjust convention which may take the form of stereotypical purities" (*Selected Essays* 204, emphasis added), a formulation that makes the Caribbean's colonial encounter but one example of such ravaging. He is thus not interested in making differentiations of degree or scale, and focuses on the shared aspects of culture rather than on their inequality and difference.

Harris's epistemology of unsettling, critique of reason, and resistance to nationalist politics thus overlap with the borderlands perspectives I have addressed; moreover, like the latter, his intervention occurs primarily at the level of epistemology. Whereas C.L.R. James focuses on political will (the Haitian Revolution) and Walcott on aesthetic will, Harris focuses on an aesthetic involving the *surrender* of will. Harris's focus on uncertainty, indeterminacy, and risk, as well as his unease with nationalist politics, share much with the postmodern and post-nationalist theorists of hybridity I have discussed. Like Bhabha, for instance, Harris is uninterested in hybridity as an instrument for developing an oppositional public identity and more interested in unintentional psychic processes of hybridization. The difference, however, is that Harris readily admits to the metaphysical and universalist implications of his position and to his interest in recovering transcultural and transhistorical archetypes. His is not a postmodern critique of nationalism, but a modernist, poeticist, and universalist one. Furthermore, unlike many contemporary academic accounts of hybridity, Harris's critique applies not only to political nationalism, but to cultural nationalism as well, resisting the reinstatement of cultural authenticity that I have identified in the work of Anzaldúa, the Créolistes, and *Puerto Rican Jam.* Of all these theorists, only Harris risks his own epistemological ground in looking for "a fiction that is consumed by its own biases." Moreover, Harris recognizes his poetics as a process of self-awareness and transformation that necessarily occurs at the level of individual subjectivities; he does not offer it as a mode of collective political practice, and therefore cannot propose his poetics as a substitute for such practice.

Édouard Glissant's influential conception of *antillanité*, developed in *Le discours antillais* (1981, translated as *Caribbean Discourse* in 1989), is instructive in the way it brings together Harris's critique of rationalism and critical deployment of premodern subjectivities with C.L.R. James's attention to the ability of a popular modern state to restructure social relations. Thus, in *Caribbean Discourse*, Glissant's celebratory invocations of Haitian marvelous realism are coupled with meditations on Martinican independence. In the epigraph to this chapter, Glissant uses Harris's language of dreams; elsewhere, his invocation of "the disturbing self-doubt that is the source of our insecurity but that also establishes our presence" (167) has distinctly Harrisian resonances. But Glissant's awareness of a dialectical relationship between settling and unsettling permits him a critically engaged relationship to oppositional nationalist politics. If, as Paget Henry argues, Afro-Caribbean philosophy is characterized by two major trends, a poeticist one exemplified by Harris and a historicist one exemplified by James, then perhaps Glissant's work is unique in the delicate equilibrium it achieves between these two positions, neither one gaining priority.

Thus, although ostensibly the Créolistes break with Glissant over the different status each accords the Creole language, underpinning that difference are radically different conceptions of the relationship of culture to economy and politics. The very structures of Glissant's *Caribbean Discourse* and the Créolistes' "Praise" are symptomatic of their divergences over the relationship of culture, politics, and economy. Like Oswald's metaphors of cannibalism, the generic hybridity of Glissant's text emphasizes the inseparability of cultural and economic analysis; it includes meditations on aesthetics, histories of plantation life, notes, litany, imaginative counter-histories, and so on. In contrast, "Praise," for all its claims to linguistic radicalism, is far less *generically* transgressive or transgressively cross-disciplinary.

Glissant declares the futility of the epistemological and artistic project of a cross-cultural poetics in the absence of the political project of gaining control of the Martinican economy: "One cannot begin cross-fertilization (to become relative, to reject origins) unless one is not lost in pseudoproduction" (46). In contrast to the Créolistes, Glissant insists that Creole cannot at the moment be a functional national language, for "a national language is the one in which a people produces" (102). Thus, for him Spanish in Cuba is a national language, and an instance where monolingualism is not reductive; in Puerto Rico, Glissant believes Spanish is a viable weapon against U.S. political and cultural dominance; of Haiti, he asserts that, while the people are unquestionably alienated from the system of production, they at least have a hinterland that prevents the disintegration of community. But Martinican Creole has none of these qualities; it is "cornered." For, according to Glissant, Creole, which encodes forms of cultural resistance structured by the plantation system and equipped to respond to that system, is helpless to resist the onslaught of the present forces of assimilation: "The dilemma of Martinican Creole is that the stage of the secret code has been passed, but language (as a new opening) has not been attained. The secretiveness of the community is no longer functional, the stage of an open community has not been reached" (125). Creole's confidential oppositionality thereby has unraveled into mere evasion. Moreover, against celebrations of trickster and *jaiba* strategies of resistance and deconstructive deferral alike, Glissant argues that

> diversion leads nowhere when the original trickster strategy does not encounter any real potential for development. . . . Diversion is not a useful ploy unless it is nourished by reversion: not a return to the longing for origins, to some immutable state of Being, but a return to the point of entanglement, from which we were forcefully turned away; that is where we must ultimately put to work the forces of creolization, or perish. (22–26)

One of the strengths of Glissant's theory of a hybrid *antillanité* is that its project of "making relative" is the very antithesis of *relativism*; instead, it is a "return to the point of entanglement" to decipher the complex *relation* of Caribbean particularity to globality. Creolization for Glissant thus becomes a method for articulating a non-relativist conception of difference.

In such a project, art and politics are two distinct but inescapably related forms of practice, each aware of its own vulnerability. "Our aim is to forge for ourselves, by either one of these not necessarily mutually exclusive ways, and based on the defective grasp of two languages whose control was never collectively mastered, a form of expression through which we could consciously face our ambiguities and fix ourselves in the uncertain possibilities of the word made ours" (168). It is this *creative* principle in politics that recedes from the vision of Harris and from Walcott's *The Antilles.*[39]

Moreover, while the Glissant of *Caribbean Discourse* is a product of the same structuring Martinican tension between nation and state that drives the Créolistes' work, he came of age in a different political era from them. A contemporary of Walcott and Brathwaite, his political horizon was shaped by the surge of Third World anti-imperialist and nationalist struggles through the 1970s, as well as the obscenities of overt American aggression toward the Caribbean and Latin America during the Cold War. In 1959, he participated in the formation of the "Front Antillo-Guyanais," which called for the decolonization of the French overseas departments and their cultural integration into the Caribbean (Dash, "Introduction" to *Caribbean Discourse* xv). In fact, the literary periodization he provides in the table "The Process of Literary Production in Martinique" (94–95) allows us to glimpse the history shaping Glissant's own intellectual formation.[40] The way he situates Martinican literary history in relation to global political sites and events (an African past, traces of African survival, the influence of African and world decolonization, deculturation by the media, contacts with the rest of the Caribbean) is an exercise in making history relative rather than absolute.

The point I want to make is that Glissant's historical and political *literacy* in the compromised histories of the Third World enables a drastically different approach to politics from that of *Puerto Rican Jam* and "Praise," for it emerges from an awareness of sites of resistance outside Francophone and U.S. cultures. The limited historical awareness in "Praise," the circumscription of political models in *Puerto Rican Jam* to those of Western Europe and the United States, become more readily apparent when read against the wealth of historical detail in *Caribbean Discourse.* The Créolistes' more narrowly Francophone points of reference noted in chapter one, for example, can be compared with Glissant's alternatively plotted pan-Caribbean and global references. Warning against any single theory's ability to encompass their diversity, Glissant references the diverse historical and political situations of Peru, Liberia, Haiti, Brazil, North America, Liberia, East Indians in the Caribbean, Palestine, South African blacks, Algeria, Armenians, Lapps, Melanesians, Micronesians, African states, Bretons or Catalans, Corsicans or Ukrainians, Australian aborigines, the British, the French, Ireland, Sicily, Cyprus, the Arab countries, Tziganes or Gypsies, Poland, Lebanese, Switzerland, Indochina, Lapps, Polynesians, and more (17–22). Also recurrent throughout *Caribbean Discourse* are meditations on politics and culture in Cuba and Haiti, two barely mentioned ghosts that haunt "Praise" and *Puerto Rican Jam*, ghosts whose historic political and cultural experiments are not engaged there with any level of seriousness. In *Caribbean Discourse*, Cuba and Haiti stand not as unqualified disasters or triumphs, but as important experiments in elaborating a Caribbean identity. Although Glissant's interpretations of the societies listed here are certainly open to question, their very *presence* in his political discourse serves an important function. These historical coordinates are simply not on the map that *Puerto Rican Jam* and "Praise" draw, the Third World appearing there largely as a blank space or space of political error. One can therefore only speculate on how the investigation of such sites might transform the political landscape and futures they map. Glissant's invocations of Chilean artist Zañartu, Cuban painter Wilfredo Lam, Anglophone and Hispanophone Caribbean poets Brathwaite, Walcott, and Guillén, and Haitian painting (114, 117, 109, 155–157) are the aesthetic equivalents of his political literacy. Créolité's abstract conception of "the world diffracted but recomposed," "an open specificity," "the nontotalitarian consciousness of a preserved diversity," "an annihilation of false universality, of monolingualism, of purity" (892) thus gains a density of historical detail and subtlety of texture in Glissant's cultural project of "making relative."

Between Glissant's *antillanité* and "Praise," then, lies a profound difference over both the agents and the sites of political resistance, and the ways in which both are shaped by relations of production. As Glissant makes clear, the "real potential for development" he desires cannot be sustained by the arts or by the enshrinement of Creole by linguists and writers; elite solidarity cannot substitute for popular mobilization. Glissant's work, with its scrupulous insistence on the limits of elite solidarity, reminds us that any notion of strategic practice must confront the limits of the academic essay and the printed word in contexts of illiteracy, limited education, and specialization of labor.

Taking their cue from Glissant, chapters three through seven thus shift the focus from the relationship of nation to state as expressed in academic and theoretical discourse, looking instead at textual representations of hybridity as a lived practice in which the traces of the "strange, stubborn presence" of a hybrid Caribbean resurface in complex ways. What resources do literary genres other than the essay—however marvelously capacious in Caribbean and Latin American literary practice—afford in such an investigation? What modes of address and action does the genre of the manifesto permit? If Walcott's poetic voice seeks to make whole, how does his theatre unsettle, disrupt, interrupt? What negotiations with omniscient narrative does the Caribbean novel undertake? What refrains occur in the give and take between music and literature? How does hybridity function in literary representations of popular cultural practices and expressions like carnival and the carnivalesque, Hosay, spirit possession, music, food, gender relations, domestic life, daily work? How can Glissant's precepts be negotiated across sexed bodies and gendered landscapes? What encounters occur in everyday practice between difference and inequality? These are the questions that animate the next several chapters, for the epistemological strength of a model of cultural hybridity is not in itself sufficient; it becomes useful only when it achieves practical and rhetorical reach. Under what circumstances, then, can the poetics and politics of Glissant's notion of cultural hybridity map onto popular desires and practices? Says Glissant: "A fragile reality (the experience of Caribbeanness, woven together from one side of the Caribbean to the other) negatively twisted together in its urgency (Caribbeanness as a dream, forever denied, often deferred, yet a strange, stubborn presence in our responses)." It is in popular practice that Glissant's subtle description in the epigraph to this chapter would find its verb.

Part II

Alternatives and Aesthetics

Chapter 3

Manifestos of Desire: Hybridity as Forced Poetics

> The *forming* of the five senses is a labor of the entire history of the world down to the present.
>
> —Karl Marx, *Economic and Philosophic Manuscripts of 1844*

I want to suggest that we may usefully think of the texts discussed thus far as manifestos of hybridity. As such, they are programmatic in intention, more properly prescriptions than descriptions, hybrid*ist* discourse rather than hybridity discourse. Whereas my focus in the previous chapters has been to specify and differentiate the contents and contexts of various discourses of hybridity, in this chapter my focus is on the genre of the manifesto as itself a particular mode of argumentation. As such, I am interested in both the generic continuities amongst different discourses of hybridity and the fluctuations in the rhetorical devices that particular discourses employ from the rhetorical repertoire of the manifesto.

This line of thought emerged as I attempted to answer my own sometimes incredulous question: why do discourses of hybridity have such a wide and enduring appeal despite their manifest theoretical inadequacies and factual errors? I submit that beyond the texts' reverberations of a racialized knowledge whose logic undoubtedly still structures our world (only the slightest sliver of conceptual time separates Gobineau's *The Inequality of Human Races* from *The Bell Curve*), beyond copyrighted neologism and academicist obfuscation, and beyond the accrued authority of Theory, the discourses of hybridity I have addressed themselves desire and testify to a desire for vital and harmonious community. It is this utopian desire, indeed this promise of acceptance, which explains the popularity and wide circulation of cultural texts on hybridity. Framed in the indicative, their appeal nonetheless derives from the subjunctive, for they resonate with the reader's own utopian desires that *it be so*. As Claude Abastado says of manifestos, they are "the foundational act of a collective subject" (7). Reading hybridist discourses as manifestos permits us to address them not only as discourses of truth that can be proven or disproven, but as documents of desire; we are thereby able to address both their truths and their erotics. My focus in this chapter is thus the aesthetic seductions of manifestos of hybridity.

First and foremost, my generic reclassification was enabled by a literary comparatism that placed the academic texts of Bhabha and Gilroy in the tradition of Latin American and Caribbean manifestos of hybridity like Oswald de Andrade's "Anthropophagite Manifesto," the Créolistes' "Praise," and Alejo Carpentier's "Prologue" to *El Reine de Este Mundo*. Second, in trying to decipher the ambivalences that haunt so many discourses of hybridity, I found very suggestive Mary Louise Pratt's study of the genre of autoethnography as one that selectively collaborated with dominant culture (*Imperial Eyes* 7) and Édouard Glissant's conception of "forced poetics" as a poetics internally divided, desire and expression at odds with one other. Both autoethnography and forced poetics helped me to think in generic terms about the constraints and desires of discourses of hybridity. Lastly, I sought to put into theoretical practice Fredric Jameson's injunction that "a Marxist negative hermeneutic, a marxïst practice of ideological analysis proper, must in the practical work of reading and interpretation be exercised *simultaneously* with a Marxist positive hermeneutic, or a decipherment of the Utopian impulses of these same still ideological cultural texts" (*The Political Unconscious* 296).

Jameson locates the utopian impulse of such discourses not in the content or ideological motifs of the discourses, but in their dawning sense of solidarity, of the unity of a collectivity (290).[1] The forms of community that manifestos of hybridity imagine differ widely, ranging from a coalition of hybrid subjects in solidarity, to an inclusionary community wherein non-hybrid and hybrid subjects coexist peacefully, to a community arising from the manifesto's act of translating between different publics (for example, translating between the academic expert or aesthetic avant-garde and the "general public").

However, it is my contention that across all these different versions of community falls the shadow of class. For from the earliest articulations of hybridity as a populist nationalist discourse to the present post-nationalist elaborations of hybridity, there has existed an intimate and vexed connection between hybridity-discourse and class-discourse. In the earlier nationalist conjuncture, as I have shown, hybridity offered a route to the cultural and political mobilization of the masses that once again skirted the issue of class equality. The present wave of hybridity discourse is inseparable from two key events: first, the rise of the New Social Movements, with their critique of class reductionism and of the prioritization of class over other forms of difference (a problem internal to and vigorously debated within the marxist tradition), and second, what might be called the predicament of the post—postcolonial, post-nationalist, post–Cold War—wherein the "post" marks an imperfect break with a past in terms of which it continues to define itself, unable to achieve an affirmative, coherent naming of the present. Just as for early anticolonial nationalists in the Caribbean, discourses of hybridity provided a rhetorical clearing-space for the assertion of a collective identity, one could read the distance that some contemporary discourses of hybridity inscribe from classical Marxist class discourse as an attempt to eke out a space for a new speaking subject, distinct from and not rendered implausible by association with the formulaic class-subject of classical Marxism. For we are at a conjuncture in which socialism and revolutionary class-consciousness are on the defensive, to many seeming to offer either an undesirable or an impossible future. Hybridity-discourse in both its nationalist and post-nationalist incarnations thus develops in part out of skepticism about the desirability or feasibility of revolutionary class equality.

But a generous reading of contemporary discourses of hybridity might see in them an attempt to create a space in which to explore and reinvent an aesthetics of equality. Against a revolutionary socialism whose traditional modes of optimism ring somewhat false at present, the discourses of hybridity I have addressed seek a new mood, accenting possibility rather than constraint, dwelling in the optative rather than the conditional, imagining conciliation rather than conflict, appealing to a present erotics rather than a deferred pleasure. They thereby seek to create new enunciative positions from which the question of equality could then be framed differently. To do so, they tend to rehearse a utopian community without rehearsing the alternative material conditions necessary to realize such a community. What I am suggesting is that a poetics of hybridity is necessary to constitute a counter-subject of equality *in the absence of equality*. Class discourse thus simultaneously underwrites the urgency of the inclusionary desires of the liberal hybridity-discourses under discussion in this book and serves as its impossible outside.[2] Read thus, class equality is part of the unconscious of liberal discourses of hybridity; "hybridity" in some senses offers a displacing translation or transfiguration of class consciousness and its desires.

Reading the discourses of hybridity I have discussed as manifestos and recognizing the discursive conventions of the manifesto in them help make legible their egalitarian desires and thus facilitate the analysis of social equality. For one common historical goal of manifestos has been precisely to critique, transform, and expand prevalent conceptions of equality so as to extend the republican promise of equality to previously disenfranchised groups. Encoded in the genre of the manifesto, then, is the historical memory of specifically egalitarian struggle, debate, agitation, and combat—as, for example, in the manifestos of the Levellers, Chartists, Suffragists, Anarchists, and Communists. In *Manifestoes: Provocations of the Modern*, the only book-length study I know to theorize the genre of the manifesto, Janet Lyon argues that "to write a manifesto is to echo a history of struggle against dominant forces; it is to link one's voice to the countless voices of previous perpetual struggles" (29). The manifesto is thus not only a genre with recognizable formal features but also a relatively stable ideological sign of political combat which can be evoked in any number of struggles or sides (29), a bridge between different episodes of the "permanent revolution" and a kind of radical Esperanto across decades and nations and cultures (60).[3]

Approached as manifestos, hybridity-discourses' contradictions, slippages, and concessions can be understood not only as signs of their failure but also as signs of their utopian designs and their generic constraints. If, as Karen Judd observes, creolization is characterized by a slippage between "1) a retrospectively observed pattern of cultural change over the colonial and postcolonial period, and 2) an active political process, occurring during periods of social or political crisis, in which individual struggles to define an ethnic identity become collective,"[4] then reading texts of creolization as manifestos enables us not only to identify their conceptual imprecisions but to interpret the *function* of those imprecisions. Indeed, the slippage between description and prescription occurs so frequently across the discourses we have read that it could well be read as a structural feature of hybridist discourse. By recasting these texts as manifestos, we may read their movement between description and prescription not as a slip or revealing accident, but as the *enabling ground*, a central structuring move, of the discourse. Martí's claim that there can be no racial animosity because there are no races, Anzaldúa's definition of the borderlands as an *already existing* space of tolerance and inclusion, and Walcott's imagining of the Caribbean as a broken vase *already* reassembled, are cases in point. Walcott's evocation of poetry as a language that "conjugates both tenses simultaneously: the past and the present" and Bhabha's invocations of the "future anterior" (95), double-time, and "time-lag" similarly attest to the complex temporality I have described.[5]

The textual definitions or quasi-definitions of hybridity often similarly straddle the descriptive and the prescriptive: When Anzaldúa says

> *Nosotros los* chicanos straddle the borderlands. On one side of us, we are constantly exposed to the Spanish of the Mexicans, on the other we hear the Anglo's incessant clamoring so that we forget our language. Among ourselves we don't say *nosotros los americanos, o nosotros los españoles, o nosotros los hispanos.* We say *nosotros los mexicanos* (by *mexicanos* we do not mean citizens of Mexico; we do not mean a national identity, but a racial one.) We distinguish between *mexicanos del otro lado* and *mexicanos de este lado.* Deep in our hearts we believe that being Mexican has nothing to do with which country one lives in. Being Mexican is a state of soul. (62)

The present indicative begins as the statement of uncontroversial fact (geographical location), slips into interpretive assertion (we do not mean x, we mean y) to still less secure speculation (deep in our hearts we believe). The present indicative is thus a powerful form of naturalizing a desired state, the repetition of "nosotros" and "we" a form of securing, of incanting into existence, the collectivity it designates. Moreover, the recurrence of verbs in the present tense ("we are," "we say," "we believe") testifies to the triumph of survival in a hostile culture, of existence itself.[6] Bhabha's apparent definitions or descriptions of hybridity as the "minus in the origin," "the perplexity of living," and so on—definitions that are continents away from any dictionary meaning of the word and that inscribe instead a complex metaphoricity; Gilroy's description of the Black Atlantic as a powerfully redemptive space—not one without communal conflict and inequality, but one where these conflicts are understood as *betrayals* of the Black Atlantic: these definitions are framed in the indicative, but appeal to the hypothetical (if it were so) or the optative (we wish it were so). The insistent repetitiveness of their definitions seeks through the power of incantation and familiarity to *make* them true; Bhabha's piling up of examples and descriptive excess produce a vivid sense of possibility in place of proof. Like many examples of the manifesto, then, these definitions restate desire as truth and truth as program, and from that restatement achieve their legitimacy. This persistent logic of definition is thus at once an act of pedagogical explanation and an act of justification.

Walcott's *The Antilles* is remarkable for the explicitness of its subjunctive in his answer to his question "What are the proportions of the ideal Caribbean city?" (17):

> Spires would pin its centre and around them would be leafy, shadowy parks. Pigeons would cross its sky in alphabetic patterns, carrying with them memories of a belief in augury, and at the heart of the city there would be horses . . . and at the centre of the city seasonally there would be races . . . Its docks would not be obscured by smoke or deafened by too much machinery, and above all, it would be so racially various that the cultures of the world—the Asiatic, the Mediterranean, the European, the African—would be represented in it, its human variety more exciting than Joyce's Dublin. Its citizens would intermarry as they chose, from instinct, not tradition, until their children find it increasingly futile to trace their genealogy. It would not have too many avenues difficult or dangerous for pedestrians, its mercantile area would be a cacophony of accents, fragments of the old language that would be silenced immediately at five o' clock, its docks resolutely vacant on Sundays. (17–18)

Having openly entered into a utopian fantasy in which hybridity plays a significant part, Walcott surprises by folding that fantasy back into the present indicative: "This is Port of Spain to me, a city ideal in its commercial and human proportions, where a citizen is a walker and not a pedestrian, and this is how Athens may have been" (19). It is perhaps one of the boldest rhetorical moves we have seen to explicitly arouse the subjunctive mood only to claim that the subjunctive ideal *already* exists in the present. In a reversal of the direction of the moves we have thus far seen, Walcott moves from the prescriptive to the descriptive.

The repetitive definitions described earlier draw attention to another feature of the manifesto: its aesthetic of excess. As Mary Ann Caws observes, the manifesto is a loud genre, "always in overdose and overdrive" (xxi). The wild weaving of images, the intensity and excitement of tone, the large font and capitalization, the propensity for an exclamatory grammar ("WORKING MEN OF ALL COUNTRIES, UNITE!"), all evoke the sense of the shout or speech from a soapbox, of argument impassioned by voice and body. This language of excess, of imagistic saturation, of radicalism, can be explained in terms of the manifesto's sense of rupture with a reactionary past and need for urgent persuasion. The manifesto's excess may be responsible for the traditional economy of length, for its intensity of pitch cannot be sustained for long, just as a symphonic finale or crescendo cannot be extended; the prolonged manifesto risks degenerating into monotony or hysteria. Indeed, the manifesto has an almost adolescent sense of its own iconoclasm and novelty. As Tristan Tzara describes the traditional manifesto (with which his own "Dada Manifesto" of course seeks to break):

> To proclaim a manifesto you have to want: A.B.C., thunder against 1,2,3, lose your patience and sharpen your wings to conquer and spread a's, b's, c's little and big, sign, scream, swear, arrange prose in a form of absolute and irrefutable evidence, prove your non-plus-ultra and maintain that novelty resembles life just as the latest appearance of a whore proves the essence of God . . .[7]

Anzaldúa's protestations fit perfectly with the manifesto's somewhat romantic railing: "So don't give me your tenets and your laws. Don't give me your luke-warm gods. What I want is an accounting with all three cultures—white, Mexican, Indian. I want the freedom to carve and chisel my own face, to staunch the bleeding with ashes, to fashion my own gods out of my entrails" (22).

The hyperbole that can be so frustrating if one reads hybridist discourse in terms of its epistemological truth-content makes sense when reframed in terms of the generic conventions of the manifesto.[8] The truth of Jean Paul's Sartre's *Being and Nothingness* and "Existentialism" (a text that can also usefully be read as a manifesto), after all, lies not in its literal claims, for the unqualified claim that "we are condemned to be free" can be disproven in a moment by reference to any one of the innumerable instances of slavery, servitude, brutalization, and abjection that scar the globe. The value of Sartre's statement, indeed of his overstatement, lies in his redefinition and exploration of the power of a freedom that is not legal, political, or physical, and in his attempt to rouse and rally to responsibility a population devastated and despairing after the cataclysmic events of World War II. Sartre's performance of political will is enabled precisely by his elision of qualification and conditionality. Thus, the value of inspirational speech lies not in its literal un/truth but in what its performance of confidence and energy might make *possible*. One structuring question of this chapter is thus: what do fantasies of hybridity enable? And concomitantly, what might more literally truthful narratives disable?

Like Sartre's manifesto, Walcott's *The Antilles* relies on its rhetorical energy rather than its truth-content to achieve its desired effects. Walcott's strategy is to use the erotic power of language to make his readers willingly enter the poetic dream when they have been abandoned by the political dream, applying to politics the balm of beauty. Thus, his act of political-via-aesthetic persuasion occurs not at the macro-societal level of policy or social program, but at the level of the individual reader. Indeed, the political nightmare of interracial conflict that motivates his narrative gains admission to it only in the phrases in which he draws attention to his ignorance of the Ramleela—"Princes and gods, *I supposed*" (3) and "nobody in Trinidad knew any more than I did . . . *apart from the Indians*" (3–4, emphasis added). These two phrases gesture outward from the text, connecting the formal textual *centrality* Walcott awards the Indo-Trinidadian performance of Ramleela to the extratextual cultural *marginality* of Indo-Trinidadians; it is precisely this marginality that *The Antilles* seeks to counter. These phrases are crucial, but equally crucially *fleeting*, moments of admission of domestic political constraint; the rest of the text dwells on a uniting, revisionary love and on the Caribbean's artistic and natural beauty that dissolve the sigh of History (7). The utopian impulse of Wilson Harris's account of the bone-flute similarly seeks to redeem History by reclaiming regenerative beauty from force.

Although I have in the previous chapters critiqued Walcott on grounds of epistemology for essentially lying about the deep inequalities and antagonisms that structure Trinidadian society, a symptomatic reading of Walcott's essay as a manifesto might shift the value attached to the word "lie," recasting it as a defiant act of imaginative and aesthetic will, an Adornian recalcitrance that gestures toward utopia precisely in its exorcism of History's inequalities from the structure of the sentence. The survivors of slavery and indentureship, the chained Cromwellian convict and Sephardic Jew, the Chinese grocer and Lebanese merchant on his bicycle (11–12), jostle together in Walcott's list, occupying identical positions in the grammar of his sentence; their oppressors are markedly absent from the list of inhabitants of Port of Spain, yet what the people listed share is precisely experiences of oppression. In keeping with my argument about the manifesto's memory of egalitarianism, then, the eulogistic evocation of specifically working-class members of different ethnicities arguably inscribes a working-class solidarity in the sentence by glossing over their mutual antagonisms and inequalities, instead paying collective tribute to them. This indeed is the "sublime stupidity" of poetry: "to fall in love with the world, in spite of History" (28). In Walcott's view, then, art provides the example that politics must learn to emulate.

Walcott's work over the decades reveals a troubled sense of the relationship of art, history, and politics—most spectacularly in his pronouncement that "the future of West Indian militancy lies in art" ("What the Twilight Says: An Overture" 18), a statement that closely parallels the Créolistes' assertion that art must take priority over politics for the present. With the shrinking of the political horizon of possibility that has accompanied the passage of time from independence, there develops in Walcott's work a corresponding expansion of the role of art in realizing or restoring the nation. In the Anglophone Caribbean in 1992, a moment so inhospitable to mass movements and popular state-formation, could any invocation of a Caribbean state sustain the optimism Walcott seeks to produce? It is the sense of political impasse that can explain why in *The Antilles* Walcott's critical, oppositional move is couched in political terms, while his reconstructive move is cast in aesthetic and sentimental terms. Similarly, the oppositional move is relegated to the international sphere, while the reconstructive move is confined to the national sphere. In other words, Walcott's language of international political economy can be made to facilitate Caribbean solidarity, providing the political Other in relation to which a nationalist Self might emerge and thereby serving as glue for the shattered vase. But addressing political economic concerns at the national level could further shatter the vase—by "breaking the dream." It is for this reason that at the national level Walcott's strategy is to revalue, rehabilitate, and reconcile warring groups in the beauty of his sentences. For economic analysis calls for redistribution, and truth needs proof or evidence, but beauty is its own argument.

Moreover, hyperbole is in most cases not a strategy that can admit to doubts. It produces instead the appearance of confidence, whether that confidence is genuine or a masquerade, and seeks to inspire in the reader a similar confidence so as to expand the collectivity projected by the manifesto. The reliance of the manifesto on overstatement is thus a rhetorical strategy conducive to persuasion and political mobilization. Read in this light, Raphaël Confiant's admission in a 1996 interview that he feared it was too late for Creole to survive testifies at once to the falsehood of his claims in the manifesto and to the utopian desire that gave rise to them.[9] If in that interview, too, he slips back into making too much of Creole cultural survival (as the language of the unconscious, emotion, etc.), I wonder whether this reinvocation is not one more attempt to persuade—albeit this time himself as much as the reader. If in chapter one I have critiqued the Créolistes for subordinating politics to art, for relegating politics to an appendix, rereading "Praise" in terms of the formal considerations of manifestos suggests that that relegation or subordination is an act of disciplining and desire. In other words, it is precisely the *priority* of politics in the world around them—a politics that in their moment evokes pessimism—that makes the Créolistes prioritize art and claim "for the moment, full knowledge of Creoleness will be reserved for Art" (893). The Créolistes' strategy is thus a compensatory reversal of relations of power between politics and art. In a similar reading, Sergio Prado Bellei reads the Brazilian O Campos brothers' Concretism, with its aestheticized postmodern version of Oswald de Andrade's anthropophagy, as a confirmation of the failure of Brazil's modernizing project (104). In all these cases, politics is what the texts repress from direct expression; it is only through a symptomatic reading of the unconscious of these texts that we can recover it.

For this reason, I suggest that several of the manifestos of hybridity we have read be considered examples of what the Martinican theorist of hybridity Édouard Glissant calls "forced poetics." In *Caribbean Discourse*, Glissant defines forced poetics or counterpoetics as a collective situation in which "a need for expression confronts an inability to achieve expression" (120). In the case of Martinique, this structural precondition for forced poetics is the absence of national control of the means of production: forced poetics is "instituted by a community whose self-expression does not emerge spontaneously, or result from the autonomous activity of the social body" (121). The term against which forced poetics takes on its meaning is "free" or "natural poetics," where there is "no incompatibility between desire and expression" (120). (Since in my understanding, natural poetics as Glissant describes it is not a condition that can be attained, I consider the difference between forced and natural poetics as one of degree rather than kind.) It is natural poetics that Glissant believes can most fully challenge the established social order, but since, according to him, the material conditions for a natural poetics do not exist in Martinique (and by extension much of the dependent capitalist Caribbean), he wants to "resist the naive optimism that glamorizes 'natural' poetics" (254). In such a situation, any apparently natural poetics can only be illusory. Thus, he self-consciously opts to use and develop a forced poetics, one task of which is to contribute to creating a situation in which natural poetics will become possible. It is Glissant's emphasis on desire that links my interests in the manifesto and forced poetics. In both cases, desire diagnoses a lack, even though the manifesto expresses an urgent desire for and/or modeling of social change, while forced poetics cannot achieve the expression it desires.

Particularly in the light of Glissant's organicist and naturalistic vocabulary, however, three interpretive cautions are necessary. First, in Glissant's thinking, forced poetics is not a romantic motif for the pathos of the individual writer; it is not some kind of grandiose writer's block: "The issue is not one of attempts at articulation (composite and 'voluntary'), through which we test our capacity for self-expression" (120). Rather, forced poetics arises out of a structural, *collective* condition. Thus, individual writers may provide examples of forced poetics, but their poetics need to be analyzed in terms of collectivities, cultures, periods, and conditions of production.[10]

In Glissant's periodization, 1960–80 is a period of "nonproduction"; it is therefore by definition a period of forced poetics. It is this period as well as the prospective one that both Glissant and the Créolistes inhabit. Given the similarities between "Praise" and *Puerto Rican Jam*, the latter, too, would fall into these categories, a claim that Grosfoguel's characterization of Puerto Rico as a "postwork society," his defense of welfare economics, and his emphasis on (the right to) consumption rather than (the right to) production support. Natural poetics, in contrast, is the direct result of activity within the social body (120). Glissant argues that the social autonomy necessary for natural poetics was possible even within the extreme forms of exploitation that characterized plantation and slave society, but that autonomy is increasingly impossible during the present onslaught of assimilation by France. Second, Glissant's goal of achieving a situation in which natural poetics becomes possible should not be read as an endorsement of mimetic referentiality; indeed, Glissant explicitly distances himself from mimeticist projects.[11] In my reading of Glissant, forced poetics does not lament the gap between word and world, for poetics itself can be said to arise from that gap. Instead, forced poetics is the mark of the inability to express *desire*. Third, the existence of forced poetics should not be confused with lack of creativity—a point that becomes quite evident if one looks at several discourses of creolization, which I contend manifest forced poetics. For while creolization as a philosophical or theoretical construct is plagued by conceptual weakness and contradiction, it has produced some of the richest aesthetics and cultural practices of the Caribbean.

Edward Kamau Brathwaite's trilogy *The Arrivants* offers an eloquent example. At the heart of his experiments with "nation language" are the attempts to reconcile voice and print and find a poetic alternative to the pentameter, one that is able to register Caribbean experience.[12] "[W]e haven't got the syllables, the syllabic intelligence, to describe the hurricane, which is our own experience; whereas we can describe the imported alien experience of the snowfall" (*History of the Voice* 263). Brathwaite analyzes this collective condition in his account of a student-essay which contained the sentence "The snow was falling on the canefields" (*History of the Voice* 264). Whilst certainly one might comment on the schizophrenic creativity possible as a result of such creole adaptation, an expression of colonized hybridity and contradiction where literary exposure and experienced landscape collide, Brathwaite thinks of it in terms akin to Glissant's forced poetics. For while the sentence may be of immense *symptomatic* interest to critics and cultural theorists (the kind of slippage in mimicry that so interests Bhabha) and might even hint at *potential* poetic fusions, potential hybrid natural poetics, by all indications such avenues were closed to the writer at the time. For that student, the sentence reflects neither self-consciousness nor empowering hybridity; it produces no active principle of poetic creation, but an inert relationship to a given reality. As such, both the expressed literary present and the absence of an alternative approach to the local landscape indicate a *truncation* of expressive possibility and desire that marks forced poetics.

In Brathwaite's own poetry, the tension between two poems in his trilogy *The Arrivants* (1967)—"Calypso" and "Pebbles"—poignantly testifies to the dilemma of forced poetics. In "Calypso," the poem that represented a breakthrough in Brathwaite's poetic method, indeed one which he hoped could lay the concerns of the previous paragraph to rest, Brathwaite lovingly takes the specks of dust shrugged off as insignificant by de Gaulle and recasts them as islands worthy of poetry's desire, worthy indeed of their own creation-myth.

> The stone had skidded arc'd and bloomed into islands:
> Cuba and San Domingo
> Jamaica and Puerto Rico
> Grenada Guadeloupe Bonaire
>
> curved stone hissed into reef
> wave teeth fanged into clay
> white splash flashed into spray
> Bathsheba Montego Bay
>
> bloom of the arcing summers (*The Arrivants* 48)

With "Calypso" Brathwaite achieves at last a relationship to the landscape that is not governed by England. He finds in the syncopated skidding of stones on water a figure at once visual and aural that registers the arc of the Caribbean archipelago and an alternative to the imperial march of the pentameter (Phaf 22, Chang 3–6).[13] The rhythms of calypso and steelband, evoked by name later in the poem, become the sound and meter of the Caribbean. The stone/word is attuned to its elements—island/water, stone/sea. In a turn very common in Caribbean literature, "Calypso" reaches back to prehistory—here to the mythic moment of the islands' creation—to own the Caribbean landscape, an act of appropriation that becomes a resource with which to survive the subsequent history of plantation, unemployment, and migration recounted in the rest of the poem; from that landscape arise the vital rhythms of creole resistance—the rhythms of the steel drum, calypso, and limbo. The process is akin to that by which, in Glissant's words, the landscape becomes a character in the process of creating history (106).[14] Brathwaite's act of resistance and intervention in history occurs here at the level of form; it consists of rearranging time, thereby altering our experience of it—and in it. Whereas Oswald de Andrade reorders history so that cannibalism, not Christianity, becomes the inaugural moment from which the clock of calendrical time starts ticking ("the year 374 after the swallowing of the Bishop of Sardinia"), Brathwaite restructures the individual unit of time.

Yet, later in the trilogy, the skidding stone of "Calypso"'s creation-myth turns into "Pebbles," a poem that admits not only creole resources but the limits upon what they can accomplish.

> But my island is a pebble.
> . . .
> You cannot crack a pebble,
> it excludes
> death. Seeds will not
> take root on its cool sur-
>
> face. It is a duck's back
> of water. A knife will not snap
> it open. It will slay giants
> but never bear children. (196)

Juxtaposing these two poems poignantly reveals the tension at the crux of creolization: the tension between creolization as a narrative of creativity and creolization as a narrative of conflict and constraint, between a resistance that can joyously overcome History and a resistance that can successfully defeat the Other but not sustain the Self. This is the lurking fear at the heart of a forced poetics.

In the academic essays we have read, the problem of forced poetics develops somewhat differently. Although the work of Gilroy and Bhabha clearly shares some of the same conjunctural constraints of the "predicament of the post" to which Walcott and Harris are subject, Bhabha and Gilroy labor under pressures particular to the location of theorists in metropolitan universities. I contend that we might think of their work as *disguised* manifestos, for the status of these texts as scholarly texts forbids them to readily acknowledge their status as manifestos; thus, they remain uneasily poised between the genre of the expository academic essay (truth/interpretation) and the political or aesthetic manifesto (rhetoric/program).[15] Bhabha's and Gilroy's work carries strong political solidarities that both the metropolitan university and the field of criticism discipline with their demands for specialization, critical distance, and positivist objectivity. It is this structure of professional expectation that makes the idea of a disguised manifesto pertinent. Their academic essays—like my own—obey the formal conventions of objectivity even as they may critique that objectivity at the level of content. The utopian function of the academic texts I have discussed, then, depends in part on erasing the signs of their own institutional conditionality and political partisanship—an erasure that permits them to circulate with the authority of Theory.[16]

However, since the aesthetic manifesto is a border-genre, typically combining criticism, codification, and art, reading academic theoretical accounts of hybridity as manifestos invites greater attention to their poetics. For example, while much has been made of the difficulty of Bhabha's prose (a difficulty that is often interpreted as being complicitous with the logic of disciplinary commodification), little attention has been paid to its intense nostalgia for the poetic word. Bhabha's circumlocutory language seems to search for a poetics for hybridity within the academic essay. The very luxuriance of his language, its often whimsical associations, its saturation with literary and filmic allusion (from Casablanca and Tangiers to "Play it Again Sam," to the ubiquitous Conrad and "Memories of Underdevelopment") stages a distinctly *literary* identification. Witness from "DissemiNation" the following passage that hybridizes Derridean deconstruction with autobiography and allusion, attempting to chart a literary genealogy quite different from the theoretical genealogy usually attributed to Bhabha:

> The title of this chapter—DissemiNation—owes something to the wit and wisdom of Jacques Derrida, but something more to my own experience of migration. I have lived that moment of the scattering of the people that in other times and other places, in the nations of others, becomes a time of gathering. Gatherings of exiles and *émigrés* and refugees; gathering on the edge of 'foreign' cultures; gathering at the frontiers; gatherings in the ghettos or cafés or city centers; gathering in the half-life, half-light of foreign tongues, or in the uncanny fluency of another's language; gathering the signs of approval and acceptance, degrees, discourses, disciplines; gathering the memories of underdevelopment, of other worlds lived retroactively; gathering the past in a ritual of revival; gathering the present. Also the gathering of people in the diaspora: indentured, migrant, interned; the gathering of incriminatory statistics, educational performance, legal statutes, immigration status—the genealogy of that lonely figure that John Berger named the seventh man. The gathering of clouds from which the Palestinian poet Mahmoud Darwish asks 'where should the birds fly after the last sky?' (139)

We may usefully think of these poetically suggestive meditations on "gathering" as an exercise in developing a poetics, as itself gathering a language of hybridity within the academic essay. With its full use of rhyme and assonance and its alliterative parallelisms, its verbless sentence-fragments may usefully be thought of as notes towards such a language.

Similarly in the passage below, alliteration is foregrounded to such an extent that it exceeds and obscures the literal meaning; the pleasure of sound and fortuitous echo becomes more urgent than the logic of theory, to whose fold the passage ultimately returns in its lapse into unpoeticized abstraction.

> This locality is . . . more complex than 'community'; more symbolic than 'society'; more connotative than 'country'; less patriotic than *patrie*; more rhetorical than the reason of State; more mythological than ideology; less homogeneous than hegemony; less centered than the citizen; more collective than 'the subject'; more psychic than civility; more hybrid in the articulation of cultural differences and identifications than can be represented in any hierarchical or binary structuring of social antagonism. (140)

If the passages I have cited hanker after a poetics less stern, more indulgent, then the following sentence is remarkable for its poetic economy: "How is historical agency enacted in the slenderness of narrative?" (198), a sentence startling in its brevity, suggestiveness, and associational logic. Forced poetics in the preceding passages from Bhabha can be thought of in terms of the conflicting desires of the poetic and theoretical discourses being stitched together and the strong structural incentive for the poetic to be subordinated to the theoretical.

Anzaldúa's formal experimentation and generic hybridization—her montage of poetry, autobiography, essay, theory, mystical antiscientific, and poeticized evolutionist discourse, her use of several languages from standard English to Tex-Mex to Chicano Spanish—constitute a definitive break with the academic essay. Gilroy's struggles are not played out primarily in the realm of form; his writing is manifesto-like primarily in terms of its use of the implicit subjunctive, definition, and a tendency toward hyperbole. It is Bhabha who most strains against the genre of academic writing from within. Part of the political interest of his work and similar academic manifestos, quite independently of the content of their assertions, lies in their momentary generic breaches of the wall between criticism and art; these breaches both recall the intellectual traditions of Oswald de Andrade, Walcott, Carpentier, and Harris, whose *oeuvres* combine theoretical and artistic practice, and hint at future modes of collaboration between aesthetic and theoretical practices.

Moreover, recognizing hybridist theoretical texts as manifestos repositions academic endeavor as unapologetically interested and as participating in political solidarities. The manifesto is a useful genre for imagining ways in which specialized knowledges become part of the public domain; it is one form of practicing public scholarship. And part of the work of a public intellectual is such *translational* labor, the labor of finding hybrid languages that bridge populations. As Lyon argues, "the manifesto occupies a distinct generic space in the arena of public discourse, and thereby aspires to a concrete form of cultural work even if it only rarely performs that work" (24).

Some additional caveats are in order here. First, the possibilities of the academic manifesto are inevitably circumscribed by structural and institutional factors—amongst them at present the marginalization of the humanities, the social privileging of reason and objectivity, the commodification of ideas and specialized language, and the tension between the collectivist logic of the manifesto (historically often a collectively or anonymously authored text) and the logic of individual stardom and celebrity that increasingly pervades the academy.[17] While Claude Abastado notes that many texts not intended as manifestos may be read as manifestos, in what he calls the "manifesto-effect," and Janet Lyon notes that manifestos are often only named as such retroactively, if they achieve the status of foundational texts (12), it is also the case that the institutional context of the reception of Bhabha's work, fully as much as its own impulse to disguise, overdetermines the conventions within which his work is read. As a result, the manifesto-like qualities of his work, its poetic strategies, go largely unnoticed. In other words, its potential to function like a manifesto is conjuncturally contained.

Second, while the invocation of translation and public intellectuals may promise a populist and democratic impulse, Marinetti's reference to the manifesto as an art form of "violence and precision" (qtd. in Perloff 65) reminds us of the erotics of power in utopian discourse, a reminder that has particular resonance for the forms of authority of academic discourse. If rhetoric persuades, it also threatens, intimidates, obfuscates, to garner authority. Marjorie Perloff notes that manifestos may be "designed, less to move the masses to action than to charm and give pleasure to one's coterie" (92). Thus, although the popular accessibility of many a manifesto offers an appealing model for theory, manifestos, like theory, are often torn amongst avant-gardist explanation, self-justification, and self-aggrandizement; their practice thus offers no secure way out of vanguardism or demagoguery. Moreover, literary theory shares the manifesto's powerful prescriptive impact on art; indeed, a hybrid poetics at present is certainly a necessary condition for and sometimes a guarantor of critical approval.

At the same time, however, the manifesto is not *merely* prescriptive; therefore, authority is not necessarily the primary axis of its acceptance or refusal. Rather, its subjunctive is imaginative, performative, exploratory, improvisational. If one of the sources of the longevity of "hybridity" is its utopian communitarian content, another is surely its formal ingenuity and flexibility. The manifesto has an erotics, its politics quickened by a poetry and performance that often exceed the political or ideological work to be done. Philosophers have only interpreted the world; the point is to change it, declared Marx in his famous eleventh thesis on Feuerbach. The manifesto promises *aesthetic* renewal of Marx' Thesis 11.

Moreover, the transience of particular manifestos has a productive dimension. As Claude Abastado has observed, if the manifesto's rhetoric depends upon the production of marginality (for example, the cutting-edge, the avant-garde, the embattled minority, the disenfranchised majority), that position of marginality is threatened when the manifesto succeeds in persuading. The manifesto's power to speak to the present is thus necessarily fleeting. Manifestos exist to be transcended; otherwise they become new orthodoxies. In Abastado's phrase, the manifesto turns managerial, "the disarmed bomb becomes a museum-piece" (6). Whereas the manifesto has a long tradition of being read conjuncturally, its contingency and contextuality well recognized, Theory has not always been read thus. Making the interpretive choice to read Theory as manifesto thus turns it outward to history, locating it inescapably in a specific situation, dated event, or conjuncture and resisting claims to transhistorical abstraction or authority. Repositioning Theory as manifesto thus decapitalizes it; it renders theory vulnerable.

While Glissant's formulation of forced poetics suggests a way of reading discourses of hybridity both symptomatically and sympathetically by understanding their deficiencies and lacks not simply as signs of failure, but as signs of desire foiled by its structural conditions, it does not absolve us of evaluating the discourses' different strategic choices and effects. For although the texts we have read are documents of a desire without which no utopian politics can exist, the existence of that desire is itself not sufficient for the realization of such politics. Nor does reading these texts as manifestos with forced poetics justify their exclusions by reading them as overdetermined, for forced poetics is a wide field inhabited by many of the vastly different theorists we have thus far read, and generating several different enunciative possibilities. Their choices have very different material consequences, ranging from the preparatory to the compensatory to the substitutional. Glissant's "dream deferred" from the epigraph to this chapter becomes in *Puerto Rican Jam* the dream deceased, for the latter's insistence on the present tense permits no Caribbean future (tense). That "strange stubborn presence in our responses," which Walcott finds in art, de Andrade finds in primitivism, Harris finds in the unconscious, and Brathwaite seeks through his reverse journeys to Africa and in premodern cultural practices such as limbo and vodun, that Caribbean breathes uneasily in "Praise" and ceases to exist in the pages of *Puerto Rican Jam.*

We need to ask which generic features from the manifesto's repertoire are employed in particular manifestos, why, and with what effect. For example, it seems to me that two dilemmas faced by post-nationalist manifestos are what collectivity to call to action and how to mobilize it. The emphasis in post-nationalist manifestos of hybridity on tropes of prophecy and inevitability, and the recession of the traditional manifesto's enumeration of specific grievances or demands and exhortations to action, may be connected to the crisis of the collective "we."[18] For institutional avenues for organizing beyond (rather than within or through) the framework of the nation-state remain only incipient. Whereas in texts like *The Communist Manifesto*, the subjunctive mood and language of prophecy aid a concrete project of opposition, in Anzaldúa's *Borderlands/La Frontera*, Benítez-Rojo's *The Repeating Island*, and for different reasons, Vasconcelos's nationalist *The Cosmic Race*, the implicit subjunctive, tropes of evolution, prophesy, and inevitability replace the manifesto's traditionally combative content. One consequence of this change is a shift in emphasis from conflict to conciliation.

Moreover, the same aesthetic or rhetorical move can have different consequences at different times; manifestos can thus only be evaluated conjuncturally. The very untruths that in Walcott's work can serve as a way of rallying energies that might be genuinely transformative in an emergent national culture can serve as an alibi or evasion in a period of nationalist consolidation; the consequence of the lie, and hence its strategic value, shifts. Similarly, if heretofore the strategy of manifestos of hybridity in the academy has been to disable the rhetoric of purism and foundations as a conceptual precondition for social equality, it may well be the case that those same manifestos now function as strategies of containment of oppositional struggles against inequality. If hybridist discourse is not to function mainly as a "forced poetics" operating as a strategy of containment, we have to find ways of combining the utopian desires of anti-purist and egalitarian discourses in a rhetorically persuasive imagination. It is my hope that interpreting these texts as manifestos can help build upon the specifically oppositional historical practice of manifestos.

Glissant's practice of forced poetics differs significantly from both the "literary" and "academic" manifestos I have addressed thus far. Part of the fascination of *Caribbean Discourse* lies in how it employs the genre of the (meta)-manifesto, the form of forced poetics, and the content of cultural hybridity. Alternately, we could think of *Caribbean Discourse* as being a self-conscious meta-manifesto of hybridity (*antillanité* or Caribbeanness imagined as a cross-cultural poetics) and forced poetics (understood as an alternative to both an illusory natural poetics and a poetics of mere capitulation). Unlike the foregoing texts, Glissant insists both that forced poetics is a problematic choice and that the resolution to the problem of forced poetics is only possible when the formal creativity of art can be linked to political creativity. That is why *Caribbean Discourse* unfolds simultaneously as a meditation on Martinican Creole *and* an impassioned argument for Martinican independence: "The independence of Martinique is . . . a form of creativity and will generate its own technology; this is where a collective sense of responsibility originates" (255).

At the heart of the differences between Glissant's manifesto and the others I have examined lies his deployment of a self-consciously forced poetics. It is as a result of this self-consciousness that, while *Caribbean Discourse* shares many of the rhetorical devices of other hybridist manifestos—for example, the implicit or explicit subjunctive, definition, repetition—it categorically rejects hyperbole. It does not permit the reader the aesthetic relief or rejuvenation of Walcott's text, nor does it make any exaggerated claims for art's victories over History; it refuses the triumphalist tones of "Praise" and the swagger and bravado of "Anthropophagite Manifesto." Against the Créoliste's rhetorical practice and linguistic program, Glissant declares: "To claim that Creole has always been our national language is to even further obscure, in this triumphant version, the disturbing self-doubt that is the source of our insecurity but that also establishes our presence" (167). Whereas the creative principle in politics recedes from the vision of Harris and Walcott, in which art becomes the home of an unfettered subjunctive, Glissant's manifesto delicately balances the optative subjunctive and the conditional, and finds both moods in both art and politics. It defamiliarizes and restlessly explores the possibilities of an art that is piercingly aware of its limits.

Glissant is modest in demarcating the limited parameters of his aesthetic interventions, recognizing that the absence of current possibilities for economic or political transformation both makes his aesthetic project necessary and limits its scope. Thus, he poses the question: "Can one, here and now, create a national economy?" and goes on to answer it thus: "If the answer is yes, theatrical reform becomes unnecessary: collective expression is channeled elsewhere" (218).

With its medley of fractured genres, *Caribbean Discourse* does not even offer the solace of complete explanation. In contrast to the magnificent—and also utopian—formal seamlessness of Walcott's prose, a counterpoint to a fractured reality, and in contrast to Walcott's "suspension of disbelief" or willed fictional dream, Glissant's manifesto of forced poetics resorts to notes, prefaces, aphorisms, to the visual use of blank space on the page, each interrupting the other to heighten our awareness of the incompleteness of his artistic project.

I want to suggest, however, that this incompleteness helps make of the reader a fellow traveler. Admittedly, it does not sweep the reader away on its triumphant tide of rhetorical energy, but its very gaps and spaces can serve as doorways through which the reader can enter the text. Unlike the building momentum and volume of the crescendo, the gaps in *Caribbean Discourse* slow one down, make one pause, puzzle, frown, linger, smile, hesitate, or murmur; they not only make one see/k the transparency of water, they invite us to savor that water's shimmering opacities.[19] Moreover, the textual techniques of echo, layering, suggestion, and association activate the reader's memory. The form of *Caribbean Discourse* thus invites the reader to collaborate in making sense of the text, making of manifesto-like translation a dialogic enterprise. For the suggestive phrase, unlike the completed argument, gives a peculiarly dialogical pleasure, requiring the reader to complete its meaning where the completed argument requires only that the reader receive and endorse it (though the resistant reader can certainly do otherwise). In *Caribbean Discourse*, the "we" that every manifesto desires takes shape as a community of interpretive laborers.

What is further interesting to me is the clarity with which Glissant understands his aesthetic project to be preparatory, that is, devoted to expanding the window of political and aesthetic opportunity for the future. Thus, he argues:

> A popular revolution would certainly make Martinique an integral part of the Caribbean, and, by freeing us from an antipoetics, would allow the Martinican people to choose either one of the two languages they use, or to combine them into a new form of expression. But in the more embattled present circumstances, the challenge of an antipoetics, deliberately creating new forms of expression, with a more limiting, less developed, less free function, would allow us from this very moment to engage in the quest for self-expression and prepare for the future. (168)

It is this notion of art as preparatory (rather than compensatory or substitutional) that explains Glissant's choice of the manifesto of forced poetics. Glissant is aware of the narrowed window for mass political movements and aware of the vulnerability of his own epistemological and aesthetic practice, but, breaking with the more settled postmodernisms represented by *Puerto Rican Jam* and "Praise," retains a memory of a larger scale of emancipatory struggle. The greatest strategic value of his manifesto, then, may lie in its insistence on gesturing towards a beyond with a memory of a before. "Creolization as an idea means the negation of creolization as a category" (141). Cultural hybridity is not a "content" (filled with, say, so many ethnicities) or a program (to write exclusively in Creole, for example). Glissant, like Maryse Condé, objects to the transformation of creolization from a process into a program, where it becomes an abstract and dogmatically decreed formula or "ism". Creolization's utopian-aesthetic possibilities vary conjuncturally.[20] Hybridity, in short, is no more than a preparatory discourse; it must not become a resting point.

To apply Fredric Jameson's terms to the context of hybridity, the utopian content of hybridity lies primarily in its "dawning sense of solidarity" with a collectivity (*The Political Unconscious* 290). Jameson's formulation is pertinent to my argument for two reasons. First, it brings home to me that I cannot follow Jameson to his epic vision of the collectivity as "Utopian not in itself, but only insofar as all such collectivities are themselves figures for the ultimate concrete collective life of an achieved Utopian or classless society" (290). In part this is because the sentence seems in some way to diminish real gains by granting them only an allegorical value. But still more, the social and political terrain we occupy has changed so radically in the twenty years since the publication of *The Political Unconscious* that, whatever nostalgia I might feel for the confident triumphalism of Jameson's words, indeed, for their sense of deliverance, I have no access to it in the present. For Jameson's performance of prophetic certainty, which echoes so closely the rhetoric of its ancestral *Communist Manifesto*, is underwritten by the geopolitical presence (if not exemplary practice) of the Soviet Union and Communist China.[21] What, I wonder, would a communist manifesto for the present moment look like? It would almost certainly evince a forced poetics (although perhaps the very same manifesto read today has the effect of forced poetics). Its forced poetics would surely have to achieve a most delicate dialectic of the optative subjunctive and the conditional; it could promise no deliverance, but it would intensify our hungers for equality, our pleasure in it, and make more urgent our political desires by refusing to let them resolve or relax into irony.

Jameson's formulation also brings into focus a sharp irony. Given the claims of the postnationalist discourses I address in chapter one, the irony is that, notwithstanding their protestations to the contrary, those discourses of hybridity share with *nationalist* discourse a desire to participate in community. Indeed, Claude Abastado's description of the manifesto as "the foundational act of a collective subject" rhymes with Doris Sommer's account of nationalist narratives as "foundational fictions"[22] that are also designed to bring into existence a community. The hybridity manifestos' substitution of rhetoric for truth, desire for fact, project for present, their invocations of a long past, a unity achieved, make exactly the same moves as nationalist discourse.[23] The movement Bhabha identifies between the pedagogic and the performative impulses of nationalist narratives, their claims to a long past as a rehearsal of and consolidation of the present, applies to his own theoretical project as well. In other words, the aesthetic and conceptual arrangement of post-nationalist and nationalist discourse is fairly similar. Thus, not only the malleable meanings of hybridity but also the generic structure of some of the discourses of hybridity I have addressed, explain that hybridity can be used to both nationalist and post-nationalist ends. The manifesto itself, then, whether nationalist or hybridist, functions as a discursive rehearsal of a desired state. Moreover, each version has multiple modalities.

Reframing discourses of hybridity as utopian manifestos requires us also to concede the utopian call (and response) of nationalism; contrary to post-nationalist claims, hybridist manifestos and nationalist manifestos are *twin* forms of imagining community. This claim gains historical credence if we remember that the manifesto's emergence as a genre is inseparable from the emergence of the modern nation-state. Emerging in the seventeenth century in Europe, it flourished during political crises involving definitions of citizenship and political subjecthood (Lyon 10, 16). The enabling condition for the emergence of the manifesto was a republican public sphere that the manifesto has always sought to expand, transform, and exceed (Lyon 31–32). Like the manifesto, the post-nationalist rhetoric of borderlessness and the surfacing of its national unconscious exist in a relationship of *critical participation* to the nation-state.

Theory and manifestos, criticism and art, can be thought of as anticipatory gestures toward a community not yet imagined, a work of art that has yet to be created. If we recall Jean-Marie Gleize's observation that "every manifesto is a general preface to an ensemble of possible works" (13, qtd. in Aching 124), an observation that Carpentier makes literal in his marvelous realist novel *El Reine de Este Mundo* with its manifesto-like Prologue on marvelous realism, and that Glissant arrives at with almost uncanny similarity ["our present works are 'the preface for a literature of the future'" (190)], then we must recognize that discourses of hybridity, theoretical and aesthetic, must not be understood as the final word. Rather, like Bhabha's "gathering" and notes, they are anticipatory gestures toward a community and an aesthetic/politics that cannot be realized within their pages. In Aching's study of Latin American *modernista* manifestos usually understood to be elitist and/or politically detached, the "provisionary character of the subjunctive" points to an "ethereal territory beyond inscription" (125). Again: "Creolization as an idea requires the negation of creolization as a concept" (Glissant 141). Understanding hybridity and nationalist discourses as manifestos demands of us a different reading practice: Instead of reading them as truth-claims whose meaning can be found within the text, it requires us to understand that their political mission, their own textual desires, will achieve fruition only in their transcendence. In this reading, discourses of nationalism and hybridity alike would be no more than small steps toward as yet unscripted alphabets of desire.

Chapter 4

Beyond Resistance: Rehearsing Opposition in Derek Walcott's *Pantomime*

> We never operated in the first, the most significant of the "modes of connection". The "active-literal" passed us by.
>
> —Salman Rushdie, *Midnight's Children*

If the manifesto is a genre of preparation, not only enabling people to imagine some better world, but also mobilizing their energies for producing it, so too is theater specially endowed with political possibilities—not least because of the collective nature of both theatrical performance and theater-going. This chapter combines an analysis of theatrical performance with an alternative to those conceptions of cultural hybridity which privilege resistance and transgression over opposition. (Such conceptions, I demonstrated in chapter one, conflate political opposition with linguistic binary opposition, and in trying to deconstruct the latter, often delegitimize specifically oppositional agency. They stem from post/marxist critiques of class reductionism and a fascination with the political possibilities excluded by it.) I argue here that resistance and transgression are better understood as potential preludes to political opposition than as superior alternatives to it. My discussion will culminate in a close reading of Derek Walcott's play *Pantomime*, which stages an especially rich and reciprocal relationship amongst cultural hybridity, staged performance, and political opposition.

Let me offer some clarification of my terminology here. Although the *Oxford English Dictionary* (OED) defines both resistance and opposition in overlapping relation to collective politics, it is possible to identify in its usage a difference of nuance between the two. For example, resistance entails covert opposition (as in the French resistance to Nazi occupation), whilst opposition is overt resistance (for example, in the form of a political party that is not in governmental office). The very covertness of resistance and its quality of disguise may give it greater semantic and political flexibility and ambiguity; indeed, these very features may be part of the attraction of resistance for contemporary theorists.

But it is in the psychoanalytic connotation of word resistance that a key ambiguity affecting its critical usage becomes most evident. The OED records one meaning of resistance in psychoanalysis as being "opposition, frequently unconscious, to allowing memories or desires which have been repressed as unacceptable or disruptive to emerge into the conscious mind." If resistance is understood thus, then the goal of psychoanalysis is to overcome it. (Here the OED is, of course, less reliable as a guide to psychoanalytic theory than to the ways in which psychoanalysis has entered popular usage.) Two distinctions between opposition and resistance are noteworthy here: first, that resistance in this sense is usually *unconscious* opposition—hidden, that is, not only from others, but from oneself; it is an attempt to block knowledge; and, second, that which it resists is not the status quo, but the disruption of the status quo. On the other hand, to be "in the opposition" typically carries the connotation of being anti-status quoist. The term resistance, then, holds in tension two conflicting tendencies: the sense of a political movement aimed at dismantling the status quo (as in the French Resistance to Nazi occupation) and the sense of it as aiming to maintain the status quo (as in Freudian psychoanalysis).

Furthermore, different forms of agency are involved in resistance and opposition. Resistance may be a natural or essential property; it may be exerted by a medium; it can be a state of being or a property of a material (as in "the resistance of fluids"; "rocks with varying degrees of resistance to erosion," and "the resistance of a disease to a drug"). To use an example from cultural theory, in Bhabha's "DissemiNation," minorities are "themselves the mark of a shifting boundary that alienates the frontiers of the modern nation" (315); in other words, by their very existence they resist the national narrative. But this is quite independent of whether or not they oppose it. Resistance may thus be an ontological category. In contrast, opposition is more typically understood not as a state of being but as an action, as indicated by the OED's synonyms "encounter, combat"; it is neither inherent nor inevitable. As meanings of "opposition," the OED lists inquisition, inquiry, and examination. Resistance, then, may or may not be conscious or intentional, while opposition is necessarily so. The politics of resistance are thus much more ambiguous and ambivalent than those of opposition.

A few words are in order here about the relationship of transgression to resistance. Unlike resistance, transgression cannot be considered to be ontological, a state of being, medium, or property; rather, it is a performative act of boundary-crossing. Unlike resistance, also, transgression is always directed against the status quo, law, or established norm; the OED lists amongst its meanings disobedience, violation of law, duty, or command. However, transgression does share resistance's more anti-systemic qualities and that has indeed been one source of its recent appeal.[1] Like resistance, transgression remains unassimilable to the logic of contradiction, dialectics, and revolutionary transcendence.

An example of recent theoretical practice may be helpful here. In *Domination and the Arts of Resistance: Hidden Transcripts*, James Scott theorizes those forms of resistance that fall short of direct military or paramilitary confrontation by asserting that such low-key forms of resistance are the iceberg of which all-out direct armed combat is only the tip. Scott's goal is to study the relationship and movement between what he calls "hidden transcripts" and "public transcripts." The former refers to the "off-stage," disguised discourse of subordinates, the latter to the "on-stage" discourse of subordinates, that is, the discourse of subordinates in the presence of their superiors. The significance of the distinction is that although open opposition in the public transcript is relatively rare, the public transcript need not be an index of the subordinate classes' conformity or consent; rather, it is an art form of deliberate mis-representation (33). Not the public transcript but the discrepancy between the hidden and the public transcript actually offers a more accurate sense of the attitudes to power that the subordinates hold. The hidden transcript thus offers a record of disguised resistance that continually threatens to erupt into the public transcript; indeed, the boundary between hidden and public transcripts is continually negotiated, contested, and redrawn. Persuasively arguing against the safety-valve theory of practices like Carnival, Scott holds that the hidden transcript is better thought of "as a condition of practical resistance rather than a substitute for it" (191). "Why," he asks, "is it that a ritual modeling of revolt should necessarily diminish the likelihood of actual revolt? Why couldn't it just as easily serve as a *dress rehearsal* or a provocation for actual defiance?" (178, emphasis added).

Though Scott's work suffers from a deeply flawed reading of Gramsci, and the absence of a plausible theory of ideology, his theatrical metaphor of the "dress rehearsal" is a richly suggestive one, which offers potential ways out of some of the weaknesses of several contemporary conceptions of resistance, but raises new problems of its own.[2] To take the example of Carnival, in the logic of Scott's argument, the performance of Carnival would be the dress rehearsal or symbolic coding of some subsequent "material," public, or openly declared political contest that, as a convenient shorthand, I will call an "opening night" (a term which Scott does not use). First and foremost, the notion of rehearsal has the virtue of drawing attention to the collective *work* involved in developing a hidden transcript. With its insistence on laborious collective articulation, the term offers a helpful alternative to the spontaneism and individualism of many contemporary accounts of resistance. For implicit in the metaphor of the dress rehearsal are the ideas of both choreography and revision. Although rehearsals prior to the dress rehearsal might offer still more scope for exploring the process of revision, the theatrical metaphor remains generally useful in enabling us to identify what modifications are necessary in both the hidden and public transcripts.

On the other hand, the metaphor of the "dress rehearsal," if followed through to its logical conclusion, might require us to problematize Scott's central distinction between "on-stage" and "off-stage" discourse. For although Scott claims that the hidden transcript should not be mistaken for "the truth" (5), he nonetheless tends to read it as the sign of subordinates' true knowledge of, and refusal of, their oppression. But if the hidden transcripts are in fact not unproblematically "the truth," it is presumably because the rehearsal is both on-stage and off. The metaphor of the dress rehearsal could be developed to explore the networks of power amongst the producers of the hidden transcripts—for which the hierarchies amongst director, principal actors, and stage hands, as well as the audience, might provide a suggestive vocabulary.

Scott's metaphor of the dress rehearsal also brings into focus the thorny question of teleology implicit in many conceptions of resistance. Although Scott insists that he does "not mean to imply that carnivals or rituals of reversal cause revolt; they most certainly do not" (181), the metaphor of the "dress rehearsal" does assume some subsequent public performance or opening night. In fact, it is the existence of a narratively deferred but *implicitly imminent* opening night that motors the metaphor of the dress rehearsal and gives it its persuasive charge. In other words, the surreptitious reintroduction of teleology (even in accounts that seek to break with a teleological understanding of revolutionary agency) enables many critical narratives to culminate with the triumphant identification of resistance or dress rehearsals, while remaining resoundingly silent about the opening night itself. In such narratives, then, symbolic resistance functions curiously as *both* a substitute for political opposition *and* a refusal of it. Microcosmic resistance becomes a metaphor for a macrocosmic transformation that is deferred from discussion. Moreover, the hidden transcript in question, say, Carnival, functions as both tenor and vehicle of the metaphor of transformation; it is both the agent of transformation and the model for an imagined alternative. Without these metaphorical substitutions and slippages, without the transformation beyond the pages of the essay toward which transformation the critic nonetheless gestures, one would presumably have to scale down the more grandiose claims made for the resistance in question.

Peter Stallybrass and Allon White have insightfully cautioned against similar inflations in our discussions of transgression, faulting Julia Kristeva for confusing transgression with opposition: "[W]hen Julia Kristeva returns to the carnivalesque scene as the potential site of political subversion she confuses the projection of bourgeois desire with the destruction of its class identity. The bourgeoisie, as we have seen throughout this book, is perpetually rediscovering the carnivalesque as a radical source of transcendence" (201). The path from resistance to opposition is thus much more messy, ambiguous, and often abortive than many models recognize.

Thus, instead of focusing primarily on symbolic or disguised resistance and deferring and delegitimizing more explicitly political opposition, we need to investigate precisely the ways and means by which one can be elaborated and articulated into the other. Rather than resting content with the identification or recovery, correct or mistaken, of a hidden transcript of resistance, I propose we shift the emphasis to the process of articulating the revisions in such transcripts, that is, to the changes from one rehearsal to the next.[3] What work is done between the dress/rehearsal and the public performance? What *labors* are necessary to transform, elaborate, or articulate a moment of resistance into a moment of opposition? How do the raw materials and conditions of production of the rehearsal shape the opening night? It is clear that a particular hidden transcript might open up several possibilities for changes in the public transcript, but what possibilities might it close off? Is a given hidden transcript equally likely to translate into reform, riot, revolt, or revolution? Such attention to the distinctions between different forms of resistance in the hidden transcript would also enable us to ask what blockages might lie along the path from hidden to public resistance. In Stuart Hall's impassioned formulation, "[t]he capacity to *constitute* classes and individuals as a popular force—that is the nature of political and cultural struggle: to *make* the divided classes and the separated peoples—divided and separated by culture as much as by other factors—into a popular-democratic cultural force."[4] It is this act of elaboration, articulation, and transformation that I refer to when I speak of a movement from resistance to opposition.

Caribbean Cultural Studies has suffered particularly acutely from the critical emphasis on resistance and transgression, of which Carnival has been the privileged critical site. I do not wish to underestimate the immense cultural, aesthetic, and economic importance of Carnival. What concerns me, however, is the critical *divorce* of Carnival from other aspects of everyday life, for this divorce risks missing the tension between mass performances of transgression and mass desires for acceptance and assimilation, between popular desires for work and popular celebration of respite from its exploitative conditions. To put the problematic in the terms of Peter Wilson's influential study of Caribbean society entitled *Crab Antics* (1973), dominant critical practice focuses on "reputation" to the neglect of "respectability."[5]

Both the scholarly focus on "reputation" in Caribbean Studies and the fascination with resistance and transgression in Cultural Studies more generally express, as I have indicated earlier, a critique of the class reductionism of orthodox marxism and an interest in the political possibilities it neglected, such as the proliferation of the New Social Movements of the 1960s, subcultures, and styles of consumption. Not least, there has been a shift in interest from studying proletarian liberation from capitalism through the organization of labor to studying lumpen-proletarian resistance to capitalism through the refusal to work.[6] Paul Gilroy, for example, has asserted in *The Black Atlantic* that for the descendants of slaves, with their historical memory of forced labor, the centerpiece of hopes for emancipation cannot be labor, but rather must be artistic expression. The point is a significant and suggestive one, and goes a long way in explaining the intense outpouring of creative energies, and concentration of artistic expertise and expressive desires in Carnival. But it does shrug aside the complex contemporary cultures of *work* in the Caribbean and the contestations of dominant ideology that occur within the realm of respectability. And it does not really engage the structuring tension between reputation and respectability which Wilson shows to be so fundamental to Caribbean societies.

In enthroning Carnival as the example par excellence of Caribbean resistance, not only do we risk reinscribing colonial and neo-colonial tourist images of merry and idle natives, and of the Caribbean as the site of play, the binary "Other" of metropolises implicitly constructed as the sites of work, productivity, and instrumental reason, we also minimize the resistant and/or oppositional possibilities of a whole host of other cultural practices. Whether or not Carnival acts as safety-valve for political tensions, then (a point which has been debated at great length), at the risk of being uncharitable, I venture that Carnival *Studies* (and Resistance Studies more generally) might act as a safety-valve, displacing, even delegitimizing, the study of "material" resistance or publicly declared opposition.

Moreover, the present critical emphasis on reputation carries its own problematic gender politics. For to the extent that "respectability" historically and discursively has been associated with the feminine, with mothers and wives promoting religiosity, economy, and the cultivation of domestic virtues, the current critical erasure or downright denigration of respectability (as simply buying into dominant ideology) devalues the feminine. In some senses, then, contemporary cultural theory's celebration of reputation positions women as acquiescing to the status quo and men as resisting it.[7] In response to such readings, several excellent feminist studies have contested the discursive association of respectability with women, pointing out that such discourses take middle-class women as the implicit norm. Such studies may adopt the strategy of demonstrating the participation of working-class women in transgressive "street culture" or Caribbean "yard" culture. Alternatively, they might point to the transgressive practices of women in Carnival, from the famed and sometimes feared jammettes of Carnival in nineteenth-century Trinidad, to the erotic public display in the dance form known as wining, to the chutney-soca debates; or they might explore the transgressive "slackness" of working-class dance-hall culture in Jamaica.[8]

My concern at present, however, is less to demonstrate the participation of women in the "reputation" pole of the Caribbean dualism than to question the *privileging* of that pole by critics and the consequent shrinkage of the field of contestation. Ironically, although the original impulse behind studying everyday forms of resistance was to expand the field of recognized resistance in order to include everyday practices, the current emphasis on carnivalesque transgression again constricts it, for it is a very select everyday that we now study. The information people exchange on the daily bus-ride to work, queues outside ration-shops or rum shops where discontent may surface, the resources of respectability through which a group of village women may mount a campaign against the drunkenness of their husbands, the informally institutionalized networks of daycare, the struggles for clean water and access to medical care, the practice of second jobs after work, the thousand small generosities and gestures of community made by people divided by caste, class, sexuality: these instances of the everyday rarely enter the pages of cultural theory.

If we approach respectability and reputation as mutually constitutive poles, we can also acknowledge the many ways in which the performance of reputation *depends* upon other performances of respectability. Indeed, the rebel's refusal to work for the "shitstem" may be enabled by the "respectable" labor of an unacknowledged person, often a woman—a lover, spouse, mother, sister, grandmother, or neighbor. Earl Lovelace's novel *The Dragon Can't Dance* is exceptional in that it reveals both the utopian edge of the Afro-Caribbean lumpen-proletarian men's practice of "reputation" and the frequent reliance of this practice upon the respectable labor of women characters like Yvonne, Daphne, the nameless old woman who gives Fisheye a yam, and JoAnne. But the novel is more typical in that these "respectable" characters remain marginal to the novel.[9]

I contend that we need to both dethrone Carnival as the privileged site of study in the Caribbean and change the nature of the questions we ask about it. I want to emphasize that in doing so, my goal is to break with both orthodox Marxist models that dismiss resistance as either insignificant or else as a pale shadow of opposition and those post-Marxist models that tend to substitute resistance or transgression for opposition. One proviso is necessary here: it is crucial to remember that Carnival in the *academy* might serve a very different function from that which it serves in Caribbean *societies*. The voluminous debates on Carnival since its earliest inception in the Caribbean have been dominated by the question of whether Carnival serves or threatens the status quo. The binary frame and abstract formulation "radical or conservative?", "threat or safety-valve?", which has dominated Carnival Studies blocks off a whole range of questions about both Carnival's ritual structure and its specific performances.[10] More productive is what Clifford Geertz calls "thick description" of particular historical performances of Carnival.[11] Such work makes clear that Carnival is very far from being the harmonious whole implied by each pole of the "for or against" positions. Different aspects of the same Carnival may enact reversal, compensation, and continuation or intensification of existing relations of power. In fact, the same performance of Carnival may be internally split, inextricably hybridizing the moment of consolidation and the moment of subversion of power. Carnival may well in many situations enable an *ironic* stance, in which radical knowledge is yoked to reformist or conservative action.

Whereas most of the "for or against" arguments about Carnival tend to emphasize either Carnival's ritual structure or its often transgressive content, our understanding of Carnival would benefit from attending to the often tense interplay of a given Carnival's structure, content, artistic context of performance, and historical conjuncture. Such an approach could bring into focus rather than disperse the contradictions of Carnival. Although this chapter will contribute only obliquely to the scholarship on Carnival, let me suggest some questions such an approach might open up: How do the different dates of Santiago de

Cuba's July Carnival and Havana's Lenten Carnival encode different political histories, possibilities, and relationships with the socialist state? How do Jouvay, Mas', Steelband, and other components of Trinidad Carnival embody different impulses? In the New Orleans Mardi Gras, by what logic do the dissenting placards and lifesized crosses of Christian fundamentalists become incorporated into the spectacle? How are they subverted by a spectacular, nonrealist context? What can a consideration of the shift in occasions for the celebration of Canboulay tell us about the emergence, decline, disappearance, and metamorphoses of particular Carnival rituals, and the significance of their articulation and disarticulation with other rituals?[12]

Since the literature on Carnival and literary representations of it is voluminous and offers several examples of the kind of approach I find productive, I will not duplicate that work here. Instead, I will undertake a limited and indirect exploration of the interplay of Carnival's form, content, context, and conjuncture by investigating what possibilities for cultural and political resistance open up when carnivalesque arts or agency are transposed to a *different* site of performance: theater. Derek Walcott's play *Pantomime* (1978) can be considered a study of the forms of political agency the carnivalesque arts can offer in a non-carnivalesque context. Though not "about" Carnival, the play can contribute to our understanding of Carnival. At the levels of both form and content, *Pantomime* stages the transposition of Carnival into theater, illuminating as few texts I know the political opportunities afforded by that transposition.

In the influential study *The Trinidad Carnival: Mandate for a National Theatre* (1972), Errol Hill holds out Carnival as a resource for developing an alternative to Eurocentric conceptions of the theater and/or elite theatrical traditions. To this end, he provides a detailed analysis of the artistic components of Carnival with a view to adopting and adapting them for an indigenous national theater, and sketches the kinds of modifications that might be needed for stage presentation, sound projection, audience reflection, and so on. In invoking Carnival as the basis for national theater, Hill admits that carnival is not *itself* theater. To transcode Hill's argument into James Scott's terms, we might say that Carnival is a kind of *dress rehearsal* for a national theater. Carnival is both transient and seasonal, whereas, according to Hill, stage-theater requires transcendence. Derek Walcott has made a similar argument, identifying a "central stillness in all serious art, the classics," which is at odds with "the essential law of carnival [which is] movement."[13] Although Walcott has been a vitriolic critic of the folklorization to which Carnival has been subject, and has polemically voiced his reservations about Carnival's theatrical potential, his theatrical practice deploys stylized elements of the carnivalesque in ways similar to those which Hill advocates. Like Hill, too, Walcott identifies theater as a privileged forum for the development of a national spirit.[14]

Neither Walcott's nor Hill's position is uncontroversial;[15] moreover, they may well disagree in more respects than they agree, but that is not relevant to my present argument. What is important for my purposes here is that the *aesthetic* argument that Carnival is a resource for developing a national theater, but is not a substitute for theater, is also an implicit argument for the limits of Carnival as *politics*, for both politics and theater require a certain level of transcendence. Their arguments suggest the need to attend to the process and labor (or rehearsals) through which the carnivalesque arts can be molded for specifically oppositional purposes. *Pantomime* illuminates precisely this process.

The character page of the play signals a series of structuring correspondences between its two characters:

> HARRY TREWE, English, mid-forties, owner of the Castaways Guest House, retired actor
> JACKSON PHILLIP, Trinidadian, forty, his factotum, retired calypsonian

Since each element of each character's identity has a corresponding element in the other character, their identities are unmistakably relational. However, the elements are not all related *in the same way*. In nationality and class position (which the play makes clear is raced, Harry being white and Jackson black), they are opposed: master and servant, neocolonizer and neocolonized. But their ages and identities as performing artists overlap. The collision of these relationships of opposition and similarity is mirrored by the relationship of art and life in the play, a relationship *Pantomime* formalizes through its double frame as a play about a play. The relationship of the inner and outer frames (art and life, pretend and real, joke and serious) changes continually, art and life sometimes corresponding to one another, sometimes opposing one another through reversal or inversion, sometimes transgressively crossing the divide, sometimes blurring it. The contestations between Harry and Jackson over their identities take place in both frames. In the outer frame, Harry Trewe is trying to pressure Jackson to act in a light pantomime of *Robinson Crusoe* to provide entertainment for the imminently arriving tourists. In the course of these negotiations, it occurs to Harry to racially reverse the roles of Crusoe and Friday, so that Harry would play Friday and Jackson Crusoe.[16] The pantomime becomes, to use Mary Louise Pratt's term, a contact zone where their relational oppositions and correspondences face off. What becomes clear is that negotiations in one frame impact the other in numerous ways.

Both the plot and the play's setting in the Castaways guesthouse on the island of Tobago clearly place the staging of the pantomime in the context of a tourist economy. That Harry expects Jackson to perform in the pantomime *in addition* to performing all his regular duties enables the play's first caution to Carnival scholarship. For while many studies of Carnival treat it as a release from work, reading it in its historical Caribbean context as a respite in the cycle of plantation labor, *Pantomime* reminds us that in the present economy, and particularly for the large numbers involved in the tourist sector, Carnival can represent not a break from exploitative labor, but an intensification of that labor.

Moreover, whereas most studies tend to focus on the performance of Carnival, one source of *Pantomime*'s value is that it focuses on the rehearsals before a final performance. In many ways, *Pantomime* can be thought of as a refinement of James Scott's metaphor of the hidden transcripts as a "dress rehearsal" for material resistance. For by the time of the dress rehearsal, the performance of the opening night is largely decided or agreed upon, the content, if not the context, of the performance relatively stable. In contrast, *Pantomime* focuses on negotiations over and in prior rehearsals, looking at the kinds of contestations, moments of transgression, and forms of understanding that emerge amongst antagonists and collaborators in the act of rehearsing together. *Pantomime* is thus less interested in the stage, and more interested in *backstage* as a site where successive transformations and revisions occur, where script and performance are contested, and the conditions for the production of the rehearsal themselves are negotiated.[17]

Finally, *Pantomime* offers an unusual and richly nuanced account of the relationship between hybridity and opposition, two terms that occupy a deeply vexed position in Carnival scholarship and in Cultural Studies more generally. The majority of studies of *Pantomime* replicates the majority of studies of Carnival in emphasizing either hybridity or opposition. Thus, for example, literary criticism on *Pantomime* that reads it sympathetically as an anti-(neo)colonial nationalist allegory often focuses on the structuring oppositions in *Pantomime*—colonizer/colonized, white/black, and master/servant—and on its nationalist revision and reversal of the colonial master-narrative *Robinson Crusoe*. This focus on the overarching oppositions, however, neglects the correspondences between Harry and Jackson (both in their forties, both retired performing artists). As a result, essays emphasizing the oppositions are not well equipped to read the functioning of complicity and collaboration, of transgression rather than reversal. Such liberational readings are homologous to celebratory accounts of Carnival scholarship that locate Carnival's radicalism in its structures of reversal and opposition. Moreover, such readings often are tinged with a triumphalism, which I will argue the play eschews.[18] On the other hand, there is the criticism that emphasizes the functioning of mimicry, improvisation, and transgression in the play. These accounts tend to be somewhat inattentive to the ways in which, if certain oppositions are dislodged in the play, they are invariably reintroduced. Focusing on Bakhtinian, Derridean, and Bhabhaesque moments in the play in which word play, deferral of meaning, pun, ambiguity, and so on, take center stage, these critics sometimes neglect the play's attention to the broader system of oppositions in which these local utterances are inscribed.[19] In other words, what recedes from view is the precise nature of the alteration of the systemic relations of power that occurs as a result of these negotiations. Such readings are homologous to Benítez-Rojo's celebratory account of Carnival, which applauds carnivalesque hybridity as the transcendence of conflict, the displacement of opposition.[20] They tend to overlook Foucault's and Stallybrass and White's worthwhile reminders that transgressing oppositions is quite distinct from dismantling them. My own interest lies in how the local acts of resistance in *Pantomime* manipulate a broader system of oppositions. To my knowledge, no study of *Pantomime* focuses on the relationship the play forges between hybridity and opposition. It is this aspect of the play upon which I shall dwell.

If, as I have argued, the character page invites us to understand Harry's and Jackson's identities as relational, and relational not only in terms of mutually constitutive oppositions, but also in terms of vexed similarities, there is one *apparent* similarity that the play rigorously interrogates: "man to man," a phrase that recurs throughout the play, with subtly shifting resonances. It is a phrase we first hear Harry Trewe uttering (134). At best, Harry's use of the phrase suggests a naive individualism, which believes that the two characters can interact as equals unconstrained by history. But such a belief itself signals Harry's power, for certainly Jackson's experience of subordination will not sustain such an illusion. Thus, when Harry threatens suicide, Jackson reminds him: "They go say I push you" (97). Jackson thus recognizes that the interpretations of their individual actions are inescapably pre-scripted by a history much larger than their "man to man" encounter. This is also the import of the oft-quoted "shadow" speech, which locates their individual utterances in a three-hundred-year history of imperialism. From within the relatively protected confines of his role in the pantomime, Jackson can say:

> For three hundred years I served you. Three hundred years I served you breakfast in ... in my white jacket on a white veranda, boss, bwana, effendi, bacra, sahib ... in that sun that never set on your empire I was your shadow, I did what you did, boss, bwana, effendi, bacra, sahib ... that was my pantomime. Every movement you made, your shadow copied. (112)

In lines that recall Hegel's master/slave dialectic, Jackson goes on to specify the means by which this mimicry, this elaborate miming of obedience, begins to threaten the master: "He cannot get rid of it [the shadow], no matter what, and that is the power and black magic of the shadow, boss, bwana, effendi, bacra, sahib, until it is the shadow that start dominating the child, it is the servant that start dominating the master" (113). The two are thus locked into a relationship and a larger historical struggle that neither can escape.

In fact, Harry's own belief in the phrase "man to man" is belied by the historically enabled racial condescension with which he says of the proposed pantomime: "I can bring it all down to your level, with just two characters" (98–99) as well as by his horror when the full implications of the twist "heavy with irony" dawn upon him: "This cannibal, who is a Christian, would have to start unlearning his Christianity. He would have to be taught by this—African ... that everything was wrong, that what he was doing ... I mean, for nearly two thousand years ... was wrong" (126). In the play's pattern of blurring art and life, Harry's claim to artistic superiority is enabled by his unacknowledged and unexamined belief in his racial superiority. The apparent correspondence "man to man," then, Jackson insists, is the mask of a superficially courteous liberal humanism, a mask that enables Harry to evade his own privilege and power, to disguise an opposition as a correspondence or equivalence. "Man to man" is like Harry's perfunctory "no offense" (142), which invariably prefaces a racially offensive statement. By such means, Harry wallows in a feel-good racial generosity, as for example when he offers to let Jackson use his bathroom rather than the servants' one. But Jackson shipwrecks Harry's words on the barely submerged jagged rocks of racial power, acidly accusing Harry of making the offer only to get more work out of him by placing a time-limit on his piss-break, something that even the segregated bathrooms of the United States did not do.

Thus, Jackson's response to "man to man" is to insist on making the power relation between them glaringly visible. While Harry poses the pantomime as a matter of camaraderie and mutual artistic interest,

Jackson makes clear that if he participates it will be because his master ordered him to. For Jackson, it is a job—and one in which he has no interest, to boot: "Mr. Trewe, I keep begging you to stop trying to make an entertainer out of me. I finish with show business.... If you ain't want me to resign, best drop the topic" (102). When Harry wants to regale Jackson with a self-aggrandizing story and hopefully asks if Jackson wants to hear it, Jackson pointedly says: "My shift is seven-thirty to one" (107). In other words: as an employer, Harry can dispose of Jackson's on-duty time as he likes, but Jackson would be listening neither out of interest nor out of an artist's admiration for Harry's ability to tell a good story, but because he is a subordinate following orders. Similarly, when Harry says "I'd say, Jackson, that we've come closer to a mutual respect, and that things need not get that hostile. Sit, and let me explain what I had in mind," Jackson tartly observes "I take it that's an order?" (107–108). Jackson thus reveals "man to man" as an alibi for one who is squeamish about *acknowledging* his own power, but not about exercising it. Boss, bwana, effendi, bacra, sahib: these titles slap Harry in the face with his own power.

Jackson's strategy, then, is to call Harry's bluff by following through on the full implications of "man to man" in the little details: he calls Harry by his first name and notes Harry's jaw twitch (138); he paints in parodically graphic detail a verbal image of himself urinating in Harry's bathroom to see the latter revoke his offer of letting Jackson use his bathroom; he goads Harry into slips that reveal his racial prejudice. All these maneuvers demonstrate that "man to man" is misleading because Harry can stop the play whenever he likes, pull rank, and revert to being master instead of servant or equal.

Thus, although Harry uses the phrase to defuse conflict—"let's have a drink, man to man, and try to work out what happened this morning, all right?"(134)—the truth of the phrase lies in the way that large historical conflicts are worked out in the bodies of two men. Indeed, the play's reference to the genre of the Western (131), as well as its humorous references to Crusoe's killing of a goat "*mano a mano*, man to man, man to goat" (148) reinforce the reading of "man to man" in combative terms. "Man to man," then, names a form of masculine combat, a battle of wits between two unequal combatants, each of whom will try to use his strengths and find the other's weaknesses.[21]

Moreover, as I hope my language in the preceding lines suggests, the individualist rhetoric of "man to man," with its recourse to the generic "he," relies upon another set of historical inequalities: that of gender. Another way in which *Pantomime* renders the opposition "man to man" ironic is through its gender subplot "man to woman," a subplot whose critical neglect may reflect feminism's subordination in a nationalist canon of criticism which continues to subordinate gender to race. The gender subplot, I contend, is absolutely crucial to the play's rewriting of *Robinson Crusoe.* It rewrites Crusoe not as a heroic, nor even an ambitiously opportunistic, risk taker, but as a henpecked husband whose mediocrity as an actor ensured his subordination to his wife both in their marriage and on the stage. In fact, Ellen, the off-stage ex-wife of Harry, strangely "corresponds" to Sycorax, the crucial off-stage native woman of another colonial master-narrative; each woman sets key events in motion, haunting the scene from different sides of the colonial divide without ever appearing on-stage.

In the dramatically tense scene in Act II, where Jackson playacts Ellen, holding her photograph in front of his face in a kind of pantomime mask and replaying scenes from her marriage, Harry characteristically confuses role-play with reality. In what becomes a kind of psychological regression-cum-flashback that borders on nervous breakdown, Harry bursts out:

> All right. I'll tell you what I'm going to do next, Ellen: you're such a big star, you're such a luminary, I'm going to leave you to shine by yourself. I'm giving up this bloody rat-race and I'm going to take up Mike's offer, I'm leaving "the theatuh," which destroyed my confidence, screwed up my marriage, and made you a star. I'm going somewhere where I can get pissed every day and watch the sun set, like Robinson bloody Crusoe. That's what I'm going to bloody do. You always said it's the only part I could play. (161–162)

He also reveals that he cast away to Tobago after the traumatic death of his son, in an attempt to reconstruct his life and gain some control over it. In other words, he seeks in the colonies a place for emotional convalescence after the disastrous dissolution of his family. Thus, in Walcott's play (neo)colonialism, far from arising out of a natural racial or cultural superiority, is rewritten as a compensatory fantasy of superiority.

That fantasy is belied by Jackson's superior linguistic and artistic abilities. For it is through Jackson's manipulation of the subplot with Ellen that Harry is forced into admitting his own mediocrity as an actor. This cathartic admission finally undoes his initial pretence of being the superior actor who would "bring it all down" to Jackson's level. Harry confesses to the photograph of Ellen: "That's the real reason I wanted to do the panto. To do it better than you ever did. You played Crusoe in the panto, Ellen. I was Friday. Black bloody greasepaint that made you howl. You wiped the stage with me... Ellen... well. Why not? I was no bloody good" (164).

In England, Harry's subordination as husband and subordination as actor reinforce one another. The subordination is doubly humiliating because it reverses both gender and artistic norms: the gender norm of the dominance of the husband, the artistic norm that in a pantomime, the man plays even the woman's roles.[22] The crowning humiliation is perhaps that this should occur even in *Robinson Crusoe*, which, as Ellen crushingly told him, was the only part he could play. In Tobago, that humiliation is compounded when Harry is forced to admit to himself that Jackson is, in some respects, another Ellen, another superior actor. This admission is the precondition for the brief but consequential artistic collaboration—man to man? artist to artist?—that they do enjoy.

The "substitution" of Jackson for Ellen, of course, also satirically echoes the homoerotic undertones of *Robinson Crusoe*. The play comments on these early on: When Jackson objects to Harry's undressing to try out the role of Friday, Harry responds: "What're you afraid of? Think I'm bent? That's such a corny interpretation of the Crusoe–Friday relationship, boy. My son's been dead three years, Jackson, and I'vn't had much interest in women since, but I haven't gone queer, either. And to be a flasher, you need an audience" (103). I will pass over the racial implications of Harry's failure to register Jackson as an audience, and go on to Jackson's response: "[i]f anybody should happen to pass, my name is immediately mud" (103)..."Don't bother getting into the part, get into the pants. Please" (104). The play exploits pantomime's conventions of cross-dressing to further the play's ironic comment on this twist on "man to man." And in the light of the importance that *Pantomime* accords word-play, *double entendre*, rhyme, and deliberate mispronunciation as ways of infiltrating dominant texts (we recall the parrot's calling "Heinegger," which rhymes with "Heidegger" and, which Jackson interprets as "Hi, nigger," two instances of a framing racial signification), when Harry mockingly mispronounces "comedy" as "codemy," one hears the rhyme, "sodomy."

What is interesting about these various evocations of homosexuality—again, scarcely commented upon in most of the criticism[23]—is that both Jackson and Harry are determined not to let art and life blur in regard to sexuality. If Jackson is insistent that no passerby should mistake him for gay, Harry invents a story of how, when he played the Vamp in a Christmas Panto called "Aladdin and His Wonderful Vamp" for the RAF, and a sergeant made advances upon him, he avenged his heterosexual honor by beating the sergeant up (107). The very same Jackson who shrewdly blurs the lines dividing art and life to negotiate his advantage, will risk no such blurring in regard to his sexuality. (Indeed, one displaced racial/class insult occurs when Jackson threatens to resign and get Harry "someone more to your sexual taste" [105].) Jackson's insistence, then, is particularly striking, since the deliberate blurring of art and life, or transposing events from one context to the other, is one of his central strategies for resisting Harry. Both characters' peculiar desire for clarity on this subject, then, emerges from and reinforces a heterosexist accord between these two men who otherwise are antagonists in so many regards. Heteronormativity and homophobia form an unnamed common ground, a site of correspondence between Jackson and Harry, that is not readily apparent from the character page.[24]

That the play's commentary on homosexuality takes place largely in terms of art and genre (cross-dressing as a convention of pantomime, the man playing the woman's roles, Harry's supposed pantomime of "Aladdin and his Wonderful Vamp," a queer interpretation of *Robinson Crusoe*) brings me to the importance of artistic performance in the negotiations between the two men. If "man to man" is a ruse that is challenged, satirized, and returned to in many ways, "artist to artist" (110) performs a no less complex function. When Harry gets a tape-recorder to record Jackson's improvised calypso, Jackson responds: "You start to exploit me already?" (119), again inscribing Harry's appropriative act in a longer tradition of exploitation of black entertainers. The proposed artistic collaboration, then, opens up yet another site of exploitative labor.

But "artist to artist" also names a genuinely shared artistic ground, which Jackson forces Harry to recognize and revalue. While Harry at times appears to set up their artistic genres as being in opposition, making a distinction between classical and Creole acting in response to Jackson's criticism of Harry's script (146), the play's complex and sustained commentary on artistic genre complicates any such distinctions. In the course of the play, we are given meditations upon classical and Creole acting, pantomime, calypso, Carnival, the Western, music hall, cabaret, improvisation, entertainment, and a capitalized Art. The play underscores and puts to work the formal similarities between the respective performance-genres of Harry and Jackson. Both British pantomime and the Carnival arts/events are popular art forms; both feature traditions of masking, humor that is often bawdy, cross-dressing, hybrid variety shows, frequent combination of music, song, and dance, and ample opportunity for improvisation. Thus Harry's music hall song and Jackson's calypso version mirror each other formally (93–94, 117, 132, 170). Harry's admission of experience (albeit as a failure) with both classical and Creole acting (136), moreover, evokes the rich tradition of creolized forms of British pantomime in the Caribbean.[25] Jackson's corresponding ability to manipulate language through double entendre, innuendo, picong,[26] humor, and skilled improvisation, derive from his training and experience as a calypsonian and a veteran of Carnival.

"Artist to artist" they can speak certain truths from the protection of the mask/role, that they dare not otherwise utter. Walcott has approvingly quoted Yeats as saying: "Give a man a mask, and he will talk the truth."[27] Thus, for example, when Harry solicits Jackson's opinion of his idea for the pantomime, Jackson succinctly provides his "honest, professional opinion": " I think is shit" (110–111)—an assessment that both men know extends beyond the particulars of Harry's plan for the pantomime. Emerging only after Harry confronts Jackson's evaluation, Harry's honest admissions about his family, artistic vulnerability and artistic in/abilities are, in fact, accomplished through the role-play techniques of pantomime and Carnival; these admissions and the accompanying recognition of what the two men share as artists enable one of the few truly collaborative (and playfully rather than combatively competitive) moments in the play—an interlude of improvised punning (168–169).

Jackson's assessment of Harry's art effects a radical revaluation of artistic forms and genres within the play. After parodically reading Harry's script, with its rhetoric of pathos, psychological interiority expressed through soliloquy, epic description of the landscape, somewhat cloying sentimentality, and self-aggrandizing comparisons of Crusoe to Job and Adam, Jackson declares: "Touching. Very sad. But something missing... Goats. You leave out the goats... [this] man ain't facing reality. *There are goats* all around him" (145–146). Harry's omission of the goats becomes an occasion for what I consider to be a meditation on the differences between classical and Creole poetics and politics. Dissenting from Harry's interpretation of Crusoe, Jackson insists:

> He not sitting on his shipwrecked arse bawling out... 'O silent sea, O wondrous sunset,' and all that shit. No. He shipwrecked. He desperate, he hungry. He look up and he see this fucking goat with its fucking beard watching him and smiling, this goat with its forked fucking beard and square yellow eye, just like the fucking devil standing up there...
> (*Pantomimes the goat and Crusoe in turn*)
> smiling at him, and putting out its tongue and letting go one fucking *bleeeeeh!* And Robbie ent thinking 'bout his wife and son and O silent sea and O wondrous sunset; no, Robbie is the First True Creole, so he watching the goat with his eyes narrow, narrow, and he say *blehhh*, eh? You mother-fucker, I go show you *blehhh* in your goat-ass, and vam, vam, next thing is Robbie and the goat, *mano a mano*, man to man, man

> to goat, goat to man, wrestling on the sand, and next thing we know we hearing one last faint, feeble *bleeeeeeehhhhhhhhhhhh*, and Robbie is next seen walking up the beach with a goatskin hat and a goatskin umbrella, feeling like a million dollars because he have faith! (148)

To be sure, no trace of divine beauty or linguistic transport casts its glow over this version! Jackson creolizes both the vocabulary and the grammar, depoeticizes the language, and borrows freely from Spanish and slang alike.[28] Moreover, the combat that Harry is squeamish about naming in art as well as life, Jackson converts into the very motor that propels the narrative forward—very much in keeping with the artistic traditions of calypso and Carnival.

This peculiar speech about the goats has a narrative precedent. We recall that the first time a goat is mentioned in *Pantomime* it is in relation to the practicalities of stage direction: Jackson points out that Crusoe needs to kill the goat immediately after being shipwrecked, so that he can clothe himself and not have to parade naked before an audience. In both the earlier and the later instance, the goats appear as an injunction for realistic and pragmatic engagement with the prosaic, mundane, and ordinary. These, in turn, Jackson shows, offer our best resources for survival. The appropriately absurd image of the goat, with its simultaneous refusal of heroism and pathos, thus becomes emblematic of Creoleness and Creole acting alike. It directs us, moreover to the two features Jackson identifies with Creoleness: practicality and faith (146–147).[29] It is therefore no coincidence that Harry's and Jackson's interlude of collaborative artistry involved punning on the word "goat" (168–169).

It is also important to remember that when Jackson describes Crusoe as "the First True Creole" and recodes Harry's script in terms of Creole acting, he does so not as an anticolonial exercise in deflating Crusoe, but rather as an expression of admiration. Bridget Jones has observed that part of the complexity of the play lies in its refusal to generate a simple artistic opposition between Harry as classical actor and Jackson as Creole. With this I concur. The play shows Harry's experience with pantomime, whose analogs to Creole acting I have demonstrated. What Jones does not emphasize, however, is that in at least two significant ways the play nonetheless positions Harry and Jackson differently with regard to Creole acting: first, Harry is simply not as *good* a Creole actor as Jackson—a belief borne out by Jackson's superior linguistic control, his management of improvised dialogue, and his deliberate manipulation of the lines separating art and life. Second, although Harry participates in Creole acting, he values it differently from the way Jackson does. Harry indeed has experience with the popular–cultural artistic forms of pantomime and music hall, but he is ambivalent toward them, not always assigning them the same value he does Shakespeare and the classics. His sense of racial and civilizational superiority, moreover, does not stem from any high valuation of British pantomime, but rather from an association of British with high or classical culture. There is thus a sense in which Harry considers the arts he practices a poor substitute for something grander after which he hankers. Thus, while it is Harry who advocates entertainment over "committing Art," a pantomime over a play, he does so not necessarily out of recognition of the artistic merits of these genres, but rather out of a wish to indulge a tourist-audience, whose desire to avoid "serious politics" he shares. His choice of the genre of pantomime may even arise from skepticism about his and Jackson's artistic abilities ("I can bring it all down to your level," "I was no bloody good"). Although Harry does "boast" to Jackson of having dined with the greats, coming as he did from a family of actors, this claim, too, is undercut if one reads it in the light of Harry's other ego-preserving artistic fibs, which are laid bare when he admits to being a second-rate actor. Moreover, unlike the conscious comedy of "Aladdin and his Wonderful Vamp," the pomposity and self-aggrandizement of Harry's language in *Crusoe* betray no hint of intentional irony. In the section of Harry's script of *Robinson Crusoe* which Jackson mocks, then, whatever aesthetic distance we might achieve from the epic or classical emerges by reading it against the grain of Harry's intention. Jackson's identification of Crusoe as the "First True Creole," in fact, draws attention to Harry's lack of understanding of the ways in which Harry is himself deeply Creole. It is a misguided system of value that makes Harry hanker after England and despise the colonies, yet, Crusoe-like, choose to stay, even when he has the opportunity to "return" to England. Jackson is proudly Creole; Harry is unconsciously or apologetically so.

One reason for Harry's disdain may be found in his disparaging comment about mimicry: "You people create nothing. You imitate everything" (156).[30] This view of mimicry is very likely responsible for Harry's devaluation of Creole art and pantomime alike. *Pantomime*'s revindication of mimicry has been the subject of much insightful critical analysis. (The shadow speech and the parrot's role in the plot have frequently been read in this light.) What has received less comment is the degree of individual agency involved in mimicry. It seems to me that at the heart of *Pantomime*'s revaluation of Creole art and politics is an affirmation not just of mimicry, but of a particular kind of mimicry: improvisation. It is this form of mimicry which the play casts as a defining feature of Creole art and politics. Crusoe's technique for survival—improvisation—must also be Jackson's and Harry's. The faith of which Jackson speaks in the goat speech is faith in his own ability to survive, to improvise, and to survive by improvising. When Harry falls apart, Jackson reminds him that Crusoe always got up and faced the next day. Moreover, it is significant that both Harry and Jackson gain access to improvisations through their training as performance artists. Improvisation thus emerges as both an aesthetic credo and a political survival strategy.

From Jackson's very first appearance, significantly, barefoot and in an open white waiter's jacket and black trousers, to his subsequent ingenious improvisations of stage sets, we see *Pantomime* cast improvisation and cultural hybridity as acts of creativity rather than inability. (Jackson's first speech throws out any association of Creole with linguistic inability. He can speak "perfect" English, but, more to the point, he can create all kinds of combinations and recombinations of English and Creole across the Creole continuum.) As a result, Jackson's role as a factotum must be reimagined, not as lack ("jack of all trades, master of none"), but as a combination of two essential features of improvisation: versatility and virtuosity.[31] In these traits, Jackson may be more Crusoe than Crusoe; he is certainly more Crusoe than Harry is. "Man to man" resurfaces, then, in that, Crusoe-like, both characters are thrown back upon their own resources, and survive by the virtuosity of their improvised performances which is all they have to hurl at History.

In fact, in *Pantomime*, improvisation holds the key to understanding the relationship in both art and life between the individual and the historical. For the artistic virtuosity of their individual performances ("man to man" and "artist to artist") is consistently placed within the frame of a political macro-history which includes class, race, nation, gender, and sexuality. Similarly, the discussion of genre (classical, Creole, music hall, pantomime, cabaret, Carnival, improvisation) provides the artistic macro-history which their individual performances must negotiate.

The formal play between the individual and the structural has been a much-noted feature of Afro-Caribbean and African-American music.[32] Such work addresses improvisation and call-and-response as techniques that allow for both individual and communal voices. But such accounts are typically not concerned with analyzing the full violence of History, reaching as they sometimes do for celebratory and conciliatory accounts of community. The applicability of these accounts to *Pantomime* is limited, since in the play Jackson and Harry clearly dissent from one another, but do not necessarily even belong to the same social community. What I want to distill from the aforementioned accounts is their acknowledgment of improvisation as deliberate, intentional, purposeful play with boundaries.

For whereas both mimicry and improvisation imply a relationship of constraint to pre-texts and inherited forms, what is specific and essential to improvisation is the idea of intent. Thus, for example, while Homi Bhabha's suggestive account of the menace and creativity of mimicry is very much in the spirit of *Pantomime*'s "shadow" speech, in Bhabha's work, the unpredictable acts of agency that elude will and conscious intent tend to stand in for all forms of mimicry.[33] As Tejumola Olaniyan has pointed out:

> [T]here is one profound difference between Walcott and Bhabha on mimicry. The latter is far more equivocal. Bhabha's mimics are not engaged in acts of conscious resistance—they are not agents of deliberate subversion or liberation, and both the condition of their production and their mimicry are spectrally overdetermined by the contradictions of the colonial context. The menace these mimics carry, because they do so unconsciously, can only result in endless compromises—there is no possibility of a new order on the horizon. It is pure process without an agent. On the other hand, Walcott's mimics are conscious agents with a dire if incoherent sense of need, Adams impelled to conscious invention by the vulgar needs of survival. (205)

In *Pantomime*, the mimicry of the parrot, the shadow, Harry, and Jackson, all entail different degrees and kinds of agency. *Pantomime* is thus Bakhtinian in the distinctions it draws between an intentional, conflictual hybridity and an unconscious, organic hybridity; in Robert Young's words, the former is dialogically contestatory, "the authorial unmasking of another's speech, through a language that is 'double-accented' and 'double-styled,' the latter an imperceptible process of amalgamation" (*Colonial Desire* 20–22). The play's emphasis on improvisation as a specific form of mimicry permits us to consider the interplay of conscious agency and structured constraint. In Judith Butler's terms, we might say that part of Jackson's agency (and the play's work) lies in resignifying mimicry as improvisation.[34]

Within the play, the question of intentional mimicry or improvisation is framed as a matter of artistic control. That Harry's familial traumas intrude into his script is deemed a failure of artistic control that compromises his script. Harry's confusion between self and role often weakens his position both artistically and politically. From the very beginning of the play, Harry is apt to slip, as for example, when he absently addresses Jackson as Friday; or, most painfully, in the scene when Jackson role-plays Harry's ex-wife Ellen, and Harry responds as though Jackson were truly Ellen. Improvisation, then, admits unpredictabilities as well as creative manipulation of those unpredictabilities as part of the process of performance; it thus offers a form of agency that is properly performative and context-sensitive. But while Jackson by no means predicts all the possible outcomes of the rehearsal, he is better able to hold apart role and reality; when he transgresses their boundaries, it is usually by design. Unlike Harry, then, Jackson rarely "forgets" himself; more often, he masks himself.[35]

What is often overlooked in readings of the play is that improvisation can also be oppositional. Jackson's experience of improvisation derives specifically from calypso, where improvisation finds its most concentrated form in the type of performance known as Extempore. In its current form, Extempore involves two well-matched calypsonians engaging in competitive improvisation within narrative parameters laid out by an M.C. (The audience and/or M.C. may judge who the winner is.) The event thus combines reciprocal artistic admiration and commitment with artistic *battle*, recognizing in the other artist a worthy opponent, as it were.[36] Read properly, then, improvisation in *Pantomime* permits both an irreverent and subversive hybridization of pre-texts or inter-texts as well as a structuring competitive logic that sharpens oppositions. Thus does improvisation constitute a formal means by which to think hybridity and opposition together. In summary, improvisation draws together several features of Creole opposition as the play understands the term: it is fully performative; it is pragmatic and strategic; it is intentional; and it typically practices a hybridizing inter-textuality.

All these features of improvisation are brought into focus by the play's conclusion. Jackson's terse concluding line encodes a stunningly intricate lesson in Creole opposition. Feeling the tug of epic or heroic agency, or, alternatively, staging a threat (much would depend on the interpretive choice of the actor and director), Jackson initially declares a total refusal of the exploitative relationship with Harry: "I going back to the gift that's my God-given calling. I benignly resign, you fire me. With inspiration. Caiso is my true life." But then he appears to change his mind, in the process reaping the benefits of the element of surprise:

> "Wait! Wait! Hold it!"
> (*Silence: walks over to Harry*)
> "Starting from Friday, Robinson, we could talk 'bout a raise?" (170)

At the most obvious level, of course, if the (outer) play began with Harry Trewe/Crusoe, this moment of Creole opposition begins with Jackson Phillip/Friday. The play in some senses declares its solidarities by giving Jackson the last word.

But far more than that is played out in those last lines. Jackson's punning reference to Friday acknowledges his historical inability to achieve a complete break out of the relationship defined by domination and subordination. What it accomplishes is not the "inspirational" result or epic victory, but a distinct, if small and subtle, shift in that relationship. One of the things that makes this opposition Creole rather than epic, then, is its scale. The strategic wisdom of Jackson's move may well lie in its combination of courage and modesty.[37] Thus, the last line of the play begins with the promise of an ultimatum ("Starting from Friday, Robinson. . . ."), only to grammatically backtrack into a question ("we could talk 'bout a raise?"). In the light of the play's mobilization of ambiguity as a weapon of resistance, it may well be that the tone of the delivery is at odds with the grammatical structure of the sentence. In other words, tonally, the second half of the sentence might continue to function as a threat or ultimatum.

The play's complex commentary on the politics of address further complicates the last line. Harry's forms of address through the play range from the stiff formality of Mr. Phillip (135, 153) to the informal but probably sarcastic "mate" and "friend" to the racially laden "boy," "ape," and "Big Chief" (153, 149, 114), as well as more straightforward expletives (147, 155). Jackson hurls back expletives equal in force (147), invents rhymes such as "Crusoe-Trusoe, Robinson Trewe-so!" (133), which implicate Harry in domination, and refers to Harry at various times as "Mr Harry," "sir," "pardner," "man" (152, 170, 104). Most spectacularly, in a single speech, in the space of a few lines, he goes from "Mr Trewe" to "Trewe" to "Harry, boy" (154), that last word suggesting a reversal of Harry's racial insult. In the light of the subtle manipulation of forms of address, it becomes significant that in the concluding line Jackson addresses Harry in his (neo)colonial role/history not as "Crusoe," but as "Robinson." While the phrasing of the sentence reminds us that Jackson remains locked into the position of Friday (for the conclusion does not offer even the perverse satisfaction of an earlier moment in the play where Jackson demands that he be named Thursday), there is a hint of insolence and intimacy in addressing the scripted "master" by his first name. That shift in address simultaneously performs and metonymically registers the precarious gains Jackson has made in the balance of power.

Moreover, while the *Crusoe* narrative retains its grip, one could argue that that grip is loosened by the introduction of another inter-text, Molière's *Don Juan*, which ends with Sganarelle lamenting "My wages, what about my wages? . . . I'm the only one who's unhappy. My wages. My wages. My wages" (87).[38] The allusion underscores the value Creole opposition places on an improvisational creativity understood in terms of inter-textual recombination, infiltration, and hybridization rather than originality, *per se*.

Whichever way we read the sentence, however, what is clear is that it subverts any recourse to epic agency or classical artistry. Even Harry early on in the play observes with wry desperation, after (playing at?) a suicide attempt, that the Third World frustrates all attempts at heroism: "You can't even leave a note because the pencils break, you can't cut your wrist with the local blades . . . " (97). If the classical Crusoe as Harry scripts him was excessively self-indulgent in his poetic eulogy to self, son, and sunset, where the Creole Crusoe, as Jackson points out, would pragmatically and prosaically focus on the goat as his hope for immediate survival, so in the concluding lines Jackson momentarily moves toward the epic or classical mode of resignation with honor only to give it up in favor of a Creole strategic pragmatism, which would offer perhaps morally smaller but materially more certain gains. For Jackson no less than for Crusoe, this is a move toward the pragmatics of staying alive, staying employed. The same imperative prompts Jackson not to demand a raise, but to explicitly demand a conversation about it.

Nonetheless, the move from implicit to explicit constitutes an escalation. Jackson's first reference to overtime occurs early in the play, but significantly, it is not in relation to himself. Rather, he surmises that the carpenter has not showed up in part because of "the peanuts you does pay him for overtime" (96). It is not long, however, before Jackson shrewdly transposes the topic of overtime to his own situation. He refuses Harry's invitation/order to act in the pantomime, saying "Breakfast, sir. Or else is overtime" (98). At several points in the play, he threatens to resign (102) or get someone more to Harry's sexual taste (105), draws attention to the duration of his work-shift (107), and says in response to Harry's proposal that Harry "ain't start to talk money yet" (110), a comment that prompts Harry to offer Jackson "half the gate" which he later ungraciously ups to $20 a day without dialogue (116). Jackson taunts Harry, calling his attempt at tape-recording Jackson's calypso "exploitation" (119); he somewhat huffily reminds Harry that Jackson would be doing him a favor by acting in the pantomime (121), again suggesting a framework of debt, although this time not a monetary one. When Jackson's *Pantomime* rapidly spins out of Harry's control, Harry orders him to stop or be fired, an order that Jackson simply flouts (123–124; see also 153). Later, Jackson introduces the possibility that his refusal to accept Harry's invitation to use his bathroom could be read as a go-slow agitation (151, 154). When Jackson tries to reenter the stage set he had invented (an overturned table to represent both boat and shelter) and Harry forbids him to, saying it's his property, a tense discussion is initiated about physical versus intellectual property (156–157). Each of these steps in their linguistic war dance could be analyzed in detail, but my point here is to note the pattern and momentum they cumulatively create. Read separately, each comment might be understood variously as the diffuse resistance of complaint and grumble, idle threat, bluff, or posturing (which, of course the play reveals to be far from innocuous). But arranged the way they are and read collectively, they are transformed from diffuse or local resistance into a rehearsal or preparation for more pointed negotiation. In other words, a dissatisfaction that starts out as backdrop or setting develops into a primary plot-event. What makes me read the trajectory of utterances as effecting a move from resistance to opposition is the escalation of scale, the intensification of argument, the increasingly pointed statements of dissatisfaction, and the move from expression of sentiment or opinion to an undisguised political demand that seeks the redistribution of material wealth.[39]

The slow escalation I have described is enabled by a series of substitutions between art and life. Jackson's and Harry's antagonisms begin with the *symbolic* violence of verbal insult and violent metaphor (playing man to man while intending to take the feller by the crotch, rip out he stones, dig out he eye, and leave him for corbeaux to pick (139); a smile that is a dagger (140)). They go on to narratives about *material* violence, for instance, the nursery rhyme "Fee fi fo fum, I smell the blood of an Englishman" (155), and still more pointedly, Jackson's story about putting an ice-pick through the hand of an Indian fellow who wanted to "play nigger" (106) and Harry's story of taking a wrench to the sergeant who came onto him (107). In both these latter cases, their having committed physical violence against someone else nonetheless threatens the present antagonist; in other words, the target of physical violence in the narrative is displaced. Jackson makes Harry play a seabird and a goat, which Jackson-as-Crusoe plans to kill (107); here the (appearance of) physical violence would be inflicted upon Harry's body, but while he is in character, that is, while he is Harry-as-animal. Harry says to Jackson in a line ambiguously poised at the intersection of inner and outer frame: "I'll tell you one thing, friend. If you want me to learn your language, you'd better have a gun" (116). The narratives about physical violence thus gradually close in, metamorphosing into instances of actual physical violence visited on substitute targets, such as Jackson's strangling of the "prejudiced" parrot, Harry's driving an ice-pick through the table, and Harry's attempt to shatter the photograph of his wife with an ice-pick, which develops into a scene where he chases with the ice-pick *Jackson*, who is carrying the photograph. Similarly, the beginning of Act II sees Harry bolt from his chair upon finding Jackson hovering nearby with a hammer he had been using to fix the deck. Clearly, each character senses the escalation of violence from the symbolic to the literal, the role to the real, and fears that he is about to become its target. Jackson's apparently nonconfrontational concluding demand, pitched somewhere between conversation and low-level challenge, takes on a sharper edge when read with the memory of these prior stagings of violence. Thus the logic of development of the substitutions, like the previous references to resignation, firing, and pay-raises, need to be interpreted in their cumulative interaction.

Like many approaches to Carnival, then, *Pantomime* explores the material effects of symbolic resistance, brilliantly elaborating how the restratification of elements in the inner frame can subtly but surely restratify elements in the outer frame. Approached thus, it is possible to read the entire play retrospectively as the performative pre-history of the concluding question. This is, however, a very different claim from one that would argue the *predestination* of the concluding question. Part of the lesson of *Pantomime*'s conception of Creole opposition is precisely that it cannot be located except in particular performances. The concluding sentence's cautious and provisional push toward the redistribution of wealth is launched by symbolic resistances and made possible through several unpredictable and improvised performances of transgression (disguise, mimicry, and the blurring of boundaries between art and life). Neither Harry nor Jackson can foresee the full consequences of their rehearsals or performances. In his expectation that they will be able to "keep it light," Harry does not anticipate the implications of playacting racial reversal; when he does, he is unable to halt the events that performance has set in motion. Neither character completely controls the ways in which history bears down on their performances and mis/interpretations. (We recall, for example, "They go say I killed you.") Too, each character's performance is a response to the other's: none of the possibilities Jackson or Harry realizes preexists the performance, and unlike in chess, the field of possibilities is not finite and therefore cannot be exhaustively mapped in advance. It is the process of performance, the rehearsal, that opens up the enunciative positions Jackson and Harry are able to occupy. And it is only through the performance that their local acts of resistance are recast as the pre-history of opposition.

Equally crucial is the way the conclusion constructs the performance as ongoing. Just as when Harry first mentions in the play the idea of the Crusoe pantomime, Jackson says "Mr Trewe, you come back with that same rake *again*?" (96, emphasis added), drawing attention to the "before" of the play, so the conclusion of the play with an unanswered question draws attention to the "after" of the play. Thus, while the conclusion withholds from Harry the satisfaction of having the last word, it also denies Jackson the certainty of a declarative sentence, and both Jackson and the audience are denied the relief of resolution. Critics have expressed dissatisfaction with the conclusion of the play on precisely these grounds. Christopher Gunness, for instance, wrote: "Unfortunately... this tension is never dissolved; the ending, with which Walcott is not satisfied, does not show a clear enough picture of what has come out of this conflict. The audience is left wondering, 'where exactly has the resolution of this conflict taken us?'" (291).

I contend that *Pantomime* delivers the audience not into the security of resolution (whether in Jackson's or Harry's favor), but rather into the full experience of the political *tautness* of the moment. The conclusion of Act I (129) formally parallels this structure. There, Jackson again has the last word, saying "Don't touch anything... Mr Trewe. Please... Now that... is MY order..." The use of ellipses, the battle of wills suggested by the characters' watching each other till the lights fade, the shift of attention from Jackson to the question of whether Harry will obey or disobey Jackson's order, all make for open conclusions, which point to an ongoing plot. The result is a shift of emphasis from result to process, here understood as Jackson's Creole performative strategy. This shift offers a searching account of the performative tools that Jackson is able to craft or improvise on his desert/ed neocolonial island and the effort that goes into keeping that performative moment open. I therefore think the play might be considered a study in and of Creole oppositional method.

What the tense openness of Creole opposition makes clear is that, whoever wins this local skirmish and whatever Harry's answer, the larger battle will continue. The balance of power might shift, but only to be recontested. In the logic of the play, then, even if Harry Trewe were to "grant" Jackson the raise, it could provide only the most fleeting respite, one which would constitute less a resolution than an occasion for regrouping. Creole opposition, then, is an ongoing negotiation rather than a definitive resolution. Deglamorized, opposition emerges as slow, repetitive, persistent work, a steady chipping away at neocolonial roles, rather than a once-and-for-all definitive overturning of them. "Freedom" becomes in this situation not so much an abstract noun as a corporeal performance, not a state, but an event that must continually repeat, reinvent, and renew itself. However, its repetitive work is removed from Carnival's context of *ritual* repetition.[40]

Pantomime also offers us insight into the ways in which hybridity and opposition can be compatible terms. Part of the political shrewdness of the play lies in its allegiance to both the ethic of hybridity and the ethic of opposition. The play undoubtedly mobilizes reversal; transgression of psychological, aesthetic, and social boundaries; interludes of artistic collaboration; the artistic virtuosity of the subordinate; and a shared ground which exceeds the class positions of Harry and Jackson where, for example, Jackson admits the precariousness of his own marriage (140) and recognizes from experience Harry's loneliness and grief (167). All these devices relentlessly deconstruct any vestige of an opposition understood as essential, but they do not erase opposition *per se*. The moments of connection I have instantiated rehearse and provide a glimpse of an alternative which the play demonstrates cannot be sustained within an overarching context of inequality. Harry's attempt to use the vocabulary of performance art to disclaim responsibility for his actions in power does not wash with Jackson ("Look, I'm a liberal, Jackson. I've done the whole routine. Aldermaston, Suez, Ban the Bomb, Burn the bra, Pity the Poor Pakis, et cetera... I'd no idea I'd wind up in this ironic position of giving orders, but if the new script I've been given says: HARRY TREWE, HOTEL MANAGER, then I'm going to play Harry Trewe, Hotel Manager, to the hilt, damnit" [*sic*] (108)). If *Pantomime* frames politics in terms of roles, it will not permit any reductive reading of them as "just" roles, but rather draws attention precisely to the consequentiality of such roles. The play's dramatization of a hybridity that deconstructs essential oppositions is thus matched by its dramatization of an opposition understood as arising out of one's social location and relationship to material privilege. Thus, the hybridization of voice that occurs in and through Jackson's concluding calypso (in which he performs a creolized and improvised version of Harry's words—"let we act together with we heart and soul. / It go be man to man, and we go do it fine, / and we go give it the title of pantomime" [170]) is pressed back into the question of better wages, which are a necessary condition for any more sustained collaboration. Performing a hybrid Creole aesthetics in the play actually sharpens or crystallizes the political opposition between Harry and Jackson.

As we reimagine the contours of opposition in our present conjuncture, the epistemological subtlety, aesthetic complexity, and political suppleness of *Pantomime*'s vision of Creole opposition—de-essentialized, sensitive to micro-politics, performative, provisional, open—have much to offer. They can help us reinvigorate our conception of opposition in part by recognizing and reimagining forms of opposition beyond or in addition to, as Richard Fox puts it, "marches, speeches, rallies, strikes" (10). Clearly, not all forms of opposition share the performative intensity of *Pantomime*, and though one could explore "back-stage" as a metaphor for some of that more quiet, anonymous labor, the theatrical metaphor and aesthetic analysis may simply not be pertinent to several cases. My interest in trying to develop a theory of performative opposition, then, is not to apply it across the board, but first, to explore what aesthetics and the study of performance can contribute to oppositional practice, and second, to emphasize that political opposition need not be essential, immutable, or monolithic, and may involve much of the creative performativity that we recognize in resistance and transgression. A host of hitherto neglected acts and sites of opposition thereby come into view. For example, we position ourselves to grasp the oppositional significance of the staged anonymity of the masked and caped Superbarrio who materializes in Mexico and the United States border area to throw his support behind the grievances of the oppressed. Or the spectacular anonymity of the Ejército Zapatista Nacional de Liberación, whose participation in local soccer matches in Mexico, for example, transforms the notion of grim guerrillas and inscribes them instead in an economy of youth, pleasure, play, vigor, and competition—all of which their performative practice links to political opposition. We could turn to the environmental Chipko (tree-hugging) movement in India for its imaginative performances of civil disobedience, just as we might consider the AIDS quilt for its extraordinary fabrication of a community of the dead and the living that is at once memorial, vigil, celebration, and accusation. Or we might literalize Scott's theatrical metaphor and study activist collective, community, or street theater groups such as Sistren in Jamaica, which have a political "message"; such groups indeed illuminate the connections between acting and activism; they both build a "cast" of political actors which rehearses and develops a counterpublic and emphasize *exploratory* political/theatrical work, rather than pre-scripted work or solutions, thus advancing what might be called "engaged improvisation." Such improvisation is a key node between the local and the systemic, and offers exploratory and diagnostic moments where opposition can crystallize at the cusp of conscious and subconscious agency. Studying such performance thus permits and recognizes a kind of agency different from the intentionalist agency of the unitary Enlightenment subject (traditionally associated with the public sphere); it may yield unpredictable but substantive political knowledge and politicize subjectivities (although the allegiances of these subjectivities cannot be known in advance). Comprehending the performativity of political opposition thus can also undercut top-heavy, abstracted, or vanguardist conceptions of opposition. When political opposition is repositioned in relation to such performance, moreover, the contemporary Left's vocabulary of the scarcity of political options might yield to an appreciation of the *abundance* of performative possibilities for opposition.[41] And finally, the performative dimension of opposition foregrounds the creativity and *artistry* of practices of political opposition. In so doing, it reminds us that ideological flexibility gives breath to liberational politics no less than to performance.

Chapter 5

Marvelous Realism, Feminism, and Mulatto Aesthetics: Erna Brodber's *Myal*

> The phenomenon of the marvelous presupposes faith.
> —Alejo Carpentier,
> "On the Marvelous Real in America"

> The word in language is half someone else's.
> —Mikhail Bakhtin,
> *The Dialogic Imagination*

This chapter is occasioned by the encounter between marvelous realism and postmodernism in the North American academy. In some ways, it takes up familiar questions of how the "local" is consumed "globally." For instance, which aspects of texts cross over easily, and which are detained at the border?[1] What are the consequences of assimilating postcolonial critiques of realism, such as marvelous realism, to postmodern ones? What aspects of resistant and/or oppositional agency may be left out as a result of this transaction? These questions are further tangled by the global market's hyper-canonization of marvelous and magic realism as ideal forms of postcolonial writing—a canonization that has generated several postcolonial and/or Marxist rejections of the forms, on grounds that magic and marvelous realist texts *lend* themselves to co-optive, assimilationist, or dehistoricizing projects, whether within postmodernism or official postcolonial nationalisms.[2] Fredric Jameson has observed in "On Magic Realism in Film" that the films he studied "presuppose extensive prior knowledge of their historical framework in such a way as to eschew all exposition and also to preempt the traditional narrative gesture of the *beginning*" (304). To me, this seems a more accurate formulation than that which charges magic or marvelous realism with the elision or displacement of history, and it is a useful point from which to initiate questions of the interpretive, narrative, and translational difficulties posed by an international readership that does not have a knowledge of the national or local history in question. Can marvelous realism survive exposition? If not, is it necessarily doomed to dehistoricizing readings by readers who do not already know that history?

My answers to these questions, rather than dwelling on the problems of marvelous-realist textual practice or the very real conformist pressures and appetites of a global literary market (visible in the over-readiness with which publishers' blurbs hail numerous postcolonial texts as postmodern—and *therefore* as meritorious), will argue for the need to reorient our own reading practices. Both postmodernism and marvelous realism engage in a critique of reason, investigate alternative forms of agency to those of the liberal humanist subject, and intervene in traditional conceptions of the nation; nonetheless, they arose out of very different sets of historical stresses—stresses that leave their traces on the narrative and invite our attention. Postmodernism and marvelous realism, then, both stage critiques of modernity; what I question is whether they stage the *same* critique.[3] We need to both de-essentialize our reading of form by historicizing it (for similar formal features may encode quite different epistemologies and projects, depending on their historical *con*text) and recognize that historical context itself leaves its traces on the form of the text. Thus, for instance, the surface effects of realism (omniscient narrator, linear narrative, transparent language, centered individual subject) are not necessarily features of a realist narrative anymore than their "opposites" (fragmented narrative, decentered or unstable individual subject, problematization of representation) are necessarily features of a postmodernist narrative. This observation would perhaps be unnecessary were it not the case that it is in the context of a specifically postmodern celebration of diversity that Caribbean literature has been welcomed into metropolitan academies; it has therefore often been appended to postmodernist reading strategies and agendas.

Although in this chapter I address only that subset of postcolonial writing that is marvelous realist, I neither uphold marvelous realism as the ideal form of postcolonial writing nor wish to posit any fundamental antagonism between postmodernism and postcolonialism. It is certainly not only at the metropolitan centers and through metropolitan reading practices that texts are "postmodernized." Ironically, Glissant's remark that (literary) realism in the ex-colonies is an essentially imitative enterprise (*Caribbean Discourse* 46, 242, 256) may today apply equally to postmodernism. It is also the case that postmodernism itself can be creolized, as it were, and interact productively with postcolonial concerns (as it does, I believe, in Glissant, *Caribbean Discourse*).[4] What concerns me here is the urgency of registering the arrangement of power within which the repeated and systematic displacement of the historical and conjunctural concerns of postcolonial texts in favor of the preoccupations of Anglo/Euro-American postmodernism occurs. To distinguish between marvelous realism and postmodernism is no nativism; rather, it is to historicize both the concerns of marvelous realism and their displacement by postmodernist criticism. It is also to argue for fuller attention to the contradictory relationship of Third World literatures to Euro-American literary history, which could enable us to reconsider our criteria for literary periodization, more rigorously periodize Euroamerican literary history, and more accurately theorize Third World literatures.[5] At the very least, one must engage the *different* genealogies and epistemologies of different realisms, modernisms, and postmodernisms, which are related to different experiences, meanings, and epistemologies of (post)modernity. Thus, for example, the Caribbean's sudden "irruption into modernity" (Glissant, *Caribbean Discourse* 146) is quite different from Europe's more gradual introduction to modernity; so, too, Latin America's "truncated modernity" (García Canclini) might generate a qualititatively different relationship than that of the United States to *post*-modernity. We may think of marvelous realism's social matrix in terms of uneven development and the coexistence of different modes of production (Jameson, "On Magic Realism in Film" 311) or the "radical simultaneity" (Fabian, *Time and the Other*) of different codes. The formal consequence of this is a constitutive tension between discursive sytstems, "neither managing to subordinate or contain the other" (Slemon, "Magic Realism" 410).[6]

Marvelous realism's break with classic realism is thus quite clear. In classic realism

> there is a hierarchy amongst the discourses which compose the text and this hierarchy is defined in terms of an empirical notion of truth.... [and w]hereas other discourses within the text are considered as material which are open to re-interpretation, the narrative discourse simply allows reality to appear and denies its own status as articulation ... The unquestioned nature of the narrative discourse entails that....
> 1 The classic realist text cannot deal with the real as contradictory.
> 2 In a reciprocal movement the classic realist text ensures the position of the subject in a relation of dominant specularity. (MacCabe, "Realism and the Cinema" 35–36, 39)[7]

As Glissant puts it, in his critique of classic realism: "The surface effects of literary realism are the precise equivalent of the historian's claim to pure objectivity" (74).[8] What is crucial about this observation to the argument I will develop is that it places the critique of a poetics squarely in the context of a critique of historiography, a struggle over poetics in the context of a struggle over history. Classic realism and traditional historiography are two of the means by which the Caribbean is made to live in a "permanent state of the unreal" (Glissant, *Caribbean Discourse* 242). Thus, he asserts: "The only source of light ultimately was that of the transcendental presence of the Other, of his Visibility—colonizer or administrator—of his transparency fatally proposed as a model, because of which we have acquired a taste for obscurity, that which is not obvious, to assert for each community the right to a shared obscurity" (161).

Marvelous realism's frequent turns to myth, spirituality, faith, ritual, the miraculous, practices such as vodun and spirit possession, are amongst its resources for exploring existing alternatives to dominant valuations of abstract rationality/Reason and its primary incarnation, Science. Such alternative practices, obscure to Euro-American Reason, are sites of the contradiction that classic realism would flatten out or render as colonial defect. In contrast, in marvelous realism, contradiction emerges as the palpable form of History. Our task as readers must therefore surely include keeping that contradiction in sight. The problem with many readings of marvelous realism (postmodern, Afrocentric, and nativist celebrations, as well as marxist critiques) is that they tend to dissolve that contradiction by privileging the "marvelous" of "marvelous realism," the "magic" of "magical realism."[9] Less commented upon in discussions of marvelous realism are the ways in which it reclaims a realist project. It seems to me that the task before us is better framed thus: How does the *friction* between "marvelous" and "realism" spark meaning? How do the marvelous and the realist each interrogate the other?

In this regard, Caribbean and Latin American debates about marvelous realism overlap with modernist defenses of nonrealistic realisms.[10] Franz Roh, for instance, who is credited with first using the term "magic realism," which he did in his discussion of post-Expressionist painting, referred to it as the New Objectivity. Jacques Stephen Alexis, the Marxist Haitian novelist and theorist of marvelous realism, states quite explicitly: "The marvellous must intervene in a powerful social and dynamic realism. Myth and the marvelous can, understood in a materialist sense, become powerful levers for realistic art and literature, for the transformation of the world" (qtd. in Dash, "Marvellous Realism: The Way Out of Négritude" 92). Similarly, Alejo Carpentier, one of the major theorists of marvelous realism, in his 1949 manifesto observes:

> the marvelous begins to be unmistakably marvelous when it arises from an unexpected alteration of reality (the miracle), from a privileged revelation of reality, an unaccustomed insight that is singularly favored by the unexpected richness of reality or an amplification of the scale and categories of reality, perceived with particular intensity by virtue of an exaltation of the spirit that leads it to a kind of extreme state. (86)[11]

Glissant, for his part, at the very moment that he rejects the classic realist form, affirms a commitment to a realist epistemology:

> An almost elementary statement of our needs, if it is valuable in our daily struggle, can also prevent us from seeing the deeper structures of oppression which must nevertheless be brought to light. This act of exposure, paradoxically, is not performed each time in an open and clear way... The production of texts must also produce history, not in its capacity to facilitate something happening, but in its ability to raise a concealed world to the level of consciousness. (*Caribbean Discourse* 107)[12]

It is surely significant that the cognitive impulse in the last two passages takes recourse to the classic realist metaphors of vision and light, appearance and essence, surface and depth. Glissant turns to marvelous realism to illuminate the deep structures of oppression and mechanisms of Othering. If he favors an aesthetic of obscurity, does he not also attempt to shed light, as it were, on obscurity, to engage with precisely that which colonialist narratives render opaque? His critique of the colonizer's "light" is that, unable to explain these structures and those they oppress, it registers them as opaque, obscure, Other. Unlike postmodern conceptions of the perpetual deferral of meaning, Glissant refers to the ideological *generation* of opacity, to particular historical obfuscations of meaning. As Kum Kum Sangari has observed: "Both meaning and the need for locating meaning are conjunctural; and it is useful to maintain a distinction between the realized difficulty of knowing and the preasserted or a priori difficulty of knowing" (4–5).

For Glissant, Alexis, and Carpentier, then, marvelous realism is a *reformulation* rather than a refusal of realism. Against the transparency of a formally realist colonial narrative, they set the mysterious opacity of an epistemologically realist narrative. If the colonial narrative's surface realism de-realizes the colonized, relegating them to a "permanent state of the unreal" (*Caribbean Discourse* 242), then a knowledge of the "deeper" reality enables postcolonial subjects to realize themselves. By my choice of the verb "realize," suggesting "making real," I wish to emphasize that Glissant links the processes of exposure and production, revelation and construction, illumination and transformation. Epistemological realism in the formulations above is thus directly related to the *political* project of the collective subjectification of the colonized. As Sangari puts it: "marvelous realism is attached to a real and to a possible" (6).

Moreover, in early marvelous-realist literature, that subjectification is often understood in distinctly nationalist terms, a factor that is often overlooked in the encounter between a nationalist context of production and a post-nationalist context of consumption. (To put it very schematically: postmodernist readings tend to simply neglect the nationalist sympathies of many marvelous-realist texts, overlooking the distinctions amongst different forms of nationalisms that these texts may inscribe. Postcolonialist readings often identify the nationalism, but make it the focus of critique. Diasporic African and cultural nationalist readings address the cultural nationalist elements, but tend to be minimally interested in political nationalist issues the text may raise.) Yet while clearly critical of both authoritarian national and colonial regimes, marvelous realism has historically been sympathetic to nationalism. I read Carpentier's remarks about the vitality of community and faith in the New World as participating in just such a regenerative nationalist project, in which the emphasis on community (and the concomitant critique of individualism) gestures toward a collectivism and nationalism; similarly, the notion of faith as it appears in Carpentier, I contend, is a secularized one that stands not least as an allegory for *political* faith (in a collective).[13] In a related vein, Michael Dash has described marvelous realism as a literary refusal of Négritude, and by extension Négritudinist nationalism.[14] In the case of Haiti, as Dash points out, marvelous realism in literature developed explicitly in response to the fascist nationalism represented by Les Griots, to which René Depestre and Jacques Stéphen Alexis, amongst others, imagined an alternative. In and of itself, marvelous realism's ties to nationalism, for me, neither recommend it nor discredit it. Rather than offering a generic stamp of approval or disapproval, I am interested in the variants of marvelous realism.

I therefore turn to a specific novel to explore its particular modulations of marvelous realism and how they negotiate the set of concerns I have outlined thus far—in particular, the different demands of production and consumption, and the complex politics of institutionalization and/or co-optation. *Myal*, the second novel of the Jamaican sociologist and novelist Erna Brodber, published in 1988, has clear affinities with marvelous realism due to its interplay of obscurity and revelation, its interest in the interaction of different rationalities, its use of spirit possession, and its interest in a community that, I contend, is both intensely local and allegorized as national. Moreover, the problematic relationship between political opposition and institutionalization or co-optation forms an explicit part of the thematics of the novel. Brodber's own double vocation in the social sciences and the arts is one instance of rubbing together different rationalities to spark meaning. In her essay "Fiction in the Scientific Procedure," she sees a continuity between her scientific and her literary projects, writing of a "twinning of fiction and science" (167, 164). In fact, she describes how her first novel was an attempt at creating a sociological "case-study" where none existed. *Myal* uses the vocabulary of the marvelous to interrogate the truths of positivist science; the novel includes an extended critique of positivist objectivity and the pretended neutrality of colonialist knowledge. Its critique leads not to skepticism about the possibility of knowing the real, nor toward subjectivism, but, like Glissant's, toward the notion of an interested objectivity.[15]

In her attempt to understand Jamaican society, Brodber grapples with the bitter (post)colonial phenomenon of "prejudice against blacks in a country of blacks. The enemy was a ghost that talked through black faces" ("Fiction in the Scientific Procedure" 165). Her novel, *Myal*, is in many ways a literalization of that metaphor. Erected around the mulatto child, Ella O'Grady, the novel spans the years 1913–20, Ella's fourteenth year to her twenty-first year. To summarize the central plot-line very schematically: the novel traces Ella's alienated relationship to the black-majority community of Grove Town, which results in her turn toward imperial texts like Kipling's "White Man's Burden." She is partially adopted by the Methodist missionaries, Maydene and William Brassington, sent away to America by the latter, where she marries the Irish American Selwyn Langley for whose coon show she serves as native informant. Soon thereafter, she becomes pregnant—inexplicably so, since Selwyn has been using prophylactics to prevent the risk of parenting a colored child—and has what appears to be a nervous breakdown. She is spiritually and physically healed as a result of the Afro-Christian practice of myalism, and she becomes a teacher in the colonial educational system where, although she is obliged to teach zombifying imperial texts, she develops resistant ways of teaching them.[16]

As a story of education and coming to consciousness, *Myal* draws on the traditions of the *bildungsroman*, the postcolonial novel of childhood, which ends with the achievement of subjectivity, and the trope of the tragic mulatto. But part of the novel's critique of realism entails breaking these traditions and tropes in significant ways.

The central plot-line is criss-crossed by numerous others. Thus, for instance, the adoption of Anita by the Holness couple closely resembles Ella's adoption; Anita's sexual domination by Maas Levi's practice of obeah doubles Ella's by Langley; the dead baby doll that leaves Ella's body in the exorcism recalls the doll Levi used to possess Anita's spirit; and Anita's cure by Miss Gatha's kumina tabernacle parallels Maas Cyrus's myalist cure of Ella. There are thus two major plot-lines being advanced simultaneously. In less obvious ways, William Brassington, the Methodist preacher, is Ella's double. In fact, it is to understand William better that his wife Maydene first wants to adopt Ella. (Her own mixed motivations for the adoption mesh with the novel's pattern of doublings.) Both William and Ella, moreover, are of mixed parentage; both are alienated from their black Jamaican cultural heritage; and both attempt to pass for white. Similarly, as I will show, imperial and sexual domination are shown to double and criss-cross each other. Moreover, Ella's allegorical function in relation to Grove Town is itself doubled by Grove Town's allegorical function in relation to Jamaica. In other words, the individual, the local community, and the national community all fold into one another through acts of narrative doubling.

Myal locates the violence of colonial domination in its "halving" of mind and body, its narrative reduction of the Others to halfwits, and its suppression of "half" the story. That is why the novel is haunted by the insistent refrain: "the half has never been told" (34–35, 40). At the heart of *Myal*, then, is a critique of binaristic narratives. If indeed it is by "halving," by suppressing heterogeneity or doubleness, that domination functions, then resistance to domination must involve the recovery of doubleness. That is one reason that *Myal* refuses the linear chronology and movement through space of classic realism, which functions to "repeat and reinforce existing patterns of understanding" (MacCabe, "Realism: Balzac and Barthes" 150). Not linearity, but doubleness becomes the cornerstone of *Myal*'s poetics.

The individual subject is literally held in place by the weave of these criss-crossing narratives. Whereas in Walcott's *Pantomime*, resistance and opposition are *condensed* in the figures of two men and understood in terms of the artistic control of characters who through the virtuosity of their individual performances create individual characters from allegorical archetypes, in *Myal*, resistance and opposition are *dispersed* through a web of relations amongst a wide social cast, and are understood in terms of the repositioning of individual characters in relationship to the community. Moreover, this repositioning occurs not so much at the level of conscious will, but at the level of the unconscious, which is in turn manipulated by the community. Thus, where in *Pantomime*, role-playing is a primary site of doubleness or double-consciousness, in *Myal*, spirit possession serves that function; role-playing and spirit possession respectively become devices by which the boundaries between Self and Other are transgressed, with varying consequences.[17]

Myal's formal strategy of doubling manifests itself in the controlling concept-metaphor of spirit possession or zombification. In the novel's first example of a colonialist pre-text, Kipling portrays the colonized as half devil; the "ghost" of the colonizer speaks through the colonized. This image sets the stage for the centrality that possession by spirits will have in *Myal*. Colonialism involves not only the plunder of gold and labor, but cultural theft, "separating people from themselves, man from his labor" (37). The novel refers to this cultural theft as "spirit thievery" or "zombification," which has

> taken their knowledge of their original and natural world away from them and left them empty shells—duppies, zombies, living deads capable only of receiving orders from someone else and carrying them out....
>
> People are separated from the parts of themselves that make them think and they are left as flesh only. Flesh that takes directions from someone. (107–108)

Yet while spirit possession functions in the text as a figure for domination (again, both imperial and sexual), it also doubles as a metonymic instance of the survival of disallowed African-derived cultural practices. Spirit possession in the novel thus represents not only domination and theft but also the possibility of connection to the half that has not been told: ancestral beliefs, oral traditions, religions, and healing practices—forms of knowledge that constitute part of the "wealth of mythologies" to which Carpentier refers ("On the Marvelous Real" 88). These instances of the inexplicable and the magical disrupt the claims of Western science, and, moreover, exercise their resistant powers by making themselves opaque to official knowledges. Their very unintelligibility to colonial narratives may be what makes them a wealth as yet unplundered.[18] To the exasperation of the colonial missionary, spirit-healing frustrates the objectivity/subjectivity binarism; it is "no longer science but participation" (87–88); it offers a cure, but no theory of causation (95). The controlling image of the novel is thus itself double-valenced: if spirit possession can make the living dead, it can also make the dead live; it can signal both objectification and subjectification, both servitude and liberation. *Myal*'s poetics, then, demands a multiplication of the meanings of spirit possession so as to dramatize the complex and contradictory relations between possession, dispossession, repossession, and self-possession. The diverse forms, goals, and politics of the resistant powers of spirit possessions, then, form a large part of the novel's interest.

Myal's limited use of quotation marks and the frequent difficulty of discerning who the speakers are constitute some of the key formal means by which the text interrupts the project of individualism. The narrative voice, too, is deindividuated: it spans the linguistic Creole continuum, and functions as something like a collective community consciousness (see, for example, 9). It thus troubles the notion of an individuated omnsicient narrator, attaching to different characters in different chapters, catching up with them in different moments of in/comprehension, and witholding information or interpretations of information from the reader. It thereby neither itself occupies nor affords the reader a stable viewing position until, as I will show later, the reader herself demonstrates her faith.

Unlike the individualist conceptions of agency that are the terrain of the traditional *bildungsroman*, agency in *Myal* is made possible less by individual will than by collective ministration. It is less Ella's will, choices, or even consciousness that drive the narrative than those of the myalist spirits supported by a community of believers. Ella is, as it were, the *object* of their ministrations. Moreover, her healing itself is the result of not just one person's ministrations, but the collective participation of the entire community of believers.[19] It is collective agency that sets in motion Ella's move from the realm of the "ethereal" (17) to the real. It is surely significant that the novel does not open with chapter two, which would provide a more conventional beginning. For it is in chapter two that we first encounter Ella, the likely protagonist, reciting Kipling's poetry. (And even in this instance, we note, Ella's few words are pre-scripted.) Instead, the novel begins with the words "Maas Cyrus," one of the novel's orchestrating forces and the myalist who cures her; it describes from shifting points of view—both human and nonhuman, but never Ella's—the cosmic turbulence of the myalist healing. The novel's opening chapter, then, foregrounds the process, consequences, and costs of restoring the natural, spiritual, and human world to some measure of harmony. Only toward the end does the chapter identify the damage in alternate, quantitative terms, providing a list of trees, residences, livestock, and humans damaged or killed (4). Only toward the end does it "explain" the storm in relation to Ella: "All this sudden destruction because Ella O'Grady-Langley lying still like a grecian sacrifice upon a pyre had gone too far, had tripped out in foreign" (4). Aside from her recitation of Kipling, we do not even hear any direct speech from Ella until chapter nine.

In fact, it is arguable whether Ella is a character at all. Denise deCaires Narain's observation about Brodber's first novel *Jane and Louisa Will Soon Come Home* is pertinent to *Myal* as well: it presents us with a cacophony of voices rather than the conventional literary device of character; moreover, "Brodber forces the reader to construct a sense of a gallery of recognizable subject positions, rather than individuated, 'familiar' characters" (101). Ella O'Grady is the *site* where the many forms of spirit thievery converge (83): the violence of colonization, the neocolonial violence of the United States and her American husband Selwyn Langley, the racial and sexual domination of her marriage, and the hostility of black Jamaicans who believe that it is her "color [that] will carry her through" (10). Indeed, the light-skinned mulatto registers the purple bruises of so many kinds of violence that at one point she is actually described as being "a little stone bruise" (3). It is in a sense those accumulated marks of violence that place her at the center of the allegory, making her emblematic of Grove Town, Jamaica, which is described as a "colony of stone bruise" (2).

When we first see Ella reciting Kipling's poem "The White Man's Burden," it is quite literally the colonizer's voice that speaks through her, the spirit of the colonizers taking over her voice, as it were. At the time, she is unaware of the implications of a colonial text that describes her people, a colonized people, as "half devil, half child" (6). She does, however, know the pain of being a half-caste; like her mother, she knows what it is like to be a "long face, thin lip, pointed nose soul in a round face, thick lip, big eye country" (8).[20] With her racial doubleness born of a forced colonial coupling, Ella is not-quite-black-enough for most blacks to be comfortable with her; she is the not-quite-full-adoptee of Maydene and William Brassington; she is just-white-enough to pass in white circles and make her a respectable choice for her Irish American (just-ascended-to-white?) husband; she is just-black-enough to be exotic and exciting to him; she is not-quite-white-enough to be worthy of carrying his children. Ella is thus situated within relations of domination and inequality more tangled than those registered by the Prospero/Caliban opposition and thus becomes a site for intervening in both colonialist and nationalist narratives.

Similarly, Anita's nightly cries against sexual oppression, "Let me go," which plead against Maas Levi's rape of her, inescapably reverberate in Reverend Simpsons's "Let my people go" (36), a plea for freedom from racial and colonial domination. Moreover, the stoning of Anita is enmeshed in other narratives of sexual violence, setting the tone for the violence of sexual relations between men and women in the novel. Anita's mother, Euphemia, "still choked on the stale hurt that had brought Anita into the world" (40). In a parallel episode to Anita's, Ella O'Grady's mother, Mary Riley (whose motherhood itself testifies to her sexual possession by a white man), fears that Ella will be raped: "It worried her that some little boy's curiosity would one day get the better of him and the next thing she would know is that Ella would come home with her clothes torn off her back and something in her belly" (48). I will return to the theme of Ella's husband, Selwyn Langley's "curiosity" about Ella. For the moment, suffice it to say, in Mary Riley's words: "Marriage have teeth" (52). Anita's cries therefore serve as a reminder that spirit possession by the colonized can be used not only to anticolonial but also to misogynistic ends. The way in which colonial and gender domination amplify and echo one another in the novel, then, resists the splitting of national from feminist liberation struggles.

If one channel for spirit thievery is the colonialist church, represented by the Methodist parson William Brassington, who seeks to educate and recreate his parishioners in the image of Europe, "to exorcise and replace" (18), another channel is the colonialist educational system. In fact, the novel figures the colonialist book as an extension of the colonial merchant ships and slave ships (67)—one of the many ways it casts the struggle as that between a culture based on orality and a culture based on the written word.[21] That colonialist book comes complete with a denial of African-derived worldviews, a contorted history, a British literary canon that serves colonialism, and a brand of literature concocted specially for consumption in the colonies. The allegory of "Mr. Joe's Farm," which was actually taught in Jamaican public schools, offers us an instance of the last kind of spirit possession.[22] This allegory, with which *Myal* duels, portrays an impetuous rebellion by the animals at Mr. Joe's farm. Resentful of the rules there, the animals decide they want to be free, but soon "realize" that they cannot fend for themselves and that they were better off with their master; they return submissively to Mr. Joe's farm. Allegories such as this represent "the kind [of studying] that splits the mind from the body and both from the soul and leaves each open to infiltration" (28).

Given the novel's interest in infiltration, it is not surprising that it draws attention to borders, the points of crossover. For instance, it is drawn to the place "midway between sleep and wake" (110), between consciousness and unconsciousness. Appropriately, its favored times for the spirit communion of white and black in resistance are dusk (76), "gloaming," twilight, or nightfall (terms that, incidentally, recall the "dreams and halflight" which Alexis associated with marvelous realism [qtd. in Dash, "Marvelous Realism" 89]). These are the times when Maydene Brassington goes walking in Grove Town:

> Nightfall then. The right word. But there was something still missing. For it wasn't just the fall of the night that was hers. It was the "cusp". Her personal word. She said it under her breath. "Cusp". "Cusp" was a word that delighted her from the day they met. "A point where two curves meet," the dictionary had said. That was what she liked about the time called nightfall. The meeting of two disparate points. Then, she felt that she was at the beginning of a new phase of creation. (13)

What is particularly noteworthy about *Myal's* interest in borders is that it analyzes those "meeting points" in the context of unequal power relations, in order to redraw the lines of power. As I have shown, its central image of zombification embodies a twilight poetics that inhabits and interrogates the borders that divide the living from the dead, domination from resistance, dispossession from repossession, power from subjugation. At what point do the arcs of resistance and complicity coincide? At what point can opportunism become solidarity? *Myal* is uncompromising in acknowledging that infiltration is made possible by and occurs along lines of fracture that already exist within the community.[23] If Ella identifies with the "pale-skinned people floating" (46) in imperial texts, it is in large part because of the rejection she faces from her classmates and teachers. Ella's legitimate desire to resist the marginalization to which majority-black culture subjects her is nonetheless shown to mis-direct her resistance into collusion or complicity with imperial white culture.

One particularly provocative episode in the novel explores agency at the borders of consent and rape, problematizing the distinctions between them. Ella's mother, Mary Riley, is not absolutely powerless; the extent of her sexual consent is unclear. Of her sexual encounter(s) with her Irish employer, we are told, "she didn't object too strongly to giving O'Grady wife" (8). Neither is O'Grady absolutely powerful; indeed, his Irishness limits his position in the colonial administration to one of functionary.

> The little girl had been born to Mary Riley from Ralston O'Grady, one of those Irish police officers whose presence the authorities must have felt, kept the natives from eating each other. As is usual, this new officer came to town with no wife and needed a housekeeper. As is also usual, the housekeeper was before long in the family way. What was unusual, was for said housekeeper to refuse to move to Kingston's anonymity to be kept by her baby-father.

> ...The belly drew attention to O'Grady. He and it became the sign of misbehaving Irish policemen and O'Grady was transferred to where Mary knew not. (6–8)

The use of the passive voice and the presentation of events unconnected to agents suggest that neither Mary Riley nor Ralston O'Grady is fully the author of events in his/her life. The passage offers one more instance of *Myal's* searching the borders of power and powerlessness. Is it an instance of a not-quite-rape by a not-quite-colonizer? Or, in Reverend Brassington's unintentionally ironic words, "How can a black woman really be Eve when the God of the garden stacked the cards so that she could not say 'No'?" (87).

These questions will return in the context of Ella and Selwyn Langley. Having identified all her life with the "pale-skinned people floating" in colonialist texts (46) and dazzled by Selwyn's interest in her past, Ella readily acquiesces to Selwyn's "whitening" of her appearance and genealogy. She is "hooked" on America and marriage to Selwyn Langley (43). To Langley, on the other hand, Ella represents an alternative to managing his family's pharmaceutical empire: "A marvelously sculpted work waiting for the animator. That was what Selwyn Langley saw. It was with this vision before him that he fully realized that movie-making was indeed going to be his line. He looked at Ella long and smiled: here was the future, after all that hide and seek!" (46). It is Ella's story that this chemist wishes to bottle and sell.

Selwyn Langley controls Ella's sexuality just as he controls her story; yet again we see the conjunction of physical and mental domination: "When she was telling her stories of back home. Ella always fell into broken English. It excited Selwyn" (54). These lines reveal both the sexualization of difference and an excitement in which sexual and textual control converge: "(H)e wanted to be in that room alone with her, to light a fire and have her take him into a tropical December and have her show him its jungle and tell him its strange tales" (46). Possessing Ella sexually is linked to having her tell him strange tales; Langley plunders Ella both physically and mentally for novelty.

His efforts result in the coon show *Caribbean Nights and Days*, which he directs and produces. Ella's reactions to the show are pivotal to her story:

> They were all there. Anita, Mammy Mary, Teacher, Miss Amy, Miss Gatha, the Baptist Reverend, Ole African. Everyone of them Grove Town people whom Ella had known was there. Like an old army boot,

> they were polished, wet, polished again and burnished. The black of their skins shone on stage, relieved only by the white of their eyes and the white of the chalk around their mouths. Everybody's hair was in plaits and stood on end and everybody's clothes were the strips of cloth she had told him Ole African wore. Ella groaned. Where was Mammy Mary's cool tan-tuddy-potato skin? The major character was a white-skinned girl. Ella was the star. He had given her flowing blonde hair. Our heroine was chased by outstretched black hands grabbing at her and sliding, and being forced into somersaults as they missed their target throughout the *Caribbean Nights and Days.* "It didn't go so," she said under breath. And these were the last words that escaped her lips for sometime. (83–84)

Langley, whom we may consider an example of a self-serving and ideologically blinded reader, takes Ella's history and irons out its complexities. His is the peculiar neocolonial violence of tourism, which seeks out difference in the form of entertainment, only to force it back into comfortably familiar narrative stereotypes of black villains and blonde victims, thereby obscuring half the story. His encounter with difference, then, navigates fetishization, domination, appropriation, and neutralization. Langley's text is indeed lit by that fatal colonizer's light of which Glissant writes, for it turns the subtly shaded twilights of Ella's experience into glaring spectacle. In other words, Langley exorcizes all doubleness or hybridity from his text, *de-realizing* Ella's story, draining the marvelous from the real. To return to the controlling metaphor of the novel, in so doing, Selwyn Langley violates the *spirit* of Ella's story.

But if the novel goes to great lengths to show the twinning of Langley's bodily and mental violation of Ella, it also insists that that violation cannot in any simple way be considered rape. For while Selwyn undoubtedly objectifies Ella, she is also complicitous in her textual and sexual objectification. Aghast when she sees *Caribbean Nights and Days* and finally realizes that "it didn't go so," Ella is pushed over the edge by that knowledge. From her state of psychic dislocation, her selves struggle to understand the nature and extent of her participation in her own subjugation: "He took everything I had away . . . It was you who let him take everything. You gave him everything. . . . But I didn't even know when I was giving it, that it was mine and my everything" (84). Similarly, Maydene Brassington remarks, "Is not all the time is somebody do something; sometimes is you do your own self something" (94). The novel's twinning of the textual and the sexual, then, applies to Ella as well. Just as she enjoyed telling Langley about her past, she enjoys touching him (81) and longs for his sexual attention. At the same time, her sexual desire is inseparable from her longing to have a child, a longing which is itself not wholly autonomous, since it stems at least partly from Ella's inscription into a historically structured text of gender expectations. Simply put: "She knew that if you lived with a man, especially if you were married to him, after about a year of marriage, your stomach should be big and you should be about to bear a child" (82).

Ella's complicity in her sexualization/textualization thus occurs at the cusp of power and powerlessness. *Myal* focuses on moments of complicity because these are also the moments when the oppressed reveal their agency. And it is on this same agency that the possibility of resistance is predicated. What is crucial and unusual about this novel is that it reclaims the possibility of resistance and reversal in the very acts of complicity and domination, while at the same time acknowledging that there is no *necessary* correspondence between complicity and resistance.[24] Moreover, the combined presentation of Ella's individual complicity ("It was you who let him take everything. You gave him everything.... But I didn't even know when I was giving it, that it was mine and my everything" [84]) with the problematic of structural coercion ("How can a black woman really be Eve when the God of the garden stacked the cards so that she could not say 'No'?") reframes the problem of agency not just as one of kind ("did she resist or comply?") but as one of degree. To what degree does she resist and/or comply? To what degree are resistance and/or complicity *possible*? Through its subtle investigation of complicitous agency, *Myal* avoids both models of feminism that wave away the problem of women's complicity by pointing to their victimization and lack of choice and models that celebrate all forms of agency or self-advancement by women.

Moreover, the novel deliberately qualifies its claims for the emancipatory function of spirit possession, not only in its obvious pitting of local against imperial spirit possession, but also in its distinctions amongst the uses to which spirit possession is put locally—Maas Levi's obeah on the one hand, myalism and kumina on the other. Whereas in the work of Anzaldúa, *Puerto Rican Jam*, and James Scott, solidarity with the oppressed involves a practically blanket "faith," an ascription of perfect knowledge to the oppressed, in *Myal*, solidarity with the oppressed involves investigating precisely their political errors. Indeed, one of the projects of the novel is to narrate the process by which Ella's resistant energies and desires are redirected into specifically oppositional activity. Ella's "growing pains" arise as a result of the difficult process of redirecting her resistance. We can reconstruct the novel as tracing Ella's shifting positions with respect to the (neo)colonialist text: from unconscious quiescence through structured complicity with the imperial texts as a form of resisting majority culture, through unconscious resistance to imperial texts, through the recognition that "the half has not been told," through resistance and opposition to the text. Awareness of the qualitative differences in Ella's resistance from stage to stage is a necessary part of appreciating the gains Ella makes by the end of the novel.

The connection of agency to a politics of infiltration is also explored in terms of the relationship between disease and cure. *Myal*'s expression of desire for wholeness is imagined in an Afro-Christian vocabulary of bodily and mental healing from affliction. The novel draws out the distinctions amongst the worldviews of different kinds of healers. First, there is a group of spirit-healers: Ole African, the herbalist, who intervenes to protect Anita from stoning; Miss Gatha, who practices kumina and helps save Anita, in which process Maas Levi dies; and Maas Cyrus, the myalist, who cures Ella by techniques unknown to Western medicine. Their practices and knowledge derive from the oral tradition, which can be maintained within a small community. Second, there is Western medicine, represented in the novel by Selwyn Langley, who is "from a long line—long for America—of chemists, manufacturers of herbal medicines and today doctors and traveling medical lecturers. And this was on both sides of the family so there was quite a little empire being built up for Selwyn to inherit" (42). As we shall see, Selwyn's particular brand of drug renders the distinction between disease and cure somewhat ambiguous: he engages in the task of exorcising Ella's hybridity and appropriates her account of Jamaica to his own ends: "It was Selwyn who explained to her in simple terms that she was colored, mulatto and what that meant, taking her innocence with her hymen in return for guidance through the confusing fair that was America. Ella was hooked and she liked the drug" (43). Selwyn's association with pharmaceuticals clearly positions him close to Western science and the written word, to which Reverend Brassington also adheres. Selwyn's brand of healing, however, renders the distinctions amongst "doctor," doctoring, and indoctrinating somewhat ambiguous—to the detriment of his patient.

However, the third category of healers/healing takes advantage of that ambiguity. In the following passage, critical to Ella's achievement of knowledge, *Myal* refigures Selwyn's sexual possession of Ella as a breaking of the barrier that separated her mind from her body:

> With her hymen and a couple of months of marriage gone, there was a clean, clear passage from Ella's head through her middle and right down to outside. Poisons drained out of her body. When she flexed her

> big toe, she could feel the muscles in her head react. Her parts were at one with each other. And even her mind came into the act. It was now struggling for a balance with her body. For years there had been something like gauze in her head where she supposed her mind to be. It stretched flat across her head, separating one section of her mind from the other—the top of the head from the bottom of the head. In there were Peter Pan and Lucy Gray and Dairy Maid and at one time Selwyn—the top section. At the bottom were Mammy Mary and them Grove Town people. She knew they were there but if she ever tried to touch them or to talk to them, the gauze barrier would push back her hand or her thoughts.... Selwyn had somehow managed to push his way in to them (the Grove Town people) and it seemed that Peter and Lucy and Dairy Maid had taken some sort of holiday, or perhaps they had gone away for good since Selwyn paid them no mind, asking no questions about them, though he knew very well that they existed.
>
> ...After a couple of months of marriage there was no gauze at all and Ella seemed to be draining perpetually. And the draining brought clarity so that Ella could, after a time, see not only Mammy Mary and them people clearly but she could see the things around them. (80–81)

It is Selwyn's neocolonial interest in her stories that makes Ella value them, but having once learned to value them, she and they elude his control. Selwyn's opportunistic sexual/textual possession of Ella thus becomes the means by which she overcomes her alienation from her past. The breaking of her hymen is refigured as a reconnection of mind and body, the breaking of a mental barrier that separated the English people from the Grove Town people, and the colonialist text from the text of Ella's daily experience. For the first time, the two texts occupy the same space in Ella's head. It is that conflictual encounter which enables her to interrogate the colonialist text with the Grove Town text. She begins to read the colonialist text with neither awe nor acceptance, and the Grove Town text without alienation; she can finally "touch" (81) their textual subjects. This Bakhtinian process of inter-illumination of texts or Glissantian project of making relative is central to *Myal's* production of knowledge. Selwyn's production of *Caribbean Nights and Days* breaks through the last of the gauze, coinciding with Ella's realization that "[i]t didn't go so" (84). At the threshold of this painful knowledge, Ella "tripped out" (84) and did not utter a word for some time.

To Selwyn's horror, Ella's belly swells with a baby, but we know she has not had sex with Selwyn ever since he began to fear a visibly mixed-race child. Western medicine cannot explain or cure her condition, so Selwyn ships her back to Grove Town, and it is there that the exorcism takes place to "get that grey mass out of that rigid, staring, silent female" (1). The exorcism and its results echo through the human and natural worlds: trees remember, and weep with the wounds of history; Maas Cyrus's spittle becomes lightning; there is a huge and destructive electric storm, and much "banging and ringing and splitting and weeping" (3). Through this marvelous collaboration between Maas Cyrus the myalist, the plant world, and the community of resistance, Ella is cured. She gives birth to a white, still doll, flesh without will. The image of the doll not only doubles the description of Ella as an "alabaster baby" (4), and recalls the doll Maas Levi used to zombify Anita; it also literally embodies the stories that have left her body: "He was busy with *Caribbean Nights and Days*. . . . She would be so pleased to see what had been done with all that had left her body" (82). Ella's birthing of the doll thus exorcizes from her body a zombie as well as zombifying texts. It is this draining of zombifying texts that brings Ella clarity (81). In the peculiar doubling of meaning that we now recognize to be characteristic of *Myal*, we see the birth of a dead baby doubling as the birth of resistance. *Myal*'s theory of resistance, then, depends on being able to locate the possibility of healing in the very act of violence. To extend Evelyn O'Callaghan's observation made in another context, if Selwyn Langley's "break-in" to Ella leads to her "breakdown," it also results in a "breakthrough" ("Interior Schisms" 104). Thus Ella's "tripping out" can be understood as incapacitation or hesitation in the face of a terrifying knowledge, as well as refusal to give Selwyn more stories. If so, her nervous breakdown can be understood in part as an unconscious knowledge that facilitates a shift in the *object* of Ella's resistance. It may be likened to an earlier moment in the text when instinctively (a word I use here to evoke an acculturation or internalization of knowledge so deep that it is incorporated into one's bodily responses), Ella engages in a linguistic ritual, putting into play a resistant knowledge of race relations and a resistant facility with Afro-Jamaican linguistic ritual she did not know she had. Asked by Maydene Brassington if she knew Ole African, Ella responds with a literal and unforthcoming "No, I do not know him" (55). Though, of course, Ella knows who Ole African is, that is, knows of and about him, she deliberately misinterprets Maydene's question to mean "have you seen him before?" Her body's reaction encodes shock at her own boldness and/or knowledge: "That happening had then, and the memory of it did now, send a sharp electric shock through her body. It was her answer—'No, I do not know him'—which shocked her then and now, but Ella had not as yet reached this truth" (55).

Once Ella achieves the realization that "it did not go so," that something was missing not just from Selwyn's story but from hers (56), she is positioned to become a healer herself by taking advantage of the possibility of infiltration. Ella and the Baptist Reverend Simpson, both thoroughly trained in Western traditions, are teachers who will train students and parishioners respectively to protect themselves from the risks of the printed word. Ole African likens Simpson to a vaccine, that is, both disease and cure: "You are the smallpox, teacher. You learn the outer's ways, dish it out in little bits, an antidote man, against total absorption" (68). Ella's and Simpson's is a translational enterprise, which mediates between the interests of the local community and the epistemologies of imperialism. Whereas Selwyn Langley's science is revealed as falsification, the metaphor of the smallpox vaccine holds out the possibility of mobilizing Western scientific knowledge to inoculate Jamaicans against the former's epidemic. The metaphor of healing itself must unsettle the distinctions between disease and cure, being a "doctor," "doctoring" or falsifying, and "indoctrinating." Or, to use the novel's recurrent images of espionage and coded resistance, the Baptist minister Simpson is a "double agent," an infiltrator of the church. Says Simpson:

> My people have been separated from themselves White Hen [Maydene Brassington], by several means, one of them being the printed word and the ideas it carries. Now we have two people who are about to see through that.... People who are familiar with the print and the language of the print. Our people are now beginning to see how it and they themselves, have been used against us. Now, White Hen, now, we have people who can and are willing to correct images from the inside, destroy what should be destroyed, replace it with what it should be replaced and put us back together, give us back ourselves with which to chart our course to go where we want to go. (109–110)

This correcting of images from the inside involves doubling meanings, which in turn figures the possibility of reversal. After the exorcism, Ella learns—in stages, and with the spirits sometimes leaving her to find her own way without any shortcut to "content" and sometimes pressuring and nudging her with deadlines—how to dialogize texts and wrest new meanings from them. She learns both how to manipulate textual meanings, thus acceding to control of the coded resistance we saw operating earlier between Maydene and Holness, and to clearly identify the object in opposition to which she was intervening—in this case, the imperial text "Mr. Joe's Farm" and its analogues in the novel. Moreover, leaving her position of marginality from the Grove Town community, she learns about the importance of occupying a strategic institutional position from which to launch her oppositional attack. Ella becomes a "double agent" when she becomes a public school teacher and teaches the colonialist allegory "Mr. Joe's Farm" to the Grove Town children. Recognizing the similarities between "Mr. Joe's Farm" and *Caribbean Nights and Days* (the text by that other writer, Selwyn Langley), Ella observes that both engage in spirit thievery by robbing their characters of their possibilities (106). Indeed, the first two principles of spirit thievery are: "Let them feel that there is nowhere for them to grow to. Stunt them.... Let them see their brightest ones as the dumbest ever. Alienate them" (98). Ella's students will probably be required to continue reciting "Mr. Joe's Farm." However, when they do, it will no longer be only the colonizer's voice that sounds through them, but another, an interruptive voice.

Resistance in the text thus proceeds through a series of half measures.[25] In Bakhtinian terms, the word in language is only half someone else's; Ella and her students will learn to dialogize an authoritarian, monologic discourse. She will teach the allegory with a knowledge of the "alternatives," the obscured possibilities of the characters in the allegory. If in "Mr. Joe's Farm," "all the animals...are ignorant all the time" (106), the novel's task is to bring to light that which the colonialist narratives render opaque: the possibilities of the Other half. In other words, the standpoint toward which the reader moves, as s/he approaches that of the community of resistance, is to recognize the Other half as heterogeneous. Meanwhile, the inhabitants of the community of resistance—Maas Cyrus, Ole African, Rev. Simpson, Miss Gatha, Maydene Brassington—communicate with one another using code names: the names of the animals in the allegory. Thus the entire narrative of *Myal* also refutes the allegory, its own denouement enacting an alternative ending in which the characters return to work not for Mr. Joe, but for their collective liberation. The refutation of the allegory occurs at the levels of both form and content. As Joyce Walker-Johnson points out, "Brodber not only transforms the original story by making it function like the folktale as a model for instruction containing a moral within the story, but also reverses the significance of earlier characterizations of the Negro as animal" (60).[26] And Helen Tiffin notes, "[m]yalism also returns the Jamaicans to their African ancestry, and thus to the source of the original animal fables, which, taken via the Arab slaving routes through North Africa to the Mediterranean, were spread across Europe as Greek, as 'Aesop's fables'—a very early example of spirit thievery" (33).

Both by authoring new texts and by opening up alternative reading positions in existing texts, *Myal* tries to tell the half that has not been told. The novel is thus deeply attentive to the complex ways in which experience is textualized. Whereas classic realism, in MacCabe's definition, denies its own status as articulation, *Myal*'s realism lies precisely in its attention to the articulations that enable Ella (and the reader) to occupy new subject positions, as well as to the struggle to produce such articulations. Thus, while Jean-Francois Lyotard claims a transhistorical "irremediable opacity at the very core of language" (qtd. in Sangari 27), *Myal*'s interest is in seeing through the opacities of particular historical narratives. Its questioning of particular grand narratives does not amount to a Lyotardian war on totality, nor a relativist skepticism about the possibility of knowing the real, but rather an expansion of our understanding of the real, "an amplification of the scale and categories of reality" (Carpentier, "Prologue" 196).

In order to arrive at an appreciation of this expanded real, the reader of *Myal* has to occupy a position similar to Ella's. Both readers have to weigh competing narratives, revise and dislodge previous knowledges, and slowly piece meaning together. To use a medical metaphor from the novel, interpreting the text involves "fishing the bits out like a doctor carefully treating a wound" (90). Making sense of the texts thus involves bringing to the surface hidden stories and obfuscated truths. The reader, then, is not outside the text in a position of "dominant specularity" (MacCabe, "Realism and the Cinema" 39) like the reader of a classic realist *bildungsroman*. Rather, the reader is at first outside the text in a position of *insecure* specularity, and then given a series of partial perspectives and required to perform the same interpretive labor as Ella, thereby slowly gaining access to the text precisely to the degree that she is able to surrender herself to its possession. The narrative's shifting points of view and partial perspectives become an exercise in the *interpretive flexibility* that is necessary for empathetic participation. Faced with the opacity of the text, the reader has no recourse to critical distance, a traditional model for achieving objective knowledge. The reader of *Myal* must, instead, demonstrate *faith*: "No longer science but participation" (87–88), in William Brassington's exasperated words. For instance, chapter one does not yield up its meaning unless one participates in the performance of the rest of the book. Who or what is Nettie? What is happening to her? What is her role in the electrical storm? Who are the characters speaking? What is a "stone bruise crawling in its many colored fur" (1)? These are not questions that can be answered through the rationalist labor of repeated rereading in order to gain control of the text before one goes on. Instead, one either has to proceed on faith or abandon the book at the outset. The reader is herself occasionally positioned like William Brassington, as for example, when the narrator refers to the place of "shy shame-mi-lady, mimosa pudica to you" (2) in Maas Cyrus's healings: the Latin taxonomy evokes an abstract scientific and authoritative knowledge that carries none of the experiential intimacy and knowledge of "shy shame-mi-lady." What Maydene Brassington knows is how important it is "to let her mind lie fallow and to let the elements from the atmosphere come in and do what ordering they could" (17). At another point, we are told of Euphemia's location in that "half-sleep place where questions write themselves on blackboards before your very eyes" (39).

William Brassington himself will be subjected to the book's valorized form of learning and participation, since, in an effort to touch the "peace of those she must touch and those who must touch her" (93), Maas Cyrus stipulates that he will heal Ella only if Brassington and his sons are also present at the occasion. Having attended and seen Ella's healing, Brassington says (to Simpson, to whom he did not deign to speak at the beginning of the novel): "It would give me the greatest pleasure to *participate*" (108, emphasis added). Like Ella's and the community of believers' in Miss Gatha's tabernacle, the reader's route to knowledge in *Myal* undoes the will to rational mastery and replaces it with faith and participation as preconditions for knowledge: "It will be revealed to us," as to Maydene Brassington and Ella. It is through these means that the reader is made privy to information that is withheld from outsiders (77–78). I suggest that this participatory notion of comprehension also implies that the inter/national reader's political solidarity is not a matter of abstractly correct knowledge, but of activism through participation in and solidarity with local political struggles.

What is also important to remember is that although faith in the novel functions as one form of active agency, it is doubled into that of rational, even scientific, deliberation. If spirit possession's language of faith provides one metaphor for infiltration, the language of science provides others: the vaccine, as well as "OSMOSIS, the process by which a thin substance pulls a thick substance through a thin cell wall" (11). However, Ella has to *learn* how to *translate* osmosis from simply the inert deadweight of received knowledge into a vital metaphor for cultural resistance. The site and methods she employs for disseminating knowledge are vastly different from those of the myalists; the novel puts to work every available site. Thus William Brassington's proposal, once he begins to see the value of what Ella has learned, that she develop and continue her work in the forum of "seminars" is not to be scoffed at as an instance of the forms of imparting "Western" knowledge; rather, seminars are appropriated as sites of translation between knowledges. (Indeed, the form of the seminar might usefully be distinguished from that of the lecture precisely for permitting dialogue and exchange.) Spirit possession, osmosis, vaccination, and seminar or classroom are all in some senses translational doubles of one another. What the novel invites, then, is not any simple rejection of reason, not the repression of any one code, but rather a sensitivity to the ways in which reason and faith can fold into one another. Other occasions where the novel models for us such translational work include the way that Amy Holness and Maydene Brassington decode one another's linguistic rituals, Ella's work with colonial texts, and Reverend Simpson's use of baptism to "link them with what they knew." Just as Ella explicates colonial texts in the colonial educational system, functioning as a vaccine that makes one immune to the "disease" of print-society that threatens the spirits, so the reader/critic is invited into a translational enterprise.[27]

Translation thus requires a deliberate and responsible transformative exchange between codes, an ability to shift viewpoints with the kind of interpretive flexibility and empathy that the narrative voice of *Myal* displays. Neil Ten Kortenaar correctly observes that "[t]he achievement of Brodber's novel is to remind readers of the translation involved in moving from the local (watched over by the spirits) to the national (constituted by readers and writers)" (69). To that, I would add the international.[28]

Given all the narrative clues, stagings, and models of translation, it is our responsibility as readers to make sure that in the act of translating we do not suppress half the story. The novel thereby makes it incumbent upon readers to *develop* a translator's knowledge of all three contexts (the local, the national, the international), and their preferred languages and grammars. The novel models this for us, too. Thus, we see Maydene Brassington struggling not to produce a familiar, lazy, or imprecise translation:

> This was the time of day that Maydene liked. The gloaming. No. Twilight. Not that. Dusk. No. Nightfall. Yes. The right word at last. That was Maydene. The effort to be true to any place or situation that she found herself in. If she were in the British Isles, the time of day that meant so much to her would have been called the "gloaming" but she was in St. Thomas, Jamaica. (13)

The novel, then, is not opposed to being metaphorically translated into transnational contexts; it requires only that we attend *as well* to the opaque specificities of the local narratives rather than merely reading the novel for what is transparent to international agendas and generalizable to transnational contexts. Brassington's work of surrender and faith in letting her "mind lie fallow" (17) is thus necessarily coupled with this kind of deliberative labor. Thus, opacity in the novel functions not as an endorsement of postmodern notions of insurmountable opacity, but rather as an exhortation in the style of Glissant to engage with and illuminate the opaque.[29]

Myal signals various sites of opacity that require the reader's attention in the form of historical and geographical research. For example, the descriptions of the landscapes and traffic between Grove Town and Morant Bay, the significance of 1919 (a year that, as Walker-Johnson has noted, marked the beginning of the widespread disturbances of the interwar years in Jamaica), the complex relations in Jamaica at the time amongst Methodism, Baptism, obeah, kumina, and myalism—all these require the rational labor of further historical research if we are not simply to produce a readerly or critical equivalent of *Caribbean Nights and Days.* The novel's dense intertextual network of allusion, carefully announced, provides clues to the ideological/textual battleground on which those events took place: "The White Man's Burden," "Let My People Go," "What nigger fuh do?," "*Caribbean Nights and Days,*" "Mr. Joe's Farm," and Marx's critique of separating man from his labor (37). I contend that it is only by reading these opaque contextual specificities that we can read the novel's events as narrating a concretely oppositional politics rather than a more diffuse politics of resistance.

That the novel is set in and repeatedly refers to Morant Bay, the site of the 1865 Morant Bay Rebellion, one of the largest uprisings in Jamaican history, has far-reaching consequences for an interpretation of the novel. For the Rebellion and its suppression were the immediate causes of the abolition of the two-hundred-year-old Jamaican Assembly, the transformation of Jamaica's Constitution, and the dismissal of Governor Eyre.[30] Two other points about the Morant Bay Rebellion are essential here. First, it provides the historical matrix for the progressive political solidarities of several Baptist congregations and Ministers, as well as for the elaboration of differences amongst Orthodox and Native Baptists, and of the latter's accommodation of myalist practice. The organizational meetings for the Rebellion, for example, often took place in Baptist churches; the Royal Commission inquiring into the Rebellion noted with displeasure the links of Baptism with political activism. The role of myalism itself in the Rebellion and the resurgence of Afro-Jamaican forms of worship after the Rebellion have also been noted. Second, the Rebellion saw the political participation of mulattoes and their collaboration with black organizers. Executed for treason to the Crown were the Baptist rebel leader Paul Bogle and George William Gordon, a mulatto sympathizer and activist who had an Orthodox Baptist background, maintained ties with Saint Thomas's Native Baptists, and established his own church. Indeed, the group that marched upon the policestation and the militia was protesting the vestry's expulsion of the popular Gordon from its ranks (Heuman xiii).

It is in this historical context that we should read religious practice as a form of simultaneously religious and cultural resistance as well as political opposition. Moreover, the invocations of Morant Bay amplify for the initiated reader the novel's conception of the community of believers as an organized political underground actively engaged in recruiting and initiating new members. Thus, for example, Willie and Dan (the code-names of Maas Cyrus and Reverend Simpson) talk of "planning a strategy" (67); Maydene Brassington kneels to join the prayer group, saying "Yes I am in . . . I have something to give," to which the narrator adds "And she set herself to pulling her forces together to join in the battle" (69). The reference to strangers with a common bond, each carrying a drum and a parcel (76, 79), also offers an instance where religious and political initiation clearly double one another. Like Ella (79), the reader has to learn to hear those drums, to comprehend the codes of history.

The point I am trying to make is that without an understanding of Jamaican history, it would be all too easy to read *Myal* as an instantiation of an abstractly desirable anti-essentialism and cultural hybridity. But *Myal*'s epistemological resistance and philosophical critique of the hegemonic order are linked to a history of organized political opposition. This combination of epistemological with other forms of activism is one of the aspects of *Myal* that I find most instructive. In this, it seems to me to go further than accounts such as Bhabha's, which often position minorities as performing a structural resistance to the status quo, or Anzaldúa's, in which resistance is understood somewhat pyschologistically as occurring at the level of the *mestiza*'s unconscious through mysterious forces; *Myal*, on the other hand, dramatizes the interplay of the unconscious and the conscious in the public sphere, even as it redefines the public sphere itself. It combines the kind of linguistic ritual and coded resistance celebrated in Henry Louis Gates's *The Signifying Monkey* with more direct political intervention. I find its sensitivity to the many registers of political intervention exemplary. "Mulatto" in *Myal* becomes a term that is both contested and ultimately affirmed as simultaneously designating race, cultural history, aesthetics, and epistemology, a particular approach to cultural translation, and a politics of engagement rather than disavowal.

Moreover, an implicit corollary of the invocations of Morant Bay is the recognition that any convergences of the religious, cultural, and political are historically conjunctural and are *made*, not inevitable or generalizable. Furthermore, notwithstanding the novel's echoing of the relative political progressivism of Native Baptism as compared with Methodism, *Myal* also carefully de-essentializes the relationship of faith to identity. It hints at the political radicalization of William Brassington toward the end of the novel, and it demonstrates how Mary's and Taylor's formal practice of Methodism is a pragmatic one resulting from the complex politics of patronage and subordination. (Despite their preference for Simpson, they are obliged to be wed and instructed by Brassington, since he adopted their daughter.) Their participation in the Methodist church, therefore, is comparable to the coded linguistic rituals that take place between Amy Holness and Maydene Brassington. Finally, any declarations of religious radicalism in the novel are tempered by its presentation of Maas Levi's malevolent religious practice. Throughout, then, the novel remains aware that its weapons are double-edged, as it were.

A third point is worth mentioning here. We can usefully read the novel's references to Morant Bay as part of its politics of translation. For the place of that local rebellion as a touchstone in the iconography of Jamaican *nationalism* itself embodies a translation between the local and the national. The echoes of Morant Bay in the novel, then, permit us to read the novel as a national allegory—indeed, as occurring at the border of the local and the national. In Ten Kortenaar's acute and provocative formulation: "Ella and William are thus positioned at the frontier where the Myalist centre, a small community where everyone knows everyone else, meets the threat of literacy, which can strike from a great distance. The frontier position where colonial literacy resists imperial literacy has a name: the nation. Ella and William are the first Jamaicans in Grove Town" (68).[31]

In several respects, *Myal* reworks and expands *The Tempest*, which has for so long defined the terms of both colonialist and nationalist discourse. If the novel offers us a William Brassington who for much of the novel has powers and interests that serve Prospero's, it also offers a Miranda, Maydene Brassington, but one who casts her lot with the colonized. It offers, moreover, at least two Calibans: one, Maas Cyrus, uses his magic to heal; the other, Maas Levi, uses it to oppress. Although the novel reestablishes the presence and power of Sycorax in the form of Miss Gatha, it also introduces the mulatto girl Ella to the cast of characters in the national allegory.

But what does it mean that "the first Jamaicans," as Ten Kortenaar calls them, are racially mixed? What is the significance of exploring in the national narrative the place of one who is female, mulatto, and an adoptee? The explicit context of the Morant Bay Rebellion offers access to the historical figure of G.W. Gordon and a concrete history of mulatto political progressivism in Jamaica's struggle for liberation. Contrary to black nationalist accounts, then, *Myal* inscribes mulattoes as having played a significant role in Jamaica's struggles for national liberation. The novel thus does not generate a mechanistic materialism, no crude determinist reading of mulattoes as class conservatives; rather, to adapt Sangari's phrase, it directs our attention to a real historical *possible*. The sharp materialist edge of Brodber's pen thus slices away claims for a mulatto aesthetics built on abstract notions of inclusion, invoking instead historical precedent as present and future possibility.

This move is underscored by *Myal*'s recasting of literary conventions of the tragic mulatto. For notwithstanding the novel's tropes of passing and alienation, Ella is hardly individuated enough to function in the sentimental or classic realist traditions of the tragic mulatto.[32] We might also distinguish *Myal*'s mulatto aesthetics from that of Walcott in his famous poem "A Far Cry from Africa," with its oft-quoted lines "I who am poisoned with the blood of both / Where should I turn, divided to the vein?" The pathos of those lines is underwritten by a universalizing humanism, which is consolidated in the poem's construction of black and white violence in the Mau Mau Rebellion as equivalent. It seems to me that this liberal notion of equivalent violences is significantly different from *Myal*'s more politically radical investigation of *comparable violences*. For the latter insists on the historical specificities of different forms of violence (gender, race, and sexual violence, for example) even as it translates them. (Maydene Brassington's semantic search for a culturally appropriate vocabulary for cultural hybridity is relevant here.) Moreover, it is precisely through this comparative understanding of violence that *Myal* introduces its gender critique of both colonialism and nationalism. The way that Anita's cries of "Let me go" supplement Simpson's rendition of "Let my people go" serves as a shorthand for that comparison.

Recovered from narratives of villainy, marginality, exceptionalism, sentimentality, pathos, and racial equivalence alike, then, the mulatto in *Myal* becomes *emblematic* of Jamaica's tangled ancestry. The novel multiplies instances of nonnuclear, nonbiological, and single-mother families; legitimate and illegitimate unions; and the intricate webs with which women are tied to husbands, lovers, rapists, employers: Ella's coerced conception from the union of Ralston O'Grady and Mary Riley; her adoption by the Brassingtons; William Brassington's own mixed parentage, his possibly half-caste mother who died giving birth to him, his absent father who paid a negress to bring up his son; Anita's birth from the union of Taylor and Euphemia (Anita's father is thus Ella's stepfather); Taylor's children with other women; Anita's adoption by the Holnesses. The national community imagined by *Myal*, then, disrupts pure lines of descent and filiation, seeking to restore the doubleness of the "patchwork children" (49) of the Caribbean. To this end, *Myal* replaces conventional patriarchal narratives of the nation-as-family with a feminist narrative of the nation-as-*adoptive*-family.[33]

What are the stakes of this recasting? Despite its vigorous critique of exclusionary forms of black nationalism, *Myal*'s continuing interest in nationalism is signaled by its adherence to the nationalist trope of the family—which it transforms. Instead of serving as the fundamental building block of national sameness (or alternatively as the transcendence of difference), the family in *Myal* becomes itself a unit of difference upon which the nation is built. (The numerous marital disagreements between Maydene and William Brassington, and Maas Levi and his wife Iris, are also pertinent here.) Although the interracial unions cannot be read as signs of racial harmony, the politics of adoption in the novel nonetheless demonstrate complex linkages between families (as, for example, in the case of Ella and Anita). Moreover, both colonial ideals of respectability and nationalist myths of the patriarchal family are belied by the many single-mother families we see in the novel. The novel does not question the heteronormativity of the national narrative, but it does use adoption as a way to imagine a nationalist narrative built on difference.[34]

Moreover, family is not the only building block *Myal* explores for the nation. The novel's inscription of religious communities as another kind of adoptive family further layers its understanding of community. Characters in the novel are grouped not according to race, gender, or even family, but according to their adopted politics and solidarities, according to whether they heal or inflict disease. Maas Levi is black, but that does not stop him from using his "native knowledge" of spirit possession for sexual domination. Rev. Brassington, who passes for white, is faithful to the colonial civilizing mission, though by the end of the novel, even he begins to question his mission, tries to learn from Rev. Simpson, and is poised to join the community; but his "better half," Maydene Brassington joins the underground community that includes Ole African, Miss Gatha, Maas Cyrus, and Rev. Simpson.[35] The novel culminates in the induction of Ella O'Grady into the community of resistance. It also hints at an emergent spiritual solidarity of Miss Iris (the wife of Maas Levi) and Amy Holness (the wife of Teacher Holness) with the community of resistance. The novel reminds us that all those who now inhabit the underground community once lived in Mr. Joe's yard (93); its interest lies in mapping the process of emergence of such a diverse and de-essentialized community, that is, the process by which the allegorical farm animals adopt a new politics.

Also crucial to *Myal*'s revisionary nationalism is that these solidarities arise out of a worldview that has a certain internal coherence and a system of positive values that is not purely reactive. As Catherine McDermott observes in "Beyond Colonizing Dialectics," "The alternate reality of *Myal* is based in a community that exists in and of itself, not solely as a strategy for working against cultural hegemony" (64). The national community it imagines, therefore, is linked by something more substantial and lasting than anticolonialism. Indeed, it may well be precisely to the extent that that community has its own distinct worldview that translation is necessary and possible.

Ato Quayson has remarked upon the "fecundities of the unexpected" in magic realism, amongst which are its abilities to normalize the fantastic, grotesque, and marvelous. (These we see, for example, in Ella's giving birth to the stinking doll—a fantastic event that is naturalized.) One source of discomfort for several critics of marvelous realism is that such moves, in the process of gesturing toward fecund possibilities, let the reader off the hook. For marvelous realism's fantastic transformations and transcendence can offer a consoling escape from confronting the violent consequences of the history in which one is implicated. If, as Jameson says, marvelous realism presupposes a knowledge of history, then this risk is still greater for readers who do not carry that history with them; in some senses, the complaint is that marvelous realism does not require them to *learn* that history.

One source of my interest in *Myal* is the way the combination of its opaque difficulty, its formal valuation of historical, geographical, and political translation, and its blatantly didactic conclusion, effectively blocks any such escape. The abundant formal difficulty of *Myal* makes it resistant to easy appropriations of spirit possession and marvelous realism alike, whether by nativists, nationalists, or disengaged international readers with a passing interest in Jamaica. *Myal* not only "presupposes history," as Jameson observes his chosen magic realist films do, but, to use a metaphor consistent with *Myal*'s religious imagery, it *immerses* the reader in history. Jameson's formulation captures the intensity of that experience:

> And in general I feel that we must sharpen our consciousness of the shock of entry into narrative, which so often resembles the body's tentative immersion in an unfamiliar element, with all the subliminal anxieties of such submersion: the half-articulated fear of what the surface

> of the liquid conceals; a sense of our vulnerability along with an archaic horror of impure contact with the unclean; the anticipation of fatigue also, of the intellectual effort about to be demanded in the slow apprenticeship of unknown characters and their elaborate situations, as though, beneath the surface excitement of the adventure promised, there persisted some deep ambivalence at the dawning sacrifice of the self to the narrative text. ("On Magic Realism in Film" 304)[36]

I find it interesting that Jameson's solution also involves an injunction to the reader, rather than to the writer. What is important to me about his description is that it draws attention to the vulnerability produced by *Myal*'s form of textual practice. Its strategy also means, in effect, that it filters out readers who are not willing to perform the kind of interpretive and solidarity labor to which I have earlier referred in terms of faith, participation, and deliberation.

As the metaphor of immersion suggests, *Myal*'s dense web of coded historical reference functions largely without realist exposition as such. Except in the end. However, I contend that there, exposition acts as a form of *closure* rather than explanatory inititation and security. By giving the reader an interpretive key at the end, a definition of zombification (107, 108), a clear reading of the allegory of "Mr. Joes' Farm," and the normative judgment that colonialist texts were replaced by what they *should* be replaced, the novel shuts down readings that would privilege indeterminacy without end. Its proliferation of narratives does not ultimately assert the equivalence of narratives; rather, its introduction of new elements enables us to reevaluate and reorder those narratives.[37] We are permitted no escape into uncertainty or incommensurability, but are asked to take a side: to refuse colonialist, essentializing nationalist, and patriarchal politics.

As I have shown, *Myal* shares with postmodernism the vocabulary of doubleness, ambivalence, hybridity, and textual proliferation; its trope of doubling generates a narrative dense with possibilities. The novel's narrative strategy of doubling serves several purposes: it evokes the cultural and racial heterogeneity of Jamaica; it figures the reconnection of mind and body, the interaction of forms of agency that rely on both, and the restoration to wholeness of people who have been split in half; it is the means by which texts are hybridized and appropriated; and it signals the possibility of reversal and renewal. But the recurrent metaphors of "wholeness," of light and vision, return us to the marvelous realism of Glissant and Carpentier, and signal a continuing interest in the categories of totality and truth. The novel thus mobilizes both the mysterious insights of the "halflight" and the "clarity" of sharp illumination. *Myal*'s epistemology remains heavily invested in a realist understanding of truth and error, knowledge and ignorance, good and evil, dualisms that operate in the Afro-Christian worldview of the novel. The novel does not surrender the notion of truth, but it radically transforms the content of the truth as well as the reader's means of access to it.

Chapter 6

East Indian/West Indian: Racial Stereotype, Hosay, and the Politics of National Space

> The African and the Asiatic will not mix.
>
> —James Anthony Froude,
> *The English in the West Indies*

Why is Indo-Caribbean belonging in the Caribbean even an issue today? The answer lies in the particular circumstances of Indian arrival in the Caribbean. After the abolition of slavery in Trinidad in 1834, Indian and subsequently Chinese indentured labor was recruited from 1845 to 1917 to replace slave labor so as to keep the plantations functional. But indentured labor differed from slave labor in two crucial regards. First, indentured laborers were never considered property; their humanity was never in question. Second, at least in theory, their servitude was limited and contractual; the contract of indentureship lasted five to seven years, after which the colonial government was to pay for the laborers' return passage to India. However, the working and living conditions of indentured labor were often comparable to those of slaves. Moreover, several features of the indentured contract system combined to make the Indians captive labor: the legal obligation to work, the promotion of indebtedness through unmeetable workloads, and the requirement that they fulfill the purposes of the employer during the period of indentureship in order to secure their freedom.[1] In fact, less than a quarter of the 144,000 Indian indentured laborers returned "home." Yet in their original contract of transience lie the seeds of several subsequent colonial and postcolonial discourses about Indians, their "place" and "placelessness," their relationship to India, their relationship to the Trinidadian nation, and whether they were natives or usurpers.

Moreover, the historical specificities of indentured servitude have shaped the forms of Indo-Caribbean resistance, forms which if better understood could undo the mistaken perception of an Indo-Caribbean quiescence that contrasted with Afro-Caribbean militant opposition to colonialism. In short, when Indians first made the passage across the *kala pani*[2] in 1845, they were inserted into a colonial society that was already racially stratified and polarized; that the racialization of difference was extended to them was thus hardly surprising.

But it is one of the great ironies of decolonization in Trinidad that racial tensions have taken the form of lateral hostility between blacks and Indians (the two largest ethnic groups, with their own different but overlapping histories of exploitation), rather than vertical hostility directed by blacks and Indians together against the French Creole elite, the white ex-plantocracy, or transnational capital. Popular and party discourses alike have understated the ways in which domestic and transnational neocolonial forces continue to structure black/Indian relations. Both colonial "divide and rule" policies and the lowering of sugar wages that resulted from the increased supply of labor exacerbated race relations between these two poorest segments of Trinidadian society. Moreover, the colonial government's brief policy of granting Indians land and credit in place of a return passage to India led to a lasting perception of Indians as an affluent group.[3] For all these reasons, despite the presence of a long oppositional tradition that has attempted to unite Africans and Indians along class lines, most political discourses have consistently posed African and Indian economic advancement in mutually exclusive terms. The logic of this competition has demanded the discursive production of clearly distinguishable races, and with it, a vocabulary of "us" and "them." In terms of political parties, this logic has led to the domination through most of Trinidad's postcolonial history of competing "black" and "Indian" political parties.[4]

Colonial Discourse: Enforcing the Stereotype

A striking feature of this antagonism between a racialized "us" and "them" is that it draws heavily upon the terms of colonial racial discourse, which provides a resonant vocabulary through which postcolonial Afro- and Indo-Trinidadians structure and express their relational antagonisms today. In 1888, the British colonialist James Anthony Froude declared: "The negro does not regard the coolie as a competitor and interloper who has come to lower his wages. The coolie comes to work. The negro does not want to work, and both are satisfied" (67). Today, we continue to hear the series of oppositions that Froude mobilized: the thriftless African/the thrifty Indian; the lazy African/the hard-working Indian; the childlike African unable to control his sexual appetites/the calculating and ascetic Indian.[5]

For example, writing in the year of Trinidadian independence, V.S. Naipaul simultaneously recognizes, analyzes, and replicates colonial racial discourse. Of relations between Africans and Indians, he observes:

> It is sufficient to state that the antipathy exists. The Negro has a deep contempt, as has been said, for all that is not white; his values are the values of white imperialism at its most bigoted. The Indian despises the Negro for not being an Indian; he has, in addition, taken over all the white prejudices against the Negro and with the convert's zeal regards as Negro everyone who has any tincture of Negro blood. 'The two races,' Froude observed in 1887, 'are more absolutely apart than the white and the black. The Asiatic insists the more on his superiority in the fear perhaps that if he did not the white might forget it.' Like monkeys pleading for evolution, each claiming to be whiter than the other, Indians appeal to the unacknowledged white audience to see how much they despise one another. They despise one another by reference to the whites. (*The Middle Passage* 80)

At the most obvious level, the passage alludes to the internalization of colonial values by the colonized, who "despise one another by reference to the whites." The "monkeys" pleading for evolution share with their colonizers the view of Europe as evolutionary ideal, and difference from Europe as defect.[6] Indeed, the absence of widespread racial stereotyping of white Trinidadians may reflect both the self-representation of colonizers as the norm, and the difficulty of throwing off that representational yoke.

Yet Naipaul's own constructions of race function "by reference to the whites," beginning with his invocation of Froude's explanations and authority.[7] In important respects, Naipaul's assumptions and vocabulary mimic those of the colonialists. For example, while Froude uses a racial logic in referring to the two races as being "absolutely apart," Naipaul, although conceding that economic rivalries and manipulation by politicians exacerbated racial tensions, insists "there must have been some original antipathy for the politicians to work on" (80). Naipaul's formulation shares with Froude's a tendency to dehistoricize and naturalize race relations. Further underscoring this tendency is the overlap between Naipaul's vocabulary of evolution and that of nineteenth-century European scientific racism. Although at first glance Naipaul appears only to be reporting that Africans and Indians have internalized racist evolutionary discourse, his choice of simile suggests that he, too, participates in that discourse. Similarly, just as Froude speaks of "the African" and "the Asiatic," so Naipaul speaks of "the Negro" and "the Indian." Both construct race as internally singular, so that "the Negro" or "the Indian" is a representative of his entire race, generic and (stereo)typical.[8] In telling contrast, Naipaul often talks of "the whites," permitting them greater plurality than he permits Africans or Indians.

If Naipaul's use of Froude's stereotypes expresses a somewhat jaundiced view of Afro- and Indo-Trinidadians, abundant contrasting usages exist. For these stereotypical constructions of race form an arena of struggle over the symbolic representations of various ethnic groups. The famed "thrift" of the Indian is greatly prided in Indo-Trinidadian self-representations, and echoed by the Afro-Barbadian writer George Lamming, who is approvingly cited in several works that celebrate the Indian presence in Trinidad[9]: "[T]hose Indian hands—whether in British Guiana or Trinidad—have fed all of us. They are, perhaps, our only jewels of a true native thrift and industry. They have taught us by example the value of money; for they respect money as only people with a high sense of communal responsibility can" (69). Lamming faithfully follows colonial stereotypes in that he refers not just to a historical pattern of behavior amongst Indians in the Caribbean, but to thrift naturalized as a "native" characteristic. What is unusual about what he does, however, is that he uses that stereotype to *include* Indians in the national "we" of Trinidad and Guyana. For though his formulation claims Indians have "native" traits, it also embraces Indians as "native" to Trinidad and Guyana. The struggle is thus largely over the *value* assigned to particular ethnic stereotypes. But it is a razor's edge that divides admiration of Indian thrift, industry, and community cohesion from contempt or paranoia about Indian miserliness, cheating, cut-throat competitiveness, and communal insularity.

The widespread Caribbean belief in the existence of distinct races with clearly distinguishable racial attitudes and characteristics raises pressing questions for Trinidadian nationalism. If, as Froude claims, and Naipaul concurs, "the African" and "the Asiatic" are so "absolutely apart," then what does "the Trinidadian" come to mean?[10] Which races are included under the sign "Trinidadian," and how do they compete for inclusion? How can the opposing characteristics of African and Indian be reconciled as "Trinidadian"? How, in short, are racial character and national character reconciled?

At the same time that Naipaul alludes to—and adheres to—the notion of distinct races with distinct cultural assumptions and behavioral characteristics, he also reveals the ambiguity, arbitrariness, and tenuousness of those racial classifications. For he asks: how much

"Negro" blood does one have to have to be a "Negro"? Both his question and his repression of its implications open onto my central concerns in this chapter: the slippages in racial categorizations, the symbolic representation of racial "mixes," the ways in which post-colonial Trinidadian racial discourse redeploys colonialist discourse, and the relationship of race, place, and national belonging.

Hosay and Racial De/Segregation

What I want to suggest here is that notwithstanding the persistence of Froude's racial stereotypes into the present day, his apparently confident declaration, "the African and the Asiatic will not mix" is rendered somewhat precarious by both the anxious flurry of colonial ordinances regulating Creole and Indian cultural practices in that very period and the riotous resistance to those ordinances. That such vigorous policing of the discursive boundaries between Africans and Indians was necessary in order to incarcerate them in their separate cells suggests that the 1880s were, in fact, a period during which the races threatened to erupt out of the small, tight spaces of the stereotype. It is therefore important to read colonial law not only for how it structured white/black and white/Indian relations, but also for how it situated blacks and Indians with respect to one another.

When in 1880, in that familiar colonial cocktail of fear, ignorance, racism, and repression, the colonial government passed an ordinance suppressing Canboulay,[11] deciding that it could not risk a public procession of thousands of wronged blacks, masked and anonymous, armed with sticks, drums, and flame, the result was the biggest confrontation in Carnival history: the Canboulay Riots of 1881. Close upon the heels of these riots followed more government regulation of Carnival as well as the 1882 Ordinance Regulating the Festival of the Immigrants (modeled on similar legislation in Guyana). The immigrant festival in question was Hosay.[12]

One of the factors prompting the government to regulate Hosay was rising Creole resentment of the government's differential intervention in Creole and Indian cultural observances, a resentment that was inseparable from wider anti-immigration sentiment in Trinidad in the wake of the depression of sugar prices, increasing labor supply, plummeting wages, and increasing unrest amongst Indian labor.[13] But the government's relative noninterference with Hosay before 1884 did not, of course, derive from generosity or a sense of justice. Its primary consideration in deciding whether or not to regulate Hosay was how to ensure the continuation of indentureship. The terms of indentureship negotiated with the government of India explicitly guaranteed that the indentured laborers would be allowed to practice their religions without interference. Moreover, against a backdrop of depressed sugar prices and real wages, and increasingly militant Indian labor, there arose internal differences within the colonial government as to whether suppressing the Hosay procession would avert confrontation with Indians or catalyze it.[14] When enforced in 1884, the Ordinance and the rejection of an Indian petition to observe Hosay without interference led to the "Coolie Disturbances of 1884," better termed the Hosay massacre, which left twelve to sixteen people dead and hundred and seven wounded.

The provisions of the Ordinance pertinent to my discussion were as follows: the procession was to be barred from entering the cities of Port of Spain and San Fernando, and from walking on public roads without license; non-plantation immigrants required the permission of the magistrate in order to participate and could not bring their own tazias to the procession; carrying torches and sticks was forbidden; and only immigrants and their descendants could participate (Singh 80–81). In other words, by refusing the procession access to public streets and the city, the regulation aimed to maintain the (already racialized) urban–rural divide and to severely limit contact amongst both Indians from different plantations and Indians and Creoles. I suggest that these measures deliberately arrested the emerging hybridization of black and Indian cultural practices and retarded the emergent "nationalization" of Hosay. Moreover, the differential colonial intervention into Carnival and Hosay reveals two different approaches to managing the black and Indian populations after Emancipation: *the subordinate assimilation* of Afro-Trinidadians and the *subordinate segregation* of Indo-Trinidadians. Afro-Trinidadians thus became subordinate natives, while Indo-Trinidadians became subordinate foreigners. Ironically, then, conceding to the Indians the right to celebrate their festival was part of a larger policy of denying their rights and claims to Trinidad.

It is my contention that it was precisely when the success of colonial policies of segregating and marginalizing Indians began to falter that the 1884 enforcement became necessary. In fact, the Report of the Royal Commissioner, which inquired into the 1884 massacre and acquitted the police of any wrongdoing, acknowledges that it was precisely the desegregating ethnic and religious transformation of Hosay in the Caribbean that prompted colonial intervention. The following passage from the report significantly opposes a religious festival to a national one.

> [T]he regulations issued in no way interfered with the religious privileges of the Mahomedans. Pains were taken to be sure of this, but I must again remark that the great majority of those who take part in the Mahomedan ceremonial in Trinidad are Hindoos, while many of the Mahomedans hold aloof from it. In fact, as I have stated . . . the day of the procession had become the occasion for a sort of national demonstration on the part of the natives of India . . .
>
> . . . After a residence of some time in Trinidad the Coolie not only becomes a man of more independent spirit than he was when in India, but according to some reliable evidence, he often becomes somewhat overbearing. There is little doubt that the Indian immigrants looked upon the processions as a sort of means of demonstrating their power. It is not as if the processions were confined to Mahomedans. If they were so confined they would be of manageable dimensions, but as Hindoos and Mahomedans alike joined in them they would become unmanageable, except under special restrictions. . . . [S]ome of the Coolies took rum while others smoked ganja or took it in sweetmeats . . . Men in such a condition, and further excited by the shouting and dancing, even if they only carry the short sticks, which they themselves admit they carried, passing along high roads or through a town in which there were many Creoles, constitute a source of danger which a Government could hardly disregard. . . . it was objectionable to leave the processions of the immigrants unrestrained, while those of the Creoles were under regulation. (Singh 144–146)

According to this report, Hosay had become national in two senses: first, it was no longer a religious Muslim observance, but a secularized assertion of *pan-Indian* cultural nationalism and pride; second, it was national in the sense of expressing and developing an emergent *Trinidadian* cross-racial culture and class solidarity and auguring the possibility of joint black and Indian opposition to government, both because Islam was a common point of reference for people of African and Indian descent and because of the cross-racially swelling ranks of the unemployed.[15] As the newspapers of the time stated: "If . . . the roughs who infest our towns can join their strength to that of the coolies, the danger will be increased tenfold" (Singh 77–78). The urban dispossessed referred to are "the heterogeneous collections of loafers, prostitutes, roughs, rogues and vagabonds who infest our towns" (94). The ordinance and the Royal Comissioner's report sought to contain these threats by denying the religiosity of local observances of Hosay, invoking India as the touchstone of authentic religious practice, and repressing in the process the fact that cultural hybridization was as much a feature of Muharram in India as it was of Hosay in the Caribbean.[16]

I am suggesting that both allowing the festival prior to 1884 and enforcing the ordinance regulating it from 1884 were policies designed to limit Indian access to a public national space and identity. This amounted to a calculated policy of de-caribbeanization, the consequences of which persist into the present day. Both the discourse of Indian "cultural embeddedness" and the repression of local hybridization would subsequently be picked up and recirculated by Indo- and Afro-Caribbean cultural nationalist discourse.

Ismith Khan's novel *The Jumbie Bird*, one of the few Caribbean literary texts to address Hosay, bears out my reading of Hosay as a site of struggle for Indo-Caribbean access to national space. Published in 1961 on the eve of Trinidadian independence, the novel uses Hosay as a device for emplotting Indo-Trinidadians in the national Trinidadian landscape from the 1884 riots to the post-1947 novelistic present.[17]

At the core of the novel is the tender relationship between Kale Khan, Pathan warrior from India and free immigrant to Trinidad, and his grandson, Jamini; the narrative consciousness is closest to Jamini. Their relationship is framed by the memory of Kale Khan's legendary militancy in the 1884 Hosay uprising (77–82), and his dream of returning to India, a dream in which Jamini is eager to participate: "Dada, how soon before we get to go to Hindustan?" (55), he asks repeatedly. The novel ends with the death of the dream of repatriation, for soon after Kale Khan meets the Indian high commissioner of newly independent India and is informed by him that India does not want its indentured children back, Kale Khan dies, fighting futilely in another Hosay (163–182). Sobbing "Dada . . . Dada . . . You gone to sleep, and who will take us back to Hindustan? Who?" (175), Jamini, along with his parents and his grandmother, is left to forge a new relationship with Trinidad, one that requires less the militant warrior-masculinity of Kale Khan's form of opposition than the delicacy of the filigree work of his jewelry-making. Hosay in the novel provides a sacred vocabulary for the themes of betrayal, militant resistance, and martyrdom; in the Caribbean context, the betrayal and martyrdom of Hussain offer an evocative idiom for mourning the double injustice of the betrayal and martyrdom of Indians at the hands of both the colonial British government of Trinidad and the government of postcolonial India.

The locale of *The Jumbie Bird* centers around Woodford Square with its statue of Sir Ralph Woodford (governor, and an architect of the system of indentureship), the Church, the Town Hall, and the Red House, seat of government; Indo-Trinidadians have to negotiate their relation to all of these. The novel's landscape is marked by conflicting Indian desires. The recurrent descriptions of the Square and the statue waver between fantasies of recognition and fantasies of retribution. On the one hand:

> The Red House meant that they were all illegitimate children, that there were no legal records of their births housed in that building . . . they knew that the small plot of land their forefathers worked and toiled for was registered there . . . they knew that they would never be able to inherit that land, for in the musty parchments that the Red House kept, they did not exist, and if they were questioned, they were bastards in the eyes of the law, for there were no records of their parents' marriages either.
>
> Yes, in the Red house where names of illegitimate children were written in red ink for their lifetime, for posterity!
>
> The Red House and its bright red ink stained them at their roots. (61)

Woodford Square thus becomes the logical site for the meetings Kale Khan organizes in support of repatriation. It is there also that Mongroo and Kareem play chess, plotting their mistaken move to Trinidad, and dreaming of a return to India ("the children an' them shouldn't suffer for we wrongs" [16]). Moreover, it is Woodford Square that is the object of a debate about the rights of homeless Indians to squat there:

> Many of them had left the sugar plantations long ago and come to the city. They had lost their trade, their ways of ploughing and sowing, they had come to the city to wander, to spend the rainy nights under the Town Hall, curled into the stoops of the buildings across from the Square, dreaming dreams of rains falling and monsoons pelting at their eardrums somewhere in Hindustan, only to be awakened by boys of Jamini's age who threw stones at them from behind the bars of the Square at night, or the steel-heeled policemen who stomped and clack-clack-clacked at their ears, moving them on into the lonely wet corners of night that wept with them till morning came. (18–19)

The novel then alludes to the move to evict the squatters, unwelcome reminders of an ugly history of poverty that disturbed bourgeois sensibilities and belied the tourist images of Trinidad as a tropical paradise.[18] Despite strong opposition, the squatters won the "right" to squat in Woodford Square—a meager and ironic right, on the one hand, since it guaranteed their homelessness instead of housing them; yet, on the other hand, it was a "right" that gave them visibility and desegregated public space, asserting the claim of the most disenfranchised class of all Indians and Creoles to that *most public* space at the heart of the nation, Woodford Square. The novel further underscores their claim to the Square by suggesting that as squatters, they knew it intimately, while the "rest of Port of Spain used it only as a short cut" (21). If the "somewhere in Hindustan" is now a landscape only faintly remembered, the very intimacy of detail with which the squatters knew the landscape of Trinidad and Woodford Square suggests that it belonged to them as India no longer did.[19]

Perhaps most importantly for my present argument, it is through the symbolism of Hosay that Indians stake a claim to the Red House, and indeed bestow their *own* recognition on it:

> The Indians were particularly fond of the Red House. It reminded them of a Hussay, the papier-mache replicas of their heroes' tombs which they pulled through the streets at festive times of the year amid great ceremony, drum-beating and promenading. They said it was red because *they* liked the color.
>
> ...And so it was that they loved the Red House. Some say that the design was stolen—from Hindustan—but there were others who knew differently. (61)

Whereas in one version, the labor and blood of Indians that stain the Red House (61) and give it its color may be understood as martyrdom, in an alternative mythography, the Indian design of the Red House becomes an index of Indian creativity and art; its color becomes an index of the will of Indians. The novel accuses the Red House of rendering Indians illegitimate even as it gathers the Red House close through the intimate idiom of Hosay.

Yet the narrator's vague references to "their heroes" and "festive times of the year" and the sentimentalized description elsewhere of the tazias as "magnificent miniatures of a fairyland architecture with domes and minarets, oriental archways, studded with gems" (167), suggest not so much the continuity with India that Kale Khan invites the high commissioner to see, but rather, the immensity of the distance from India, the image of a "fairyland" aptly suggesting a *fantasy* of Indianness and one mediated by an Orientalizing Western gaze at that, albeit no less poignant or loving for being so. That this is a fantasy or idealization is borne out by an early detail: "He hated India from which he had fled, and he hated Trinidad to which he had come to find a new life" (2). In fact, I would like to speculate that if Kale Khan in the novel is cast in the idiom of romance, then his wife Binti, her son, daughter-in-law, and grandson are cast in the idiom of realism. The tensions between these two idioms are managed by having the child Jamini's perspective govern the familial narrative.

What is perhaps most moving is the novel's evocation of the possibility that the second Hosay was not resistance, but the tragic sublimation of resistance (for Kale Khan suicidally fights a youthful stickfighter rather than the High Commissioner); it is a fantasy, a romance, of resistance.[20] In ways that recall the dilemmas of *Puerto Rican Jam* and "In Praise of Creoleness," in which access to politically independent homelands seems unlikely, Kale Khan's death in the novel thus signals the need for new strategies of resistance and new ways of staking a claim to Trinidad once repatriation to India is no longer available. The title of the novel, Kale Khan's disillusioned observation that "government is a 'obeah,'" (90) and the speech patterns of the Indians, all register the creolization of Indians. Kale Khan's estranged wife Binti's use of a bindi (in India traditionally worn by Hindu women); her keeping a shop where, in violation of Muslim taboos, she sells pork to support herself and her family; the irrelevance to the characters of distinctions between India and Pakistan; and the invocation of a transnational Pathan tribal identity, all signal the emergence of a diasporic, creolized pan-Indian identity. Through Rahim's choice to continue Kale Khan's ancestral jewelry trade and Rahim's and Meena's decision that their son Jamini may go to Queen's Royal College rather than be forced into a jewelry trade, the novel also explores the viability of maintaining an ethnically marked occupation. And it holds out a fascinating possibility for thinking about Indian creolization and assimilation in terms not antithetical to Indianness. If we know and recall that the grounds of the Queen's Royal College are also the site of a Karbala (one of several symbolic Karbalas around the world that enable devotees to make a pilgrimage to a symbolic battlefield if not the real one), then Rahim's desire not to go into his father's trade but to the Queen's Royal College can be seen not so much as the loss of Indian culture that occurs in the nation's schools, nor even the choice to give up Indian culture, but rather the possibility for a renewed and transformed connection to a continually changing Hosay.

The Jumbie Bird offers a critique of self/representations of Indians as outsiders and of the mythologization of India; it points to the unavailability of repatriation for Indians, and critiques Kale Khan for his inflexible gender politics and militant solutions, gesturing toward the need for new forms of opposition that would permit love for the Trinidadian landscape and location in it. Thus, it is the project of the novel to lovingly inscribe Indians at the heart of the Trinidadian nation symbolized by Woodford Square.

And yet, even a novel so radical in so many respects bears no trace of *black* Creole participation in Hosay, bleak testimony to the success of (post)colonial historiography in severing the emergent ties between blacks and Indians and erasing their hybridized histories. Moreover, colonial policy succeeded in that, notwithstanding sporadic resistance in subsequent years, Canboulay never fully recovered after the 1881 "riots," and forms no substantial part of Carnival today, although it may occasionally be represented as part of mas'. On the other hand, in Trinidad today, Hosay has won access to public space; in fact, the Hosay procession of Saint James is Trinidad's second-largest tourist attraction (second only to Carnival), and several scholars hail it as a significant site of interracial cultural practice: for example, the tazias show the influence of Carnival floats; Afro-Caribbean drummers are a prominent presence in the processions; the names of the tassa drums are increasingly drawn from a vocabulary that spans both Indian and Creole experience. (For instance, a drum called "Poison" evokes both the poisoning of Hassan and a popular Trinidadian hard-rock group [Thaiss 46–47]; and it also conjures up the carnival mas' band called Poison, which is known for the scantily clad sculpted bodies of its mas' players.)

What is clear is that the struggle for control over the *meanings* of Hosay continues. The facts of interracial activity or cultural hybridization do not in themselves signal racial harmony. As Gordon Rohlehr cautions, the presence of both Africans and Indians on occasions such as Diwali and wedding feasts has often been recuperated into the language of stereotype. Obligatory feedings by Indians of black neighbors, beggars, and the poor are compatible with Indian stereotypes of Creoles as gluttons and freeloaders, or notions of Africans as tricksters who outsmart Indians by crashing their parties, as well as with African resentment at Indian wealth and exclusivism, which interpret the feedings as acts of religious obligation.[21] Above all, most Afro-Caribbean spectators and many Indo-Caribbean spectators view and interpret the theatricality and spectacle of Hosay through the lens or analytic of Carnival. It is thus common for the procession, enactments, and drumming to be consumed as a form of "feting" that is relatively uninterested in religious devotion or even in a secularized Islam, far less in the lives of Hassan and Hussain; it is thus a *carnivalized* version of Hosay that is consumed *en masse*. In response, "trying to maintain some degree of control in defining the Hosay situation, many Sh'ia are redefining the meaning to suit the changed circumstances" by emphasizing elation at the saving of Islam over mourning the death of Hussain (Thaiss 51). In other words, Indo-Caribbean Muslims are finding evidence from within Islam rather than from Carnival to justify and accommodate joyous celebration of Hosay. As I will show in Chapter seven, these contemporary struggles over the meaning of Hosay participate in a broader contest between creolization and douglarization.

Calypso and Early Pro-PNM Black Nationalist Discourse[22]

The cultural centrality of calypso in Trinidad gives its constructions of race wide currency and particular significance. Its prominence in Carnival has also given it a special role in the construction of identities and national memory. However, since both calypso and Carnival are perceived to be expressions of Afro-Trinidadian culture, one of the most charged questions in cultural politics for Indo-Trinidadians has been this: What does it suggest about the place of Indo-Trinidadians in the national imaginary that calypso has been seen as simultaneously Afro-Trinidadian and *national*?[23] Calypso's representation as a popular national art form makes it crucial that we study its constructions, both dominant and contestatory, of "Indianness," "Africanness," and "Trinidadianness," as well as the gendered nature of those constructions. In fact, I contend that the importance of stereotype in the popular national art form calypso, combined with the racialization of politics in postcolonial Trinidad, have resulted in a situation in which stereotypes form the bedrock of public racial discourse.

Calypso's use of "picong," a wit based on caricature and insult, is a central formal device of calypsos. Gordon Rohlehr notes:

> Race calypsos trade on racial stereotyping, and employ a caricature and humor based on the mockery of accent, gestures or music of the other race. They measure, or betray, the uncertainty with which the races have regarded one another; a latent atavistic mistrust, and the competition which has always been taking place against a background of chronic unemployment, poverty and dispossession on the part of broad masses of people, and authoritarianism, patronage and manipulation on the part of those small elitist groups who control their destiny. (*My Strangled City* 325)

What these stereotypes produce for dominant cultural nationalist discourses is the fiction of a seamless and monolithic racial community with common interests, pitted against another seamless and monolithic racial community with common interests. My analysis of dominant discourses will focus on Afro- and Indo-Trinidadian cultural nationalist negotiations over the figure of the Indo-Trinidadian woman, her simultaneous deployment and erasure.

The eve of Trinidadian independence saw an escalation of racial tensions between Africans and Indians. The emergence of racialized bourgeois-nationalist political parties formed the context for Lord Superior's 1958 calypso, "Tax them!" which I read as an example of dominant Afro-Trinidadian nationalist discourse at the time. What I find noteworthy about Superior's calypso is the way in which it *engenders* the colonial stereotype of the thrifty Indian. Lord Superior urges Dr. Eric Williams, leader of the People's National Movement (PNM) and future prime minister of Trinidad:

> Tax them doctor tax them
> Tax them like you mad
> Lord Superior say
> Don't care who feel bad
> Down to the street girls
> You should make them bawl
> Check every Yankee man that they call
> And buss tax on them and all
>
> It have some old Indian people
> Playing they like to beg
> This time they got one million dollars
> Tie between their leg
> I am telling the doctor
> I am talking the facts
> Is to chop loose the capra[24] with a sharp axe
> And haul out your income tax. (Qtd. in Trotman 391)

The recurrent theme of Indian wealth is framed here as a fear of Indian economic dislocation of Afro-Trinidadians, and a charge of Indian dishonesty; Indians are thus framed as robbing the nation. In this sense, the calypso aligns Indians with British colonialists, framing both as exploitative intruders. Clearly associating the wealth of Indians with potent sexuality, the second verse associates the bundled-up loin cloth (capra) with a bundle of money; the capra hides the Indian man's wealth/genitals. Lord Superior offers a solution to the "problem" of Indians who allegedly opposed the government's taxation program and withheld taxes by underreporting their income ("playing they like to beg"): his exhortation to "buss tax" on them becomes a fantasy of sexual violence, for recovering the wealth due to the Trinidadian nation takes the form of the castration or emasculation of the Indian man: "chop loose the capra with a sharp axe."

If the Indian man is imaged as being treacherous to Trinidad by refusing to pay taxes, the Indian woman is doubly treacherous. The "Yankee men" whom the street girls call are presumably American servicemen stationed at military bases in Trinidad after World War II, to whom a growing number of prostitutes, both African and Indian, sold their services. While the black calypsonian identifies himself as an honest citizen defending his nation from foreigners, he identifies the prostitute as collaborating with the Yankee foreigner against the interests of the Trinidadian nation. The prostitute is thus homologous to the Indian man who serves himself, against the interests of the Trinidadian nation. And since the "street girls" earn their living through commercial sex, they too can be read, like the Indian man, to have their money "tied between their leg." Still more significant is the manner in which Lord Superior urges the PNM on: "Don't care who feel bad . . . You should make them bawl." Since he seeks to recover by force the money that is between her legs, the measure he advocates to recover the taxes suggests rape; it is this that might make the street girl "bawl." With the deliberate provocation, overstatement, and combative humor that is so typical of calypso's *picong*, "Tax Them" becomes a fantasy of punishment, which takes the form of castration of the Indian man and rape of the woman.

Mighty Christo's 1961 calypso "Election War Zone" engenders the African/Indian divide similarly. In response to the call by Rudranath Capildeo for Indians to arm themselves and destroy the voting machines which he claimed were rigged to favor the PNM,[25] Christo urged:

> Whip them P.N.M. whip them
> You wearing the pants
> If these people get on top
> Well is trouble
> And we ain't got a chance
> Now we faring better
> Since we got a Premier
> So who we want? P.N.M. government.

When Superior said "tax them," it was easy to supply the implicit "us." Christo makes explicit the "us" and "them" racial divide: "They" are trouble; "we" ain't got a chance. And in the context of the racialization of political parties, he clearly sees the PNM as advancing black interests: "now we faring better/Since we got a Premier." Christo, too, figures power in gendered terms. "They" can't wear the pants; "they" have to be shown that "we," the PNM, are wearing the pants. Thus this calypso, too, seeks to feminize or emasculate the Indian. Indeed, in the light of calypso's tradition of sexualizing power, the line "if these people get on top is trouble" takes on distinctly sexual overtones: if "they" get on top, "they" will sexually/economically conquer us; their place as women/Indians is below us. The calypsos in question yoke together gender and race, constructing a masculinized African and a feminized Indian, gender dominance functioning as a metaphor for racial and national power.

In the light of the gendered and racialized logic of "us" and "them" that I have described, it is not surprising that in early postcolonial racial maneuvers for power, many conservative Africans saw the assimilation of Indians into the cultural mainstream as threatening, and resisted the official liberal ideology of Trinidad as a "callaloo."[26] As with the conservative Indian discourse, the insularity/assimilation debate takes the form of anxieties over issues of belonging and of increasing/decreasing power of Indians in the national formation. Mighty Killer's 1952 calypso "Indian People with Creole Name" is a humorous examination of these anxieties from an Afro-Trinidadian perspective. Since the titular Indians do not become Creole, but remain instead "*Indian* People with Creole Name," Killer's calypso fits squarely with the traditional usage of "Creole" to refer to only West Indian whites, blacks, and the mixed descendants of blacks and whites; this is a usage that has historically excluded East Indians, even though it claims to be a metaphor for Trinidadianness or West Indianness.[27]

> What's wrong with these Indian people
> As if their intentions is for trouble
> Long ago you'd see ah Indian by the road
> With his capra waiting to tote people load
> But I noticed there is no more Indian again
> Since the women and them take away Creole name.
>
> Long ago was Sumintra, Ramnaliwia
> Bulbasia and Oosankalia
> But now is Emily, Jean and Dinah
> And Doris and Dorothy
>
> Long ago you hadn't a chance
> To see an Indian girl at a dance
> But nowadays is big confusion
> Big fighting in the road for their Yankee man
> And see them in the market they eh making joke
> Knocking down nigger people to buy they pork
> And see them in the dances in Port of Spain
> They wouldn't watch if you call by ah Indian name.
> As for the men and them I must relate
> Long time all they work was in cane estate
> But now they own every theatre
> Yes hotel, rumshop and hired car
> Long time was Ramkaisingh, Boodoo, Poodoo, and Badoo
> Now is David, Cooper, Johnston, Caesar, Cephas Alexander.[28]

If the humor in this calypso is gentler than in "Tax Them!" or "Election War Zone," it is in part because this calypso is framed as an *after the fact* commentary on the creolization of the Indian. Thus, although Killer shares Superior and Christo's sense of the implications of the creolization of the Indian, he cannot resort to their militant and absolute refusal; rather, his tone is one of nostalgia. He continually harks back to a "long ago" when Indians "knew their place": as laborers, municipal sweepers, and sugar-estate hands, Indians in early post-emancipation Trinidad were socially and economically inferior to blacks, and they adhered to established racial divisions. But Killer expressly links the "changes of the Indian"[29] to the creolization of the Indian: "There [waiting to tote people load] is no more Indian again / Since the woman and them taking Creole name." He thus establishes a temporal link between Indian poverty and Indian cultural separateness or otherness: "long ago" they carried people's loads, "long ago" women had Indian names; "long time" they worked in the sugar fields; "long time" the men had Indian names. "But now" they are taking Creole names and causing "trouble" and "confusion," disrupting the traditional occupational division of labor by race and the traditional cultural markers of otherness such as food habits, dress, and names. Moreover, as the Indians of the song abandon roti, capra, and the strictly controlled sexuality of the Indian woman, they "confuse" or frustrate racial stereotypes which rely on these markers of difference. The parodied list of Indian names ("Boodoo, Poodoo and Badoo"), which makes the Indians the butt of humor by emphasizing difference, gives way to names that minimize difference. Killer must surely laugh at himself as "Boodoo, Poodoo and Badoo" become "Cephas Alexander," Killer's own real name. The comically evoked threat that creolized Indians pose, then, is that of reducing the gap between self and other, and encroaching upon the terrain of the Creole self. Killer constructs "Creole" as a black–white continuum; he seeks to protect his right to an Anglicized colonial name, a name that itself marks processes of hybridization and assimilation, but seeks to exclude the East Indian from sharing that hybrid identity. It is *as a creole* that Killer seeks to protect his status and wealth from Indian encroachment. He sees Indians not just as "taking" Creole names, but as "taking *away*" Creole names. Thus, upwardly mobile creolized Indians are represented as literally knocking down the Creoles, taking their place, and appropriating their wealth.

If the creolization of the Indian man is identified in terms of increased status and ownership of private property (associated with sexual potency in Lord Superior's calypso), the creolization of the Indian woman is identified in terms of a change in her sexuality.

The stereotypical Indian "girl" whose sexuality is strictly controlled by her family is now replaced by the creolized "Emily, Jean and Dinah," who go to dances and prostitute with Yankee man.[30] When the calypso refers to "fighting in the road for their Yankee man," the racially ambiguous possessive pronoun "their" appears once again. With whom are the Indian women fighting? Are they fighting amongst themselves for economic gain through commercial sex with foreigners? Or are they fighting with Creole prostitutes for the latter's clients? In the logic of the calypso, the second case may be read as *taking away* the Creole woman's access to wealth. Taking (away) Creole food, names, and business, then, functions as a metonym for controlling/consuming national resources. The issue is competition: for resources, wealth, and claims to West Indianness. And it is the racial ambiguity of the "they" when Indians are creolized that is the source of the stinging *picong* in this calypso. The range of Indo-Trinidadian responses to such Afro-Trinidadian characterizations of their ethnicity and sexuality is the concern of the chapter seven.

Chapter 7

Facing the Music: Gender, Race, and Dougla Poetics

Child does run away
Fowl does run away
Woman, cat does run away
When you treating them bad
Cow does run away
Dog does run away
What happen to you
Woman, you could run away too.
—"Runaway," Singing Francine

Conservative Indo-Trinidadian Discourse on Douglas

In their desire to keep "us" and "them" clearly demarcated, conservative Indo-Trinidadians agree with the Afro-Trinidadian calypsonians Mighty Killer and Lord Superior. In fact, crucial to my analysis is the claim that the "black" and "Indian" parties have historically shared an interest in maintaining this racial demarcation and opposition.[1] Furthermore, both conservative African and conservative Indian cultural nationalist discourse deploy the Indo-Trinidadian woman in symmetrical ways. The stereotypical distinctions that Killer makes between the Indian and creolized Indian women's sexuality, for example, coincide with the distinctions the Indo-Trinidadian orthodoxy makes.

Partha Chatterjee's essay, "The Nationalist Resolution of the Women's Question," offers a helpful framework for analyzing various discursive contestations over "Indian womanhood" in the context of cultural nationalist discourses in Trinidad. Chatterjee argues that nineteenth-century Indian nationalist discourse resolved the conflicting pulls of tradition and modernity by producing a dual discourse of the material and the spiritual, the world and the home:

> The material/spiritual dichotomy, to which the terms 'world' and 'home' corresponded, had acquired, as we have noted before, a very special significance in the nationalist mind. The world was where the European power had challenged the non-European peoples and, by virtue of its superior material culture, had subjugated them. But it had failed to colonize the inner, essential, identity of the East which lay in its distinctive, and superior, spiritual culture.... In the world, imitation of and adaptation to western norms was a necessity; at home, they were tantamount to the annihilation of one's very identity. (239)

This opposition between outer and inner, world and home, Chatterjee continues, was then hierarchized in such a way that the "home" came to be seen as the inner, true, or essential culture; accommodations to the West in the "outer" or material sphere were represented as superficial changes that did not compromise the "essential" inner culture. Since "home" has historically been gendered feminine, the place of the woman in securing this "true" nationalist culture has been crucial. The figure of the woman, then, bears an immense ideological load in nationalist discourse. And indeed, only a particular vision of "Indian" femininity is enshrined in nationalist constructions of the "Mother Culture."[2]

In conservative Indo-Trinidadian discourse, one arena where the issues of racial ambiguity and Indian women's sexuality have been played out is in debates over the figure of the dougla, the mixed descendant of Afro- and Indo-Trinidadian. These anxieties around racial ambiguity are often expressed as disavowals of the dougla—either through the discursive repression of the dougla or through explicit attack on the category.

If in colonial times the authorities engaged in an elaborate "racial accounting" of black–white mixing (for which a complex array of race, color, and hair distinctions emerged, from "white," "Trinidad white," "so-called white," "near-white," "red," "brown," "light black," "black," and "black–black") as Daniel Segal has shown, they did not track the mixing of Africans and Indians because they did not for a long time see the racial mixing of Africans and Indians as a threat to the dominant colonial order. *Post*-colonial Trinidad, however, has seen an elaboration of racial competition between Africans and Indians; in this context, the dougla now occupies a considerably different position, since s/he disrupts the racial accounting that depends on clearly differentiable races.

There is considerable evidence for my claim that the dougla constitutes what I will call a "dis-allowed identity." As Segal points out, "there seems to have been little inheritance of the 'dougla' identity': the child of a dougla and an African would probably be categorized as an African; the child of a dougla and an Indian would be an Indian; only the child of two douglas would be identified as a dougla" (97). Since Indo-Trinidadians commonly consider douglas to be creoles, attributing to them all the stereotypically undesirable characteristics of "creolized behavior," including vice, idleness, mental problems, and vagrancy, it is hardly surprising that many douglas choose not to identify as such.[3] In fact, the word "dougla" does not appear in the *Dictionary of Common Trinidad Hindi*[4]—an erasure that symptomatizes the dougla's vexed position with respect to various processes of Indian cultural reconstruction and affirmation of which the compilation of the dictionary is a part.

The fraught position that the dougla occupies in post-colonial Trinidad is poignantly evoked by the Mighty Dougla's 1961 calypso "Split Me in Two," which recounts the displacement of the dougla from dominant discourses of race:

> Because they sending Indians to India
> And the Negroes back to Africa
> Can somebody just tell me
> Where they sending poor me
> I am neither one nor the other
> Six of one, half a dozen of the other
> If they serious about sending people back for true
> They got to split me in two.
>
> . . .
>
> Some fellas having a race discussion
> I jump in to give my opinion
> A young fella watched me in meh face
> He say "you shut your mouth, you ain't got no race."
> What he said to me was a real insult
> But is not me to blame, is meh father fault.
> When he say I have no race he ain't talkin' true
> Instead of having one race you know I got two.

"Split Me in Two" stages the social and cultural displacement of the dougla, who is literally silenced in those early "race discussions." It ends by refusing to be labeled raceless and refusing, equally, to be forced into choosing one race or another. It also ruefully registers the impossibility of choosing either India or Africa and locates itself squarely in Trinidad. A comparable Afro-Trinidadian critique of racial purism is provided by Maestro's "Mr. Trinidadian," which ridicules cults of both India and Africa, wryly observing: "The conservative only talking race/ Yet so much dougla all over the place."[5]

What I would like to suggest is that the anxiety surrounding the figure of the dougla may well be a measure of the possibilities of the latter. For if "the Indian" and "the African" are discursively held apart by a series of stereotypical oppositions, then the figure of the dougla becomes an interesting site for the collision of classifications, for negotiations over the dougla's racial "value" and place in a racially hierarchized society, and for the disruption of the notions of racial purity upon which racial stereotypes depend.

Nowhere has this threat been more clearly symptomatized than in what has come to be known as the "douglarization debate." In response to the multiracial National Alliance for Reconstruction's 1990 proposal of a National Service Scheme for the nation's youth, and Archbishop Anthony Pantin's support of interracial marriage, Satnarayan Maharaj, the secretary-general of the Sanatan Dharma Maha Sabha, ran a full-page advertisement in the *Trinidad Guardian* entitled "Maha Sabha Answers Back. Debate: Douglarisation or Pluralism?"[6] In the advertisement, the Maha Sabha triumphantly declares that what Eric Williams notoriously called a "recalcitrant and hostile minority" "has now become the decisive majority in the 1990s." (No matter that the "decisiveness" of this majority consists of a mere 0.7 percent edge over the African population.) The advertisement's repeated invocation of the 1990 census is driven by the idea that there is strength in numbers; it must therefore build an opposition between douglarization and pluralism, and then endorse the latter. The advertisement makes an analytical distinction between "integration and assimilation/creolisation":

> According to David Lowenthal, integration implies the formation of a sense of belonging to a country and society within the framework of one's modified cultural identity.
>
> Integration thus suggests cultural diversity. Lowenthal continues, "When Indians speak of integration they insist on cultural integration which involves Indian as well as Euro-african culture and values."
>
> Creolisation is inacceptable [*sic*] because it requires Indians but not Creoles to forgo their identity.... Integration cannot and must not be interpreted to mean assimilation." (David Lowenthal, West Indies Societies, Oxford)

What is interesting about this terminological clarification is that it represses the very subject of the debate: douglarization. In fact, the section depends on *assuming* an identity between creolization and douglarization, and then distinguishing between *creolization* and integration. Lowenthal may well be right that creolization in contemporary Trinidad represents assimilation and "ethnological absorption," since the term "creole" historically has not included Indians, and therefore could stand for a one-way accommodation. But the question arises: if these are the problems of creolization, can douglarization overcome them? Could douglarization name the "cultural integration which involves Indian as well as Euro-African cultures" for which Lowenthal argues? Or is cultural integration acceptable, but "biological" mixing intolerable? And to what extent must these questions be framed by Afro-Creole deployments of douglarization to assimilationist ends?

I would respond to these questions by insisting that it is crucial to make a conceptual distinction between douglarization and creolization, a distinction which both the African and the Indian orthodoxies have an interest in erasing. On the one hand, the Indo-Trinidadian orthodoxy seeks to contain the douglas' threat to the logic of purist racial stereotypes by conflating "creolization" and "douglarization"—by conflating, that is, the assimilation of Indian culture into Creole culture, and the Indianization of dominant Creole culture. For the Indian orthodoxy, *any* hybridization of black and Indian identities threatens to compromise its construction of Indianness; it thus considers douglarization and creolization equally as the contamination and dilution of Indianness. On the other hand, the Maha Sabha's advertisement quotes Radica Saith, the wife of the chairman of the PNM, as saying: "We will be mixed. A brown-skinned curly-haired Trini and if we continue to push this race talk, we go 20 years backwards to the days of (Rudranath) Capildeo and (Bhadase) Maraj." In Saith's rhetoric, douglarization does function as a code word for assimilation; moreover, her insistence that it is Indian politicians who have engaged in "race talk," places her rhetoric of racial unity in the service of an already racialized PNM. Indeed, she implies that the Indian politicians of the United National Congress (UNC) will take Trinidad "backwards," whereas the PNM will take it forwards. What I am suggesting, then, is that both the Maha Sabha's refusal of douglarization and Radica Saith's endorsement of it as another name for creolization are motivated by racialist politics.

Equally interesting are the discursive overlaps between the Maha Sabha and the African Association it quotes. Both advocate racial purity, and both subscribe to the idea that douglarization represents racial "dilution" and African "self-contempt."[7] Indeed, the Maha Sabha makes its case for racial purity by mobilizing a very unlikely crew of supporters: the authority of both science and state in the form of the census and social sciences, the appeal of common-sense and stereotype, the moral authority of Hinduism (loudly announced by the large symbol "Om" in the caption), Marcus Garvey's and the African Association's black nationalism, Eric Williams's and V.S. Naipaul's observations about black self-esteem and dependency, and the language of patriotism in the form of the concluding national anthem. In fact, its motley discursive strategies and the racial mix of its supporters belie its message of racial purity and distinctiveness; its invocations of Marcus Garvey and the PNM, for instance, underscore the fact that the Indian and African orthodoxies are in many respects partners, and mark an accommodation between them which contradicts the refusal of Africanness staged in the rest of the piece.

I have shown how this refusal of Africanness does not differentiate between douglarization and creolization. In fact, the crucial "analytical" section of the Maha Sabha's advertisement to which I have referred displaces the dougla; indeed, the word "dougla" does not reappear until near the end of the advertisement. The advertisement culminates in a series of assertions in boldface, which follow (but do not follow from) the census data. I find the conclusion's implicit race and gender codings and contrasts remarkable:

> Indians in T&T will not accept any use of subtle strategies to promote a culture of disrespect for women, a promotion of single parent households and irresponsible parenting.
>
> Beauty is unity with diversity.
>
> The values of Hindu Trinidad must be preserved from the amoral forces of destruction clothed in the slogans of douglarisation.
>
> Indians find it insulting that a process of race mixing should take such priority when illiteracy, crime, depravity and unemployment are destroying the people in the urban areas.
>
> We believe in love and respect for each human being in whatever form.
>
> Indians must not be told to tolerate abuse as a call for douglarisation.
>
> Here every creed and race must have an equal place.

This manifesto-like conclusion to the advertisement is fascinating both in its complete shift in narrative strategies, and in the way in which that shift erases much of what has preceded it. Whereas the "explanations" in previous sections relied on producing the effect of neutral objectivity by invoking the authority of the census and the UN, the manifesto relies on familiarity with, if not consent to, existing racial stereotypes. The term "urban areas," for instance, is coded "African," and its references to crime, dependency, illiteracy, madness, and unemployment reproduce colonial stereotypes of the lazy African; these stereotypes are in turn to be interpreted in light of an implied contrast to Indian values of hard work and self-reliance. Moreover, the manifesto's parading of African "immorality" effectively erases its goal stated earlier of a "cultural integration which involves Indian as well as Euro-African culture and values." For in the advertisement, Creole/African values and culture seem to comprise only of low self-esteem, dependence, irresponsibility, and unbridled sexuality. In this light, it is not clear what the Maha Sabha's belief in "love and respect for each human being in whatever form" means, since it seems to have none for Africans. Instead, the text continually uses "pluralism" and "diversity" as code words for separatism and racial purity. "Integration," then, comes to mean "separate but equal." In this context, the quote from the Trinidadian national anthem, "Here every creed and race finds an equal place," translates into the assertion not just of an equal place, but of a *separate* and equal place, even as it functions as a measure of Indian patriotism and national authenticity.

The advertisement, then, resorts to exactly the strategy that Partha Chatterjee identifies: it produces a dual discourse of economic assimilation or advancement coupled with cultural separatism or purity. The power of the anti-douglarization advertisement depends precisely on its ability to translate the NAR's public policy of integration into an assault on a feminized Indian domestic/cultural sphere. It is such a translation that is effected by the advertisement's invocation of a stereotypical African sexual irresponsibility and promiscuity which threaten Indian womanhood and Hindu religion alike. Through this translation, a feminized Indian culture—the "mother culture"—is portrayed as being under threat of violation by a masculinized and predatory African culture. The declaration that "Indians in T&T will not accept any use of subtle strategies to promote a culture of disrespect for women, a promotion of single parent households and irresponsible parenting" codes interracial sex as African (but not Indian) "disrespect" for women, and African (but not Indian) lack of self-respect in diluting the race. Representing the Indian community as feminized victim also displaces discussion of *Indian* men who seek out African women.[8]

Drupatee: Gender, Cultural Nationalism, and the Chutney-Soca Debates

What these dominant constructions of douglas do is mobilize particular constructions of Indian womanhood in the service of a racial logic. But what of the Indian woman who does not carry the ideological load assigned her by the Maha Sabha's bourgeois-nationalist discourse? What of the woman who resists the discursive erasure of her active sexuality? Above all, what of the Indian woman who names *Indian* "disrespect" for Indian women? It is these historical women who are repressed from nationalist constructions of a mythic Indian womanhood and mother culture.

The entrance of the East Indian Drupatee Ramgoonai on to the calypso stage engaged these questions in fascinating ways. On account of her participation in Carnival and her sexually suggestive lyrics, Drupatee was described as "a thorn among East Indian women," "immoral and disgusting" (qtd. in Constance 51), indeed the very antithesis of conservative representations of the Hindu epic *Mahabharata*'s Draupadi after whom Drupatee is named. The stated logic behind conservative condemnation was this: "For an Indian girl to throw her high upbringing and culture to mix with vulgar music, sex and alcohol in Carnival tents tell me that something is radically wrong with her psyche. Drupatee Ramgoonai has chosen to worship the Gods of sex, wine and easy money" (qtd. in Constance 51). There is a certain literary irony to these expressions of outrage at the contamination of Indian womanhood by Creole culture, since in the *Mahabharata*, it was one of Draupadi's five husbands (and not their opponents) whose addiction to gambling led him to bet his kingdom and his wife Draupadi. Nonetheless, central to these expressions of indignation is a political fear of cultural co-optation, expressed as a Hindu high-cultural notion of intercultural contact as "contamination." The objection is clearly to an Indian woman entering a stereotypically imagined "African" or Creole domain of vice and sexuality, indeed to her moving from "respectability" to "reputation," to use Wilson's schema. These accounts of the Indian woman "before" and "after" creolization share much with Killer's in "Indian People with Creole Name." In fact, the outraged references to sexuality and easy money imply the same connection between Indian women's creolization and prostitution that Killer suggested. One could also argue that the attacks on "easy money" object to the easy spending of money on various vices, in violation of a stereotypical Indian "thrift" and to the public participation of an Indian *woman* in successful commercial activity that is stereotypically the domain of the Indian male.

The notion Chatterjee outlines of Woman as the guardian of Indian (Mother) culture might also explain why it is the participation of Indo-Trinidadian *women* in Carnival that has drawn most criticism from conservatives. Policing the behavior of women is a means of policing the construction of the Mother Culture. Certainly, it is Drupatee, far more than male Indo-Trinidadian calypso or soca-chutney singers, who was a target of condemnation by Indian religious organizations. By the logic of conservative cultural nationalists, the demand must not be that Carnival be indianized or douglarized, but that a conservative construction of a monolithic Indian culture be given the same national status as carnival. In the cultural sphere, as I have shown, the demand is to be "separate but equal."[9]

Thus, many conservative Indo-Trinidadians celebrate chutney, which they see as an authentically and distinctively Indo-Trinidadian musical form, performed as it historically has been in all-women's gatherings during Hindu wedding festivities. In a carefully demarcated space—female and/or Indian—even the ribald sexuality of chutney singing and chutney dancing is sanctioned by Indian cultural nationalists. These same conservatives, however, fiercely resist the "crossover" from chutney to the further hybridized chutney-soca, the "africanized" and carnivalized form of chutney which is performed during Carnival; for in the context of Carnival, chutney's distinctive Indo-Trinidadianness is potentially compromised, and the sexuality of the Indo-Trinidadian woman becomes the site of contest for African and Indian dominance. Thus, vigorous controversy has accompanied Indo-Trinidadian chutney-dancers accompanying Afro-Trinidadian calypsonians. The "separate but equal" formula must therefore arrest the hybridization of chutney at the point of crossover from Hindu/Indian wedding tent to Creole calypso tent.[10]

Such are the racial and cultural nationalist politics that framed Drupatee Ramgoonai's success on the national calypso stage in 1988. The Indian cultural nationalist attack on her intensified with her subsequent chutney-soca, "Lick Down Me Nani." It is in relation to this song that I will now discuss some of the ways in which conservative cultural nationalist discourse has addressed questions of women's sexuality.

The entire song "Lick Down Me Nani" is structured around two *double entendres*: "lick," which is a stock pun in calypso, and "Nani," which means "grandmother" in Hindi and "vagina" in Trinidadian slang. One source of conservative outrage was certainly that Drupatee brought the subject of Indo-Trinidadian women's sexuality into the Afro-Creole public sphere, drawing unabashed attention to her own sexuality. Moreover, the sexual vocabulary is distinctly unsanitized. (Indeed, "lick down me nani" is a far cry from the insidiously allusive and euphemistic "disrespect" for Indian women to which the Maha Sabha refers in its advertisement.) But perhaps above all, it is Drupatee's parody of that revered and idealized symbol of Indian womanhood, the grandmother, which generated most explicit outrage.[11]

I contend that the public outcry about these aspects of "Lick Down Me Nani" fails to address—indeed, *actively displaces*—another aspect of the song: its narrative of rape and violence. For what none of the condemnations of Drupatee I have encountered addresses is the fact that the refrain "Lick down me nani" functions not only as an imperative ("lick down me nani"), but also as part of a declarative description ("de man lick down me nani"). Moreover, since the *double entendre* of "lick" itself here refers to oral sex and physical beating, the song may be read both as a woman's playful demand for or description of oral sex and as a woman's description of sexual violence. Since so much of the uproar around the song hinged on repressing these narrative complexities, I here reproduce in its entirety the text of "Lick Down Me Nani":

Man mash your brakes!
Oh gosh, look at me nani!
Oh gosh, oh gosh (*repeat*)

Neighbor, neighbor come an' see
    Nani get bounce down
By a big big big maxi[12]
    Nani get bounce down
She was standin' in she cap
And the driver knock she flat.
De driver was careless, de driver was mad
To bounce down me nani right in front she yard
    (*Chorus*)
    De man lick down me nani
    De man lick down me nani, oy
    (*Repeat*)
Neighbor come and see what he do to me nani
    (*Chorus*)
It's true!
Neighbor come and see what he do to me nani
Right away de police come
    Nani get bounce down
Dey want to know what goin' on
    Nani get bounce down
The man say he brakes cut away
    Nani get bounce down
But I was standin' right there.
The driver was ruthless an' drivin' too hard
He bounce down me nani just so in she yard.
    (*Chorus*)
Neighbor here hurry, call the ambulance for me
    (*Chorus*)
Neighbor here hurry, come ah hospital with me.

He jump de drain
Now she in pain

What ah go do
If she were through?
He break she leg
He break she hand
Fracture she spine
Now she can't wine.
(*Chorus*)
Neighbor I ain't makin' sport
Nani get bounce down
I takin' the driver to court
Nani get bounce down
The doctor say she in coma
I don't know when she'll recover.
I miss she phulari, I miss she roti
And every day I grievin' for me nani.
(*Chorus*)
Neighbor don' hold me, I want to buss some lash on he
(*Chorus*)
Neighbor you eh see what he do to me nani

He fender break
On Nani waist
Now she can't move
She two knee-bruise
While he drivin' he was gazin'
Ah feeling sad, he bump she hard
(*Chorus*)
Neighbor you eh see what de maxi do to she
(*Chorus*)
Rum in the face
He take a taste
Check he permit
How much nani he hit?
Yes sarge, check de man out!

He mash she up
He break she up
De man was wrong to bump she down
No more roti, no dal curry
No more achaar or kuchela

All over town
De talk around
Nani get jam
From maxi man.
Man mash your brakes
For goodness sakes
Now she can't move
She two knee-bruise

(*Fade-out*)
But is that man, self
Yes, is he on the corner
Is that man.
Take him away!
Take way his license!
The man drivin' too hard, recklessly.

The sexual connotations of the song are unmistakable. In fact, the sexual puns on an engine/car are commonplaces of masculinist discourse in calypso and society. But if some of the song's puns refer to a sexually aroused man or an erect penis, they also refer to sexual violence: bouncing Nani down, breaking her bones, "driving too hard" because his "brakes cut away." The song alludes to that common rationalization of rape, the claim that once aroused, the man is unable to stop himself or "apply the brakes." However, cultural nationalist discourse about "Lick Down Me Nani" resolutely refuses to address this narrative of violence, dismissing or condemning the song as frivolous, vulgar, and degrading.

The position that dismisses the political content of the song as trivial does so by casting the song as a party calypso whose form and context of consumption render any serious content impossible. But such a position surely ignores the political possibilities of humor, possibilities which the art of calypso has elaborated to an extraordinary degree. Furthermore, to claim that audiences would not register the narrative of conflict and violence, focusing only on the humorous imperative "lick down me nani," is to fail to recognize that Trinidadian audiences have long experience with a calypso tradition in which sex and violence are often intertwined.[13] To be able to laugh at the pun, the audience *has* to recognize the double meaning. What one might more productively question are the formal training by which that recognition can be immediately depoliticized and the possibility that sexual violence itself may be sufficiently commonplace as to merit only passing attention. But if indeed the song is no more than shallow frivolity, it is unclear why it has merited such sustained and intense attack.

The position that actually *condemns* the song is emblematized by Kenneth Parmasad in his paper "The Wedding Tent and the Public Sphere: Towards an Understanding of Indian Cultural Practices in Trinidad." There Parmasad provides a historical argument for the contemporary importance of maintaining a separate Indian cultural space represented in his paper by the wedding tent. According to Parmasad, the tent provided a "sacred space" where Indian culture and Indian arts could be nurtured, away from the brutalizing and degrading "public space" of indentureship. In contemporary Trinidad, Parmasad argues, the public space remains an Afro-Creole space that requires that Indians degrade or renounce Indian culture as the price of admission. He points to Hindu Prince's calypso "Goodbye to India" and Drupatee's "Lick Down Me Nani" as examples of the pressure to cut ties with India as a means of gaining access to the Afro-Creole "public space" of Carnival. Parmasad thus reads the song's "degrading" parody of the Nani and violence directed against her as symbolic violence toward Indian culture, a violence enacted, we might say, by shifting representation of the Nani's body from the "classical" to the "grotesque" register (Bakhtin, *Rabelais and His World* 24–26). But significantly, what Parmasad addresses is the symbolic "equation" of Nani and vagina, not the rape of the grandmother. The refusal of conservative cultural nationalists to address the narrative of violence in "Lick Down Me Nani" is particularly troubling given the high incidence of domestic violence within diasporic Indian communities, including the Indo-Trinidadian one.[14] It seems to me that members of the orthodoxy which charges Drupatee with doing violence to Indian womanhood would do well to consider how their silencing of the narrative of violence in the song enacts its own violence.

My criticism of conservative Indian attacks on the song, however, by no means denies that the song is appropriable by racialist Afro-Caribbean agendas.[15] As we have seen, the symbolic violence of Christo's and Killer's calypsos toward Indian women participated in just such a logic of interracial antagonism. But I would argue that even the symbolic degradation is ambivalent, for it is the *incongruity* between the material authority and symbolic degradation of the object of parody that is the source of the humor. As Gordon Rohlehr points out, the humor of "Lick Down Me Nani" depends on an indirect acknowledgment or recognition of the grandmother's authority.[16] Furthermore, the "degradation of the Nani" is not reducible to those interracial antagonisms. Rather, as Mikhail Bakhtin has demonstrated, degradation is part of the very logic of Carnival.[17] Whether or not one concurs with the utopianism of Bakhtin's reading of carnivalesque degradation, whether or not one accepts that the reversal always favors the powerless, what is clear is that Carnival's reversals and degradations are symbolic reinscriptions of power along several axes. I would therefore argue that the ritual degradation enacted by the parody of the grandmother in "Lick Down Me Nani" is not *only* a racialized one; it also emerges out of fissures and inequalities within the Indian community. The Nani is not only Indian, but is also a symbol of female familial authority (an authority which is in turn compatible with patriarchal ideology). The song's hyper-embodiment of the Nani through its pun on "grandmother" and "vagina," and through its image of the grandmother wining or dancing, parodies and reverses precisely this authority and de-sexualized idealization.

Applying the classic feminist critique of the virgin/whore dichotomy to calypso's constructions of women, Gordon Rohlehr points to the anti-feminism of several calypsos that idealize women: "It is clear from calypsos such as this one [Atilla's "Women Will Rule the World"] that the very veneration of woman's role as wife, mother and helpmate was part of an ideology of control which was designed to deny women the possibility of successful movement beyond the home and the family" ("Images of Men and Women" 247). It is telling, indeed, that cultural nationalist discourse on "Lick Down Me Nani" reinscribes the virgin/whore dichotomy in its idealization of a de-sexualized Indian grandmother and its attacks on Drupatee for prostituting herself. The song's insistence on the embodied-ness of the Nani, then, participates in another kind of reversal as well—a reversal of dominant Indian cultural nationalist discourse's erasure of the sexuality of Indian women.[18] The conservative nationalist foregrounding of the racial logic of the song to the exclusion of all other logics precludes one from asking what other kinds of reversals the parody might engage in.

Furthermore, readings of "Lick Down Me Nani" which confine its context to that of interracial conflict fail to address the fact that the carnivalesque degradation and reversal are not uniquely Afro-Creole. Both the Maha Sabha advertisement and the charge that Drupatee had embraced the "gods of sex, wine and easy money" construct Indian culture as the morally superior and sexually restrained antithesis of an Afro-Creole culture of excess. This construction, however, ignores the existence of carnivalesque traditions within *Indian* culture. Not the least of these traditions is Holi or Phagwa. I am insufficiently familiar with the practices associated with Holi in Trinidad to comment on them, but it seems worth pointing out that in the Indian context, Holi offers some parallels to Carnival in Trinidad—parallels that might offer a means of thinking about the relationship of Indo-Trinidadians to Carnival differently.[19] In India, Holi celebrations, which take place in the spring (traditionally associated with rebirth and renewal) are deeply implicated in the logic of embodiment and reversal. Holi provides a space within Hindu culture in which intoxication, drunkenness, and public expressions of sensuality are much less rigidly policed; it is also a day when caste, class, and gender boundaries are relaxed. The ritual putting of color on others allows a public physical contact between castes, sexes, and classes that is otherwise taboo. There are even forms of the celebration in and around the North Indian town of Mathura in which women of the town beat the men of the town. Obviously, the transgressions permitted during Holi are not unequivocally "progressive," for the lowered gender barriers and increased physical contact between the sexes is often accompanied by sexual harassment, abduction, and rape of women, as well as by gang violence, pointing to the fact that Holi and the carnivalesque cannot be thought of as a utopian counter-world; rather, their transgressions are inscribed in negotiations for power, both utopian and dystopian, within a social context of vast inequalities.

The foregoing comments should make quite clear that I am not claiming "Lick Down Me Nani" is a definitively feminist statement; far less am I making any claims about Drupatee's personal politics or the personal politics of Barnet Henry, the Afro-Trinidadian songwriter who wrote "Lick Down Me Nani." Rather, I am resisting the absolute closure of meaning that conservative Indian nationalist discourse about the song displays—a closure of meaning that I contend is interested. My own interest in "Lick Down Me Nani" lies in drawing attention to the *range* of (often mutually contradictory) meanings it permits, as well as to the politics of the *closure* of meaning performed by conservative cultural nationalist discourse. In so doing, I am attempting to provide an account of transgression that is sensitive to the impact of that transgression on nationalist discourse, public discourses of race, and racial politics.

It will also be clear by now that my interest in the critique of violence in the song is not intended to sanitize the song nor to understate its mischievous sexuality; it is the very ambivalence (or multivalence) of carnivalesque laughter which is one source of the song's transgressive power.[20] The power of "Lick Down Me Nani" lies in its adept manipulation of calypso's, soca's, and chutney's traditions of *double entendre*, a manipulation that enables the song to simultaneously tell several conflicting narratives with shifting points of identification, opening up a contradictory and contestatory space for feminist critique within the admitted constraints of the "wine and jam" genre of calypso.[21]

The song's playful sexuality and sexual humor, as well as its party rhythm, enable it to work successfully within a commercially viable formula. Within the space of that formula, however, it offers several sets of identifications and interpretations: If one reads it in the satire-cum-boast tradition of calypso, one could consume the song by aligning oneself with the maxi-taxi driver. Read thus, the pleasure of the narrative would indeed lie in the sexual conquest and parody of the Nani, and the ridicule of the potentially ineffectual narrator. This identification with the maxi-taxi driver as rapist could indeed participate in a masculinist and/or racial logic; but even this identification should not be read in essentialist or univalent terms, for these identifications, and the enjoyment of the sexual vocabulary, could themselves be motivated by a range of different interests. In the context of the erasure of the sexual agency of Indian women by conservative Indian cultural nationalist discourse, producing and enjoying this sexual vocabulary, despite its sexist genealogy, might be productively transgressive. The idealization and de-sexualization of the Nani are embedded in a logic of coerced chastity for Indian women (the terms of the outcry against Drupatee make this logic abundantly clear); at one level, therefore, refusing that idealization might constitute a utopian transgression. The meanings of the sexual assertions in the song, or even of "identifying with the aggressor," then, should not be reduced to a single meaning. Furthermore, both the song's narrator and the neighbor in the song serve as *witnesses* to masculine violence against women, witnesses who are crucial to realizing the narrative's fantasy of revenge or justice, expressed in the song in terms of personal retaliation and recourse to the State. The song, then, yields several different feminist interpretive possibilities: it could be read as a feminist affirmation of a woman's sexual assertiveness (the imperative "lick down me nani," which refuses the erasure of her sexuality), a feminist lament of loss of control over her own sexuality (coerced chastity and rape), and a feminist attempt to reclaim control by attacking the rapist or having him arrested. All of these possibilities are glossed over in that nationalist discourse which subordinates class, feminist, and formal and aesthetic considerations to a racial-cultural nationalist agenda.

Moreover, in stark contrast to the racialization of sexual violence evidenced by the Maha Sabha's advertisement in which a virtuous Indian woman is the victim of a hyper-sexualized African "disrespect," Drupatee's song nowhere suggests that the sexual violence is interracial. A further threat that Drupatee's song poses, then, is that it allows for the intolerable suggestion that the "culture of disrespect for women," the predatory masculinity to which the Maha Sabha alludes, may be flourishing *within* the Indian community. The consistent displacement in conservative cultural nationalist discourses of the problem of *intra*-racial rape in favor of a focus on *inter*racial rape, is one of their most troubling features.[22] Unlike such discourses, Drupatee's song does not permit the question of violence against

Indo-Trinidadian women to be definitively displaced on to African men. Perhaps, then, it is not least Drupatee's disruption of the Maha Sabha's formula (of African men's "disrespect" toward Indian women and Indian men's protection of Indian women) that requires the Indian orthodoxy to denounce Drupatee as inauthentic and impure, a creolized/douglarized Indian woman.

Carnival 2002 saw Drupatee make headlines again with a new song written by the Indo-Caribbean songwriter Kenneth Supersad: "Doh Beat Your Wife," a chutney melody with a slower tempo, sung in a combination of Trinidadian Creole and Hindi. Those who scoffed at the idea that "Lick Down Me Nani" might have any serious content or critique of violence will find that the new song dispels any ambiguity in its explicit treatment of the topic. Moreover, that several lines are direct imperatives in Hindi to batterers, that the instruments of violence are also named *in Hindi* ("bandhook" or gun, "puyaa" or cutlass, and "lathi" or stick), and that "Karma" is evoked, can leave us in little doubt that the perpetrators accused of domestic violence are Indo-Caribbean men.

Although I clearly differ with the Indo-Trinidadian orthodoxy on the value and possibilities of "Lick Down Me Nani," I share its view that the song, and more generally, chutney-soca, participates in a dougla poetics. For, first, chutney-soca's musical form and instruments hybridize Indo- and Afro-Trinidadian musical traditions. Second, chutney-soca intervenes in the historically "African" calypso tent rather than in a separate "Indian" space. Third, if we think of the original sense of dougla as "bastard" or illegitimate, we can think of "Lick Down Me Nani" as articulating a dougla, that is, de-legitimized or disallowed Indian or woman's identity. It is these possibilities that interest me, possibilities I shall elaborate in the conclusion of this essay.

Writing a Dougla Feminism: Ramabai Espinet's "Barred: Trinidad 1987"

One could think of Ramabai Espinet's short story "Barred: Trinidad 1987" as a parallel attempt within the field of literature to push outward from a certain kind of "Indian" space to interrogate the possibilities of a "dougla space." I understand the story as an attempt to renegotiate constructions of Indianness by articulating that which is "barred" from dominant representations of race and sexuality. Like "Lick Down Me Nani," the story does so by addressing the question of violence against women. Exploring this question reveals a different configuration of "us" and "them," demonstrating how the Indian racial community is internally fractured along gender lines. Espinet thus shows the question of "racial interests" and racial enmities to be more complexly gender-inflected than is revealed by the dominant discourses we have seen.

My reading of "Barred" in the following pages will demonstrate considerable overlap with "Lick Down Me Nani," not only in its thematic consideration of violence against women and sexuality, but also in its formal emphasis on ambivalence. However, notwithstanding these similarities, "Barred" has not come under attack or generated the same kinds of debates that "Lick Down Me Nani" and Drupatee have. I tentatively attribute this to the following: First, the story's high literariness and its publication in North America rather than in Trinidad limit its audience in the latter to a small group of intellectuals. Drupatee, on the other hand, has vast popular appeal, and therefore makes a different kind of impact. Furthermore, her song's irreverent humor contrasts strongly with the aura of gravity in "Barred," an aura that might lend it a certain legitimacy and weight. But perhaps more importantly, whereas "Lick Down Me Nani" (and by extension chutney-soca) enacts its dougla poetics and contestation of Indianness in a space often understood simultaneously as African and national, "Barred" stages its dougla poetics in literature, a medium that is not understood to be exclusively the cultural capital of Indo- or Afro-Trinidadians. Thus, neither Espinet's nor her narrators' "Indianness" is ever in question in the way that Drupatee's and chutney-soca's "Indianness" are. What this suggests is that notwithstanding the overlaps in content of the two texts, their different genres and media might be partly responsible for their different receptions. In turn, this might signal different possibilities for a dougla poetics in the fields of literature and music.[23]

"Barred" unfolds as a series of discrete first-person narratives by unnamed Indo-Trinidadian narrators. Each narrative consists of an act of remembering that raises questions of belonging and identity. I will provide a brief sketch of each narrative before more substantially engaging the story as a whole.

The first narrative refers to three national spaces: Trinidad, India, and Canada. The narrator is an urban person, possibly a writer, since she lists paper as one of her belongings. The story begins with her jamming a chair against the door to prevent an intruder from entering her room at night; she has lost her keys and her wallet. Their loss occasions the memory of her recurrent fantasy of losing her keys and wallet, "a fantasy of being locked out and thrown absolutely upon my own primary resources" (80). Unable to sleep, she looks out at the Trinidadian landscape from her balcony and tries to identify her relationship to it.

For the narrator of the second section, the question of identity is neither so central nor so ambiguous. She begins by stating: "I am an Indian, plain and simple, not East nor West, just an Indian. I live in the West" (81). She recalls a life of fear, poverty, and physical abuse of herself and her child by her drunken husband, and narrates the events of the night she killed her husband.

The third narrative is occasioned by the sight and smell of burning canefields. The narrator associates the "live sugar smell of burning cane" with holidays, and recalls eating sweets at the "Ramdillah, later corrected to Ramleela" (83).[24] Her observation about the relationship of the Trinidadian Hindi word to the Indian Hindi word leads to a meditation on speaking and the unspeakable in a hybridized Indian culture. If the previous narrator noted that her "travel across the water to this land has not been easy" (81), this one observes that "it has not been a happy arrival" (83). She refers to the weed-killer with which Indians often committed suicide, and to the cruel naming of the weed-killer as "Indian tonic." Starting with "Indian tonic," she runs through a litany of stereotypes of Indians, their wealth, food, clothes, education, and corruption.

The fourth section begins with the birth of a nineteen-year-old narrator's second child. The narrator recounts her descent into poverty caused by the addition to the family and by her husband's taking to drink and gambling after being fired from his job. She describes how she emerged from poverty: One day, her husband accidentally left behind a full pack of cigarettes; she put the cigarettes on an upside-down empty tin in the window facing the road, and somebody bought them. With the money from the sale of the pack of cigarettes—meager capital indeed—she bought food, and some sweets with the change; then she sold the sweets. That was how she began to keep shop.

The narrator of the last section, which is only six lines long, is the same as the narrator of the first. She describes the sweet sound of rainfall, and recalls: "when you lie with someone under the sheets in a safe bed while rain pelts down on the roof above, there is no other experience on earth like that." The story ends with daybreak: "It is Sunday morning. I have lived through the long night" (85).

"Barred" thus consists of several fragmented stories of survival, of fragile shelters from adversity. It locates these shelters in different spaces: a room, a hotel room, a lepayed hut, a parlor, a shop, a canefield, a city, an island, a (sub)continent. The fragility of each of these shelters lies not only in the fact that one might lose them, but even more so in the fact that the line between shelter and prison is so thin. The story explores the many meanings of being "barred": barred from what? barred in to what? barred in by whom? The narrator of the first section bars herself in for her own safety, and yet the decision to bar herself in is not freely made; it is a choice made under threat of assault. Thus, while these shelters can represent security and relative safety, they can also represent incarceration and isolation.

It is the tension in the story between safety and incarceration that leads to the first narrator's contradictory longing for the door to open and fear that it will open. Owning those keys gives her control over a space, yet she fantasizes about losing the keys. She has this to say about her fear/fantasy of intrusion:

> And that impulse [to throw away my keys] has resurfaced over and over. All at once it happens without my consciously trying. All night long I hear a key turning in the lock downstairs, heavy footfalls on the stairs—an intruder confident and careless—what does this mean? And if someone has been dogging my footsteps and now possesses my keys, not to mention my wallet, what will I do when he appears? (81)

The passage reveals the ambivalence she feels toward the intrusion: "What does it mean?" And "what will I do?" Her own unease and recurrent worries contrast with an intruder imagined as "confident and careless." The keys that gave her a modicum of control over a space and a sense of safety may now be in the possession of someone else, thereby transferring command of the situation to him. That she does not necessarily *own* the keys or the room emphasizes the very limited control the keys give her. Still, while they assure her of no permanent or absolute security, she is yet more vulnerable to attack without them. Hence, she prepares herself to resist violence: she has insect repellent, a rape alarm, and a walking stick to protect herself from attack, and she reassures herself that she owns nothing that would be valuable to a thief. And yet, her wait for the door to open is both fearful and hopeful: "And, in between the waiting and his forced entry, I might die before the night is out of nerve-racking loneliness and anguish. All my loves, fights, anxieties, and fears have crystallized into this mournful night where I am reduced to a purple jellyfish-like consistency. I can't sleep" (81). Weighed down by the loneliness of her fortification, she longs for "footfalls of love" (85) instead of the threatening, "heavy footfalls" (81) of an intruder; she longs for some choice other than that between isolation and rape ("forced entry"). The narrative desire for sexual pleasure combined with the narrative fact of sexual violence parallels Drupatee's song; both evoke a social context in which violence permeates sexual relations.

Both texts also grapple with the difficulty of working toward new names from within the space of the formula or stereotype. It is in part the very inability of the narrator in "Barred" to name her loves, fights, anxieties, and fears, her inability to give them shape and solidity, that "reduces" her to "a jellyfish-like consistency":

> I can't sleep. And then I rise and throw open the doors to my balcony high above the ground. I look up at the peaks of the Northern Range—Morne Wash and El Tucuche. Unto the hills do I lift up my longing eyes. Only I have no idea what I'm longing for, or if I do, it's still only an apprehension of something. I'm trying to approach closure, which for me is the completion of the whatever which is necessary for living, and which remains like a door perpetually, uneasily, left ajar. (81)

Burdened by a frustrated desire to name and define, the narrator yearns for a narrative that can rest and that allows her to rest. What she desires, then, is certainty and closure, an end to her doubts. Instead, her narrative is marked by an ambiguous vocabulary, ambiguous grammar, and an ambiguous voice with ambiguous agency. And yet, certainty might return her to the claustrophobic space of the stereotype. We are thus returned to the narrator's fantasy of losing her keys and being unable to lock her door. The narrative, then, remains ambivalently divided between openness and closure; the figure of an uneasily ajar door—part open, part closed—captures the structural tension in the story as a whole.[25]

The narrative unease about leaving that door open can be understood as unease about what lies on the other side of that door: an intruder, and a Trinidadian landscape that demands that the narrators place themselves in relation to that landscape as well as in relation to an "elsewhere": India and Canada. The first narrator achieves a provisional resolution to her dilemma by jamming shut the front door, but opening up the door to her balcony, thereby opening her space out onto the Trinidadian landscape. The semi-protected, semi-private space of the balcony is that half-way space, half-open and half-closed; it offers something between complete vulnerability and complete isolation. Similarly, the hotel room offers a space poised between the public and the private.

"Barred" certainly raises many questions about the identity of the intruder, and this uncertainty may account for part of the ambivalence toward him/her. In contrast, in dominant racial discourse the intruder or enemy is always clearly defined: it is the other majority race. Hence, for Killer and Lord Superior, the intruder is the Indian. For the Maha Sabha and the UNC, the enemy is African government and cultural assimilation; the danger is in opening the door to Creole culture. But "Barred" raises the question of whether there are other, equally dangerous intruders from whom the narrators are not protected, even if the narrators erect barriers against Creole culture. The first narrator is prepared with her rape alarm and insect repellent to protect herself from an unknown intruder/intruders. (Note the vagueness with which the assailant is referred to in the sentence: "I have no idea, but under my bed I keep a tin of insect repellent which I am told is good for spraying in their eyes.") But the woman in the second narrative is attacked not by an unknown intruder or a member of another race, but by her husband. He is an intruder she had not locked out; perhaps he has locked her in. Like the previous narrator, she too is certain that an enemy exists, but is uncertain of its identity: ". . . waiting, waiting—waiting to make the next move. There is fear, poverty, and sometimes a heavy hand striking at night. The enemy waits outside. Who is the enemy? Is it rum? The boy I married turns into a strange man who hits and curses at night" (81–82). His drunken, heavy footfalls (comparable to those of the intruder in the first section) are threatening; his boot is heavy (81) as he kicks her and knocks her down. Unlike in the calypso "Indian People with Creole Name," here the Indian man "knocks down" not "nigger people," but a woman of his own race; in this story, the competition for survival takes place between an Indian man and an Indian woman. And just as the previous narrator's longing to "lie with someone under the sheets in a safe bed" (85) existed in the context of the threat of rape and assault, so too does the violence of the second section culminate in the "Slumberking," where the narrator finally kills her drunken husband. In this manner, the second narrative also achieves a resolution of sorts: the narrator makes her bed a "safe bed," thus shutting the door on one threat to her survival. But like the first narrator's longing memory of lying peacefully in bed with someone, this story highlights the tension between safety and isolation: she has gained a safe bed, but not a shared bed. "The man dead" (83), and his death is part—and only part—of the "completion of the whatever which is necessary for living."

The third narrative begins with the sensual pleasure of the scent of sugarcane:

> All around us the cane fires are burning—rising and falling, smoke and soot. Nothing on earth has the live sugar smell of burning cane. And when the cane-sugar boils in the vats the smell is like all the holidays rolled into one fragrant ball—amber and crystalline on the outside and

> full of honeyed liquid in the center. We bought those balls at the Ramdillah, later corrected to Ramleela. (83)

This is the narrative that opens most fully out onto a public space, a landscape, a collective. Perhaps it is significant, then, that this narrative is the least explicitly marked by gender. (Indeed, it is only in the context of the other three narratives and on account of the absence of a gender-neutral third-person singular pronoun in English that I have chosen to refer to this narrator as a woman.) Perhaps the most unguarded and exuberant moment in the story, the cited passage provides the only "we" that is momentarily secure, even if in the next clause it fractures internally again, and again faces assault from the outside.

"Barred" goes on to bring together in one section a compelling, contradictory, and occasionally comical discourse that alludes to the murders and suicides that have long been part of the cultural vocabulary about Indians in Trinidad. Stories abound of indentured laborers who committed suicide by drinking weed-killer, Indian men who murder their wives for adultering with African men, and star-crossed Indian lovers:

> Indians ain't have no backbone, no stamina. You ain't see how at the slightest sign of stress they does run and drink Indian tonic? (Boy meets and loves girl but the arranged marriage gets in the way. Boy and girl drink GRAMAZONE and perish together—desire literally burning a hole through their bowels.) Indians ain't fraid to die. They does kill easy too. Is because they believe in reincarnation, don't doubt it. If you look in the hospitals is mostly Indians you go see. They there for accident, chopping and poor guts. Is all the dhal and bhaji[26] they eat. And all the time the bitches and them have all kinda money hide up and save up. Yuh see all them sadhu and babu all yuh see walking the streets. Them is millionaires, man, millionaires. How you think Indians have so much business in this country? Them controlling the business community, you know, is only me and you stupid enough to think is white people. We born yesterday, we can't see what in front of we eye. Them controlling ninety-five percent of the business in this country. They smart too bad. And all they children does do is study, study. I went to school with plenty Cramlal Booksingh and them you hear. And when they can't get in the good schools they does bribe the man, bribe. Even in the university they does buy the test paper. Is true they don't have no big job and money, but them people low, they ain't bong for that. They ain't know how to live, they don't even spend money on food. Is only dhal and bhaji day and night. (83–84)

This is the available popular Afro-Trinidadian racial discourse about Indians. It brings all the familiar cultural markers of Indianness tumbling out: the timid, cowardly, wily and deceitful Indian, the miserly millionaire dressed like a poor man who eats simple and strange food, the brilliant student, the get-ahead mentality, and above all, the rich man.[27]

If dominant racial discourse, both Afro- and Indo-Trinidadian, works within the logic of the stereotype, "Barred" is acutely conscious of the *assault* of these stereotypes, and tries to rewrite existing discourses of Indianness. In light of the stubborn social and textual motif of the wealthy Indian, I read the key and wallet in the story as metonyms for ownership of private property and money. Read thus, the Indian narrator's fantasy of losing her keys and her wallet can be understood as a desire to break out of the symbolic space to which Indians are confined. Also, the second narrative presents us with an Indian space, an Indian family/home which is clearly oppressive and from which the narrator seeks relief. Thus, if the Indian space is familiar and can provide a limited sense of community and belonging, it can also oppress, as the unhappy brooding about identity and the intense violence of the narratives reveal. That is perhaps one reason that the narrator fantasizes not about locking herself in but about "being locked out and thrown absolutely upon my own primary resources" (80). What she seeks, then, are not the stereotypical resources of the Indian community, but the chance to remake herself using her own "primary resources." One goal of the story is thus to articulate a different Indian identity, one which makes room for Indian women.

One way the story does this is by disrupting some of those stereotypes we read. The woman of the second narrative, for instance, does not fit the image of the submissive Indian wife who takes endless abuse, nor is it she who is killed by a jealous Indian husband; she kills him to end her abuse. Similarly, the first narrator who keeps the tin of insect repellent as a weapon for survival significantly rewrites the stereotype of the Indian who commits suicide by drinking Gramazone. Moreover, contrary to popular opinion, the narrators of at least three sections are very poor. The first points out that "[t]he valuables were pretty meager: a bit of makeup, a few dollars, the key to a shabby little room" (80). The second narrator is not only poor, but is inserted into a history of poverty: "My travel across the water to this land has not been easy and many a time I have squatted in this or that lepayed hut, a few coins knotted in the corner of my ohrni" (81).[28] And we know that the third narrator has nothing but a stolen pack of cigarettes and a few empty Klim tins that mark her infant's hunger. Contrary to the popular images of Indians, her introduction to the field of commerce is marked by desperation rather than avarice. And it is desperation caused in part by her thrift*less* husband, who spends his time drinking and gambling. When she does become a shopkeeper, she is a far cry from the archetypal Ram Kirpalani—not only because she is a woman, but also because her modest shop hardly represents a transformation from rags to riches. Perhaps it is in the context of this history of poverty that we can read the fact that, her fantasies notwithstanding, the first narrator does not actually throw away her valuables. "The valuables were pretty meager: a bit of makeup, a few dollars, the key to a shabby room in a little hotel. But what would I have done without them?" (80). And more, what would she have done without her walking stick, rape alarm and insect repellent? There is a very obvious way in which these belongings secure survival.

The image of the key captures the tense relationship between belonging and belongings.[29] The key is a sign that the room/space belongs *to* the narrator, as well as a sign that, unlike the intruder, *she* belongs in the room. The story is, however, attentive to the tenuousness of both belonging and belongings: as we have seen, the first narrator's key is to a rented hotel-room; she is more a transient tenant than an owner; nor are the shopkeeper's belongings and wealth secure; rather, her accession to her new role as shopkeeper results from desperation to feed her baby, and a chance occurrence (her husband's leaving his cigarettes behind). Yet it is through those meager belongings—a few empty tins and a packet of cigarettes—that she locates herself with respect to the space outside her home, and takes up a place as part of the community.[30] Significantly, the cigarettes are the local Trinidadian brand "Anchor," a word which suggests how they serve to locate her or root her in the landscape. It is also a word that evokes the voyage across the seas of Indian indentured labor and suggests that her ship can now come to rest. To use one of the dominant figures of the story: the pack of cigarettes is the key to her participation and fragile belonging in the community.

It is important to remember that her participation in the community is severely limited. The fact that she becomes a shopkeeper does not necessarily mean that she participates in other aspects of community life. The open window that serves as the shop window functions rather like the open balcony door in the first narrative; it both lets in a non-Indian world and provides some protection against it; it is a space that is both public and private as well as one implicated in the market. Indeed, the price she pays for her survival and for a "way out" of her poverty is being "barred in" to the role of Indian shopkeeper. Moreover, while she opens a window to a multiracial community by selling cigarettes to a "Negro gentleman" and learning how to bake cakes to sell from a Creole woman, it is primarily in their capacity as people implicated in commodified consumption that she has access to them. "People came and bought in my little parlor" (85). It is only as clients that their race ceases to matter; their exchange is confined to the commercial. Thus, on the one hand, survival for this woman comes not from barring herself in, but from opening out onto the community, but on the other hand, she "belongs" to the community only insofar as she confines herself to the role of shopkeeper.[31]

The passage where the Creole woman teaches the narrator how to bake cakes, however, suggests the possibility of an interracial community of working-class women. The interaction between the Creole woman and the Indian narrator provides the only instance of interaction between races that is neither fraught with danger nor limited to commercial exchange. It is in the context of the gender and class equality of the two women that contact is reconciled with safety; the unequal situation within the marriages the narrative describes makes it impossible to achieve safe communication purely on the basis of racial identity.

If "Barred" grapples throughout with the terms of belonging, it also grapples with the terminology of belonging, and registers the inadequacy of that terminology.

> We bought those balls at Ramdillah, later corrected to Ramleela. Which one is right, what the books now say or what we uttered in the peasant newness of this settlement? We are lost here, have not found the words to utter our newness, our strangeness, our unfound being. Our clothes are strange, our names are strange. And it is not possible for anyone to coax or help us. Our utterance can only come roaring out of our mouths when it is ready, set, and can go. (83)

The passage points to the absence of an adequate vocabulary of Indianness and belonging. In terms of the relationship between belonging and belongings, one might say the narrator expresses the need for a language that belongs to her and allows her to belong in it. At the moment, however, she says: "we are lost"; the words are lost; the key to our identity is lost; her quest, then, is for her "unfound being." The passage thus recalls the uncertain vocabulary of the first narrative.

Indeed, the entire story is held together by a profound sense of waiting and anticipation: "Our utterance can only come roaring out of our mouths when it is ready, set, and can go." Similarly, the second narrator speaks of "waiting, waiting—waiting to make the next move." And the first narrator speaks of "the waiting"—to discover the identity of the intruder, and to discover how she will react to him. Will she find the words to write on the paper she keeps? Above all, whose "being" is unfound and whose is found? For a narrative that has so problematized community, the "us," "we," and "our" of this passage seem to stage a *fantasy* of security, for the identity, as well as the security, of the community is uncertain. The "we" could refer to Indians, to Indo-Trinidadians, to Indo-Trinidadian women, or to poor Indo-Trinidadian women. In the sentence, "We bought those balls at Ramdillah, later corrected to Ramleela," *who* corrected the word? Was it someone from within or without the community implied by "we"? And what construction of Indianness is legitimized when "Ramdillah" is "corrected" to "Ramleela"? The passage associates "Ramdillah" with a dialect of Hindi and with the speech of peasants; moreover, it associates "Ramdillah" with the speech of peasants *in Trinidad* ("the peasant newness of this settlement"). "Ramleela," on the other hand, is the "pure," Sanskritized version of the word, institutionalized through the book in Trinidad by priests, scholars, and political conservatives (together symbolized, perhaps, by the Maha Sabha). "Ramleela," then, represents the hegemonic form of Indian cultural nationalism in Trinidad. The tension between "Ramdillah" and "Ramleela," then, metonymically represents the struggle within the *Indian* community over how Indianness will be defined, and by whom.

On the Possibilities of a Dougla Poetics

The issue staged in Espinet's story as well as in the Drupatee debate, then, is which utterances will be heard, recorded, and valued: peasant's, priest's, or entrepreneur's, low caste or high caste, oral or written, pure or hybrid, masculinist or feminist. "Barred" and "Lick Down Me Nani" attempt to carve out a space of contestation from within available formulae, for the logic of the stereotype is too deeply entrenched for simple refusal to be an option; rather, both texts engage, contest, and re-configure stereotypes. Moreover, both texts struggle to articulate alternatives barred from dominant racial representations, alternatives other than "isolation or rape," "insularity or assimilation," "no exchange or commercial exchange," "stereotype or silence," serving as witnesses to the inadequacy of dominant vocabularies of "Indianness" and "belonging" (whether to Trinidad or the "Mother Culture"). Indeed, they challenge both the "separateness" and the "equality" of the purists' "separate but equal" formula by showing how purist racial identities and constructions of the Mother Culture repress the problem of gender and class inequalities within the Indo-Trinidadian community and de-legitimize many identities and cultural possibilities as "un-Indian." Part of their struggle against the stereotype, then, is a struggle against the narrowing of the range of meanings of Indianness.

However, if a dougla poetics plays a key role in articulating a third alternative to opposing stereotypes, neither "Barred" nor "Lick Down Me Nani" represents an unqualified endorsement of a dougla space. Rather, as I have argued, both texts remain marked by a fundamental ambivalence. In "Lick Down Me Nani," the violence can be read as constituting both feminist and masculinist transgression. Similarly, in "Barred," both the purist "Indian" space and the douglarized "outside" space are marked by violence; shutting the door *and* opening the door both risk violence. Against the enforced segregation of the plantation, "Barred" explores the limited possibilities of the space afforded by the shop, the balcony, and the Creole woman's house; so, too, does "Lick Down Me Nani" carve out a very uneasy space for feminist critique. If one consequence of my readings of "Barred" and "Lick Down Me Nani" is a privileging of ambiguity and ambivalence, it is because in the context of the erasures and simplifications of cultural nationalist discourse and in the light of the fragile emergence of a dougla discourse, to borrow a phrase from novelist Fiona Cheong, "ambiguity may be the only precision there is."[32] Ambiguity offers a *mode of entrance* which "Barred" craves. An exploratory politics and poetics cannot afford the closure of meaning.

My claims for the two texts I have read at length are strengthened if one situates Drupatee's dougla poetics in relation to a minor history in which the figure of the dougla has served as a means to rethink cultural hybridity in relation to projects of political equality and critiques of the racialized national-bourgeoisies. The Mighty Dougla's 1961 calypso "Split Me in Two" is one early example that ruefully recounts the position of douglas in a society marked by black/Indian political division. In both his stage-name and his song, the Mighty Dougla resists both the characterization of "dougla" as raceless and the pressure to choose one race or the other. Nearly thirty years later, Delamo's "Soca Chutney" (1989) uses the figure of the dougla to refuse "divide and rule" politics:

> Mix a bassman from Laventille
> With a dhantal from Caroni[33] . . .
>
> Now who come to divide and rule
> Eh go use we as no tool

Any time they comin' racial
I dougla, I staying neutral. (qtd. in Constance 43)

Delamo's song deploys popular and official expressions of Trinidad as a land of harmonious mixing, drawing on the motto "all o' we is one," and on popular formulations of Trinidad as a festive party. But he inflects those images in a particularly Indian way. For instance, he replaces the "callaloo" as an image of harmonious diversity with that of "chutney" and "dhal curry." His treatment of the "racelessness" of the dougla also plays with dominant constructions of the dougla. But the dougla's racial "neutrality" in "Soca Chutney" is the very opposite of political neutrality. The song clearly recognizes contemporary race politics as an opportunistic continuation of colonial "divide and rule" policies. Where the Mighty Dougla refuted dominant race politics by insisting that he had not one but two races, Delamo refutes dominant politics using its own vocabulary of "racelessness"; he opposes racial neutrality to racial polarization; his recourse to the language of racial "neutrality" thus attempts to neutralize a divisive discourse. What we see in the years between the Mighty Dougla's "Split Me in Two" and Delamo's "Soca Chutney" is a shift from articulating an anxious dougla identity to articulating a celebratory one.

Similarly, Bally's song "Dougla" fuses Afro- and Indo-Trinidadian musical vocabularies, and explicitly refers to the dougla as a figure for the linked interests of the majority of Afro- and Indo-Trinidadians:

Dougla—a mutual link, absolute bond, the symbol of unity
The hope for him, the hope for her, the hope for you and me.

More recently, in the 1996 Carnival, Brother Marvin's "Jahaji Bhai" employs rhythms and instruments deriving from India and Africa, to make a claim for Indian and African unity based on their shared conditions of entrance into Trinidad and the impossibility of separating out those two histories:

The indentureship and the slavery
Bind together two race in unity
...For those who playing ignorant
Talking 'bout true African descendant
If yuh want to know the truth
Take a trip back to yuh roots
And somewhere on that journey
You go see a man in a dhoti
Saying he prayers in front of a jhandi.[34]

The song ends with the refrain: "Let us live under one sky / As 'Jahaji Bhai'."

The Hindustani phrase *jahaji bhai*, meaning brothers or brotherhood of the boat, has historically referred to the relationships forged on the Fatel Rozack and later ships that brought Indian indentured labor to Trinidad. Brother Marvin's song, however, deploys the phrase to inscribe a broader brotherhood, one that is also forged in history rather than underwritten by race or assured by blood. Moreover, I contend that "Jahaji Bhai" is also a rewriting of Black Stalin's controversial 1979 calypso "Caribbean Unity," a call for unity based on a black nationalist vision of the Caribbean as the inheritance of the descendants of slaves:

> Dem is one race—De Caribbean Man
> From de same place—De Caribbean Man
> That make the same trip—De Caribbean Man
> On the same ship—De Caribbean Man."[35]

Whereas Black Stalin's Caribbean unity was achieved through an implicit exclusion of Indians, "Jahaji Bhai," in its conjoining of Indian journeys across the *kala pani* and African journeys across the middle passage, refutes Black Stalin's purist history with a dougla history.

I have tried to outline the political reasons for the popular and academic erasure of what we might call dougla histories. In order to further specify, elaborate, and delimit the possibilities of a dougla poetics, more scholarship and artistic elaboration of the figure of the dougla is needed. For, at present, the entrenchment of racialized political discourse in Trinidad is such that simple disidentification with it does not seem a strategically sound option. Instead, negotiating and reconfiguring racial discourse seems necessary. Based on the various examples I have discussed so far, then, what general claims might one make for the political possibilities of a dougla poetics?

I am emphatically not suggesting a dougla poetics as somehow paradigmatic of postcolonial, West Indian, or even Trinidadian aesthetics; indeed, the example of a dougla poetics does not necessarily offer a way of thinking about the place of minority groups such as the Chinese, Syrians, or Lebanese in the national imaginary.[36] Rather, I am making a conjunctural—and conjuncturally circumscribed—claim about the possibilities of a dougla poetics in Trinidad today; to claim more would be to repeat the aggrandizing claims for cultural hybridity I have critiqued, and to forget that any political project or aesthetics can be co-opted.

It is also likely that a dougla poetics offers different possibilities and faces different challenges in the fields of literature and music: Certainly, dougla poetics has generated much less controversy in the field of literature. For this there are probably several reasons, to which I have alluded earlier: literature in Trinidad has a relatively small audience in comparison to music; its popular impact is therefore significantly narrower. But perhaps more importantly, in the context of an ethnic politics which has entailed the "objectification" and "commodification of ethnicity" (Yelvington, "Introduction" 11), music is often seen as part of the cultural capital of particular ethnic groups; blurring the ethnic boundaries of the music therefore potentially risks both a loss of cultural capital and its appropriation by the culturally dominant group. In contrast, in the field of literature, although particular authors might be seen as ethnic cultural capital, the literary genres of the novel, short story, and poem are not so clearly marked as African or Indian, and can therefore escape some of the controversies around hybrid music.

In the field of literature, one might begin with C.L.R. James's *Minty Alley*, the first novel I know of in which the dougla ethnicity of one of the characters is understood as causally relevant to the action; its racial portrait of the dougla is, however, by no means revisionary or affirmative. Other literary attempts to negotiate dominant constructions of race and gender in a way that fits with the kind of project I have outlined include the work of Earl Lovelace, Sam Selvon, Ismith Khan, Ramabai Espinet, and Rajkumari Singh's manifesto-like "I am a Coolie."[37] Arising out of the Mauritian experience of Indian indeturedship, Khal Torabully's conception of "coolitude," like Singh's "I am a Coolie" and my own arguments for a dougla poetics, revalues and appropriates a previously pejorative term.[38] According to Torabully, "[c]oolitude also seeks to emphasize the community of visions between the slave and the indentured labourer, shared by their descendants, despite the fact that these two groups, were placed in an situation of competition and conflict" (*Coolitude* 150). With its evocation of a specifically working-class identity, coolitude, like many examples of dougla poetics, also productively distances itself from the potential exoticism and elitism of *indianité*.[39] Returning to the Caribbean, the films of the Trinidadian film-maker Robert Yao Ramesar, and paintings such as Parma and Prabhu Singh's "Brian Lara as Hindu deity" constitute suggestive developments in a dougla aesthetic.

Besides the arts, other areas of inquiry might include: the multiethnic celebration of Indian cultural practices such as Hosay, which, as I have shown, has hybridized not only Hindu and Muslim cultural practices to forge a pan-Indian identity but also Afro- and Indo-Caribbean cultural practices; comparative analyses of barely remembered, overlapping black and Indian histories of regulation by colonial government and joint opposition to it; Indo-Trinidadian worship of and Easter pilgrimages to the black Virgin in Siparia whom they call Sipari Mai;[40] social scientific studies such as those of Khan and Reddock on the experience of douglas; and various attempts at labor organizing across racial lines by James, Rienzi, Butler, Hosein, and the oil and sugar unions.

I have been suggesting that the very anxiety surrounding the figure of the dougla is a measure of its radical possibilities. If creolization as a figure for hybridity has exhausted its radicalism in contemporary Trinidad (leading some to refer ironically to "Afro-Saxon" culture), now serving status quoist class agendas and perhaps racially exclusive ones, and if, as Aisha Khan's work suggests, the fluid hybridity designated "Spanish" is non-threatening in part because it functions as a euphemism for more conflictual identities, then a dougla hybridity might offer some useful alternatives.

The word "dougla" can be thought of as capturing the triple discourse of illegitimacy that has haunted Indo-Caribbean history: the colonial state's policy not to recognize Indian marriages, which therefore deemed Indian children illegitimate (a policy from which several Creole constructions of Indians as outsiders with no legitimate claims upon Trinidad took their cue); independent India's rejection of the requests of some Indo-Caribbeans for repatriation, which rendered Indo-Caribbeans illegitimate children of India; and finally Indo-Caribbeans' own exclusionary and disciplining pejorative that demonizes the mixed descendants of Indo- and Afro-Caribbean as illegitimate. Based on several examples from Trinidadian musical and literary traditions, I suggest that the figure of the dougla and a dougla poetics could provide a vocabulary for disallowed, delegitimized racial identities; furthermore, they could offer ways—and have offered ways—of reframing the problematic of black-Indian party politics as well as race, gender, and sexual relations.

It is, however, undeniable that "dougla" carries many sedimented meanings, not all of which are politically suggestive or progressive. The figure of the dougla often functions in both African and Indian purist discourses, as well as in some pro-PNM discourses, as a codeword for assimilation and racial "dilution."[41] Some of the political usefulness of the term "dougla" arises simply from its bringing into representation and public discourse a repressed reality. Beyond that, the political possibilities of the term will depend on the specific kinds of elaborations and symbologies that emerge in the arts and politics.

However, in a cultural context of marginalization of Indians, I think it important to make visible *as Indian* the Indian elements of a dougla poetics such as chutney-soca's, in other words, to contest rather than acquiesce to assimilationist deployments. This contestation is doubly important because pejorative readings of cultural douglarization all too often name "biological" douglas pejoratively as well; behind anti-assimilationist disavowals of cultural douglarization sometimes lurks a more insidious set of practices of exclusion and de-legitimization directed against "biological" douglas. Anti-(cultural) douglarization, then, can both deploy and mask an underlying racism.

Keeping in mind, then, that the original meaning of the word "dougla" was "bastard," or "illegitimate," I suggest that one might think of a dougla poetics as a means for articulating potentially progressive cultural projects de-legitimized by both the Afro-Creole dominant culture and the Indian "Mother Culture." For, first, as against purist racial discourse, the figure of the dougla draws attention to the reality of interracial contact; it names a contact that already exists. Second, a dougla poetics can provide a rich symbolic resource for interracial unity, as it does in Bally's soca-chutney melody "Dougla" and in Brother Marvin's "Jahaji Bhai." To break the stranglehold of the racial politics of the PNM and the UNC, any egalitarian politics clearly needs to emphasize the shared histories of oppression of Afro- and Indo-Trinidadians, just as it needs to articulate their economic advancement in non-exclusive racial terms. What distinguishes a dougla hybridity at this conjuncture from liberal multiculturalist tropes of hybridity such as callaloo, "Spanish," and, arguably, Creole, is the ability of the term to place cultural hybridity in relation to equality, and the potential of a dougla poetics to unmask power and symbolically redraw its lines. A dougla poetics thus offers a vocabulary for a political identity, not a primarily biological one.

Moreover, in its confusion of stereotypes, a dougla poetics could elaborate alternative discourses of femininity, as it does in Drupatee's "Lick Down Me Nani." On the one hand, it seems important to caution that we have no reason to think a dougla identity would *necessarily* be any less masculinist than existing racial identities; however, on the other hand, because constructions of race are gendered in very particular ways, the dougla's potential disruption of dominant racial stereotypes could provide an opportunity for specifically feminist contestations of dominant gender and race imagery. Whether such discursive resistances translate into a specifically oppositional politics cannot be predicted in advance. Elaborating a dougla poetics offers no guarantees, then, but it does offer a symbolic *resource* in the reconfiguration of racial and gender identities.

The unstable and diverse functions of different mobilizations of a dougla hybridity caution against making inflationary generalizations, and point instead to the need for more careful contextual and conjunctural claims for cultural hybridity. My purpose here, then, is not to set up a dougla identity or a dougla poetics as some kind of "ideal" hybridity; rather, I have tried to shift the kinds of questions we ask about cultural hybridity and to historicize our answers. I offer my exploration of a dougla poetics, therefore, as but one of many possible elaborations and experiments whose goal is to analyze the poetics and politics of cultural hybridity and to interrogate the articulations and disarticulations between them.

Notes

Introduction

1. I include in the Caribbean not only the islands of the Caribbean archipelago but the circum-Caribbean coasts of the mainland Americas, which were characterized by plantation and slave societies; thus, parts of Brazil, Mexico, Guyana, and other mainland nations are included in my discussion. Although I have made a conscious effort not to generalize on the basis of the English-speaking Caribbean, and have drawn on the discursive histories of hybridity in the French and Spanish Caribbean, my linguistic competence does not extend to all of the region's numerous colonial, indigenous, and contact languages. Regrettably, this study repeats Caribbean Studies' marginalization of the Dutch Caribbean—a marginalization that arises from the number of local Dutch Caribbean contact/languages, the paucity of translations, and the Netherlands' own relative marginality to the centers of European power. I also dwell only briefly in this book on the large diasporic Caribbean populations and hybridities. Both these omissions are corrected in Puri, ed., *Marginal Migrations: The Circulation of Cultures within the Caribbean*.
2. *The Predicament of Culture* 173. Conversely, García Canclini, writing from within the discipline of Latin American Studies, writes "All cultures are frontier cultures."
3. For an argument that shares my critique, see Mimi Sheller, "Theoretical Piracy on the High Seas of Global Culture."
4. Nor did this usage die with the nineteenth century. In South Africa, the rhetoric of pluralism often operated as a code word for apartheid. In the context of tensions between Afro- and Indo-Caribbean populations in the present-day Caribbean, the invocation of "pluralism" by some conservative cultural nationalists is also a euphemism for "separate but equal." (See chapters six and seven.) Although the emphasis today may have shifted from racial to cultural hybridity, the distinctions between race and culture—or for that matter between race and ethnicity—are far from secure. See Young 53–54, 88, 92–93.

5. To the extent that hybridity and homosexuality were related in discourse, it was as two forms of degeneration (Young 26).
6. See also Coombes 221. Begun in 1990, my study shares the spirit and hopes to complement the work of Coombes, Shohat, and Young; Stallybrass and White's *The Poetics and Politics of Transgression*, a study of English popular culture from the seventeenth century on, which treats transgression as a phenomenon of the hybridization of high and low culture; Pratt's *Imperial Eyes*, which discusses cultural and generic hybridization in the "arts of the contact zone" in a context of unequal relations of power; Fraser's *Justice Interruptus*, which examines the relationship of difference and inequality; Brah and Coombes, eds., *Hybridity and its Discontents* and Werbner and Madood, eds., *Debating Cultural Hybridity*.
7. For examples of transnationalist theory, see Boehmer and Moore-Gilbert, eds. Brennan, *At Home in the World*, Featherstone, ed., Grewal and Kaplan, Robbins, Rediker and Linebaugh, and Spivak's "Culture" in *Toward a Critique of Postcolonial Reason*. In my thinking, transnational corporations, the Internet, CNN, MTV, movements such as Pan-Africanism and the pan-Americanism of the Latin American modernists, the EZLN's transnationally aided nationalism, identities such as "South Asian," and the organization "Doctors without Borders" that represents an active attempt to cross in solidarity borders whose power it recognizes, all constitute examples of transnationalism. See "Encancaranublado," a short story by the Puerto Rican feminist writer Ana Lydia Vega, for insight into the tense coexistence of transnational regional Caribbean solidarities and nationalist Caribbean rivalries.

   For examples of post-nationalism, see Albrow, Appadurai, Guéhenno, and Ohmae. When post-nationalism is simply an orientation—that is a desire or a program, but not a description of an existing reality—then it approaches the transnationalism with which I have no quarrel. For key positions developed in classical marxism on the status of the nation, see Marx, Lenin, Stalin, Trotsky, and Luxemburg. For other debates informed by marxism, see Fanon; James, *The Black Jacobins*; Nairn; Poulantzas; Eagleton, "Nationalism"; and Jameson, "Conclusion," *The Political Unconscious*. On the core-periphery model see World-Systems and Dependency School Theory (Wallerstein et al.; Gunder Frank, Rodney, Amin); for a marxist critique of Third Worldism that reads the Non-Aligned Movement in terms of a politics of communist containment, see Ahmad, chapter 8. For an argument that appropriates "cosmopolitanism" from the traditionally pejorative value given it by nationalists, see Robbins, "Comparative Cosmopolitanisms" and *Feeling Global*. For overviews of Marxist debates on the subject of nationalism, see Tom Bottomore, *A Dictionary of Marxist Thought*.
8. Recounted in Vincent, "The Future of the Debate" 180.
9. For excellent and accessible overviews of the economic debates, fuller than the brief summary I offer here, see Kiely, "Introduction" and

chapter 2, to which this section is indebted; Golding and Harris, eds., Klak, ed., Harvey, "Globalization in Question," and Alan Scott, ed.

10. UNCTAD 1995, qtd. in Kiely 49. The ten nations that accounted for 68 percent of Direct Foreign Investment in the Third World in the early 1990s: Singapore, Mexico, Brazil, China, Hong Kong, Malaysia, Egypt, Argentina, Thailand and Taiwan (*New Internationalist*, qtd. in Kiely 49). The Asian tigers' rise to prominence in the global market, moreover, is in part the result of a strongly planned and protected *national* economy. Employment in Export Processing Zones that are so often invoked as signs of postnationalism typically accounts for about 5 percent of total industrial employment in individual countries, and in many cases less than 10 percent of total manufactured exports originate there (Gereffi and Hempel, Jenkins, qtd. in Kiely 54). Kiely also points out that various transnational free-trade groupings like NAFTA and the EC not only may be subject to national regulations based on considerations of product quality and health regulations, but themselves act as regional protectionist groupings (51).
11. International Organization for Migration and U.N., *World Migration Report 2000* 5, 55. The numbers of migrants within nations presumably would be substantially larger.
12. See Puri, "Introduction," *Marginal Migrations.*
13. UNDP Report cited in *Le Monde Diplomatique*, Paris, November 1998. Qtd. in *World Press Review*, February 1999, 47.
14. Vincent 195; Klak and Conway 259.
15. Vincent 178–181.
16. (*New Internationalist* 1992, qtd. in Kiely 13). These statistics do not, of course, imply uniform levels of consumption or access to wealth within a nation-state; nation-states have always been and continue to be marked by greater or lesser degrees of class inequality. Notwithstanding the increasing gaps between rich and poor within many First World nation-states, their relatively developed infrastructures and welfare safety nets provide some protections against the experience of *mass* poverty that characterizes so many Third World nation-states. The statistics should also not be interpreted to suggest a static situation in the Third World. Clearly, *selected segments* of more and more Third World nations are being incorporated into global communications networks. For instance, in 1996 eight African countries had no Internet access at all; in 1999 only one (Somalia) had none; in 1996, 13 African nations had "full" Internet access; in 1999, 42 did (*Discover* May 1999, 28). Moreover, the Internet has become a crucial resource for many Third World activisms, perhaps most spectacularly the Ejército Zapatista de Liberación Nacional.
17. See Boehmer and Moore-Gilbert, eds., Malkki and Ong (particularly the notion of "flexible citizenship") for the argument that nationalism and internationalism are compatible.
18. See also Kiely's suggestion that we revise our understanding of core and periphery, treating them as effects rather than causes of

the world system (9). So doing avoids simplified notions of intentionality or central planning of the kind that characterized the era of classical imperialism. For other accounts of the hierarchical reinscription of space, see David Harvey, Edward Soja, and Neil Smith.

19. That cultural theory today can continue to declare the nation dead, untroubled by the kind of data I have laid out above, stems in part from skepticism toward empiricist and positivist methodologies. However, this skepticism risks turning into a wholesale disregard for history and political economy. The point of my own invocation of statistics is not to hold them out as incontrovertible truths (indeed, the manipulability of statistics has long been recognized within the social sciences). Rather, I wish to draw upon an early conception of Theory as a transdisciplinary project, a conception that requires one to engage discourses governed by different legitimating rules from those of one's own. Without such engagement and mutual disciplinary interrogation, Theory becomes simply a self-endorsing grand narrative in its own right. To avert such a situation, I further suggest the value of fieldwork for Cultural Studies in the humanities. For the transdisciplinary responsibilities of Theory, see Jameson, "Metacommentary" and Spivak, "Scattered Speculations on the Question of Culture Studies."
20. The second of these questions modifies a question posed by Marcus Rediker in discussion at a Symposium on Linebaugh and Rediker, *The Many Headed Hydra*; University of Pittsburgh, October 4, 2001.
21. Anderson, *Imagined Communities* 14–15. See also Yadav for a productive reframing of the problematic of nationalism in relation to popular struggles for self-determination.
22. See Goodwin's account of both the role of the prerevolutionary Cuban state in generating "popular" support for the Cuban Revolution and the limitations of Cuban statism.
23. Marxist-informed debates about "popular culture" have been central to the emergence of the field of Cultural Studies; see Raymond Williams, Stuart Hall, Colin MacCabe, ed., and the South Asian and Latin American Subaltern Studies groups. "Popular culture is neither, in a 'pure' sense, the popular traditions of resistance to these processes [of moralisation, demoralization, and re-education]; nor is it the forms which are superimposed on and over them. It is the ground on which the transformations are worked" (Hall, "Notes on Deconstructing the Popular" 228). See García Canclini, *Hybrid Cultures* chapters 5 and 6, especially his discussion of different disciplinary conceptions of the popular. According to him, the market prefers "the popular" or better yet, "popularity" to "the people," for "[w]hile the people may be the place tumult and danger, popularity—adhesion to an order, consensus on a system of values—is measured and regulated by opinion polls" (188). Recently the word "popular" has achieved currency in post-marxist circles skeptical of the term "the people." But "the popular" is

no more or less an instrumentalizing and homogenizing fabrication than "the people." In it, "the people" return surreptitiously, displaced, as an adjectivalized noun, notwithstanding the recalibration of agency as product without people.

24. For a similar project, see Klak, ed., *Globalization and Neo-liberalism: The Caribbean Context*. For an account of the historical difficulties such a project faces, see Knight, *The Caribbean: The Genesis of a Fragmented Nationalism*.

Chapter 1 Theorizing Hybridity: The Post-Nationalist Moment

1. My discussion will treat undecidability, radical constructionism, critiques of Reason, and skepticism toward the idea of "totality" as features common to diverse currents of postmodernism and post-structuralism. See, for example, Foucault's advocacy of anti-systemic movements and refusal of the totalization involved in any definite political project (*Foucault Reader* 375–376), Lyotard's famous slogan "Let us wage a war on totality" (82), and Derrida's critique of the metaphysics of presence and "absolute knowledge" (188).
2. This formulation of mine is clearly indebted to Fredric Jameson's conceptions of the political unconscious and national allegory in *The Political Unconscious: Narrative as a Socially Symbolic Act* and "Third World Literature in the Era of Multinational Capitalism" respectively. For critiques of the latter, see Ahmad, Colás, and Larsen.
3. The now institutionalized field of Postcolonial Studies is complicitous in this displacement. For various critical reflections on the "postcolonial" and the politics of the post, see Ahmad, "Literary Postcoloniality"; Appiah; Klor de Alva, "The Postcolonization of Latin American Experience"; Dirlik; Frankenberg and Mani; Lazarus; McClintock; Mignolo; Mishra and Hodge; Quayson, "Postmodernism and Postcolonialism" and *Postcolonialism: Theory, Practice, or Process?*; Radhakrishnan, *Diasporic Mediations*; E. San Juan Jr.; Shohat; Slemon, "Post-colonial Critical Theories"; and Spivak, *A Critique of Postcolonial Reason*.
4. For example, he finds it in his analyses of interdisciplinarity, mimicry, colonial subjectivity, stereotype, and modes of signification in the 1857 Indian Mutiny—the subjects of various essays collected in *The Location of Culture*. Although Bhabha's work has been enormously helpful in opening up our understanding of the operation of political agency beyond intentionalism, his casting of hybridity as a master-trope of formal resistance—notwithstanding his critique of master-narratives—limits that work. For several insightful critiques of Bhabha, see Cheah, Gikandi, "The Location of Culture," Kraniauskas, Lazarus, Loomba, Moore-Gilbert, Parry, Radhakrishnan, *Diasporic*

Mediations, and Young, *White Mythologies*. Unless otherwise stated, all quotations from Bhabha are from *The Location of Culture*. When quoting from his essay "DissemiNation," I occasionally quote from the earlier version which appeared in *Nation and Narration*, since the section on "Cultural Difference" is longer in that earlier version.

5. In fact, Anne McClintock and Rob Nixon take issue with Derrida's account of apartheid in South Africa on grounds that his primarily formal deconstruction of the word "apartheid" ignores the historical conditions of production of discourses of apartheid. See their "No Names Apart: The Separation of Word and History in Derrida's 'Le dernier Mot du Racisme.'" Peter Stallybrass and Allon White's refutation of abstract Saussurean conceptions of difference offers a similar cautionary reminder:

> Whilst it is true that meaning does indeed slip away down a chain of substitutions because of the relational and differential nature of linguistic signs, the smooth metaphor of 'chain' wrongly suggests a certain regularity and equality of the 'links' which make up each different term. On the contrary, the most significant kinds of displacements are across diverse territories of semantic material and always appear to involve steep gradients, even precipitous leaps, between socially unequal discursive domains. (198)

6. "Traddutora, Traditora: A Paradigmatic Figure of Chicana Feminism." For other histories, elaborations and appropriations of the figure of La Malinche, see Cortéz' contemporary, Bernal Díaz del Castillo, *The Conquest of New Spain*; Octavio Paz, *The Labyrinth of Solitude*; and Mary Louise Pratt, "Yo soy la Malinche: Chicana Writers and the Poetics of Ethnonationalism."
7. See, for example, Rendon, *Chicano Manifesto.*
8. For an excellent critique of this tendency in Angloamerican feminisms, see Adrienne Rich, "Notes Toward a Politics of Location" and "North American Tunnel Vision," and Caren Kaplan, "Deterritorializations: The Rewriting of Home and Exile in Western Feminist Discourse" and "The Politics of Location as Transnational Feminist Practice." In my opinion their critiques are applicable to many post-colonial and minority discourses of border-crossing and placelessness.
9. Thus, Robert Young reminds us in his critique of Deleuze and Guattari's celebration of nomadism that "if we recall the enforced dislocations of the peoples of the South, it means that we cannot concur with the idea that 'nomadism' is a radically anti-capitalist strategy; nomadism is, rather, one brutal characteristic mode of capitalism itself" (173). As Doris Sommer puts it, borders may be erected as a deliberate means of installing or maintaining distance (*Proceed with Caution* 9–10). Sherry Ortner's succinct summary of the strengths and pitfalls of borderland perspectives in anthropology applies well to Anzaldúa's

work ("Specifying Agency"). For further analyses of Anzaldúa's work, see Alarcón, Grewal (in *Scattered Hegemonies*), Moya and Hames-García, eds., Pratt, "Soy La Malinche," and the select bibliography in the second edition of *Borderlands/La Frontera*. For some of the few critical accounts of it, see Michaelson and Johnson, eds., *Border Theory: The Limits of Cultural Politics.*

10. See "Introduction," *Nation and Narration.*
11. This formulation was suggested to me by Yadav's observation of the tendency of respected Western theorists of nationalism to construct a typological distinction between "pathological" ethnically heterogeneous Eastern nationalisms and "natural" ethnically homogeneous Western nationalisms (200, 216–217).
12. In "A Question of Survival: Nations and Psychic States," through a reading of Edward Said's *After the Last Sky*, Bhabha develops a discussion of the exiled or diasporic Palestinian situation which brings it into line with his treatment elsewhere of nationalism as an internally and impossibly divided narrative. That the problematic of division and dispersal is necessarily an explicit part of Palestinian national narratives perhaps permits Bhabha the note of tragic pathos he strikes in speaking of the Palestinians. However, the crushing material violence of Israeli occupation goes unacknowledged as a source of the impossibility of Palestinian nationalist success.
13. For some exemplary discussions of Gilroy's work, see the special issue of *Research in African Literatures* edited by Gikandi; *Debating Cultural Hybridity*, many of the essays of which are in dialogue with Gilroy's work; and Lazarus. Since Gilroy has helped inaugurate an entire field, it is impossible to cite all the discussions of his work.
14. For an attempt to counter this tendency by exploring the histories and specificities of intra-Caribbean migratory cultural practices, see Puri, ed., *Marginal Migrations: The Circulation of Cultures within the Caribbean.*
15. Some of Gilroy's specific examples, such as his analysis of Martin Delany's modernizing and civilizing impulses toward Africa, admit and take into account the complex inequalities mediated by the nation-state in the transatlantic world; yet the generalizations he draws tend to repress the implications of these insights. It may well be his close readings rather than his generalizations, then, that provide the most helpful methodological cues for a comparatist transatlanticist project.
16. In 1990, "Éloge de la Créolité" was translated into English as "In Praise of Creoleness." All subsequent citations are to this translation, abbreviated as "Praise." For critical accounts of the work of the Créolistes, see Condé, "Order, Disorder, Freedom"; Glissant, *Caribbean Discourse*; Walcott, "An Open Letter to Chamoiseau"; Dash, *Édouard Glissant*; Britton, *Édouard Glissant and Postcolonial Thought*; Burton, "The Idea of Difference in French West Indian Thought"; and Richard and Sally Price, "Shadowboxing in the Mangrove." For a collection of

influential essays informing pro-independence positions and therefore at odds with *Puerto Rican Jam*, see Zavala and Rodriguez, eds. Not many critiques of *Puerto Rican Jam* have been published to date.

17. The United States invaded Puerto Rico in 1898 and imposed U.S. citizenship in 1917 (which was unanimously rejected by the Puerto Rican Congress at the time). Until 1950, when the United States made Puerto Rico a "commonwealth" of the United States, Puerto Rico was on the United Nations schedule of non-sovereign peoples. There has been widespread sentiment within the United Nations that Puerto Rico remains a colony; moreover, Puerto Rican political parties, bitterly divided on the subject of what relationship Puerto Rico should have to the United States, all agree on one thing: that Puerto Rico today is still a colony of the United States. For such arguments, from ideologically opposed authors, see Carlos Romero Barceló, *La estadidad es para los pobres*; Raymond Carr, *Puerto Rico: A Colonial Experiment*; and José Trías Monge, *Puerto Rico: The Oldest Colony in the World.*

    For a similar set of reasons, Martinique and Guadeloupe officially ended their status as colonies of France, when in 1946 they were made "Overseas Departments" (DOM's) of France. The historical similarities between Puerto Rico and the French DOM's have led to social formations that are comparably contradictory: they are not even nominally independent politically or economically; they hold strategic and symbolic value for the metropolitan states; and they are characterized by little local agricultural or industrial production, dense urban populations, a high standard of living relative to many independent Caribbean islands, and high unemployment offset by large metropolitan transfers. In both islands, the debate is often framed as a problem of balancing economic survival against cultural assimilation by the metropoles.

18. Thus, the multidisciplinary anthology includes feminist and gay critiques of nationalism, critiques of nationalist historiography, a revisionary history of the democratic opportunities enabled by the U.S. invasion, arguments on the advantages of rap and corporate sponsorship over salsa (the musical form preferred by nationalists) and government support of the arts, the advantages of functional bilingualism over Spanish, and the status of the Puerto Rican diaspora in the national imaginary.

19. See, for example, 76 n. 24 for a particularly personal attack on Juan Mari Bras. In the context of the current resurgence of the Right in the United States, Grosfoguel's brief outline of a political–economic platform (72–74) looks far from pragmatic. He argues for a reduced workday; welfare as a form of lumpen resistance to capitalism (in contrast to traditional leftist calls for employment); the legalization and free distribution of addictive drugs; organizing against environmental pollution by claiming autonomy from federal environmental laws (although historically federal environment laws have been stricter than Puerto Rican ones); the elimination of a

federal minimum wage so that it could be increased (suspect for a similar reason); a monorail to resolve Puerto Rico's traffic problem; and a vaguely invoked struggle for women's rights, the only concrete example of which is the creation of child-care centers with joint public and private funding. There may be many things to recommend such a platform, but pragmatic realpolitik is not amongst them. Indeed, the only economist in the anthology, Jaime Benson-Arias, also insists that the current forms of federal transfers and tax incentives cannot be sustained in the medium run, let alone the long run, and argues for the island to become economically self-reliant.

20. Despite the Créolistes' intent to exalt the people by representing and enshrining the masses and popular culture in their writing, the version of Art that embodies the solution seems to be remote from popular participation. In such a context, the Creole woman and keeper of oral histories, who turns out to be "The Source" in Chamoiseau's *Texaco* (in a deliberate contrast to the Négritudinist idea that Africa is the source), is likely to become a version of the traditional female inspirational muse for a eulogizing male author. The people will be protected, represented, and heroically defended by the male author. Although Mother Africa has been replaced by a local Creole woman as The Source, the gender politics of this feminized nation remain similarly conservative, and cultural resistance, far from being a mass movement, risks becoming the preserve of a male elite. Michael Dash has addressed the politics of the Créolistes' shift of emphasis from maroon to writer; Richard and Sally Price have critiqued their gender politics and their claims to represent the people.
21. It might seem that the Créoliste emphasis on the islands as sites of cultural reconstruction and on the Creole language rather than on French places them at odds with *Puerto Rican Jam*'s emphasis on Puerto Ricans in the U.S. mainland and on English and Spanglish. But Spanglish and bilingualism function in *Puerto Rican Jam* in much the same way as Creole does in "Praise": as sites of hybrid resistance to the purism represented by French for the Créolistes and by Spanish for *Puerto Rican Jam*.
22. As with *Puerto Rican Jam* on the topic of independence, the Créolistes shift from the pragmatic belief that the hinterland upon which maroon politics depended is no longer available, making it no longer a viable option, to a vitriolic delegitimation of maroon politics as purist.
23. Bhabha, for example, describes the postcolonial perspective as a break with the sociology of underdevelopment or "dependency" theory, which advanced influential versions of the thesis of cultural imperialism: "As a mode of analysis, it attempts to revise those nationalist or 'nativist' pedagogies that set up the relation of Third World and First World as a structure of opposition" (173). For an account that takes Bhabha to task for transforming Fanon from a theorist of opposition into a theorist of ambivalence, see Lazarus. For variants of the

aforementioned move delegitimizing opposition and the cultural imperialism thesis, see Fuguet, "Magical Neoliberalism?" and Fuguet and Gómez, eds., *McOndo*; Antonio Benítez-Rojo, *The Repeating Island* (for example, page 20); and Howes, ed., *Cross-Cultural Consumption* (for example, 179). A similar logic regards as unfashionably oppositional Ngũgĩ wa Thiong'o's decision to write in Gikuyu, preferring Salman Rushdie's hybridization or "chutnification" of a Global English. My point is both that these individual choices should not be hypostatized and that Ngũgĩ's decision itself could be read more productively not as an essentialist choice, but as an attempt to reach a larger national Gikuyu-speaking public and as an act that involves the mutual hybridization of Gikuyu and English. For a thorough and subtle account of Ngũgĩ's shifting language politics, see Gikandi, *Ngũgĩ wa Thiong'o*. See also the special issue of *Research in African Literatures* on "The Language Question," edited by Bjornson. The most persuasive intellectual critique I have seen of the cultural imperialism thesis is Tomlinson, *Cultural Imperialism*.

24. *A Critique of Postcolonial Reason*.
25. *Outside in the Teaching Machine* 279; see also 64, 278–280 and *A Critique of Post-colonial Reason* 382, 395–396.
26. See, for example, Ann DuCille's polemical account of the relationship of Postcolonial Studies and African American Studies.

Chapter 2 Theorizing Hybridity: Caribbean Nationalisms

1. For a summary of the scientific positions, see Young, *Colonial Desire* 18.
2. See Dash, *The Other America* for an account of how marvelous realism emerged historically in the Caribbean islands as an alternative to Cesairean négritude.
3. He lists the American Revolution of 1776, the Hatian and French Revolutions of 1790 and 1789 respectively, and the revolutions in Latin America from 1806 to 1826 (Phaf, "Preface" *Creole Presence* 13–14).
4. Dessaline's constitution of 1805 (and subsequent constitutions through 1918) used the term "noir" to refer to all citizens of the nation. That constitution prohibited foreign whites from citizenship and ownership of property, and offered citizenship to non-Haitians of African descent. (See Lewis 285.)
5. Thus, the fact that Haiti's independence resulted in its isolation from the world-system by the colonial powers rather than its fuller integration into that system should not detract from the recognition of the modern, modernizing, and integrative impulse of the Haitian Revolution. As James points out, moreover, what Toussaint L'Ouverture sought was absolute local independence combined with access to French capital and commissioners—not a protectorate, but dominion status ("The Making of the Caribbean People" 183).

6. Callaloo, a stew or soup made from many different ingredients, is regarded as a distinctively Trinidadian dish. Other culinary metaphors for Trinidadian hybridity include chutney and pelau.
7. Beverley, "Populism and Nationalism: Some Reservations" 153.
8. See, for example: Mariátegui; Hale (who discusses the relationship of Nicaragua's Sandinistas and Miskitu Indians); Stutzman (who criticizes the Ecuadoran government on the grounds that ethnic difference for Ecuadoran Indians includes their right *not* to participate in nationalist identities); Gordon; Sommer; Richard Jackson, Torres-Saillant; and the journal *Afro-Hispanic Review*.
9. Ironically, the ambiguous interchange of Native American and African in anticolonial nationalist discourse echoes colonial discourse. If Fernández Retamar's "Caliban" enacts a kind of trade-off between Caliban as a figure for our mestizo America and African America (overwriting Caliban onto Martí's notion of "nuestra américa mestiza," our mestizo america,) it is worth remembering that Shakespeare's Caliban, too, is racially ambiguous: In *The Tempest*, the animalization and enslavement of Caliban suggest traditional colonial tropes of Africanness, yet the name "Caliban" refers us back to "Carib." The location of the island of the shipwreck itself is ambiguous, with some evidence pointing to the Old World and some to the New World. Fernández Retamar's and *mestizaje*'s nationalist move thus repeats a long colonial history of racial conflation, confusion, and substitution. See, for example, Defoe and Behn. See Hulme, *Colonial Encounters* for a more detailed account of the significance of such substitutions. Fernández Retamar's "Caliban" through this move also tends to subsume race under class and make the figure of progressive resistance a masculine one. See Nixon for an overview of anti-colonial/postcolonial appropriations of Shakespeare's "The Tempest" and Busia, Donaldson, Saunders, and Wynter for the gender implications of the canonization of Caliban as a figure for anticolonial/anti-imperial oppositional nationalisms.
10. I am thinking especially of the journal *Afro-Hispanic Review*, launched in the United States in 1982, which has been a formative journal of the field and instrumental in developing an Afro-Hispanic literary canon. Carlos Guillermo Wilson, Yvonne Captain, and Richard Jackson regularly contribute to the journal in the spirit of its founding statement. For dissidents from their configuration of the field, see Rosemary Feal and Vera Kutzinski. I distinguish Afro-Hispanic criticism from earlier schools of thought like *Negrismo* and *Negritud* that were led by Afro-Hispanics on the grounds that Afro-Hispanism is, first, a professionalized disciplinary formation and second, it is located largely in the United States, where it responds to and expresses U.S. African-American and Latino identity politics, particularly in terms of claiming various sites of the African diaspora in service of that identity.
11. Qtd. in Kutzinski 14, 205. Kutzinski remarks upon the way in which the analogy to lynching erases the bodies of non-white women to

focus instead on the very different form of violence visited upon black male bodies.

12. See Sorenson, Martínez, and Torres-Saillant. See Burton, "The Idea of Difference" and Dash, "Marvellous Realism" and *The Other America* for critiques of Négritude as official ideology in Martinique.
13. In a similar move, the Trinidadian J.J. Thomas's *Froudacity* refutes the stereotypical racist allegations of Froude by pointing precisely to the mixed mulatto class, which he claimed made black and white racial conflict impossible in the British West Indies, unlike in Haiti. Vera Kutzinski has shown brilliantly how the figure of the Cuban *mulata* belies Martí's claims of transcendence, reading the literary prominence of the *mulata* as a symptom of Cuba's racial anxiety. She demonstrates how in nineteenth-century literary versions of these discourses, the *mulata* "indexes areas of structural instability and ideological volatility in Cuban society, areas that have to be hidden from view to maintain the political fiction of cultural cohesion and synthesis" (172). Kutzinski provides an indispensable study of the relationships amongst *mestizaje*, *cubanidad*, *cubanía*, *mulatez*, and Afro-Cubanism in terms of their race, gender, and sexual politics. For thoughtful, historicized readings of Martí in the context of regional politics at the time, see Lewis and Foner. See also Dash 59–60 for an account of how *mestizaje* was compromised both internally by its own shifting agendas and externally by the effects of the expansion of U.S. capitalism.
14. That several subsequent independent Latin American governments, independently or in collusion with the United States, performed their own massacres of Indians is a bitter irony—but one for which surely Martí cannot be held responsible. The urgent question of how the rhetoric of *mestizaje* intervenes in shaping the relations between the Third and the Fourth Worlds needs to be considered in relation to the discursive practices of the particular states in question. The Cuban case is obviously not the place for such an investigation, since the extermination of Native Americans there long preceded the rise of nationalism. Regarding Martí's choice of the term *mestizaje*, while it would be interesting to determine the moment at which *mestizaje* shifted from being a *metaphor* for other forms of hybridity (particularly *mulatez*) to becoming a *synonym* for them, what appears certain is that by the time Martí was writing, that shift had already occurred.
15. See Stepan and Young, *Colonial Desire*.
16. Similarly, as Gordon Lewis has pointed out in relation to other nationalist literatures, Dominican nationalism in the nineteenth century was significantly less Hispanophobic than Cuban or Puerto Rican nationalisms, in part because of the relative brevity of Spanish rule in the Dominican Republic and in part because of the association of the rival French tradition with Haiti (283). These different relationships to Spain (and France and Haiti) resulted in significant differences in inflection of Dominican, Cuban, and Puerto Rican nationalist discourses of hybridity.

17. See 21–22, where Vasconcelos explains in terms of fairly predictable racial essences what each race contributes. For similar notions of hybridity as a racial composite of a hierarchy of races, see the Brazilian writers Gilberto Freyre and Cassiano Ricardo. See Moreira for an account of how the "mestizo bandeirante" of Cassiano's nonfictional text *Marcha para Oeste* legitimated the authoritarian corporatism of the *Estado Novo* government in Brazil in the 1940s.
18. I thank Susan Andrade for suggesting to me that there might be a rhetorical relationship between India and China in Vasconcelos's work. Other factors that may have influenced the honorific invocations of India may have included the Indian independence movement, particularly in its Gandhian incarnations, and the history of translation of Sanskrit literature into Spanish. Vasconcelos's racist anti-Chinese immigration policy is very similar to that which he criticizes in the United States, notwithstanding the unsuccessful rhetorical gymnastics he performs to try and distinguish his anti-Chinese stance from that of the United States (19–20). Martí shares Vasconcelos's silence on the subject of the substantial Chinese Cuban minority. See the 1876 *Cuba Commission Report* on the hidden history of the Chinese in Cuba.
19. There are innumerable such instances where hybridity has been recuperated to serve conservative and anti-egalitarian social arrangements. In the cases of Jamaica and Trinidad, for instance, the racial hybridization represented by mulattoes did not disrupt the racial stratification of society, but was absorbed into that structure: mulattoes came to comprise the middle class, situated between a white upper class and a largely black and Indian lower class.
20. See Hale and Stutzman.
21. Like Williams' "Mother Trinidad," it promotes a cultural rather than a racial hybridity. For a classic critique of *jibarismo*, see José Luís González, *El País de Cuatro Pisos*. For recent and insightful analyses of *jibarista* discourse (including a sympathetic critique of González), see Lillian Guerra and Roberto Márquez. For a reading of how the monument "*El Jíbaro*," erected in the 1970s, embodies a racialized and gendered national narrative, see Den Tandt 1994.
22. See Den Tandt 1999 for an account of how PPD populism sought to bring the black and mulatto working-class population into line with the Commonwealth project through the image of "*la gran familia puertorriqueña*" or the Great Puerto Rican Family.
23. Coexisting with the image of the *jíbaro* and interacting with it are others: for example, the three-race discourse, that is the discourse that imagines Puerto Ricans to be the descendants of Spanish, Blacks, and Indians. It seems telling that the numerous monuments depicting this rarely represent a recognizably racially mixed Puerto Rican. Thus, once again, the visual emphasis on diverse but distinct racial ancestry does not quite *confront* racial mixing; rather it sustains several suggestions—of

racial hybrids, cultural hybrids, racial composites, or cultural composites. To markedly different degrees, then, both *jibarismo* and the three-race discourse gloss over racial hybridity.

24. The idea of a Creole identity and indeed the term Creole, of course, long precede these developments. Competing academic models of Anglophone Caribbean society included the creole society model, the plural society model, and the plantation society model. See Edward Kamau Brathwaite, *The Development of Creole Society in Jamaica*; Orlando Patterson, *The Sociology of Slavery: An Analysis of the Origins, Development, and Structure of Negro Slave Society in Jamaica*; M.G. Smith, *The Plural Society in the British West Indies*; George Beckford, *Persistent Poverty: Underdevelopment in Plantation Economies of the Third World.*
25. Notably absent from Brathwaite's etymological account of the Spanish verb *criar* is its prominent meaning "to breed"; Brathwaite's history thus writes out the sense in which creolization draws on the categories of animal husbandry.
26. C.L.R. James's emphasis on the state and state-formation stands out as a remarkable discursive exception, though not a practical exception, since, as we have seen, the rhetoric of hybridity has in practice often complemented nation- and state-building activity. One of the aspects of James's work that is valuable is the way that his analyses of Creole states and Creole cultural practices like cricket supplement each other.
27. For a celebratory account of creolization that dwells on the acculturation of white to black Creole norms, see the Curaçaoan intellectual Frank Martinus Arion, who addresses the role of black nannies and concubines in (cultural) reproduction. From these women, and in their care in the slave-quarters, he claims, the children of the Great-House learned the language and culture of the Afro-Creole. Arion traces the linguistic survival of Creole and Papiamentu in English nursery rhymes.
28. In recent years, Brathwaite has become increasingly aware of the tenuousness of claims to cultural unity made in the name of the African heritage. See his exchange with Édouard Glissant in "A Dialogue: Nation Language and Poetics of Creolization" 32.
29. Nigel Bolland attributes the tension between the creolizing impulse in Brathwaite and the (re-)Africanizing impulse in Brathwaite's work to Brathwaite's adherence to the simple dualism "colonial or creole" signaled by his chapter title "Jamaica: Colonial or Creole?" Brathwaite associates "colonial" with metropolitan and reactionary, and creole with local and creative. As Bolland points out, "colonial creole" would be a more accurate characterization of Jamaican society (71). Several critics have argued also that Brathwaite tends to over-state the degree to which interculturation (rather than acculturation) was possible, given the stark inequalities of power. (See Smith, Patterson, Bolland.)

30. In chapters 6 and 7, I discuss how this notion of creolization functions to construct Indo-Trinidadians as outsiders or non-natives.
31. Walcott's critiques of black nationalism share much with Glissant's and the Créolistes' critiques of Négritude. All fault Négritude for its focus on an African elsewhere rather than a Caribbean here, and on the pure rather than the hybrid. The Créolistes declare Europeanness and Africanness "two forms of exteriority" (888). Similarly, Glissant speaks of the "struggle against a single History for the cross-fertilization of histories" (93). Antillanité and Créolité for the Martinicans and "mulatto" aesthetics for Walcott ("What the Twilight Says: An Overture") offer alternatives that incorporate the cultural legacies and dynamics of all the ancestral cultures of the Caribbean.
32. The Guadeloupean and Martinican versions of Créolité offer comparable differences in emphasis. (See Burton, "The Idea of Difference.")
33. Here I allude to Samir Amin's concept of "delinking" outlined in his book of that name.
34. In Chapter Seven I will suggest that the Ramleela that Walcott mobilizes as a sign of hybridity and inclusion may actually be better understood as part of a politics of racial purism and separatism. The cultural politics of the organizers of the Ramleela have less to do with hybridizing projects (though they necessarily have hybrid poetics) than with an ethnic politics that claims cultural continuity with India.
35. The Brazilian Concretist poet Haroldo de Campos who was instrumental in the resurrection of cannibalist discourse in the 1950s through the 1970s similarly switches the nations associated with raw materials and manufactured goods, nature and technology, in his reference to "crushing the raw matter or tradition with the teeth of a sugar-cane machine, transforming sugar cane fibre into rich juice" (qtd. in Prado Bellei 100.) Prado Bellei charges the Concretist reappropriation of anthropophagy with an aestheticism that severed anthropophagy from its matrix of emancipatory social programs. For illuminating discussions of Oswald de Andrade and the discourse of cannibalism in Brazil, see Prado Bellei, Madureira, Johnson, and Schwarz. For a broader discussion of cannibalism and a bibliography, see Barker, Hulme, and Iverson, ed., *Cannibalism and the Colonial World.*
36. "Down with social reality, dressed and oppressive" (313); Brazil's is "a participating consciousness, a religious rhythm" (312).
37. "The word 'chasm' is adopted therefore in this exploratory essay to imply that within the gulfs that divide cultures—gulfs which some societies seek to bypass by the logic of an institutional self-division of humanity or by the practice of ethnic cleansing—there exists, I feel, a storage of creative possibility that, once tapped, may energize the unfinished genesis of the imagination" ("Creoleness" 239).

38. Conrad's *Heart of Darkness* becomes another site for Harris's recovery of connection through shared archetypes. Thus, whereas Chinua Achebe is sharply critical of the politics of Conrad's novel and opposes its being taught, Harris praises it, looking for ground *shared* with Conrad's novel and finding in it gestures towards deep cross-cultural affinities, orchestral reverberations, and archetypal resemblances. His own novel *Palace of the Peacock*, part of the *Guyana Quartet*, might be thought of as a creolized rewriting of *Heart of Darkness*. See also Harris's essay "Benito Cereno," which he characterizes as part of an attempt "to make intuitive connections between apparently irreconcilable imaginative "writers in the past and the present" (123).
39. I focus on *Caribbean Discourse* in this book precisely because the conjunction of art and politics is more prominent there than in Glissant's more recent work. Although he describes his 1990 *Poétique de la Relation (Poetics of Relation)* as "a reconstituted echo or a spiral retelling" of *Caribbean Discourse* (16), in fact, it is much less grounded in the specificities of Martinican and Caribbean culture; the focus on conflict and political opposition so characteristic of *Caribbean Discourse* disappears in *Poetics of Relation*—a disappearance that is intimately connected to Glissant's silence there on the subject of Martinican independence. As Peter Hallward points out, it is telling that the word "Martinique" scarcely appears in that book (118). "La relation" or "Relation" tends to become in *Poetics of Relation* an abstract and inevitable force. The careful equilibrium Glissant achieves in *Caribbean Discourse* between epistemology and economics, art and politics, disintegrates in *Poetics of Relation*. I do not include an extended discussion of that work since its results are fairly similar to those I have already problematized in relation to Bhabha and the Créolistes. Analyzing the subsequent trajectory of Glissant's work—in particular, the reasons that he has moved away from the kinds of political engagement he showed in the 1970s and early 1980s—is beyond the scope of this study. However, for sharp critiques of Glissant's recent work, see Hallward, especially Chapter Two and Excursus Two; Richard Watts; and Richard Clarke.
40. Glissant's periodization shares much with Fredric Jameson's ambitious and justly famous periodization of realism, modernism, and postmodernism as the literary forms corresponding to different stages in the development of capitalism (*Postmodernism Or, The Cultural Logic of Late Capitalism*). If, however, Jameson's periodization has been faulted for inadequately taking into account the Third World at the levels of both economic and literary production, Glissant's periodization might be thought of as an anterior corrective. Glissant centers the history of Martinique, characteristically both making classificatory generalizations and checking the impulse to do so. His method might be construed as using classification as an illustrative

example rather than as a total/izing explanation (as in Jameson) or an ideal model (as Martinique becomes in "Praise"). For although Glissant clearly situates Martinique in a global context, consistent with his belief that cross-cultural poetics, *antillanité*, and hybridity necessarily call for relational understanding, he does not generalize from Martinique to the rest of the Caribbean, far less to the Third World or the globe in its entirety.

Chapter 3 Manifestos of Desire: Hybridity as Forced Poetics

1. See also Jameson, "Reification and Utopia in Mass Culture." Jameson identifies this utopian element in phenomena as extreme and monstrous as Nazism ("Reification and Utopia" 144) as well as in phenomena so routinized and degraded as advertising (*The Political Unconscious* 287). Given the connections I am drawing between utopianism and the manifesto, Jameson's claim for advertising becomes more suggestive still when conjoined with Alice Yaeger Kaplan's characterization of advertising as the mass-cultural heir to the manifesto (77).
2. Here I confine myself to addressing liberal discourses of hybridity. For an analysis of explicitly racist and right-wing discourses of hybridity, see Young, *Colonial Desire*, particularly his discussion of the place of hybridity in debates on the monogenist or polygenist origins of humankind.
3. In fact, Lyon argues that it was the association of the manifesto form with radical political struggle that enabled the intersection of the political and aesthetic avant-gardes.
4. "Who will define us? Creolization in Belize," qtd. in Bolland 72.
5. Walcott, *The Antilles* 10; Bhabha, "A Question of Survival," "DissemiNation," and "The Postcolonial and the Postmodern."
6. I noted with interest the inclusion of an excerpt from Anzaldúa's *Borderlands/La Frontera* in the anthology of manifestos entitled *Manifesto: A Century of Isms*, since it seems to support my generic assertion—although, of course, any such anthology must include both typical examples and examples that stretch the definition of the genre. (The anthology's inclusion of Eudora Welty's "Place in Fiction" may be an example of the latter.) Excerpting and abbreviating texts like Anzaldúa's may also have the effect of intensifying their manifesto-like qualities.
7. *Manifesto: A Century of Isms* 297.
8. Thus far, I have identified the subjunctive mood, slippages between description and prescription, definition, overstatement, and repetition as features of the manifesto. To these, Claude Abastado adds: "the tense of utopia," of prophesies, of certainties to come, the future indicative, the imperative or wish, the injunctive, the auxiliary mode, exclamation, exhortation, invective, polemic, intimidation, citation,

and assertive adverbs (9–11). Janet Lyon describes a set of characteristics of the manifesto that include: the signature pronoun "we" (11); the declaration of a position in ardent disregard for good manners and reasoned civility (12); newly invigorated metaphors that help create new enunciative positions within ideology (15); an "apocalyptic present tense" (*now* is the time for action) (30); discourses of religious prophecy, chiliasm, or millenialism, the martial language of war or siege, and the forensic mode of persuasive rhetoric (13); a forceful enumeration of grievances or demands; and the parataxis of the list or epigrammatic declaratives refusing mediated forms or synthesized transitions (15). Lyon cautions that these features function as "family resemblances" rather than a rigid checklist of features found in every manifesto, since genre "describes groups of texts whose similarities fluctuate into differences with changing historical pressures and reading practices" (12–13). Part of the work of this chapter is to note which formal features are foregrounded at particular moments and speculate about why.

9. Julia H. Watts, "An Interview with Raphaël Confiant" 44.
10. For analysis of these structural conditions that shape artistic practice, see Glissant's periodizing table "The Process of Literary Production" (94).
11. See chapter six for an account of Glissant's relationship to mimetic realism, critiques of which are scattered through all of *Caribbean Discourse* and *Poetics of Relation*.
12. See Brathwaite, *History of the Voice*; and Brathwaite's commentary in Phaf, ed., and Chang, ed. For other examples of experiments in relating spoken and written word, see the anthology of West Indian poetry *Voiceprint*, edited by Stewart Brown et al.
13. Of "Calypso" Brathwaite says: "And so this poem, which is at the heart of my concept of *nation language* because I could relate the skidding stone to calypso, freed me of Milton and the pentameter and Michelangelo and anybody else. It celebrates the rhythms of our own people permitting [*sic*] to enter in the experience that the rhythms correspond to" (Phaf 22).
14. See Glissant 106 where, for reasons similar to Brathwaite's, he argues that the Caribbean landscape and climate cannot be stuffed into a sonnet.
15. Two prominent exceptions come to mind: Donna Haraway's "A Manifesto for Cyborgs: Science, Technology, and Socialist Feminism in the 1980's" and Cary Nelson's *Manifesto of a Tenured Radical*. In principle, however, the claims I am making for academic manifestos could be extended to include such texts as Lyotard's *The Postmodern Condition*, Deleuze and Guattari's *Kafka: Toward a Minor Literature*, and much of the first wave of academic writing that celebrated postmodernism.

16. I am making a distinction between a decapitalized theory and a capitalized Theory. The former in my usage refers to a particular explanatory practice; to the extent that it seeks to make visible truths at odds with the prevailing wisdom, it may pose considerable difficulty to the reader in its methodology, terminology, and level of abstraction. In contrast, capitalized Theory refers to a commodified form judged primarily by its exchange value. In such a context, its difficulty may be fetishized as a form of professional armor or capital, the *source* of its authority.
17. In such a context, the manifesto form with its hyperbolic claims, including those of its radical newness, may begin to approach that other form of academic translational labor and source of celebrity: the academic grant proposal.
18. See Lyon's discussion of the responses of two different postmodern manifestos—Donna Haraway's and Jenny Holzer's—to this problem (195–202).
19. See Doris Sommer, *Proceed with Caution* for a deeply suggestive and extended argument about the value and methods of texts that slow the reader down. See also chapter five of this book for a meditation on opacity.
20. See Condé's "Créolité without Creole?" Glissant and Condé both write in French, though they include Creole in their novelistic practice; their Anglophone equivalents might be writers such as Merle Collins, Merle Hodge, and Sam Selvon, who move between Creole and standard English. According to Michael Dash, one measure of Glissant's concerns is his subsequent move away from the term "creolization" to the term "relation" ("Psychology, Creolization, Hybridization" 51).
21. See David Scott for an account of the new problem-space we occupy in the post–Soviet/Communist Chinese era. Scott argues that we have gone as far as we can in Postcolonial Studies with the decolonization of representation. Moreover, he argues, that strategy was made possible precisely because we could believe socialism had our political futures "covered," so to speak. In the present post–Cold War era, which permits no such political guarantee, he calls for a foregrounding of politics. Though I disagree with Scott's belief that we are in a definitively post-socialist era, what does seem clear is that socialism cannot be breathed into being with the same triumphalist rhetoric or the same manifestos.
22. See Sommer, *Foundational Fictions*.
23. See Mary Layoun's account of nationalism (especially 411) that treats the terms "grammar" and "rhetoric" as roughly equivalent to my categories of truth and persuasion, description and prescription.

Chapter 4 Beyond Resistance: Rehearsing Opposition in Derek Walcott's *Pantomime*

1. Foucault's formulation is helpful here: "[t]ransgression does not seek to *oppose* one thing to another, nor does it achieve its purpose through mockery or by upsetting the solidity of foundations; it does not transform the other side of the mirror.... Transgression is neither violence in a divided world (in an ethical world) nor a victory over limits (in a dialectical or revolutionary world)" ("A Preface to Transgression" 35, emphasis added).
2. As an intervention in the disciplines of History and the Social Sciences, which have been notoriously blind to informal and noninstitutional forms of political resistance, Scott's project is a useful corrective. However, in Cultural and Post-colonial Studies, the fields out of which I write, as well as in Anthropology, the disciplinary emphases have been quite the reverse. For in recent years, these fields have seen a real fetishization of the notion of resistance and, as I argued in chapter one, a concomitant delegitimation of opposition. Moreover, appropriations of Scott's work in Cultural Studies often lack the careful and thorough empirical work that undergirds his theoretical arguments in both *Domination and the Arts of Resistance* and the earlier *Weapons of the Weak*. It is this disciplinary emphasis that frames many of my reservations about Scott's study.

   My critique of the overvaluation of resistance shares the concerns of such diverse theorists as Lila Abu-Lughod, Talal Asad, Michael Brown, Jean Franco, Abdul JanMohamed, Martha Kaplan and John Kelly, Neil Lazarus, Meaghan Morris, Sherry Ortner, Benita Parry, Gayatri Spivak, and Peter Stallybrass and Allon White. See also David Harris's scathing critique of "designer Gramscianism" in *From Class Struggle to the Politics of Pleasure: The Effect of Gramscianism on Cultural Studies* and Robert Young's "Back to Bakhtin," both of which object to the critical dehistoricization and decontextualization of Gramsci's and Bakhtin's claims and the repression of their specifically Marxist politics. For examples of rigorously historicized social science case studies, which also theorize forms of resistance that fall short of revolutionary action, and which avoid some of the problems of Scott's work, see Susan Eckstein, ed., *Power and Popular Protest: Latin American Social Movements*; Richard Fox and Orin Starn, eds., *Between Resistance and Revolution: Cultural Politics and Social Protest*; and Jonathan Glassman, *Feasts and Riot: Revelry, Rebellion, and Popular Consciousness on the Swahili Coast, 1856–1888*. Interestingly, none of these titles has achieved the kind of circulation in English or cultural studies that Scott's work has.

   For Scott's taxonomic summary of kinds of resistance, see the chart on 198.

3. One example of a text that does this with great analytical gains is Johannes Fabian's *Power and Performance: Ethnographic Explorations through Proverbial Wisdom and Theater in Shaba, Zaire.*
4. Hall, "Notes on Deconstructing the Popular" 239.
5. Broadly speaking, "reputation" refers to the pleasurable, performative, and often transgressive dimensions of street culture that emphasize transience, whilst "respectability" refers to bourgeois ideals of character, decorum, deferral, and transcendence. Wilson interprets Caribbean societies as being structured by a polarity between the values of "reputation" and "respectability." As with any schematic opposition, the reputation/respectability dualism is not all-encompassing, yet it is useful in making visible two related and conflicting sets of cultural desires, practices, and allegiances that are elaborated to an unusual degree in the Caribbean. The schema is also particularly pertinent as a measure of the allegiances of cultural *criticism*, which is the object of my critique here. For a productive gloss on Wilson's schema, see Burton, *Afro-Creole* 162. For an overview of the impact of Wilson's study on Caribbean anthropology, see Miller, *Modernity* 259–264, who notes that the privileging of values of reputation is visible in the disproportionate study of Carnival as compared with Christmas, even though the latter may well involve more Trinidadians. Burton's and Miller's are amongst the only studies I know that both draw on Wilson's model and critique and modify its gender politics.
6. For some theories and practices of that shift, see Foucault, *The History of Sexuality*; deCerteau, *The Practice of Everyday Life*; Guha, *Elementary Forms of Peasant Insurgency*; Hall, "Metaphors of Transformation"; Hall and Jefferson, eds., *Resistance through Rituals: Youth Subcultures in Post-War Britain*; Hebdige, *Subculture: The Meaning of Style*; Fiske, *Reading the Popular* and *Understanding Popular Culture*; Chambers, *Popular Culture: The Metropolitan Experience.* For an interest in "post-work" social contexts, see Aronowitz, Milagros López, and Grosfoguel.
7. Thus, for example, dominant critical discourses on Trinidadian Mas'—in which today women vastly outnumber men—treat it as a commodified, co-opted, homogenizing, and nonthreatening aspect of Carnival, which they contrast to steelband, Jouvay Mas, and stickfighting—in all of which men predominate. See, for example, Lovelace, "The Emancipation–Jouvay Tradition and the Almost Loss of Pan."
8. See Barnes, Pamela Franco, Miller, and chapter 7 of this book. For feminist studies of Jamaican dance-hall, see Cooper and Saunders.
9. See in contrast Elma Napier's story "Carnival in Martinique," in which the female character's marginality is not accidental, but the pointed force of the story. Carnival offers scarcely an interlude in the maid Jeannette's daily chores, and even in that interlude her desires are divided between the rewards of reputation and those of respectability. The conclusion of the story jolts her back to the unflinching present of

coerced labor: "What did Jules [her beau] matter or Josephine [Empress of France], or the spirit of carnival? She had forgotten to bring the fowls back into the yard" (230).

10. Central to the safety-valve theory is the notion that Carnival's release is sanctioned by the authorities to secure their interests; its ritual or symbolic inversion of material inequalities compensates or substitutes for a material transformation of social relations. In pre-Lenten Carnivals, anarchic energies and excesses are immediately recontained by Lent, which in turn represents not just the reaffirmation of the existing social order, but the intensification of it in the form of socio-religious imperatives of duty, guilt, atonement, and subordination. The safety-valve theory has had currency in orthodox Marxism cultural theory, where ritual has long occupied an uneasy position and carnival is often cast as a kind of "opiate of the masses," its ritual economy and ritual expenditure proving resistant or irreducible to the logic of political economy except as waste or distraction. Proponents of the "safety-valve" model include Gluckman and Eagleton 1981. Opponents of the safety-valve model, on the other hand, argue that the anxious regulation of carnival by the ruling classes, combined with the actual rise in incidence of riots and rebellions during Carnival season, suggest the transformative or anti-status quoist nature of Carnival. Opponents of the safety-valve model include Roberto da Matta, Robert Stam, and James Scott. These two antithetical visions of Carnival have informed colonial discourse and policy, popular opinion, and cultural criticism alike.
11. For insightful examples of such studies, see Birth, Burton's *Afro-Creole*, van Koningsbruggen, Frank Manning, Miller, Roach, and Gordon Rohlehr. Earl Lovelace's novel *The Dragon Can't Dance* is one of the richest literary explorations of Carnival available. I think of the novel as a critical tribute to the lumpen dispossessed of an urban slum; a study of gender and ethnic relations; an exploration of Carnival as a repository of cultural memory, self-expression, creativity, and collectivity, confrontation and joyous release from confrontation; finally, it bears eloquent and sympathetic witness to the limits of the spontaneism, the transient energies, and diffuse ideologies and goals that coalesced in the conjunction of Carnival and the 1970 Black Power uprising in Trinidad, known as the February Revolution, with its creation of a "People's Parliament" at Woodford Square. (The relationship of that uprising to the 1970 Carnival has been the subject of some critical scholarship, as well.) On *Dragon*, see Brydon, O'Callaghan, "The Lovelace 'Prologue'," and Miller.
12. Very schematically, canboulay consisted of a performative representation of the burning of the cane, performed first by the white plantocracy, later by free blacks on Emancipation Day; recently canboulay has been represented in different Carnival events.
13. "Carnival: The Theatre of the Streets" (1964), qtd. in Robert Hammer 141.

14. "More than any other art, the theater can express the national spirit, and it needs intense concentration of purpose." "Future of Art Promising," qtd. in Hammer 139.
15. For instance, the great Trinidadian mas' designer Peter Minshall disagrees with them, insisting that all performance, all theater, is transient, and that Carnival is the people's theater. In conversation, September 11, 1998.
16. For an earlier, poetic dialogue with the figure of Robinson Crusoe, see Walcott's *The Castaway and Other Poems* (1956).
17. Studies of Carnival that address the mas' camps where the costumes are made, or the daily rehearsals in neighborhood pan yards, could offer a different view of participation, an account more attuned to the work that sustains carnivalesque performance, and to the many different sites of community-formation in carnival. *Dragon* is once again helpful here in focusing not so much on Aldrick's brief mas' as dragon, but on the laborious making of the dragon costume, the shifting relations within the slum of Laventille, and the multiple and changing meanings of "all o' we is one." In a related vein, Lovelace distinguishes his notion of Carnival from "bacchanal" or abandon before Lent, a vision of Carnival that applies only to the mas' of Carnival Tuesday. He argues persuasively that those who think of Carnival as hedonistic play and abandon ignore the fact that if you look at what Carnival characters actually do (particularly the ones from jouvay such as the midnight robber, the jab jab, the dragon, the bat), the idea of abandon does not work well. Instead, he argues, they are possessed or *achieve* possession by entering into a rhythm that links them to themselves, their community, to those who share the experience with them, and to God. In this rhythm, he claims, we begin to find ourselves. (Presentation at World Carnival Conference, September 9–13, 1998; and "The Emancipation–Jouvay Tradition and the Almost Loss of Pan").
18. See, for example, Patrick Taylor: "Derek Walcott takes that old but enduring European myth of Crusoe and Friday (Prospero and Caliban, if you like) and transforms it to bring Caribbean man to a true confrontation with his freedom in history" (293). "Paradoxically, this self-consciousness makes Jackson the master *in reality*" (297, emphasis added).
19. Biodun Jeyifo's claim that the play displaces opposition is representative of this second kind of reading, though his reading is unusual in that it *faults* the play on precisely these counts:

> *Pantomime*, I think, implies a radical relativism in its complete deconstruction of both Eurocentrism and nativism; this evidently recalls certain forms of post-structuralist and deconstructivist assault on essentialism and the "metaphysics of presence" in the canons, and the celebration of indeterminacy. As analogically dramatized in *Pantomime* this position invites its own

> "deconstruction" and interrogation: what is the value of a radical relativism which carries out a necessary demythologization of essentialized Eurocentrism and nativism but evades or occludes the violence of the power relations between them by tacitly assuming an equivalence of either actual power consolidation between them, or the will-to-power of their pundits and adherents? (*Critical Perspectives on Derek Walcott* 387).

It seems to me that parts of this argument could more legitimately be pitched against *The Antilles* than against *Pantomime*.

The extraordinary insights of Bridget Jones's and Graham Huggan's essays on *Pantomime* are enabled precisely because they escape the dichotomies of the aforementioned approaches.

20. Declares Benítez-Rojo:

> No matter how postmodern or postideological we might feel, how can we keep from admiring works like C.L.R. James's *The Black Jacobins*, Frantz Fanon's *The Wretched of the Earth*, or Manuel Moreno Fraginal's *El Ingenio*, not to speak of the magnificent books written by Aimé Césaire and other confrontational writers and poets? And, nevertheless, every Caribbean person knows, at least intuitively, that the Caribbean is *much more* than a system of binary oppositions. (295, emphasis added)

The sense that these oppositional or "confrontational" thinkers enact a reduction is further developed in Benítez-Rojo's reading of Derek Walcott's 1958 play *Drums and Colors*, in which the characters at an imagined Carnival include Columbus, the discoverer; Raleigh, the conqueror; Touissant L'Ouverture, the rebel; and Gordon, instigator of the Morant Bay Rebellion in Jamaica (300–304).

Benítez-Rojo also collapses Walcott's violence and counterviolence into the familiar liberal notion of equivalent violences ("ultimately it is not important that Mano . . . should have picked out Raleigh and Gordon; he could equally have chosen Henry Morgan or José Martí, this person or another") (302). In place of Walcott's carnival marred by "neopositivist manipulation" (302), Benítez-Rojo celebrates the ostensibly "postmodern carnival" of Carpentier's *Concierto Barroco*, which "dismantles the binary oppositions that Walcott's play had constructed, converting them into differences" (304). See also 20–21. "From opposition to difference," from Revolution to Carnival, becomes Benítez-Rojo's slogan. See Fuguet and Gomez for a similar move.

21. As Jackson notes: "We having one of them 'playing man-to-man' talks, where a feller does look a feller in the eye and say, 'Le' we settle this thing, man to man,' and this time the feller who smiling and saying it, his whole honest intention is to take the feller by the crotch

and rip out he stones, and dig out he eyes and leave him for corbeaux to pick" (139).

22. Note that whereas for Harry in relation to Ellen, the relations of domination in art and life repeat and reinforce one another, for Jackson in his relationship with Harry, they are a counterpoint, Jackson's superior artistic ability serving as a tool with which to offset his racial subordination.
23. Bridget Jones' essay is the only one I have come across that does so.
24. I thank Lisa Coxson for first suggesting to me the importance of the heterosexual accord of Jackson and Harry.
25. I owe this observation about British and Caribbean theater history to Bridget Jones. See Jones 230–231.
26. In Trinidadian Creole, picong refers to the practice of engaging in witty and stinging insult.
27. See Walcott's 1965 lecture "The Figure of Crusoe" 39.
28. Elsewhere, Jackson satirizes the classical script with hilarious effect when, in an example par excellence of the carnivalesque inversion/hybridization of the classical and the grotesque, he uses the elevated language of the classics to describe the process of urinating (149–154).
29. Walcott has in more than one instance opposed the Creole to the epic. In *The Antilles* the fragment represents an incisive critique of the epic scale. See also Gregson Davis, "'With No Homeric Shadow': The Disavowal of Epic in Derek Walcott's *Omeros*."
30. Harry's sentence is a close echo of a remark Naipaul made about the West Indies, which Walcott has contested explicitly in "The Caribbean: Culture or Mimicry" and implicitly in almost all his artistic practice.
31. The actor of not British but Roman Pantomime, in which a single actor played all the roles, might well be considered the artistic equivalent of a factotum.
32. See, for example, Brathwaite, Gilroy, Rohlehr on improvisation and call and response in jazz, hip-hop, and calypso respectively.
33. See Bhabha, "Of Mimicry and Man: The Ambivalence of Colonial Discourse."
34. Published a decade before Butler's *Gender Trouble*, *Pantomime*'s conception of improvisational agency shares much with Butler's conception of agency as a variation on the process of repetition through which identity is constructed. *Pantomime* gives artistic form to Butler's theoretical account of the complex relationship between the imitation and the original in the performance of drag, and of how the imitation reveals the radical contingency of the original. See Butler 137–138, 143–147.
35. Although it is certainly true that Harry's "slip" enables an honest insight and admission that Harry needs to make, and that the slip therefore serves productive cathartic and analytical functions, which enable Harry to regroup and set in motion a harmonious interlude

between the two men, these advantageous consequences may arise because Harry's conscious self will not permit the honesty that a mask does or the *surrender* of self that a role requires. Thus, the breakdown of Harry's control offers cathartic relief in the play Walcott has described as "confessional psychodrama" (qtd. in Christopher Gunness, "White Man, Black Man" 290–291) As Jackson says to Harry, "[t]hat stiff upper lip goin' have to quiver a little" (137). "Slippage" is not as significant a factor in Jackson's role-playing; more often, he *stages* slips or fortuitously gains leverage from them; it is rarely his route to self-knowledge.

36. In the context of Extempore, the tradition of picong, which we see in *Pantomime*, is particularly highly developed. (The tradition of calypso more generally—in its lyrics, in its construction of race and sexual relations, in the stage-names of calypsonians, and its contexts of performance—has a strong element of violence.) Extempore shares several features of the African American practice of the dozens, which stages the virtuosity of improvised competitive insult; the dozens could also provide an illuminating lens through which to read several of the exchanges in *Pantomime*.
37. I do not intend my claims about improvisation and Creole opposition to be understood as a formula that works in all contexts; my claims are more limited in scope, emerging from and explicating *Pantomime*. One could equally consider the *grandeur* of scale, the swagger and bravado of, for instance, several calypsonians' stage-names (such as Black Stalin, Invader, Attilla the Hun) and the bombastic prose of the Carnival character the Midnight Robber as being implicated in a Creole notion of opposition. It is, however, worth noting, that these examples all have an element of self-conscious or ironic hyperbole.
38. I learned of the echoes of Molière's *Don Juan* from Bridget Jones's essay on *Pantomime*. Walcott's interest in the figure of Don Juan is amply displayed in his creolized adaptation of Tirso de Molino's *El Burlador de Seville* entitled *The Joker of Seville* (1979) and written fairly close in time to *Pantomime*.
39. One could undertake a similar close reading of the differences in the versions of the calypso Jackson improvises.
40. I owe the idea of freedom as an event to Daniel Miller, who, in his study of the Trinidadian dance-form or movement known as wining (from "winding down the waist") treats wining as a ritual repetition of freedom. The idea also resonates with Judith Butler's notion of a performativity which participates in a repetitive temporality.
41. I owe this idea to Randy Martin, *Critical Moves: Dance Studies in Theory and Politics* 2.

Chapter 5 Marvelous Realism, Feminism, and Mulatto Aesthetics: Erna Brodber's *Myal*

1. For a thoughtful study of this question in relation to literary textual production about Dominican–Haitian relations, see Den Tandt 2003.
2. See, for example, Brennan 1989, Durix, Fuguet and Gomez.

   It may be worth distinguishing between earlier and later variants of marvelous realism; it is the Latin American Boom and post-Boom marvelous-realist novels that have been canonized thus internationally. The relationship between marvelous realism and magic realism has itself also been contested. Alejo Carpentier, whose Prologue to *El Reine de Este Mundo* is a key manifesto of marvelous realism, distanced himself from magic realism, arguing that magic realism was essentially a mode of narration that employed stylistic virtuosity and modernist techniques of defamiliarization, and shared much with the artificial qualities of surrealism (the object of his vitriolic assault). In contrast, he argued, marvelous realism was the form of New World reality itself. García Márquez's own view of magic realism, however, is fairly close to Carpentier's (see for example, his Nobel Prize acceptance speech). See *Magical Realism: Theory, History, Community*, which collects many of the most influential writings and debates on the subject, in all their definitional slipperiness, and more recently Ato Quayson. There is a certain irony to writing a chapter that puts into dialogue two terms—postmodernism and marvelous realism—upon whose definitions there is no consensus; indeed, their definitional fuzziness is comparable only to their longevity.
3. For related investigations see Appiah; Gikandi, *Writing in Limbo*; Gilroy, *The Black Atlantic;* JanMohamed; Lubiano; Quayson, "Postmodernism and Postcolonialism"; and Radhakrishnan, "Postmodernism and the Rest of the World."
4. For perspectives that argue for a postmodern epistemology in the Caribbean and Latin America respectively, see Antonio Benítez-Rojo and Beverley and Oviedo, eds.
5. Pertinent here is Fredric Jameson's periodization of literature into realism, modernism, and postmodernism, corresponding to three stages in the expansion of capitalism. Notwithstanding its many strengths, *Postmodernism or, The Cultural Logic of Late Capitalism* often leaves under-specified the place of Third World cultural production in its tripartite schema. See Santiago Colás's astute critique of Jameson's periodization, where he points out:

   > The "Third World" performs a paradoxical double function in Fredric Jameson's theory of postmodernism. It is both the space whose final elimination by the inexorable logic of late capitalist development consolidates the social moment—late capitalism—whose cultural dominant is postmodernism, and the space that remains somehow untainted by and oppositional to those

> repressive social processes which have homogenized the real and imaginative terrain of the "First World" subject. (258)

This contradictory function of Third World literature reappears in Jameson's essay "Third World Literature in the Era of Multinational Capital," where it is unclear how the category "Third World Literature" relates to the realism–modernism–postmodernism schema. For extended critiques of Jameson's theory of Third World literature, see Ahmad, *In Theory* 95–122 and Larsen. Ahmad has criticized Jameson's tendency to define the First World in terms of production (whether of goods or theoretical practices) but the Third World as an experience (99–100). He thus raises the vexed question of the relationship of literature to theory, and the absence of attention to Third World theoretical production in First World academies, which Jean Franco has observed replicates the economic division between Third World producers of raw materials and First World producers of manufactured goods ("Beyond Ethnocentrism" 503). In "The Nation as Imagined Community" Franco dispenses with both "postmodernism" and "national allegory" as analytic terms with which to understand Latin American literature.

All too often, to the extent that "the postcolonial" is a field or object of study, it is read via poststructuralist theory; to the extent that "the postcolonial" refers to a reading practice, it is not differentiated from poststructuralist reading practices. (See, for example, Frankenberg and Mani. Their use of the word "postcoloniality" in its strict etymological sense of a "state" or "condition" of being postcolonial underscores the problem [294].) Vivek Dhareshwar points out that poststructuralist theory when applied to postcolonial situations has on occasion actually blocked an analysis of postcolonial problematics. He argues that the postcolonial problematics of "detour" and "return" (as theorized by Glissant), have too often been recuperated in to the "movement of delay, relay, delegation, differánce, discontinuity, dissemination, etc." (156). Instead of attending to the differences of postcolonial situations, such theories often turn the concrete experience of detour into a "figure of system," he argues. There is thus a critical difference between Dhareshwar's usage and Benítez-Rojo's: in Dhareshwar's work (Third World) narrative has an *interruptive* relationship to (First World) theory or any "figure of system," whereas in Benítez-Rojo's, Caribbean narrative *endorses* postmodern theory, thereby losing its critical stance. Despite the many strengths and suggestive insights of Dhareshwar's essay, I hesitate to accept his framing of the First World as the space of theory and the Third World as the space of narrative, even if it is an interruptive narrative. (One could usefully consider interruptive First World narratives and Third World theory.) In defining "theory" narrowly as post-1960s poststructuralism, he may too readily accept the terms of hegemonic U.S. academic discourse. My hesitations about Mani and Frankenberg's conflation of postcolonial and postmodern theory are similar: it acquiesces to the particular way in which post-colonial studies has been institutionalized in the U.S. academy.

6. This constitutive tension between codes seems to me qualititatively different from the eclecticism and pastiche at the level of *style* of Anglo-American postmodernism, which itself arises out of what we might call the historical experience of dehistoricization. Sangari similarly distinguishes the "cultural simultaneity" of Latin America from the "cultural synchronicity" available in the so-called First World (3–4).
7. What MacCabe calls "classic realism," Glissant calls "literary realism" or mimesis. Glissant also associates literary realism with the "clarity" of a linear narrative, a transparent and harmonious narrative, a pre-occupation with the inner self of a transcendental individual subject, and the omniscient authority of "objectivity" (73, 107, 236). Throughout this chapter I use the terms "classic realism" and "literary realism" interchangeably.
8. See also Glissant, *Caribbean Discourse* 75–76.
9. This tendency is realized not so much in published articles, for these usually require a certain level of specialization in Caribbean or Latin American culture and history, but in the way these texts are taught in multiculturalist undergraduate courses, where detailed cultural and contextual research is not always part of pedagogical preparation.
10. For attempts to theorize the epistemological breaks and continuities between realism, modernism, and postmodernism in European literature, see Brecht's defense of modernism in "Against Georg Lukács," and Jameson's notion of "cognitive mapping" (*Postmodernism* 399–418), both of which attempt to theorize what we might call nonrealistic realisms.
11. In the Spanish original, this passage remains the same in both Carpentier's 1949 Prologue and his later elaboration of that into "On the Marvelous Real in America." I have therefore used the less awkward translation of the passage from the latter, in *Magical Realism: Theory, History, Community*.
12. See also Gikandi, *Writing in Limbo*, which locates marvelous realism within a revisionary Caribbean modernism that is compatible with a realist epistemology.
13. In fact, Carpentier's energetic denunciations of European surrealism and claims for the distinctiveness of marvelous realism can be understood as part of his nationalist and regionalist project. Taking up his overstated distinctions between surrealism and marvelous realism is not necessary for my argument here. See Durix for a vigorous critique of the lurking Eurocentrism of Carpentier's vision of marvelous realism.
14. See René Depestre, qtd. in Dash, "Marvellous Realism."
15. For a related project, see Mohanty, *Literary Theory and the Claims of History*.
16. *The Dictionary of Jamaican English* defines myal variously as sorcerer, wizard, intoxication, return, formal possession by the spirit of a dead ancestor, and the dance done under possession. Myalism is almost always

curative, and can be used to counter obeah, which can cause sickness or death. The anthropologist Diane Austin-Broos defines myalism as neither simply nativistic nor even consistently millenialist, but instead "a complex of rite and belief that sought to sustain the logic of affliction by assimilating elements of Christianity to it" (54). She understands myalism as an intervention in the ethical rationalism of Protestantism. (In the novel this element receives its most concentrated treatment in the encounter of the Methodist parson William Brassington with myalism.) Austin-Broos and others have noted the historically close connection in Jamaica between myalism and Native Baptism (a connection we see played out in the figure of the Baptist minister Reverend Simpson in the novel) and have documented the resurgence of myalism in Jamaica after the 1865 Morant Bay Rebellion, which both discredited orthodox Christianity and saw the participation of myalists and Baptists (71).

See also Nelson-McDermott (65) on the relationship between the Morant Bay Rebellion and Myalism. See Cooper ("Something Ancestral Recaptured" 70) for an account that places *Myal* in a tradition of writing that uses spirit possession as a figure for liberation. Cooper astutely observes, "the accreted negative connotations of the word 'zombie'—in English—thus encode the acculturation or zombification process itself."

17. There are also overlaps between *Pantomime*'s model of improvisation and *Myal*'s model of textual infiltration. See Evelyn O' Callaghan's *Woman Version* for the idea of the "dub version" or musical remix as a metaphor for cultural resistance.
18. One could well ask whether the disastrous coon show Selwyn produces is his attempt at translating as transparent that which is unintelligible to his code.
19. The grammar of the novel underscores this. Of Maydene Brassington's accession to the community of spirits, we are told: "It was revealed to her" (88), a sentence with unmistakable biblical resonances. The subject of the action remains mysterious as a result of the passive voice, and Brassington is the indirect object of the action.
20. This particular description refers to Ella's maternal grandparents and mother, who are light-skinned and fine-featured Africans, but it applies with equal poignancy to Ella's acute sense of her own racial "strangeness."
21. For a helpful reading of the novel, which focuses on the tension between voice and print, orality and literacy, see Collette Maximin, "Distinction and Dialogism in Jamaica."
22. It was from Evelyn O'Callaghan's essay on *Myal* that I learned that the allegory was on colonial Jamaican school syllabi. When it was introduced, what the immediate historical considerations were, whether for example it had any connection to the Morant Bay Rebellion, I have been unable to learn.

23. In this regard, it recalls Chinua Achebe's *Things Fall Apart*, in which the Christian missionaries are able to obtain converts as a direct result of inequalities and exclusionary practices within Igbo culture.
24. Useful in understanding this last point is Kumkum Sangari's distinction between two forms of women's agency: consent and feminist agency. The former works by "appropriating available hegemonic or legitimating languages" within patriarchy which enable individual women to exercise power over other women or men; the latter consists of the "organized initiatives of women and men committed to gender justice within an egalitarian framework" ("Consent, Agency, and Rhetorics of Incitement" 365). She further distinguishes amongst consent resting on material arrangements, ideological ensembles, and forms of coercion which push women toward normative behavior; and suggests study of women from the upper layers of social hierarchy for "the full range of complicities and extracted compensations" (374). That phrase "complicities and extracted compensations" offers, I think, an ideal framework for understanding Ella and her allegorical doubles.
25. In one example of the way the text transforms the reader's system of values, we realize that saying that Maas Levi did not accept any half-measures (61), far from being testimony to his moral virtue, is in fact a clue to his puritanical inflexibility. We are, in fact, meant to revise our initial (mis)judgment of him, a misjudgment we share with the community (31–34).
26. I would modify Walker-Johnson's observation only to the extent of saying that the formal restructuration of "Mr. Joe's Farm" into a folktale occurs not so much as a result of making it provide coded moral instruction (for such coded moral instruction is also performed by the colonialist text), but by rendering the authoritative imperial text "Mr Joe's Farm" dialogical, manipulable, and increasingly proximate to the spoken word. Walker-Johnson's claims elsewhere in her essay implicitly make this point as well (54).
27. This enterprise may well also extend to the present-day Jamaican reader, since the novel's setting in 1900–19 and many of its allusions are temporally and possibly experientially distant even to them.
28. Neil Ten Kortenaar faults an earlier version of my essay on *Myal* ("An 'Other' Realism") for reductively translating spirit possession into a metaphor for a cultural imperialism; he advances the genuinely suggestive formulation that Brodber "posits a literal spirit possession for which cultural imperialism is a metaphor" (51). Although I do refer, as charged, to spirit possession as a "controlling concept-metaphor" (101) (albeit for the recovery of doubleness, not for cultural imperialism as Kortenaar charges), that claim is accompanied by the converse assertion that spirit possession in *Myal* "is in many ways a literalization of that metaphor" (99). Moreover, my analysis of the politics of gender inequality within the black community should make clear that I do not think the theme of cultural imperialism exhausts the politics of the

novel. However, I would argue that the novel's poetics of doubling invites metaphorical readings, with the significant proviso that those metaphorical readings should not erase the literal meanings. Thus, if Ella can be "translated" into an allegory for Grove Town, and Grove Town into an allegory for the nation, I see no reason that the nation cannot be translated further into an allegory of global resistance. What *Myal* requires of us in these translations is that we keep the literal and the metaphorical dimensions of the text, tenor and vehicle, operational simultaneously, and that we become aware of the process of translation.

For another reading of the relationship of the metaphorical to the literal in magic realism, see Ato Quayson, "Fecundities of the Unexpected."

29. Mariolina Salvatori's conception of a hermeneutics and pedagogy of difficulty is comparable and relevant to the pedagogical practice of both Ella and the novel as a whole. See also Doris Sommer, *Proceed with Caution*, for an insightful recent investigation of the difficulties posed by and readerly practices demanded by texts concerned with cultural difference.
30. This summary and all my references to the Morant Bay Rebellion closely follow Gad Heuman's and Diane Austin-Broos's accounts. Both authors document the role of religion, particularly myalism and Baptism, in the carefully planned Rebellion. (Heuman's study also refutes accounts that treat the Rebellion as a spontaneous riot.)
31. Ten Kortenaar clarifies that the subnational or local agent has access to these texts through orality or face-to-face communication; s/he does they do not rely on the medium of the written word, nor on the anonymous community of the "nation." For a theoretical and historical account that connects print-capitalism to the rise of imagined national communities, see Benedict Anderson. In a similar vein to Ten Kortenaar, Joyce Walker-Johnson has suggested that Simpson (and by extension Ella) can be thought of as part of the new nationalist intellectual vanguard (61).

Of course, the novel's many references to colonialism and imperialism themselves *imply* a unit larger than Grove Town; they imply the existence of "Jamaica," that unit of colonial administration. I note as an aside that it may well be significant that it is at the moment of the rational labor of deliberate translation that the idea of the *nation* becomes operational.

32. Denise deCaires Narain connects the disembodiedness of Brodber's female characters to their de-individuation (101); certainly, despite the accounts of Ella's sexual encounter with Selwyn, we are given only a minimal physical description of Ella. This disembodiedness is yet another means by which Brodber rewrites the trope of the tragic mulatto—typically a beautiful, highly sexualized or hyper-embodied woman. For a history of literary representations of the mulatto in the United States, see Berzon. For Cuban representations, see Kutzinski, *Sugar's Secrets.*

33. See Doris Sommer's *Foundational Fictions* for a feminist literary history of the trope of the nation-as-family as it intersects with racial hybridity in Latin American and Caribbean literature.
34. In Brodber's third novel, *Louisiana*, the interfamilial narrative and linkages are further complicated by the experience of migration and the trans-diasporic family or community. For other attempts to think nationalism and feminism together, see West, ed.
35. Helen Tiffin remarks,

    > [t]hrough the English character, Maydene Brassington (White Hen), Brodber seems to suggest a possible reading position for the former imperialists which is not one of *absolute exclusion*.... Brodber's portrait of the Englishwoman indicates to a white audience the *minor role* a genuinely involved local sympathizer might play in the process [of recuperating the Jamaican community from a destructive history of English political and textual control]. (34, emphasis added)

    I believe, however, that not only is Maydene Brassington's role more than a "minor role" of partial inclusion, it is fundamental to *Myal*'s anti-essentialist politics that Maydene Brassington have a role on par with that of the others in the underground. It is certainly true that her interventions are at first viewed with a historically justifiable suspicion. But, as Amy Holness observes when Maydene offers her reasons for wanting to adopt Ella, "you never know who is going to set the balance right" (26). Later, it is Maydene Brassington whom Miss Gatha chooses to carry "classified information" (77). Maydene Brassington's crucial role in setting the balance right is asserted both at the level of plot and at the level of the valorized themes of hybridization and infiltration as means of resistance.
36. In a similar vein, Joan Dayan's study of vodou in *Haiti, History, and the Gods* also emphasizes "the intensely intellectual puzzlement, the process of thought working itself through terror [which] accounts for what I have always recognized as the materiality of vodou practice, its concreteness, its obsession with details and fragments, with the very things that might seem to block or hinder belief" (Dayan xvii).
37. This raises the question of whether Brodber *breaks* with marvelous realism in her conclusion. It seems to me, however, that her move is quite consistent with marvelous realism. This point might be clarified by a brief look at a passage from Carpentier's novel *El Reine de Este Mundo*, which was inspired by Haitian marvelous realism and features his manifesto on marvelous realism; he refers in that manifesto to this section of the novel: when narrating the burning of the Haitian folkhero Macandal, the narrator describes the collective faith of the crowd, which believes Macandal transforms himself into a mosquito that alights on the tricorne of the commander of troops from where it laughs at the whites. At the moment Macandal is being burned, the

crowd cries out : "Macandal saved!" It is this passage's unmistakable celebration of the slave's counter-cultural belief system and faith that is usually remarked upon (not least by Carpentier himself). What receives less attention, however, is the quiet assertion of the narrator: "And the noise and screaming and uproar were such that very few saw that Macandal, held by ten soldiers, had been thrust head first into the fire, and that a flame fed by his burning hair had drowned his last cry" (52). In other words, at the "literal" level, the narrator subscribes to a European rationalist conception of what happened, which he expands to include an account of what happened to the crowd; his rationalist reading leaves us in no doubt that Macandal's physical body was killed. The *marvel* of the story, then, lies not in Macandal's literal survival, but perhaps in the transformation through faith of the literal event of Macandal's execution and in the deepening of collective faith at the moment of his execution.

I thank Carlos Cañuelas for pointing out the narrator's differentiation of his vision of the events from that of the crowd.

Chapter 6 East Indian/West Indian: Racial Stereotype, Hosay, and the Politics of National Space

1. Haraksingh, "Control and Resistance" 62–64. See Hugh Tinker, Madhavi Kale, and Basdeo Mangru for extensive analyses of the system of indentured labor.

   Following common Trinidadian usage, I use the terms "East Indian," "Indian," and "Indo-Trinidadian" synonymously and "African," "black," and "Afro-Trinidadian" synonymously.
2. *kala pani*: black waters.
3. See Yelvington's *Producing Power* 66–68 and Ryan and Barclay's *Sharks and Sardines* 144 for evidence that reports of income disparities between Africans and Indians are greatly overstated. African and Indian incomes have in fact been roughly equal. In terms of land ownership, in the 1970s, East Indians owned about 9 percent of available land, Africans 4 percent, and French Creoles 87 percent (Constance 3). The class/race stratification that colonial rule installed, and which, broadly speaking, endures today, consisted of: (1) Whites, including (a) "principal whites" (wealthy European and Creole planters and merchants, and British officials), (b) "secondary whites" (wage-earning employees of principal whites) and (c) Syrian, Lebanese, Portuguese, and Jewish small-business owners; (2) colored descendants of black and white unions who comprised the bulk of the middle class; and (3) blacks and Indian indentured laborers (Khan, "What is a 'Spanish'?" 187).

   The wealth of different segments of the population is inversely related to their numerical strength. According to the 1980 census, people of European descent constituted only 0.5 percent of the population. People of African descent constituted 40.8 percent of the population;

people of Indian descent 40.7 percent. The remainder of the population consisted of Mixed 16.3 percent; Syrians, Lebanese, and Jews 1.8 percent; and Chinese 0.9 percent. It was in the 1990 census, which was not released for some time for fear of precipitating racial violence, that Indians overtook Africans in numerical strength by a fraction of a percentage point, thereby making the transition from an ethnic minority to an ethnic majority. In 1990, Indians comprised 40.3 percent of the population and Africans 39.6 percent.

4. Control of government by the "black" party, the People's National Movement, has led East Indians to accuse the government of promoting "black" interests and discriminating against Indians in cultural policy, education, and public sector employment. If the "Indian" United National Congress historically has charged the PNM with dominating the public sector, PNM popular discourse has represented Indians as dominating the private sector. In 1995, however, not long after the release of the population census in which the Indo-Caribbean population overtook the Afro-Caribbean, the UNC won the elections for the first time and Basdeo Panday became Trindad's first Indo-Trinidadian prime minister. Recent years in Trinidad have seen the fall of several precarious coalition-governments, and racial polarization approaching that of Guyana.
5. For an authoritative historical account of the functions of the stereotype of the lazy native in colonial legitimation, see Alatas, *The Myth of the Lazy Native.* For two later theoretical accounts of stereotypes of the native, see JanMohamed, "The Economy of Manichean Allegory" and Homi Bhabha, "The Other Question." Both of these texts, however, focus on the opposition between the colonizer and the colonized, rather than on oppositions among the colonized. However, in the Trinidadian context, it is the differences among the colonized that have been elaborated at length. See John Stewart's "Ethnic Image and Ideology in Rural Trinidad" for an analysis of contemporary deployments of racial stereotypes there.

   My own emphasis on colonial stereotypes does not posit colonialism as the founding moment of racial difference; it indicates, rather, that it was in the context of a particularly colonial racialization of difference that Africans and Indians encountered one another in Trinidad, and that it was colonial policies that determined and signified the terms of their incorporation into Trinidadian society. Thus, while tribalist and casteist vocabularies from India and Africa predate colonialism, in Trinidad (as well as in India and Africa), these vocabularies were reconfigured during the colonial period. For example, the Hindi word "dougla," meaning "bastard," was used in India to designate descendants of intercaste or interreligious unions, but in Trinidad it refers specifically to the descendants of Indian and African unions.
6. In a more sympathetic formulation, Frantz Fanon observed: "The Negro is comparison.... Whenever he comes into contact with someone else, the question of value, or merit, arises. The Antilleans

have no inherent value of their own, they are always contingent on the presence of the other" (*Black Skins, White Masks* 211).

7. In the course of *The Middle Passage*, Naipaul invokes other colonialist writers, including Charles Kingsley and Anthony Trollope.
8. For a similar usage, see also Naipaul's "East Indian."
9. See for example the epigraph of Dabydeen and Samaroo, eds., *India in the Caribbean* and Jagan 24–25.
10. For Naipaul's meditations on "the Trinidadian" see *The Middle Passage* 77. See also C.L.R. James's *Beyond a Boundary* for the place of cricket in race relations, decolonization, and symbols of West Indianness.
11. Prior to Emancipation, during Canboulay (from the French *cannes brulées*), the French Creole plantocracy would dress as slaves and roam the streets with drums and lit torches, imitating the burning of the cane fields by slaves. After Emancipation, however, Canboulay became the proud preserve of Afro-Caribbeans, and came to symbolize freedom from slavery. In it, they enacted scenes of a brutalizing slavery, in a potentially subversive black mimicry of white mimicry of black slaves. See Cowley and Hill for detailed accounts of Canboulay, its regulation, and its relationship to Carnival.
12. Elaborated in the Caribbean as Hosay, Hussein, Tazia, or Tadjah, Muharram is the occasion on which Shia Muslims traditionally commemorate the martyrdom of Hussain and Hassan, the grandsons of the Prophet Mohammed, who died in the struggles for succession after the death of the Prophet—Hassan by poison and Hussain in the Battle of Karbala. In Shia practice, the mourning for the martyrdom is emphasized over the merriment and feasting that otherwise characterize the tenth day of Muharram (the "Ashura") in celebration of the first rainfall, the creation of Adam and Eve and the ninth heaven, and the assignment of the divine mission to the spirits of 10,000 prophets (Singh 5). Although Hosay's Shia origins are known in Trinidad, it is not observed as a Shia event, but reflects, rather, Shia influence on Sunni practice (Khan, "Homeland, Motherland" 126). The procession, for example, has little of the self-flagellation that characterizes it in India; instead, the mood is often one of gaiety. According to Juneja, there is drinking, and some of the tazias may even be sponsored by rum shops. (Literally meaning grief or consoling, tazias are the imaginative recreations of the tombs of the martyrs.) The procession itself takes place by torchlight, with drumming, enactments of scenes from the life and martyrdom of Hassan and Hussein, and stick-fighting. On Little Hosay night the green moon of Hassan and the red moon of Hussain "kiss." The main procession occurs on the tenth night, destined for the symbolic Karbala at the Queen's Royal College. Three days later, on Teej, the tazias are immersed in the Gulf of Paria.

    For studies of Hosay, see Bettelheim and Nunley, Chelkowski and Korom, Mangru, Mohapatra, Singh, and Thaiss.

13. Cowley documents evidence of Creole resentment as early as 1859 at the regulation of Canboulay and Carnival but not Hosay (56). Analyzing the editorials of various contemporary dailies and periodicals such as *New Era, Sentinel, Port of Spain Gazette, Fair Play*, and *San Fernando Gazette* offers a way of reading Hosay regulation within the matrix of Creole/Indian relations and debates on immigration. See, for example, Singh, especially 23–25, 26, 64–65, 95–96. My comparison of Canboulay and Hosay is indebted to Cowley and Singh; although neither extensively compares the two or addresses the implications of the comparison, their books provide the archival materials about each practice, which have enabled my comparison.
14. For example, 1882 saw the Cedar Hill Disturbances, in which Indians revolted against their overseers. See *Port of Spain Gazette*'s editorials urging the suppression of Hosay, and the Anti-Slavery Society's letter to *The London Times* urging nonintervention.
15. Evidence of black participation in Hosay dates back to the 1850s (Singh 7), and in Saint James in particular there was substantial black working-class participation. Carnival masquerades from as far back as 1878 included Creole depictions of Hosay processions (Cowley 83–84). In Guyana there is even evidence of black tazias and of Creoles being tried for observing their own Hosay, which incorporated African rites (Mangru 22). Finally, there is evidence of Creole encouragement and support of Indian resistance to the police suppression of Hosay in 1884 (Singh 87, 120).
16. For example, as Kale and Thaiss point out, the immersion of the tazias into water seems to have been inspired by Hindu religious practices; furthermore, there is evidence of large-scale Sunni participation and some Hindu participation in Muharram in India. See Kale, "Projecting Identities" for a detailed account of the reifying function of invocations of Indian Islam in Trinidadian legislation; see also Khan, Chelkowski and Korom, and Thaiss.
17. I will not address in this condensed and selective reading the relationship of Indo-Caribbeans to England and Empire, which is explored in the novel through the Empire Day celebrations. For more extended readings of the novel, see Cobham and Juneja.
18. See Singh for newspaper accounts of the eviction debates.
19. See also *The Jumbie Bird* 48–49.
20. I intentionally play here on the title of Lila Abu-Lughod's essay "The Romance of Resistance."
21. Rohlehr, in conversation, August 17, 1995.
22. Ever since the early years of independence there has been a tradition of "nation-building," "national unity," and "callaloo" calypsos. The subtitle of this section is in part intended to caution that I do not address that tradition in this chapter. For a sample of Afro-Trinidadian calypsos that dissent from PNM party politics, are more conciliatory toward Indo-Trinidadians and more tolerant of interracial and

intercultural mixing, see the work of the contemporary popular calypsonian Chalkdust, who in 1995 became the UNC's Minister of Culture.

The following discussion of a range of race calypsos is intended to quickly identify some recurrent racial tropes and broadly map the terrain of racial discourse; it does not seek to provide close readings of the calypsos, far less to take into account their musical features or performances. (In many cases only fragmentary print-texts of the calypsos survive; many of the calypsos were never recorded.)

23. Similarly, women calypsonians and feminists have had to confront the issue of what kinds of constraints are placed on calypso by the fact that it has historically been a black *male* art form.
24. "Capra" is Hindi for cloth; in Trinidadian Hindi it often refers to the loincloth or dhoti that men wear. In popular and political discourse in Trinidad, dress and eating habits have frequently been used as markers of racial difference and an occasion for ridicule. Hence the reference to Indian food in the 1961 election slogan, "We don't want no roti government" (Constance 28). For an account of pre-independence calypso's constructions of race relations, see Rohlehr, *Calypso and Society in Pre-Independence Trinidad*, esp. 493–508.
25. See Constance 28. Capildeo was the leader of the predominantly Indian Democratic Labor Party. His call to violence is evidence that if in the calypsos I cite the violence is directed primarily against Indians, it is not because Indians were passive victims of racial aggression, but rather that calypso, a historically black cultural form, was not the medium in which they expressed their racial antagonisms. I address problematic Indian constructions of blackness in chapter seven.
26. Callaloo: a common liberal metaphor for nonconflictual hybridity and unity-in-diversity.
27. For a further elaboration of the term "Creole," see Segal.
28. Qtd. in Constance 7–8, where he also provides a reading of the calypso.
29. I allude here to Mighty Cobra's 1958 hit "The Changes of the Indian," which makes many of the same moves as Killer's calypso.
30. "Jean and Dinah" was the name of Sparrow's famous 1956 calypso about the fate of prostitution after the departure of the Americans from the island. In this context, Jean and Dinah are all but synonyms for prostitutes.

Chapter 7 Facing the Music: Gender, Race, and Dougla Poetics

1. See Raffique Shah for an account of the convergent class interests of the predominantly Indian Democratic Labor Party and the predominantly Creole PNM, and for evidence of the collusion between their leaderships to crush the Black Power struggles in 1970, when it appeared that the mostly Indian sugar workers would join the Black

Power demonstrators. In 1965, the government passed the Industrial Stabilization Act which forbade workers from two essential racialized industries, sugar and oil, from joining (Shah 8).

2. Anannya Bhattacharjee's essay, "The Habit of Ex-Nomination: Nation, Woman and the Indian Immigrant Bourgeoisie," which applies and extends Chatterjee's work to Indian cultural nationalist discourse in the United States, first suggested to me the relevance of Chatterjee's framework to the Indo-Trinidadian context. Caitrin Lynch's response to Bhattacharjee's essay is a useful complement to the latter's argument.
3. Aisha Khan provides ample data to support this claim. For instance, one dougla interviewee identifies himself as Indian, because "dougla" is "kind of negative" (204). Another interview proceeds as follows:

   Indo-Trinidadian woman: "My boyfriend is a Spanish-Indian and Negro."
   AK: "Isn't that a *dougla*?"
   Woman: "Well, I don't use that word, I calls it Spanish.
   He have grey eyes, like, and soft hair. I doesn't say *dougla*."
   AK: "How about if he had dark eyes and hard hair?"
   Woman: "Oh! Then he'd be *dougla*, not Spanish." (198)

   The interview is cited in the context of an argument which demonstrates the positive social value of the ambiguous racial/ethnic mixed category "Spanish" as opposed to the negative social value often placed on the racial ambiguity implied by "dougla." See also Segal 97; Sampath 237–239. Bridget Brereton and Rhoda Reddock trace contemporary Indian disavowals of the dougla back to the highly skewed sex ratios within the Indian population during the period of indentureship, as well as to Hindu notions of caste endogamy. It is in that context that the pejorative Hindi term "dougla" or bastard was applied to people of mixed Indian and African descent. Today, most people in Trinidad are not aware of its literal meaning, and it remains the only word to specifically designate the mix of Afro- and Indo-Caribbean.
4. Kumar and Sita Mahabir. *A Dictionary of Common Trinidad Hindi.*
5. For a longer excerpt, see Trotman 396.
6. The Sanatan Dharma Maha Sabha has historically been and continues to be the dominant voice of organized Hinduism in Trinidad today. Originally the religious wing of the bourgeois-nationalist Indian Democratic Labor Party, the Maha Sabha has historically represented bourgeois-nationalist economic interests, orthodox Hinduism, and conservative or reactionary cultural politics. Although today the Maha Sabha has no formal ties with the leadership of the UNC, as Carol Prorok observes, "associating with the SDMS formally precludes a certain political position." According to Prorok's data, in 1985, 46 of 186 Hindu temples were affiliated with the Maha Sabha–more than with any other organization. (E-mail to the author.)

I address the Maha Sabha's advertisement for several reasons. First, the Maha Sabha is the most vocal and visible orthodox Indian presence in Trinidad; it claims to speak for all Indo-Trinidadians. Second, while the Maha Sabha probably does not represent the opinions of all the people whom it claims to represent, it cannot be dismissed as a fringe group either, as Prorok's data show. Third, even though some of the positions of the Maha Sabha may be extremist, its position on douglas and douglarization falls well within mainstream Indo-Trinidadian opinion. Moreover, the advertisement relies on the logic of the racial stereotype, a logic which I have argued forms the bedrock of commonsensical racial discourse in Trinidad. It is the racial stereotype and its foregrounding of racial inequalities to the exclusion of gender and class inequalities with which this chapter is centrally concerned. For these reasons, I here consider the Maha Sabha as a metonym for Indian bourgeois-nationalist economic and cultural ideology.

7. See C.L.R James's Minty Alley for a novel that dramatizes the perception of the "dougla" as racially "diluted." Both the Maha Sabha and the African Association mobilize racist colonial scientific discourses that understand racial mixing as degeneration. In the context of the contemporary United States, arguments about racial "dilution" and "race suicide" are persistent and familiar in debates over interracial relationships and adoptions.
8. Here, too, the Maha Sabha's strategy in imagining the dougla as the offspring of a (forced) union between an African man and an Indian woman mirrors the strategy of the conservative African discourse represented by Superior, Killer, and Christo.

   Rhoda Reddock has shown that this construction of the dougla continues in the 1980s. Referring to the spate of 1980s calypsos portraying "the male African calypsonian in a love/marriage/sexual relationship with an Indian woman," Reddock writes: "these songs really represented a metaphor for the anxiety and tension ridden love–hate relationship which exists between the two groups, but to a large extent they were seen by Indian men as another example of the African man's desire to take their women while to a lesser extent to African women it was seen as another reflection of their rejection by African men" (109). In other words, many Indians read interracial relationships as a sign of cultural/sexual conquest of Indian women by African men, while many African women read African men's desire for Indian women as a sign of the internalized racism or self-contempt of African men. Reddock's interviews with douglas born to Indian *fathers* and African *mothers* help contest some of the assumptions accompanying dominant constructions of the dougla as the descendant of an African father and an Indian mother.
9. To continue my discussion of economic assimilation and cultural separatism, if conservative Indians objected to the *exclusion* of Indians from the calypsonian Black Stalin's vision of a black Caribbean in "Caribbean Man," they also objected to the *inclusion* of Indian culture

in Carnival. Thus, Shorty's "Om Shanti" drew criticism from the Maha Sabha for insulting Hinduism by bringing its holy prayers into the "vulgar streets" of Carnival. "Om Shanti" went on to become a hit in the Bombay film "Karz." The song's incorporation into popular/mass culture in India failed to generate comparable objections in India, probably because of Hinduism's cultural dominance there.

10. For a fuller statement of this cultural nationalist position, see Kenneth Parmasad's paper, "The Wedding Tent and the Public Space: Towards an Understanding of Indian Cultural Practices in Trinidad," which I have here summarized. I offer a critique of his argument below, in the course of my reading of Drupatee's chutney-soca. For other feminist analyses of the chutney-dancing phenomenon, see the CAFRA archives, Tejaswini Niranjana, and Rosanne Kanhai. My own sense is that the transgressive public performance of chutney dancing is neither definitively liberatory nor definitively oppressive.
11. This was certainly the most sustained objection made to my qualified defense of the song at the Conference on the Indian Diaspora in Trinidad in August 1995.
12. "Maxi" is a short form of "maxi-taxi," one of the quickest and cheapest forms of transportation in Trinidad; it is a private van which serves as a route taxi. The central event that the song describes, as well as many of the puns, is to be read in the context of the several fatal accidents caused by maxi-taxi drivers' speeding and reckless driving. At the most literal level, therefore, the song criticizes the government's failure to effectively regulate the maxi-taxi industry.
13. See Rohlehr, "Images of Men and Women in the 1930's Calypsos," especially the section entitled "The Battered Woman" (292–296). Dismissals of the song as mindless party music participate in a larger debate about whether the "rise of highly rhythmic, celebratory, but verbally simplistic 'soca' tunes has led to a depoliticization of the Trinidad Calypso" (Rohlehr, *My Strangled City* 328). Rather than understanding the comic and the overtly political as mutually exclusive, Rohlehr places gender and ethnic conflict at the heart of a Trinidadian comic tradition ("Images of Men and Women" 308).
14. According to Bhiku Parekh, domestic violence within the Indian diasporic community is the highest amongst all diasporic communities.
15. Many invoke the fact that the calypso was written by an Afro-Trinidadian man (Barnet Henry) as evidence that its agenda is to degrade Indian culture. It is common for calypsonians, both Afro-and Indo-Trinidadian, to sing calypsos written by others. However, I am less interested here in questions of the songwriter's intent than in the performance and reception of the song.
16. Rohlehr, in conversation. August 17, 1995.
17. Thus Bakhtin writes:

> Degradation here means coming down to earth, the contact with earth as an element that swallows up and gives birth at the same

time. To degrade is to bury, to sow, and to kill simultaneously, in order to bring forth something more and better. To degrade also means to concern oneself with the lower stratum of the body, the life of the belly and the reproductive organs; it therefore relates to acts of defecation and copulation, conception, pregnancy, birth.... To degrade an object does not imply merely hurling it into the void of non-existence, into absolute destruction, but to hurl it down to the reproductive lower stratum, the zone in which conception and a new birth takes place. (*Rabelais and His World* 20–22)

18. One of the cultural nationalist objections to Rosanne Kanhai's paper "The Masala-Stone Sings: Indo-Caribbean Women Coming into Voice," where Kanhai appropriated the Bhowjee figure for a feminist Indo-Caribbean aesthetics, was that the Bhowjee (sister-in-law) is "the product of a male gaze." The proposed alternative was "why not Nani or Bahin (grandmother or sister) instead of Bhowjee?" Although it might be possible to appropriate the terms Nani and Bahin from within a patriarchal framework (as indeed Kanhai does with the Bhowjee figure), it seems to me that, once again, the objection erases the sexuality of Indo-Trinidadian women. Kanhai's response was that the Nani and Bahin are desexualized figures and were thus not as useful to her project of thinking sexuality and artistic creativity together. I would add that Nani and Bahin are *de*sexualized by the male gaze, just as the Bhowjee is *sexualized* by the male gaze.
19. For an insightful study of the shifting functions of Holi in another diasporic Indian context, see Kelly, "From Holi to Diwali in Fiji."
20. See Bakhtin, *Rabelais* 11–12. In fact, Bakhtin's critique of then-hegemonic and monologic readings of Rabelais is applicable to contemporary Trinidadian cultural nationalist dismissals of "Lick Down Me Nani" as frivolous or apolitical on grounds of its festive humor.
21. "Wining" is the gyrating dancing done to calypso. "Jamming" refers to making music and improvising. Both "wine" and "jam," however, are also used as stock sexual *double entendres*, as, for example, "I want to jam you," or "Nani get jam from maxi man." "Wine and jam" calypsos are the target of annual lamentations, from both Afro-Creole and Indian sections of the population, about the state of public morality and the decay of calypso as a serious art form.
22. The media coverage and political statements made by Hulsie Bhaggan, a UNC parliamentary representative, about the March 1993 bandit rapes of Indo-Trinidadian women by Afro-Trinidadian men are a case in point. To my knowledge, no public discussion of *intra*-racial rape has received such extensive national coverage, although intra-racial rapes are almost certainly far more numerous. For an analysis of the rapes which provides an alternative to the mainstream media's, see Maharaj et al., "Report on Bandit Rape, Crime and Race in Central Trinidad." For an account of what is at stake in suppressing the figure of the woman who is the victim of intra-racial

violence, see Anannya Bhattacharjee's and Caitrin Lynch's analyses of how dominant Indian American cultural nationalists responded to the shelters for battered South Asian or Indian-American women.

23. I am grateful to Carol Prorok for encouraging me to think this issue through.
24. "Ramleela" is the (performance of) the story of the Hindu god/king Rama. Given the marginalization of Indian culture and festivals from a national imaginary that centers Afro-Creole culture, it is not surprising that the Ramleela plays an important part in Indo-Trinidadian cultural politics.
25. Amy Andrews insightfully reads "Barred" as a stanzic poem in which each stanza, self-contained and marked off from the others, serves as a room or stopping place. Presentation in graduate course, February 26, 2001.
26. "dhal": lentils; "bhaji": vegetables.
27. See the Afro-Trinidadian Mighty Chalkdust's "Ram the Magician" of 1984, a tribute to the real-life Ram Kirpalani, now an archetypal figure of Indian "rags to riches" success. The calypso's chorus playfully insists: "If you cyan run the country/Call in Kirpalani" (Trotman 398). Kirpalani is the image par excellence of someone who can profitably manage resources. Criticizing the failed economic policies of the African-dominated PNM government and the Prime Minister George Chambers, Chalkdust actually advocates remaking Trinidad in the image of the Indian businessman. Kirpalani is neither a scholar nor a professional politician, but he can bring to politics a practical knowledge of financial management: he "never went to a school/but he have a Ph.D in money." Ironically, Kirpalani's business went bankrupt and folded within three years of Chalkdust's calypso. (I thank Kevin Yelvington for pointing this fact out to me.) It tells us much about the way in which stereotype functions that the fact of the failure of Kirpalani, the very symbol of Indian economic success, did not for a moment weaken the discourse of Indian economic success.
28. "Ohrni": long cloth worn by women to cover the head and chest.
29. We recall that Lord Superior's and Killer's calypsos, among others, frame the problem as one of Indian "intruders" acquiring too much wealth, that is of people who do not "belong" having too many "belongings." For an Afro-Caribbean literary text that explores the dialectic of possession and dispossession in relation to race and gender in ways that overlap with Espinet's, see Lovelace, *The Dragon Can't Dance.*
30. Like the Indians in "Indian People With Creole Name," she did "make her way up" by stealing someone else's belongings, but she stole from another Indian and she did so in part to feed him. In fact, her theft results in his restoration to economic productivity, since thereafter he improves the shop and participates in the shopkeeping.
31. See Stewart for a study of images of Indo-Caribbeans as shopkeepers.
32. Cheong, "Notes on the Eve of a Green Card." Unpublished ms.

33. "Laventille" is a largely Afro-Trinidadian slum near Port of Spain; Caroni is a poor rural Indo-Trinidadian county; they function as markers of "Africanness" and "Indianness" respectively.
34. "Dhoti": draped clothing worn by Indian men; "jhandi": Hindu prayer flags. Both words are commonly used markers of Indian difference. In Brother Marvin's song, however, they are used to mark the inseparability of Self and Other.
35. For an account of the controversy surrounding this calypso, see Constance 46–48 and Warner 282–290.
36. For one of the first and only book-length histories of the Chinese Caribbean presence, see Look Lai. For a literary exploration of the Chinese in the national imaginary of Trinidad, see Chen.
37. See Espinet's recent play "Indian Robber Talk" and her poems "Mama Glo" and "Hosay Night."
38. See Torabully, *Cale d'étoiles-coolitude* (1992) and *Coolitude* (2002).
39. Torabully's assertion that "Creoleness is to *négritude* what coolitude is to *indianité*" (Coolitude 152), however, also points up some of the same conceptual problems in his conception of coolitude that I have identified in Créolité.
40. See Vertovec 219–220.
41. The dougla poetics of Chris Garcia's 1996 "Chutney Bacchanal," for example, is only marginally different from any number of "all oh we is one" or "wine and jam" tunes. That being said, however, lest "Chutney Bacchanal's" "frivolity" be chalked up to the corrupting influence of Creole carnival, I note that the video of the song, with its construction of a coyly titillating femininity, probably owes more to the song-and-dance sequences of commercial Bombay cinema than to Creole carnival.

Works Cited

Abastado, Claude. "Introduction a l'analyse des manifestes." Special issue on "L'Écriture manifestaire." *Littérature* 39.3 (October 1980): 3–11.

Abu-Lughod, Lila. "The Romance of Resistance: Tracing Transformations of Power through Bedouin Women." *American Ethnologist* 17.1 (February 1990): 41–55.

Aching, Gerard. *The Politics of Spanish American "Modernismo": By Exquisite Design*. Cambridge University Press, 1997.

Ahmad, Aijaz. *In Theory: Classes, Nations, Literatures*. London and New York: Verso, 1992.

——. "The Politics of Literary Postcoloniality." *Contemporary Postcolonial Theory: A Reader*. Ed. Padmini Mongia. London and New York: Arnold, 1996. 276–293.

Alarcón, Norma. "Traddutora, Traditora: A Paradigmatic Figure of Chicana Feminism." *Dangerous Liaisons: Gender, Nation, and Postcolonial Perspectives*. Ed. Anne McClintock, Aamir Mufti, and Ella Shohat. Minneapolis and London: University of Minnesota Press, 1997. 278–297.

Alatas, Syed Hussein. *The Myth of the Lazy Native: A Study of the Image of the Malays, Filipinos and Javanese from the 16th to the 20th Century and Its Function in the Ideology of Colonial Capitalism*. London: Frank Cass, 1977.

Amin, Samir. *Capitalism in the Age of Globalization: The Management of Contemporary Society*. London and New Jersey: Zed, 1997.

——. *Delinking: Towards a Polycentric World*. London and New Jersey: Zed Books, 1990.

Anderson, Benedict. *Imagined Communities: Reflections on the Origin and Spread of Nationalism*. London and New York: Verso, 1990.

Anzaldúa, Gloria. *Borderlands/La Frontera: The New Mestiza*. San Francisco: Spinsters/Aunt Lute, 1987.

Appadurai, Arjun. *Modernity at Large: Cultural Dimensions of Globalization*. Minneapolis, Minnesota: University of Minnesota Press, 1996.

Appiah, Kwame Anthony. "Is the Post in Postmodernism the Post in Postcolonial?" *Contemporary Postcolonial Theory: A Reader*. Ed. Padmini Mongia. London and New York: Arnold, 1996. 55–71.

Arion, Frank Martinus. "The Victory of the Concubines and the Nannies." *Caribbean Creolization: Reflections on the Cultural Dynamics of*

Language, Literature, and Identity. Ed. Kathleen M. Balutansky and Marie-Agnes Sourieau. Gainesville: University Press of Florida, 1998. 110–117.

Aronowitz, Stanley. *Post-Work: The Wages of Cybernation*. London and New York: Routledge, 1997.

Asad, Talal. "Introduction." *Genealogies of Religion: Discipline and Reasons of Power in Christianity and Islam*. Johns Hopkins University Press, 1993. 1–24.

Ashcroft, Bill, Gareth Griffiths, and Helen Tiffin. *The Empire Writes Back: Theory and Practice in Post-colonial Literatures*. London and New York: Routledge, 1989.

Austin-Broos, Diane. *Jamaica Genesis: Religion and the Politics of Moral Orders*. Chicago: University of Chicago Press, 1997.

Bakhtin, Mikhail. *Rabelais and His World*. Cambridge, Massachussetts: MIT Press, 1968.

——. *The Dialogic Imagination: Four Essays*. Ed. Michael Holquist. Trans. Caryl Emerson and Michael Holquist. Austin: University of Texas Press, 1981.

Barker, Francis, Peter Hulme, and Margaret Iverson, eds. *Cannibalism and the Colonial World*. Cambridge: Cambridge University Press, 1998.

Barnes, Natasha. "Body Talk: Notes on Women and Spectacle in Contemporary Trinidad carnival." *Small Axe* 7 (March 2000): 93–105.

Beckford, George. *Persistent Poverty: Underdevelopment in Plantation Economies of the Third World*. New York: Oxford University Press, 1972.

Behn, Aphra. *Oroonoko Or, The Royal Slave*. New York and London: Norton, 1997.

Benítez-Rojo, Antonio. *The Repeating Island: The Caribbean and the Postmodern Perspective*. Trans. James Maraniss. Durham: Duke University Press, 1992.

Bernabé, Jean, Patrick Chamoiseau, and Raphaël Confiant. *Éloge de la Créolite*. Paris: Gallimard, 1989.

——. "In Praise of Creoleness." Trans. Mohamed B. Taleb Khyar. *Callaloo* 13 (1990): 886–909.

Berzon, Judith R. *Neither Black Nor White: The Mulatto Character in American Fiction*. New York: New York University Press, 1978.

Bettelheim, Judith and John Nunley. "The Hosay Festival." *Caribbean Festival Arts: Each and Every Bit of Difference*. Ed. John Nunley and Judith Bettelheim. Saint Louis Art Museum in association with University of Washington Press, 1988. 119–135.

Beverley, John. "Populism and Nationalism: Some Reservations." *Process of Unity in Caribbean Society: Ideologies and Literature*. Ed. Ileana Rodriguez and Marc Zimmerman. Minneapolis, Minnesota: Institute for the Study of Ideologies and Literatures, 1983. 141–157.

——and José Oviedo, eds. *The Postmodernism Debate in Latin America*. Special issue of *boundary* 2 20.3 (Fall 1993).

Bhabha, Homi. *The Location of Culture*. London and New York: Routledge, 1994.

——. "A Question of Survival: Nations and Psychic States." *Pyschoanalysis and Cultural Theory: Thresholds.* Ed. James Donald. New York: St. Martin's Press: 1991. 89–103.

——. "DissemiNation: Time, Narrative, and the Margins of the Modern Nation." *Nation and Narration.* Ed. Homi Bhabha. London and New York: Routledge, 1990. 291–322.

——. "The Other Question." *Screen* 24.6 (1983): 18–36.

——, ed. *Nation and Narration.* London and New York: Routledge, 1990.

Bhattacharjee, Anannya. "The Habit of Ex-Nomination: Nation, Woman and the Indian Immigrant Bourgeoisie." *Public Culture* 5.1 (Fall 1992): 19–44.

Birbalsingh, Frank, ed. *From Pillar to Post: The Indo-Caribbean Diaspora.* Toronto: TSAR, 1997.

Birth, Kevin. "Bakrnal: Coup, Carnival, and Calypso in Trinidad." *Ethnology* 33.2 (Spring 1994): 165–178.

Bjornson, Richard, ed. *The Language Question.* Special issue of *Research in African Literatures* 23.1 (Spring 1992).

Boehmer, Elleke, and Bart Moore-Gilbert, eds. *Postcolonial Studies and Transnational Resistance.* Special issue of *Interventions: International Journal of Postcolonial Studies* 4.1 (2002).

Bolland, O. Nigel. "Creolization and Creole Societies: A Cultural Nationalist View of Caribbean Social History." *Intellectuals in the Twentieth Century v.1: The Commonwealth Caribbean.* Ed. Alistair Hennessy. London: Macmillan, 1992. 50–79.

Borneman, John. *Belonging in the Two Berlins: Kin, State, Nation.* Cambridge: Cambridge University Press, 1992.

Bottomore, Tom. *A Dictionary of Marxist Thought.* Cambridge: Harvard University Press, 1983.

Bourne, Randolph. "Transnational America." *Atlantic Monthly* July 1916 v. 118 (July–Dec). 86–97.

Brah, Avtar and Annie Coombes, eds. *Hybridity and Its Discontents: Politics, Science, and Culture.* London and New York: Routledge, 2000.

Brathwaite, Edward Kamau. *Contradictory Omens: Cultural Diversity and Integration in the Caribbean.* Mona, Jamaica: Savacou Publications, 1974.

——. *The Development of Creole Society in Jamaica 1770–1820.* Oxford: Clarendon, 1971.

——. *The Arrivants: A New World Trilogy.* London and New York: Oxford University Press, 1973.

——. "History of the Voice." *Roots.* Ann Arbor: University of Michigan Press, 1993. 259–304.

—— and Édouard Glissant. "A Dialogue: Nation Language and Poetics of Creolization." *Presencia Criolla en el Caribe y América Latina/Creole Presence in the Caribbean and Latin America.* Ed. Ineke Phaf. Frankfurt am Main: Verveurt, 1996. 19–35.

Brecht, Bertolt. "Against Georg Lukács." *Aesthetics and Politics.* London: Verso, 1980. 68–85.

Brennan, Timothy. *At Home in the World: Cosmopolitanism Now.* Cambridge, Massachussetts: Harvard, 1997.

Brennan, Timothy. *Salman Rushdie and the Third World: Myths of the Nation.* New York: St. Martin's Press, 1989.

Brereton, Bridget. *Race Relations in Colonial Trinidad: 1870–1900.* Cambridge: Cambridge University Press, 1979.

Britton, Celia. *Édouard Glissant and Postcolonial Theory: Strategies of Language and Resistance.* Charlottesville and London: University Press of Virginia, 1999.

Brodber, Erna. *Louisiana.* London and Port of Spain: New Beacon, 1994.

——. *Myal.* London and New York: New Beacon Books, 1988.

——. "Fiction in the Scientific Procedure." *Caribbean Women Writers: Essays from the First International Conference.* Ed. Selwyn Cudjoe. Wellesley, Massachusetts: Calaloux Publications, 1990. 164–168.

Brown, Michael F. "On Resisting Resistance." *American Anthropologist* 98.4 (December 1996): 729–735.

Brown, Stewart, Mervyn Morris, and Gordon Rohlehr, eds. *VoicePrint: An Anthology of Oral and Related Poetry from the Caribbean.* Essex and Kingston: Longman, 1989.

Brydon, Diana. "Trusting the Contradictions: Competing Ideologies in Earl Lovelace's *The Dragon Can't Dance.*" *English Studies in Canada* 15.3 (September 1989): 319–335.

Busia, Abena. "Silencing Sycorax: On African Colonial Discourse and the Unvoiced Female." *Cultural Critique* 14 (Winter 1989–90). 81–104.

Burton, Richard D.E. *Afro-Creole: Power, Opposition, and Play in the Caribbean.* Ithaca and London: Cornell University Press, 1997.

——. "The Idea of Difference in Contemporary French West Indian Thought: Négritude, Antillanité, Créolité" *French and West Indian: Martinique, Guadeloupe and French Guiana Today.* Ed. Richard D.E. Burton and Fred Reno. London: Macmillan, 1995. 137–166.

Butler, Judith. *Gender Trouble: Feminism and the Subversion of Identity.* New York: Routledge, 1990.

Carpentier, Alejo. "Prólogo." *El Reino de Este Mundo.* Havana, Cuba: Editorial Letras Cubanas, 1984. 5–11.

——. "Prologue to *The Kingdom of This World.*" *The Oxford Book of Latin American Essays.* Ed. Ilan Stavans. New York and Oxford: Oxford University Press, 1997. 194–198.

——. *The Kingdom of This World.* Trans. Harriet de Onís. New York: Noonday Press, 1989.

——. "On the Marvelous Real in America." *Magical Realism: Theory, History, Community.* Ed. Lois Parkinson Zamora and Wendy B. Faris. Durham and London: Duke, 1995. 75–88.

Carr, Raymond. *Puerto Rico: A Colonial Experiment.* New York: Vintage, 1984.

Caws, Mary Ann, "The Poetics of the Manifesto: Nowness and Newness." *Manifesto: A Century of Isms.* Ed. Mary Ann Caws. Lincoln and London: University of Nebraska Press, 2001. xix–xxxi.

Césaire, Aimé. *Discourse on Colonialism.* New York: Monthly Review Press, 1972.

——. "Notebook of a Return to the Native Land." *Aimé Césaire: The Collected Poetry*. Trans. Clayton Eshleman and Annette Smith. Berkeley: University of California Press, 1983. 32–85.

Chambers, Iain. *Popular Culture: The Metropolitan Experience*. London and New York: Methuen, 1986.

Chamoiseau, Patrick. *Texaco*. Trans. Rose-Myriam Réjouis and Val Vinokurov. New York: Vintage, 1997.

Chang, Victor L., ed. *Three Caribbean Poets on Their Work: E. Kamau Brathwaite, Mervyn Morris, Lorna Goodison*. Mona, Jamaica: Institute of Caribbean studies, University of the West Indies, 1993.

Chatterjee, Partha. "The Nationalist Resolution of the Women's Question." *Recasting Women: Essays in Indian Colonial History*. Ed. Kum Kum Sangari and Sudesh Vaid. New Delhi: Kali for Women, 1989. 233–253.

Cheah, Pheng. "Given Culture." *Cosmopolitics: Thinking and Feeling Beyond the Nation*. Ed. Pheng Cheah and Bruce Robbins. Minneapolis and London: University of Minnesota Press, 1998. 290–328.

—— and Bruce Robbins, eds. *Cosmopolitics: Thinking and Feeling Beyond the Nation*. Minneapolis and London: University of Minnesota Press, 1998.

Chelkowski, Peter J. and Frank Korom. "Community Process and the Performance of Muharram Observances in Trinidad." *The Drama Review* 38.2 (Summer 1994): 150–175.

Chen, Willie. *King of the Carnival*. London: Hansib Publishing, 1988.

Cheong, Fiona. "Notes on the Eve of a Green Card." Unpublished ms.

Clarke, Colin. *East Indians in a West Indian Town*. San Fernando, Trinidad: 1930–70. London and Boston: Allen and Unwin, 1986.

Clarke, Richard L.W. "Root Versus Rhizome: An 'Epistemological Break' in Francophone Caribbean Thought." *Journal of West Indian Literature* 9.1 (April 2000): 12–41.

Clifford, James. *The Predicament of Culture: Twentieth Century Ethnography, Literature, and Art*. Cambridge: Harvard University Press, 1988.

Cobham, Rhonda. "*The Jumbie Bird* by Ismith Khan: A New Assessment." *Journal of Commonwealth Literature* 21.1 (1986): 240–249.

Colás, Santiago. "The Third World in Jameson's Postmodernism or, the Cultural Logic of Late Capitalism." *Social Text* 31–32 (1992): 258–270.

Condé, Maryse. "Order, Disorder, Freedom, and the West Indian Writer." *Yale French Studies* 83 (1993): 121–135. Special issue *Post/Colonial Conditions*. Ed. Lionnet and Scharfman.

Conrad, Joseph. *Heart of Darkness: An Authoritative Text, Backgrounds, and Sources, Criticism*. Ed. Robert Kimbrough. New York: Norton, 1988.

Constance, Zeno Obi. *Tassa, Chutney and Soca: The East Indian Contribution to the Calypso*. San Fernando, Trinidad: pvt. publication (Jordan's Printing Service), 1991.

Coombes, Annie. *Reinventing Africa: Museums, Material Culture and Popular Imagination in Late Victorial and Edwardian England*. New Haven: Yale University Press, 1997.

Cooper, Carolyn. *Noises in the Blood: Orality, Gender and the "Vulgar" Body of Jamaican Popular Culture*. London and Basingstoke: Macmillan, 1995.

Cooper, Carolyn. "Something Ancestral Recaptured: Spirit Possession as Trope in Selected Feminist Fictions of the African Diaspora." *Motherlands: Black Women's Writing from Africa, the Caribbean and South Asia.* Ed. Susheila Nasta. New Jersey: Rutgers University Press, 1992. 64–87.

Cowley, John. *Carnival, Canboulay and Calypso: Traditions in the Making.* Cambridge: Cambridge University Press, 1996.

Cuba Commission. *The Cuba Commission Report: A Hidden History of the Chinese in Cuba.* The Original English-Language Text of 1876. Introduction by Denise Helly. Baltimore and London: Johns Hopkins University Press, 1993.

Dabydeen, David and Brinsley Samaroo, eds. *India in the Caribbean.* London: Hansib, 1987.

Da Matta, Roberto. "*Carnaval* as a Cultural Problem: Towards a Theory of Formal Events and their Magic." Helen Kellog Institute for International Studies. Working Paper 79 (September 1986).

Dash, Michael. *The Other America: Caribbean Literature in a New World Context.* Charlottesville and London: University Press of Virginia, 1998.

——. *Édouard Glissant.* Cambridge: Cambridge University Press, 1995.

——. "Psychology, Creolization, and Hybridization." *New National and Post-Colonial Literatures: An Introduction.* Ed. Bruce King. Oxford: Clarendon, 1996. 45–58.

——. "Marvellous Realism: The Way Out of Négritude." Special Issue: Between Negritude and Marvellous Realism. *Black Images* 3.2 (1974): 80–95.

Davis, Gregson. " 'With No Homeric Shadow': The Disavowal of Epic in Derek Walcott's Omeros." *The Poetics of Derek Walcott: Intertextual Perspectives.* Ed. Gregson Davis. *South Atlantic Quarterly* 96.2 (Spring 1997): 321–334.

Dayan, Joan. *Haiti, History, and the Gods.* Berkeley: University of California, 1998.

de Andrade, Oswald. "Anthropophagite Manifesto." *Art in Latin America: The Modern Era. 1820–1980.* Ed. Dawn Ades. New Haven, Connecticut: South Bank Centre and Yale University Press, 1989. 312–313.

——. "Manifesto of Pau-Brazil Poetry." *Latin American Review* 14.27 (January–June 1986): 184–187.

DeCerteau, Michel. *The Practice of Everyday Life.* Berkeley: University of California, 1988.

Defoe, Daniel. *Robinson Crusoe.* London: Penguin, 1985.

Deleuze, Gilles and Felix Guattari. *Kafka: Toward a Minor Literature.* Trans. Dana Poland. Minneapolis: University of Minnesota Press, 1986.

Den Tandt, Catherine. " 'El masacre se pasa a pie': Haitian and Dominican Border Talk." *Marginal Migrations: The Circulation of Cultures within the Caribbean.* Ed. Shalini Puri. London: Macmillan, 2003. 165–189.

——. "All That is Black Melts into Air: Negritud and Nation in Puerto Rico." *Caribbean Romances: The Politics of Regional Representation.* Ed. Belinda Edmondson. Charlottesville and London: University Press of Virginia, 1999. 76–91.

——. "Tracing Nation and Gender: Ana Lydia Vega." *Revista de Estudios Hispánicos* 28 (1994): 3–24.

Derrida, Jacques. "The Double Session." *A Derrida Reader: Between the Blinds*. Ed. Peggy Kamuf. New York: Columbia University Press, 1991. 172–199.

deVerteuil, Anthony. *Sir Louis deVerteuil. His Life and Times: Trinidad 1800–1900*. Trinidad: Columbus Publishers, 1973.

Dhareshwar, Vivek. "Toward a Narrative Epistemology of the Postcolonial Predicament." *Traveling Theories, Traveling Theorists*. Ed. James Clifford and Vivek Dhareshwar. *Inscriptions* 5 (1989): 135–157.

Díaz del Castillo, Bernal. *The Conquest of New Spain*. London: Viking, 1963.

Dirlik, Arif. "The Postcolonial Aura: Third World Criticism in the Age of Global Capitalism." *Contemporary Postcolonial Theory: A Reader*. Ed. Padmini Mongia. London and New York: Arnold, 1996. 294–321.

Donaldson, Laura. "The Miranda Complex: Colonialism and the Question of Feminist Reading." *Diacritics* (Fall 1998): 65–77.

DuCille, Anne. "Postcolonialism and Afrocentricity: Discourse and Dat Course." *The Black Columbiad: Defining Moments in African American Literature and Culture*. Ed. Werner Sollors and Maria Diedrich. Cambridge and London: Harvard University Press, 1994. 28–41.

Durix, Jean. *Mimesis, Genres, and Post-Colonial Discourse: Deconstructing Magic Realism*. New York: Palgrave, 1998.

Eagleton, Terry. "Nationalism: Irony and Commitment." *Nationalism, Colonialism, and Literature*. Ed. Terry Eagleton, Fredric Jameson, and Edward Said. Minneapolis: University of Minnesota Press, 1990. 23–39.

——. *Walter Benjamin, Or, Towards a Revolutionary Criticism*. London: Verso, 1981.

Eckstein, Susan, ed. *Power and Popular Protest: Latin American Social Movements. Updated and Expanded Edition*. Berkeley and London: University of California Press, 2001.

Espinet, Ramabai. "Barred: Trinidad 1987." *Green Cane and Juicy Flotsam: Short Stories by Caribbean Women*. Ed. Carmen C. Estevez and Lizabeth Paravisini-Gebert. New Brunswick, New Jersey: Rutgers University Press, 1991. 80–85.

——. "Hosay Night" and "Mama Glo." *Nuclear Seasons*. Toronto: Sister Vision, 1991. 9–10, 27–29.

——. "Indian Robber Talk." Unpublished play.

Fabian, Johannes. *Power and Performance: Ethnographic Explorations through Proverbial Wisdom and Theater in Shaba, Zaire*. Madison: Wisconsin University Press, 1990.

——. *Time and the Other: How Anthropology Makes Its Object*. New York: Columbia University Press, 1983.

Fanon, Frantz. *Black Skins, White Masks*. Trans. Charles Lam Markmann. New York: Grove Press, 1967.

——. "The Pitfalls of National Consciousness." *The Wretched of the Earth*. Trans. Constance Farrington. New York: Grove Press, 1968. 148–205.

Feal, Rosemary Geisdorfer. "Feminism and Afro-Hispanism: The Double Bind." *Afro-Hispanic Review* 10.1 (1991): 25–29.

——. "Afro-Hispanic Literature and Feminist Theories: Thinking Ethics." *Postcolonial Literatures: Expanding the Canon.* Ed. Deborah Madsen. London: Pluto, 1999. 148–163.

——. "Reading against the Cane: Afro-Hispanic Studies and Mestizaje." *Diacritics: A Review of Contemporary Criticism* 25.1 (Spring 1995): 82–98.

Featherstone, Mike, ed. *Global Culture: Nationalism, Globalization, and Modernity.* London: Sage Publications, 1990.

Fernández Retamar, Roberto. "Caliban: Notes Towards a Discussion of Culture in Our America." *Caliban and Other Essays.* Trans. Edward Baker. Minneapolis, Minnesota: University of Minnesota Press, 1989. 3–45.

Fiske, John. *Reading the Popular.* Boston: Unwin Hyman, 1989.

——. *Understanding Popular Culture.* Boston: Unwin Hyman, 1989.

Forgacs, David. "National-Popular: Genealogy of a Concept." *The Cultural Studies Reader.* Ed. Simon During. London: Routledge, 1993. 177–190.

Foucault, Michel. "Politics and Ethics: An Interview." *The Foucault Reader.* Ed. Paul Rabinow. New York, Pantheon: 1984. 373–380.

——. *The History of Sexuality.* Trans. Robert Hurley. New York: Pantheon Books, 1978.

——. "A Preface to Transgression." *Language, Counter-Memory, Practice: Selected Essays and Interviews.* Ed. Donald Bouchard. Ithaca, New York: Cornell University Press, 1980. 29–52.

Fox, Richard and Orin Starn, eds. *Between Resistance and Revolution: Cultural Politics and Social Protest.* New Jersey and London: Rutgers University Press, 1997.

Franco, Jean. "The Nation as Imagined Community." *Dangerous Liaisons: Gender, Nation, and Postcolonial Perspectives.* Ed. Anne McClintock, Aamir Mufti, and Ella Shohat. Minneapolis and London: University of Minnesota Press, 1997. 130–137.

——. "What's in a Name? Popular Culture Theories and Their Limitations." *Critical Passions: Selected Essays.* Ed. Mary Louise Pratt and Kathleen Newman. Durham and London: Duke University Press, 1999. 169–180.

——. "Globalization and the Crisis of the Popular." *Critical Passions: Selected Essays.* Ed. Mary Louise Pratt and Kathleen Newman. Durham and London: Duke University Press, 1999. 208–220.

——. "Beyond Ethnocentrism: Gender, Power, and the Third-World Intellegentsia." *Marxism and the Interpretation of Culture.* Ed. Cary Nelson and Lawrence Grossberg. Urbana and Chicago: University of Illinois Press, 1988. 503–515.

Franco, Pamela. "The 'Unruly Woman' in Nineteenth-Century Trinidad Carnival." *Small Axe* 7 (March 2000): 60–76.

Frankenberg, Ruth and Lata Mani. "Crosscurrents, Crosstalk: Race, 'Postcoloniality' and the Politics of Location." *Cultural Studies* 7.2 (May 1993): 292–310.

Fraser, Nancy. *Justice Interruptus: Critical Reflections on the "Postsocialist" Condition*. London and New York: Routledge, 1997.

Freyre, Gilberto. *The Masters and the Slaves: A Study in the Development of Brazilian Civilization*. Trans. Samuel Putnam. New York: Knopf, 1956.

Froude, James Anthony. *The English in the West Indies Or The Bow of Ulysses*. London: Longmans, Green and Co., 1888.

Fuguet, Sergio. "Magical Neoliberalism." *Foreign Policy: The Magazine of Global Politics, Economics, and Ideas*. http://www.foreignpolicy.com/issue-julyaug-2001.

Fuguet, Alberto and Sergio Gómez, eds. *McOndo*. Barcelona: Grijalbo, 1996.

García Canclini, Néstor. *Consumers and Citizens: Globalization and Multicultural Conflicts*. Trans. George Yúdice. Minneapolis and London: University of Minnesota Press, 2001.

——. *Hybrid Cultures: Strategies for Entering and Leaving Modernity*. Trans. Christopher Chiappari and Silvia López. Minneapolis and London: University of Minnesota Press, 1995.

García Márquez, Gabriel. "The Solitude of Latin America." Nobel Prize Lecture. December 8, 1982. Nobel e-museum. http://www.nobel.se/literature/laureates/1982/marquez-lecture.html.

Gates, Henry Louis, Jr. *The Signifying Monkey: A Theory of African-American Literary Criticism*. New York: Oxford University Press, 1988.

Geertz, Clifford. "Thick Description: Toward an Interpretive Theory of Culture." *The Interpretation of Cultures*. New York: Basic Books, 2000. 3–30.

Gikandi, Simon. *Ngũgĩ Wa Thiong'o*. Cambridge: Cambridge University Press, 2000.

——. *Writing in Limbo: Modernism and Caribbean Literature*. Ithaca, New York: Cornell University Press, 1992.

——, ed. "Introduction: Africa, Diaspora, and the Discourse of Modernity." *Research in African Literatures* 27.4 (Winter 1996): 1–17. (Special Issue on *The Black Atlantic*.)

——. "The Location of Culture." Review article. *Research in African Literatures* 27.2 (Summer 1996): 139–151.

Gilroy, Paul. "Diaspora, Utopia, and the Critique of Capitalism." *The Subcultures Reader*. Ed. Ken Gelder and Sarah Thornton. London and New York: Routledge, 1997.

——. *The Black Atlantic: Modernity and Double Consciousness*. Cambridge: Harvard University Press, 1993.

Glassman, Jonathan. *Feasts and Riot: Revelry, Rebellion, and Popular Consciousness on the Swahili Coast, 1856–1888*. Portsmouth, New Hampshire: Heinemann, 1995.

Glissant, Édouard. *Poetics of Relation*. Trans. Betsy Wing. Ann Arbor: Michigan, 1997.

——. *Le discours antillais*. Paris: Seuil, 1981.

——. *Caribbean Discourse: Selected Essays*. Trans. J. Michael Dash. Charlottesville: University Press of Virginia, 1989.

Gluckman, Max. *Order and Rebellion in Tribal Africa: Collected Essays with an Autobiographical Introduction*. London: Cohen, 1963.

——. *Custom and Conflict in Africa*. Oxford: Basil Blackwell, 1965.

Gobineau, Joseph Arthur Comte de. *The Inequality of the Human Races (v.1)*. Trans. Adrian Collins. London: Heinemann, 1915.

González, José Luís. *El País de Cuatro Pisos*. Rio Piédras: Huracán, 1980.

Goodwin, Jeff. "State-Centered Approaches to Social Revolutions: Strengths and Limitations of a Theoretical Tradition." *Theorizing Revolutions*. London and New York: Routledge, 1997. 11–37.

Gordon, Edmund. *Disparate Diasporas: Identity and Politics in an African-Nicaraguan Community*. University of Texas Press, 1998.

Gramsci, Antonio. *Selections from Cultural Writings*. Ed. David Forgacs and Geoffrey Nowell-Smith. Trans. William Boelhower. London: Lawrence and Wishart, 1985.

Grewal, Inderpal and Caren Kaplan, eds. *Scattered Hegemonies: Postmodernity and Transnational Feminist Practices*. Minneapolis: University of Minnesota Press, 1994.

Grosfoguel, Ramón and Frances Negrón-Muntaner, eds. *Puerto Rican Jam: Rethinking Colonialism and Nationalism*. Minneapolis: University of Minnesota Press, 1997.

Guerra, Lillian. *Popular Expression and National Identity in Puerto Rico: The Struggle for Self, Community, and Nation*. Gainesville: University Press of Florida, 1998.

Guha, Ranajit. *Elementary Aspects of Peasant Insurgency*. Delhi and New York: Oxford, 1994.

——. and Gayatri Spivak, eds. *Selected Subaltern Studies*. New York and Oxford: Oxford University Press, 1988.

Guéhenno, Jean-Marie. *The End of the Nation-State*. Trans. Victoria Elliott. Minneapolis: University of Minnesota Press, 1995.

Gunder Frank, Andre. *Capitalism and Underdevelopment in Latin America: Historical Studies of Chile and Brazil*. New York: Monthly Review Press, 1969.

Gunness, Christopher. "White Man, Black Man." *Critical Perspectives on Derek Walcott*. Ed. Robert D. Hammer. Washington, DC: Three Continents Press, 1993. 290–291.

Gupta, Akhil. "The Song of the Non-Aligned World: Transnational Identities and the Reinscription of Space in Late Capitalism." *Cultural Anthropology* 7.1 (February 1992): 63–79.

Guzmán, Manuel. " 'Pa' la Escuelita Con Mucho Cuida'o y por la Orillita': A Journey through the Contested Terrains of Nation and Sexuality." *Puerto Rican Jam*. Ed. Ramón Grosfoguel and Francés Negrón-Muntaner. Minneapolis: University of Minnesota Press, 1997. 209–228.

Hale, Charles. *Resistance and Contradiction: Miskitu Indians and the Nicaraguan State 1894–1987*. Stanford: Stanford University Press, 1994.

Hall, Stuart. "For Allon White: Metaphors of Transformation." *Introduction to Allon White, Carnival, Hysteria and Writing*. Oxford: Clarendon, 1993. 1–25.

——. "Notes on Deconstructing 'The Popular.'" *People's History and Socialist Theory*. Ed. Raphael Samuel. London: Routledge and Kegan Paul, 1981. 227–240.

—— and Tony Jefferson, eds. *Resistance Through Rituals: Youth Subcultures in Post-War Britain*. London: Routledge, 1993.

Hallward, Peter. *Absolutely Postcolonial: Writing Between the Singular and the Specific*. Manchester and New York: Manchester University Press, 2001.

Hammer, Robert. "Archipelagos of Man: The Critic." *Derek Walcott*. Boston: Twayne Publishers, 1981. 150–164.

Haraksingh, Kusha. "Control and Resistance among Indian Workers: A Study of Labour on the Sugar Plantations of Trinidad, 1875–1917." *India in the Caribbean*. Ed. David Dabydeen and Brinsley Samaroo. London: Hansib, 1987. 61–77.

Haraway, Donna. "A Manifesto for Cyborgs: Science, Technology, and Socialist Feminism in the 1980's." *Socialist Review* 80 (1985): 65–107.

Harris, David. *From Class Struggle to the Politics of Pleasure: The Effect of Gramscianism in Cultural Studies*. London and New York: Routledge, 1992.

Harris, Wilson. "Creoleness: The Crossroads of a Civilization." *Selected Essays of Wilson Harris: The Unfinished Genesis of the Imagination*. Ed. A.J.M. Bundy. London and New York: Routledge, 1999. 237–247.

——. "Benito Cereno." *Selected Essays of Wilson Harris: The Unfinished Genesis of the Imagination*. Ed. A.J.M. Bundy. London and New York: Routledge, 1999. 123–133.

——. *The Guyana Quartet*. London and Boston: Faber and Faber, 1985.

Harvey, David. "Globalization in Question." *Rethinking Marxism* 8.4 (Winter 1995): 1–17.

——. *The Condition of Postmodernity: An Inquiry into the Origins of Cultural Change*. London: Blackwell, 1990.

Hebdige, Dick. *Subculture: The Meaning of Style*. London and New York: Routledge, 1981.

Henry, Paget. *Caliban's Reason: Introducing Afro-Caribbean Philosophy*. New York and London: Routledge, 2001.

Heuman, Gad. *"The Killing Time": The Morant Bay Rebellion in Jamaica*. London: Macmillan, 1994.

Hill, Errol. *The Trinidad Carnival: Mandate for a National Theatre*. London: New Beacon, 1997.

Howes, David, ed. *Cross-Cultural Consumption: Global Markets, Local Realities*. London and New York: Routledge, 1996.

Huggan, Graham. "A Tale of Two Parrots: Walcott, Rhys, and the Uses of Colonial Mimicry." *Contemporary Literature* 35.4 (1994): 643–660.

Hulme, Peter. *Colonial Encounters: Europe and the Native Caribbean 1492–1797*. London and New York: Routledge, 1986.

Hutnyk, John. "Adorno at Womad: South Asian Crossovers and the Limits of Hybridity-Talk." *Debating Cultural Hybridity: Multi-Cultural Identities and the Politics of Anti-Racism*. Ed. Pnina Werbner and Tariq Madood. London and New Jersey: Zed, 1997. 106–136.

International Organization for Migration, and United Nations. *World Migration Report 2000*. Geneva: Switzerland, 2000.

Jackson, Richard. "'Mestizaje' vs. Black Identity: The Color Crisis in Latin America." *Black World* 24.9 (1975): 4–21.

Jagan, Cheddi. "Indo-Caribbean Political Leadership." *Indenture and Exile: The Indo-Caribbean Experience*. Ed. Frank Birbalsingh. Toronto: TSAR, 1989. 15–25.

James, C.L.R. *Beyond a Boundary*. Durham: Duke University Press, 1993.

——. "From Touissant L'Ouverture to Fidel Castro." *The C.L.R. James Reader*. Ed. Anna Grimshaw. Oxford: Blackwell, 1992. 296–314.

——. "The Making of the Caribbean People." *Spheres of Existence: Selected Writings*. Westport, Connecticut: L. Hill, 1980. 173–190.

——. *Minty Alley*. London and Port of Spain: New Beacon, 1971.

Jameson, Fredric. *Postmodernism Or, The Cultural Logic of Late Capitalism*. Durham: Duke University Press, 1991.

——. "Third World Literature in the Era of Multinational Capital." *Social Text* (Fall 1986): 65–88.

——. "Metacommentary." *The Ideologies of Theory v.1*. Minneapolis: University of Minnesota Press, 1988. 3–16.

——. "On Magic Realism in Film." *Critical Inquiry* 12 (Winter 1986): 301–325.

——. *The Political Unconscious: Narrative as a Socially Symbolic Act*. Ithaca, New York: Cornell University Press, 1981.

——. "Reification and Utopia in Mass Culture." *Social Text* 1 (1979): 130–148.

JanMohamed, Abdul. "The Economy of Manichean Allegory: The Function of Racial Difference in Colonialist Literature." *"Race," Writing, and Difference*. Ed. Henry Louis Gates, Jr. Chicago and London: University of Chicago Press, 1986. 78–106.

Jeyifo, Biodun. "On Eurocentric Critical Theory: Some Paradigms from the Texts and Sub-Texts of Post-colonial Writing." *Critical Perspectives on Derek Walcott*. Ed. Robert D. Hammer. Washington, DC: Three Continents Press, 1993. 376–387.

Jones, Bridget. "'With Crusoe the Slave and Friday the Boss': Derek Walcott's Pantomime." *Robinson Crusoe: Myths and Metamorphoses*. Ed. Lieve Spaas and Brian Stimpson. London: Macmillan, 1996. 225–238.

Johnson, Randall. "Tupy or Not Tupy: Cannibalism and Nationalism in Contemporary Brazilian Literature and Culture." *Modern Latin American Fiction: A Survey*. Ed. John King. London and Boston: Faber and Faber, 1987. 41–59.

Juneja, Renu. "Representing History in The Jumbie Bird." *World Literature Written in English* 30.1 (1990): 17–28.

Kale, Madhavi. *Fragments of Empire: Capital, Slavery, and Indian Indentured Labor Migration in the British Caribbean*. Philadelphia: University of Pennsylvania Press, 1999.

——. "Projecting Identities: Empire and Indentured Labor Migration from India to Trinidad and British Guiana, 1836–1885." *Nation and*

Migration: The Politics of Space in the South Asian Diaspora. Ed. Peter Van der Veer. Philadelphia, University of Pennsylvania Press, 1995. 73–92.

Kanhai, Rosanne. "The Masala Stone Sings: Poetry, Performance and Film by Indo-Caribbean Women." *Matikor: The Politics of Identity for Indo-Caribbean Women*. Ed. Rosanne Kanhai. St Augustine, Trinidad: University of the West Indies School of Continuing Studies, 1999. 209–237.

Kaplan, Alice Yaeger. "Review Article: Recent Theoretical Work with Pamphlets and Manifestoes." *L'Esprit Créateur* 23.4 (1983): 74–82.

Kaplan, Caren. "The Politics of Location as Transnational Feminist Practice." *Scattered Hegemonies: Postmodernity and Transnational Feminist Practices*. Ed. Inderpal Grewal and Caren Kaplan. Minneapolis: University of Minnesota Press, 1994. 137–152.

——. "Deterritorializations: The Rewriting of Home and Exile in Western Feminist Discourse." *The Nature and Context of Minority Discourse*. Ed. Abdul Jan Mohamed and David Lloyd. New York: Oxford University Press, 1990. 357–368.

——. *Questions of Travel: Postmodern Discourses of Displacement*. Durham and London: Duke University Press, 1996.

Kaplan, Martha and John Kelly. "Rethinking Resistance: Dialogics of 'Disaffection' in colonial Fiji." *American Ethnologist* 21.1 (1994): 123–151.

Kelly, John. "From Holi to Diwali in Fiji: An Essay on Ritual and History." *Man* 23 (1988): 40–55.

Khan, Aisha. "Homeland, Motherland: Authenticity, Legitimacy, and Ideologies of Place among Muslims in Trinidad." *Nation and Migration: The Politics of Space in the South Asian Diaspora*. Ed. Peter Van der eer. Philadelphia, University of Pennsylvania Press, 1995. 93–131.

——. "What is a 'Spanish'? Ambiguity and 'Mixed' Ethnicity in Trinidad." *Trinidad Ethnicity*. Ed. Kevin A. Yelvington. Knoxville, Tennessee: University of Tennessee Press, 1993. 180–207.

Khan, Ismith. *The Jumbie Bird*. Essex and New York: Longman Caribbean, 1961.

Kiely, Ray. "Introduction" and "Chapter Two." *Globalisation and the Third World*. Ed. Ray Kiely and Phil Marfleet. London and New York: Routledge, 1998. 1–22, 45–66.

—— and Phil Marfleet, eds. *Globalisation and the Third World*. London and New York: Routledge, 1998.

Kincaid, Jamaica. *A Small Place*. New York: Plume, 1988.

Klak, Thomas, ed. *Globalization and Neoliberalism: The Caribbean Context*. New York and Oxford: Rowman and Littlefield, 1998.

—— and Dennis Conway. "From Neoliberalism to Sustainable Development?" *Globalization and Neoliberalism: The Caribbean Context*. Ed. Thomas Klak. New York and Oxford: Rowman and Littlefield, 1998. 257–275.

Klor de Alva, Jorge. "The Postcolonization of the (Latin) American Experience: A Reconsideration of 'Colonialism,' 'Postcolonialism,' and 'Mestizaje'." *After Colonialism: Imperial Histories and Postcolonial Displacements*. Ed. Gyan Prakash. Princeton, New Jersey: Princeton, 1995. 241–275.

Knight, Franklin W. *The Caribbean: The Genesis of a Fragmented Nationalism.* Second edition. New York: Oxford, 1990.

Koningsbruggen, Peter van. *Trinidad Carnival: A Quest for National Identity.* London: Macmillan, 1997.

Korom, Frank. "Memory, Innovation, and Emergent Ethnicity: The Creolization of an Indo-Trinidadian Performance." *Diaspora* 3.2 (1994): 135–155.

Kortenaar, Neil Ten. "Foreign Possessions: Erna Brodber's *Myal*, the Medium, and her Message." *ARIEL: A Review of International English Literature* 30.4 (October 1999): 51–73.

Kraniauskas, John. "Hybridity in a Transnational Frame: Latin Americanist and Post-colonial Perspectives on Cultural Studies." *Hybridity and Its Discontents: Politics, Science, and Culture.* Ed. Avtar Brah and Annie Coombes. London and New York: Routledge, 2000. 235–256.

Kutzinski, Vera. *Sugar's Secrets: Race and the Erotics of Cuban Nationalism.* Charlottesville and London: University Press of Virginia, 1993.

Lamming, George. "The West Indian People." *New World Quarterly* 2.1 (1966): 63–74.

Latin American Subaltern Studies Group. "Founding Statement". John Beverley and José Oviedo, eds. *Boundary* 2 20.3 (Fall 1993): 110–121. (Special issue entitled *The Postmodernism Debate in Latin America.*)

Lao, Agustín. "Islands at the Crossroads: Puerto Ricans Traveling Between the Translocal Nation and the Global City." *Puerto Rican Jam.* Ed. Ramón Grosfoguel and Francés Negrón-Muntaner, Minneapolis: University of Minnesota Press, 1997. 169–188.

Larsen, Neil. "Imperialism, Colonialism, Postcolonialism." *A Companion to Postcolonial Studies.* Ed. Henry Schwarz and Sangeeta Ray. Oxford: Blackwell, 2000. 23–52.

Layoun, Mary. "Telling Spaces: Palestinian Women and the Engendering of National Narratives." *Nationalisms and Sexualities.* Ed. Andrew Parker et al. New York and London: Routledge, 1992. 407–423.

Lazarus, Emma. "The New Colossus." *The Heath Anthology of American Literature. Volume II.* Fourth edition. Ed. Paul Lauter. Boston and New York: Houghton Mifflin, 2002. 27.

Lazarus, Neil. *Nationalism and Cultural Practice in the Postcolonial World.* Cambridge: Cambridge University Press, 1999.

Lenin, Vladimir. I. *Questions of National Policy and Proletarian Internationalism.* Moscow: Progress Publishers, 1970.

Lewis, Gordon. *Main Currents in Caribbean Thought: The Historical Evolution of Caribbean Society in Its Ideological Aspects, 1492–1900.* Baltimore and London: Johns Hopkins University Press, 1983.

Linebaugh, Peter and Marcus Rediker. *The Many-Headed Hydra: Sailors, Slaves, Commoners, and the Hidden History of the Revolutionary Atlantic.* Boston: Beacon Press, 2000.

Look Lai, Walton. *The Chinese in the West Indies, 1806–1995: A Documentary History.* Barbados, Jamaica, Trindad: University of the West Indies Press, 1998.

Loomba, Ania. *Colonialism/Postcolonialism*. London and New York: Routledge, 1998.

Lovelace, Earl. "The Emancipation-Jouvay Tradition and the Almost Loss of Pan." Special Expanded Issue on Trinidad and Tobago Carnival. *The Drama Review* 42.3 (Fall 1998): 54–60.

——. *The Dragon Can't Dance*. Essex, England: Longman, 1979.

Lubiano, Wahneema. "Shuckin' Off the African-American Native Other: What's "Po-Mo" Got to Do with It?" *Dangerous Liaisons: Gender, Nation, and Postcolonial Perspectives*. Ed. Anne McClintock, Aamir Mufti, and Ella Shohat. Minneapolis and London: University of Minnesota Press, 1997. 204–229.

Luxemburg, Rosa. *The National Question: Selected Writings*. New York: Monthly Review Press, 1976.

Lynch, Caitrin. "Nation, Woman, and the Indian Immigrant Bourgeoisie: An Alternative Formulation." *Public Culture* 6 (1994): 425–437.

Lyon, Janet. *Manifestoes: Provocations of the Modern*. Ithaca and London: Cornell University Press, 1999.

Lyotard, Jean-Francois. *The Postmodern Condition: A Report on the Condition of Knowledge*. Trans. Geoff Bennington and Brian Massumi. Minneapolis, Minnesota: University of Minnesota Press, 1984.

MacCabe, Colin. "Realism and the Cinema: Notes on Some Brechtian Theses." *Tracking the Signifier: Theoretical Essays: Film, Linguistics, Literature*. Minneapolis: University of Minnesota Press, 1985. 33–57.

——. "Realism: Balzac and Barthes." *Tracking the Signifier: Theoretical Essays: Film, Linguistics, Literature*. Minneapolis: University of Minnesota Press, 1985. 131–150.

——, Ed. *High Theory/Low Culture: Anzalyzing Popular Television and Film*. New York and London: Palgrave, 1986.

Madureira, Luís. "Lapses in Taste: 'Cannibal-Tropicalist' Cinema and the Brazilian Aesthetic of Underdevelopment." *Cannibalism and the Colonial World*. Ed. Francis Barker, Peter Hulme, and Margaret Iverson. Cambridge: Cambridge University Press, 1998. 110–125.

Mahabir, Kumar and Sita. *A Dictionary of Common Trinidad Hindi*. El Dorado, Trinidad: Chakra, 1990.

Maharaj, Indira et. al. "Report on Bandit Rape, Crime and Race in Central Trinidad for the Period April to May 1993: Study Conducted by a Group of Concerned Citizens of Religious and Spiritual Persuasion." Unpublished typescript, 1993.

Maharaj, Satnarayan. "Mahasabha Answer Back. Debate: Douglarisation or Pluralism." *Trinidad Guardian* October 7, 1993: 25.

Malkki, Liisa. "Citizens of Humanity: Internationalism and the Imagined Community of Nations." *Diaspora* 3.1 (1994): 41–68.

Mangru, Basdeo. "Tadjah in British Guiana." *Indo-Caribbean Resistance*. Ed. Frank Birbalsingh. Toronto: TSAR, 1993.

Mann, Michael. "As the Twentieth Century Ages." *New Left Review* 214 (Nov/Dec 1995): 104–124.

Manning, Frank. "Carnival in Antigua: An Indigenous Festival in a Tourist Economy." *Anthropos* 73.1–2 (1978): 191–204.

Mariátegui, José Carlos. "The Problem of the Indian" and "The Problem of Land." *Seven Interpretative Essays on the Peruvian Reality*. Trans. Marjorie Urquidi. Austin and London: University of Texas Press, 1971. 22–30, 31–79.

Márquez, Roberto. "Nationalism, Nation, and Ideology: Trends in the Emergence of a Caribbean Literature." *The Modern Caribbean*. Ed. Franklin W. Knight and Colin A. Palmer. Chapel Hill and London: University of North Carolina Press, 1989. 293–340.

Martí, José. "Our America." *Our America: Writings on Latin America and the Struggle for Cuban Independence*. Ed. Philip S. Foner. Trans. Elinor Randall with additional translations by Juan de Onis and Roslyn Held Foner. New York and London: Monthly Review Press, 1977. 84–94.

——. "Manifesto of Montecristi: The Cuban Revolutionary Party in Cuba." *Our America: Writings on Latin America and the Struggle for Cuban Independence*. Ed. Philip S. Foner. Trans. Elinor Randall with additional translations by Juan de Onis and Roslyn Held Foner. New York and London: Monthly Review Press, 1977. 390–400.

——. "My Race." *The America of José Martí: Selected Writings*. Ed. Philip Sheldon Foner. Trans. Juan de Onis. New York: Noonday Press, 1953. 308–312.

Martínez, Samuel. "Identities at the Dominican and Puerto Rican International Migrant Crossroads." *Marginal Migrations: The Circulation of Cultures within the Caribbean*. Ed. Shalini Puri. London: Macmillan, 2003.

Marx, Karl and Friedrich Engels. "Manifesto of the Communist Party." *The Marx-Engels Reader*. Ed. Robert C. Tucker. New York and London: Norton, 1978. 469–500.

Maximin, Collette. "Distinction and Dialogism in Jamaica: Erna Brodber's *Myal*." *Commonwealth Essays and Studies* 21.2 (Spring 1999): 49–62.

McClintock, Anne. "The Angel of Progress: Pitfalls of the Term 'Post-Colonialism.'" *Social Text* 10.2–3 (1992): 84–98.

——and Rob Nixon. "No Names Apart: The Separation of Word and History in Derrida's 'Le Dernier Mot du Racisme.'" *"Race," Writing, and Difference*. Ed. Henry Louis Gates, Jr. Chicago and London: University of Chicago Press, 1986. 339–353.

Menchú, Rigoberta. *I, Rigoberta Menchú*. London: Verso, 1984.

Michaelson, Scott and David Johnson, eds. *Border Theory: The Limits of Cultural Politics*. Minneapolis and London: University of Minnesota Press, 1997.

Mignolo, Walter. "(Post)Occidentalism, (Post)Coloniality, and (Post)Subaltern Rationality." *The Pre-occupation of Postcolonial Studies*. Ed. Fawzia Afzal Khan and Kalpana Seshadri-Crooks. Durham and London: Duke University Press, 2000. 86–118.

Milagros López, Maria. "Postwork Society and Postmodern Subjects." *The Postmodernism Debate in Latin America*. Ed. Michael Aronna and John Beverley. Durham: Duke University Press, 1995. 165–191.

Miller, Daniel. *Modernity: An Ethnographic Approach: Dualism and Mass Consumption in Trinidad.* Oxford: Berg, 1994.

——. "Absolute Freedom in Trinidad." *Man* 26.2 (1991): 323–341.

Mishra, Vijay and Bob Hodge. "What is Post(-)Colonialism?" *Textual Practice* 5.3 (Winter 1991): 399–414.

Mohanty, Satya P. *Literary Theory and the Claims of History: Postmodernism, Objectivity, Multicultural Politics.* Ithaca: Cornell University Press, 1997.

Mohapatra, Prabhu. "The Hosay Massacre of 1884" Class and Community among Indian Immigrants in Trinidad." *Work and Social Change in Asia: Essays in Honour of Jan Breman.* Ed. Arvind N. Das and Marcel van der Linden. Delhi: Manohar, 2002.

Moore-Gilbert, Bart. *Postcolonial Theory: Contexts, Practices, Politics.* London: Verso, 1997.

Molière, Jean-Baptiste P. *Don Juan.* Trans. Christopher Hampton. London: Faber and Faber, 1974.

Moreira, Luiza. " 'Biological Democracy': Corporatism, Miscegenation, and Poetry in Cassiano Ricardo's *Marcha para Oeste.*" *Brasil/Brazil*, forthcoming.

——. " 'All Silent . . . Only One Singing': The Brazil of Cassiano Ricardo's Martim Cererê." *Cultural Critique* 38 (Winter 1997–97): 107–135.

Morris, Meaghan. "Banality in Cultural Studies." *What is Cultural Studies?: A Reader.* Ed. John Storey. London and New York: Arnold, 1996. 147–167.

Moya, Paula and Michael Hames-García, eds. *Reclaiming Identity: Realist Theory and the Predicament of Postmodernism.* Berkeley: University of California Press, 2000.

Murray, Charles and Richard J. Herrnstein. *The Bell Curve: Intelligence and Class Structures in American Life.* New York: The Free Press, 1994.

Naipaul, Vidia S. *The Middle Passage: Impressions of Five Societies—British, French and Dutch—in the West Indies and South America.* New York: Vintage Books, 1981. (1962)

Naipaul, Vidia S. "East Indian." *The Overcrowded Barracoon.* New York: Vintage: 1984. 30–38.

Nairn, Tom. *The Break-up of Britain: Crisis and Neo-Nationalism.* London: New Left Books, 1977.

Napier, Elma. "Carnival in Martinique." *The Routledge Reader in Caribbean Literature.* Ed. Alison Donnell and Sarah Lawson Welsh. London and New York: Routledge, 1996. 228–230.

Narain, Denise deCaires. "The Body of the Woman in the Body of the Text: The Novels of Erna Brodber." *Caribbean Women Writers: Fiction in English.* Ed. Maryse Condé and Thorunn Lonsdale. New York: St. Martin's Press, 1999. 97–116.

Nelson, Cary. *Manifesto of a Tenured Radical.* New York: New York University Press, 1997.

Nelson-McDermott, Catherine. "Myal-ing Criticism: Beyond Colonizing Dialectics." *ARIEL: A Review of International English Literature* 24.4 (October 1993): 53–67.

Niranjana, Tejaswini. "'The Indian in Me': Gender, Identity, and Cultural Politics in Trinidad." *Conference on Challenge and Change: The Indian Diaspora in its Historical and Contemporary Contexts.* University of the West Indies, Trinidad. August 11–18, 1995.

Nixon, Rob. "Caribbean and African Appropriations of *The Tempest.*" *Critical Inquiry* 13 (Spring 1987): 557–578.

O'Callaghan, Evelyn. *Woman Version: Theoretical Approaches to West Indian Fiction by Women.* London: Macmillan, 1993.

——. "Interior Schisms Dramatized: The Treatment of the 'Mad' Woman in the Work of Some Female Caribbean Novelists." *Out of the Kumbla: Caribbean Women and Literature.* Ed. Carol Boyce Davies and Elaine Savory Fido. Trenton, New Jersey: Africa World Press, 1990. 89–109.

——. "The Lovelace 'Prologue': Ideology in a Nutshell." *Occasional Papers in Caribbean Studies Number 2*: 1–9. Center for Caribbean Studies, University of Warwick.

Ohmae, Kenichi. *Borderless World: Power and Strategy in the Interlinked Economy.* New York: Harper Business, 1999.

Olaniyan, Tejumola. "Derek Walcott: Liminal Spaces/Substantive Histories." *Caribbean Romances: The Politics of Regional Representation.* Ed. Belinda Edmondson. Charlottesville and London: University Press of Virginia, 1999. 199–214.

Ong, Aihwa. "Flexible Citizenship Among Chinese Cosmopolitans." *Cosmopolitics: Thinking and Feeling Beyond the Nation.* Ed. Pheng Cheah and Bruce Robbins. Minneapolis and London: University of Minnesota Press, 1998. 134–162.

Ortíz, Fernando. *Cuban Counterpoint*: Tobacco and Sugar. Trans. Harriet de Onis. Charlottesville, North Carolina: Duke University Press, 1995.

Ortner, Sherry. "Specifying Agency: The Comaroffs and Their Critics." *Interventions* 3.1 (2001): 76–84.

——. *Making Gender: The Politics and Erotics of Culture.* Boston: Beacon, 1996.

——. "Resistance and the Problem of Ethnographic Refusal." *Comparative Studies in Society and History* 37.1 (January 1995): 173–193.

Parekh, Bhiku. "Feature Address." *Conference on Challenge and Change: The Indian Diaspora in Its Historical and Contemporary Contexts.* University of the West Indies, Trinidad. August 11–18, 1995.

Parmasad, Kenneth. "The Wedding Tent and the Public Space: Towards an Understanding of Indian Cultural Practices in Trinidad." *Conference on Challenge and Change: The Indian Diaspora in Its Historical and Contemporary Contexts.* University of the West Indies, Trinidad. August 11–18, 1995.

Parker, Andrew et al., eds. *Nationalisms and Sexualities.* New York and London: Routledge, 1992.

Parry, Benita. "Signs of Our Times: A Discussion of Homi Bhabha's The Location of Culture." *Third Text* 28/29 (Autumn/Winter 1994): 5–24.

——. "Resistance Theory/Theorizing Resistance, Or Two Cheers for Nativism." *Contemporary Postcolonial Theory: A Reader.* Ed. Padmini Mongia. London and New York: Arnold, 1996. 84–109.

Patterson, Orlando. *The Sociology of Slavery: An Analysis of the Origins, Development, and Structure of Negro Slave Society in Jamaica*. London: MacGibbon and Kee, 1967.

Paz, Octavio. *The Labyrinth of Solitude: Life and Thought in Mexico*. Trans. Lysander Kemp. New York: Grove, 1984.

Perloff, Marjorie. "'Violence and Precision': The Manifesto as Art Form." *Chicago Review* 34.2 (1984): 65–101.

Phaf, Ineke, ed. *Presencia Criolla en el Caribe y América Latina/Creole Presence in the Caribbean and Latin America*. Frankfurt am Main: Verveurt, 1996.

Poulantzas, Nicos. *Political Power and Social Classes*. Trans. Timothy O'Hagan. London: New Left Books, 1973.

Prado Bellei, Sergio. "Brazilian Anthropophagy Revisited." *Cannibalism and the Colonial World*. Ed. Francis Barker, Peter Hulme, and Margaret Iverson. Cambridge: Cambridge University Press, 1998. 87–109.

Pratt, Mary Louise. *Imperial Eyes: Travel Writing and Transculturation*. New York: Routledge, 1992.

——. "Yo soy la Malinche: Chicana Writers and the Poetics of Ethnonationalism;" *Callaloo* 16.4 (Fall 1993): 859–873.

Price, Richard and Sally, "Shadowboxing in the Mangrove: The Politics of Identity in Postcolonial Martinique." *Caribbean Romances: The Politics of Regional Representation*. Ed. Belinda Edmondson. Charlottesville and London: University Press of Virginia, 1999. 123–162.

Prorok, Carol. E-mail to the author. August 30, 1995.

Puri, Shalini, ed. *Marginal Migrations: The Circulation of Cultures within the Caribbean*. London: Macmillan, 2003.

——. "An 'Other' Realism: Erna Brodber's Myal." *ARIEL: A Review of International English Literature* 24.3 (July 1993): 95–116.

Quayson, Ato. "Fecundities of the Unexpected: Magical Realism, Narrative, and History." *Il Romanzo: An Encyclopedia of the Novel*. Ed. Franco Moretti, Fredric Jameson et. al. Princeton: Princeton University Press, forthcoming.

——. "Postmodernism and Postcolonialism." *A Companion to Postcolonial Studies*. Ed. Henry Schwarz and Sangeeta Ray. Oxford: Blackwell, 2000. 87–111.

——. *Postcolonialism: Theory, Practice, or Process?* Malden, Massachusetts: Polity Press, 2000.

Radhakrishnan, R. *Diasporic Mediations: Between Home and Location*. Minneapolis and London: University of Minnesota Press, 1996.

——. "Postmodernism and the Rest of the World." *The Pre-occupation of Postcolonial Studies*. Ed. Fawzia Afzal Khan and Kalpana Seshadri-Crooks. Durham and London: Duke University Press, 2000. 37–70.

Rama, Ángel. *Transculturación en América Latina*. Siglo XXI: México, D.F., 1987.

Reddock, Rhoda. "'Douglarisation' and the Politics of Gender Relations in Contemporary Trinidad and Tobago: A Preliminary Exploration." Ed. Ramesh Deosaran, Nasser Mustapha, and Rhoda Reddock. *Contemporary Sociology* 1.1 (1994): 98–127.

Rendon, Armando. *Chicano Manifesto*. New York: Macmillan, 1971.

Ricardo, Cassiano. *Marcha para Oeste v.1 and 2.* Fourth edition. Rio de Janeiro: Editora de Universidade de São Paulo and Livraria José Olympio Editora, 1970.

Rich, Adrienne. "Notes Toward a Politics of Location." *Blood, Bread, and Poetry: Selected Prose, 1979–85.* New York: Norton, 1986. 210–231.

——. "North American Tunnel Vision." *Blood, Bread, and Poetry: Selected Prose, 1979–85.* New York: Norton, 1986. 160–166.

Roach, Joseph. *Cities of the Dead: Circum-Atlantic Performance.* New York: Columbia University Press, 1996.

Robbins, Bruce. *Feeling Global: Internationalism in Distress.* New York: New York University Press, 1999.

——. "Comparative Cosmopolitanism." *Social Text* 10.2–3 (1992): 169–186.

Rodney, Walter. *How Europe Underdeveloped Africa.* Washington, D.C. Howard University Press, 1981.

Rodriguez, Ileana. "Introduction: Towards a Theory of Caribbean Unity." *Process of Unity in Caribbean Society: Ideologies and Literature.* Ed. Ileana Rodriguez and Marc Zimmerman. Minneapolis, Minnesota: Institute for the Study of Ideologies and Literatures, 1983. 13–24.

Rohlehr, Gordon. *The Shape of that Hurt and Other Essays.* Port of Spain, Trinidad: Longman Trinidad Limited, 1992.

——. *My Strangled City and Other Essays.* Port of Spain, Trinidad: Longman Trinidad, 1992.

——. *Calypso and Society in Pre-Independence Trinidad.* Port of Spain, Trinidad: Gordon Rohlehr, 1990.

——. "Images of Men and Women in the 1930's Calypsoes." *Gender in Caribbean Development.* Ed. Patricia Mohamed and Catherine Shepherd. Mona, Kingston, Jamaica: Institute of Social and Economic Research, 1991. 235–309.

Romero Barceló, Carlos. *La estadidad es para los pobres.* San Juan, PR: s.n., 1976.

Rouse, Roger. "Mexican Migration and the Social Space of Postmodernism." *Diaspora* 1.1 (Spring 1991): 8–23.

Rushdie, Salman. *Midnight's Children.* London and New York: Penguin, 1980.

Ryan, Selwyn. "Race and Occupational Stratification in Trinidad and Tobago." *Social and Occupational Stratification in Contemporary Trinidad and Tobago.* Ed. Selwyn Ryan. St. Augustine, Trinidad: Institute of Social and Economic Research, University of the West Indies, 1991. 166–190.

Ryan, Selwyn and Lou Anne Barclay. *Sharks and Sardines: Blacks in Business in Trinidad and Tobago.* St. Augustine, Trinidad: Institute of Social and Economic Research, University of the West Indies, 1992.

Salvatori, Mariolina. "Towards a Hermeneutics of Difficulty." *Audits of Meaning.* Ed. Louise Z. Smith. Portsmouth, New Hamsphire: Boynton/Cook and Heinemann, 1988. 80–95.

Sampath, Niels M. "An Evaluation of the 'Creolisation' of Trinidad East Indian Adolescent Masculinity." *Trinidad Ethnicity.* Ed. Kevin A. Yelvington. Knoxville, Tennessee: University of Tennessee Press, 1993. 235–253.

Sangari, Kumkum. *Politics of the Possible: Essays on Gender, History, Narrative, Colonial English*. New Delhi: Tulika, 1999.

San Juan Jr., E. *Beyond Postcolonial Theory*. New York: St. Martin's Press, 1998.

Sartre, Jean Paul. *Being and Nothingness: An Essay on Phenomenological Ontology*. Trans. Hazel E. Barnes. New York: Washington Square Press, 1969.

——. "Existentialism." *The Norton Reader*. Seventh edition. Ed. Arthur M. Eastman et al. New York and London: Norton, 1988. 1193–1202.

Saunders, Patricia Jane. "Nah Go Bow Down Low: Market Values, Cultural Values, and National Identity." Paper presented at the Conference on Caribbean Culture and Festival of the Word. University of the West Indies, Mona, Jamaica. January 9–12, 2002.

——. *Beyond Caliban: (Dis)Forming Identity and Being in Contemporary Anglophone Caribbean Literature*. Ph.D. Dissertation. University of Pittsburgh, 1999.

Scott, Alan, ed. *The Limits of Globalization: Cases and Arguments*. London: Routledge, 1997.

Scott, David. *Refashioning Futures: Criticism After Postcoloniality*. Princeton: Princeton University Press, 1999.

Scott, James C. *Domination and the Arts of Resistance: Hidden Transcripts*. New Haven and London: Yale University Press, 1990.

——. *Weapons of the Weak: Everyday Forms of Peasant Resistance*. New Haven: Yale University Press, 1985.

Schwarz, Roberto. *Misplaced Ideas: Essays on Brazilian Culture*. London and New York: Verso, 1992.

Sedgwick, Eve Kosofsky. "Nationalisms and Sexualities in the Age of Wilde." *Nationalisms and Sexualities*. Ed. Andrew Parker et al. New York and London: Routledge, 1992. 235–245.

Segal, Daniel A. "'Race' and 'Colour' in Pre-Independence Trinidad and Tobago." *Trinidad Ethnicity*. Ed. Kevin A. Yelvington. Knoxville, Tennessee: University of Tennessee Press, 1993. 81–115.

Shah, Raffique. *Race Relations in Trinidad: Some Aspects*. San Fernando?, Trinidad: Classline Publications for the Committee for Labour Solidarity, 1988.

Shakespeare, William. *The Tempest*. New York and London: Signet Classic, Penguin, 1987.

Sheller, Mimi. "Theoretical Piracy on the High Seas of Global Culture: Creolization in Discourses of Globalization." *Uprootings/Groundings: Questions of Home and Migration*. Ed. Sara Ahmed et. al. Oxford: Berg, forthcoming.

Shohat, Ella. "Notes on the 'Post-colonial.'" *Social Text* 10.2–3 (1992): 99–113.

Singh, Kelvin. *Bloodstained Tombs: The Muharram Massacre 1884*. London and Basingstoke: Macmillan Caribbean, 1988.

Slemon, Stephen. "Post-Colonial Critical Theories." *New National and Post-Colonial Literatures: An Introduction*. Ed. Bruce King. Oxford: Clarendon, 1996. 178–197.

Slemon, Stephen. "Magic Realism as Postcolonial Discourse." *Magical Realism: Theory, History, Community*. Ed. Lois Parkinson Zamora and Wendy B. Faris. Durham and London: Duke, 1995.

Smith, M.G. *The Plural Society in the British West Indies*. Berkeley: University of California Press, 1965.

Smith, Neil. *Uneven Development: Nature, Capital, and the Production of Space*. Oxford: Blackwell, 1990.

Soja, Edward. *Postmodern Geographies: The Reassertion of Space in Critical Social Theory*. London and New York: Verso, 1989.

Sommer, Doris. *Proceed with Caution when Engaged by Minority Writing in the Americas*. Cambridge: Harvard University Press, 1999.

——. *Foundational Fictions: The National Romances of Latin America*. Berkeley: University of California Press, 1991.

Sorenson, Ninna Nyberg. "There are no Indians in the Dominican Republic: The Cultural Construction of Dominican Identities." *Siting Cultures: The Shifting Anthropological Object*. Ed. Karen Fog Olwig and Kirsten Hastrup. London and New York: Routledge, 1997. 292–310.

Spivak, Gayatri Chakravorty. *A Critique of Postcolonial Reason: Toward a History of the Vanishing Present*. Cambridge: Harvard University Press, 1999.

——. *Outside in the Teaching Machine*. New York and London: Routledge, 1993.

——. "Can the Subaltern Speak?" *Marxism and the Interpretation of Culture*. Ed. Cary Nelson and Lawrence Grossberg. Urbana and Chicago: University of Illinois Press, 1988. 271–313.

Stalin, J.V. *Marxism and the National and Colonial Question*. London: Lawrence and Wishart, 1936.

Stallybrass, Peter and Allon White. *The Politics and Poetics of Transgression*. Ithaca, New York: Cornell University Press, 1986.

Stam, Roberto. "On the Carnivalesque." *Wedge* 1 (1982): 47–55.

Stepan, Nancy. "Biological Degeneration: Races and Proper Places." *Degeneration: The Dark Side of Progress*. Ed. J. Edward Chamberlin and Sander L. Gilman. New York: Columbia University Press, 1985. 97–120.

Stewart, John. "Ethnic Image and Ideology in Rural Trinidad." *Social and Occupational Stratification in Contemporary Trinidad and Tobago*. Ed. Selwyn Ryan. St. Augustine, Trinidad: Institute of Social and Economic Research, University of the West Indies, 1991. 149–65.

Stutzman, Ronald. "*El Mestizaje*: An All-Inclusive Ideology of Exclusion." *Cultural Transformations and Ethnicity in Modern Ecuador*. Urbana, Chicago, and London: University of Illinois Press, 1981. 45–94.

Taylor, Patrick. "Myth and Reality in Caribbean Narrative: Derek Walcott's Pantomime." *Critical Perspectives on Derek Walcott*. Ed. Robert D. Hammer. Washington DC: Three Continents Press, 1993. 292–299.

Thaiss, Gustav. "Contested Meanings and the Politics of Authenticity: The 'Hosay' in Trinidad." *Islam, Globalization and Postmodernity*. Ed. Akbar S. Ahmed and Hastings Donnan. London and New York: Routledge, 1994. 38–62.

Thomas, J.J. *Froudacity: West Indian Fables by James Anthony Froude Explained by J.J. Thomas*. London and Port of Spain: New Beacon Books, 1969.

Tiffin, Helen. "Decolonization and Audience: Erna Brodber's *Myal* and Jamaica Kincaid's *A Small Place*." *SPAN* 30 (1990). 27–38.

Tinker, Hugh. *A New System of Slavery: The Export of Indian Labour Overseas 1830–1920*. London: Hansib Publishing Ltd, 1993 [1974].

Tomlinson, John. *Cultural Imperialism: A Critical Introduction*. Baltimore: Johns Hopkins University Press, 1991.

Torabully, Khal. *Cale d'étoiles-coolitude*. Reunion: Editions Azalées, 1992.

——and Marina Carter. *Coolitude: An Anthology of the Indian Labour Diaspora*. London: Anthem Press, 2002.

Torres-Saillant, Rafael. "Creoleness or Blackness: A Dominican Dilemma." *Plantation Society in the Americas* 5.1 (Spring 1998) (Special issue on "Who/What is Creole?"): 29–40.

Trías Monge, José. *Puerto Rico: The Trials of the Oldest Colony in the World*. New Haven: Yale University Press, 1997.

Trotman, D.V. "The Image of Indians in Calypso: Trinidad 1946–1986." *Social and Occupational Stratification in Contemporary Trinidad and Tobago*. Ed. Selwyn Ryan. St. Augustine, Trinidad: Institute of Social and Economic Research, University of the West Indies, 1991. 385–398.

Trotsky, Leon. *Leon Trotsky on Black Nationalism and Self-Determination*. Ed. George Breitman. New York: Merit, 1967.

Tzara, Tristan. "Dada Manifesto." *Manifesto: A Century of Isms*. Ed. Mary Ann Caws. Lincoln and London: University of Nebraska Press, 2001. 297–304.

Vasconcelos, José. *La Raza Cósmica/The Cosmic Race: A Bilingual Edition*. Trans. Didier T. Jaén. Baltimore and London: Johns Hopkins Press, 1997.

Vega, Ana Lydia. "Encancaranublado." *Encancaranublado y Otro Cuentos de Naufragio*. Río Piédras: Editorial Antillana, 1983. 11–20.

——. "Cloud Cover Caribbean." *Her True-True Name: An Anthology of Women's Writing from the Caribbean*. Ed. Pamela Mordecai and Betty Wilson. London: Heinemann, 1990. 105–111.

Vertovec, Steven. *Hindu Trinidad: Religion, Ethnicity and Socio-Economic Change*. London: Macmillan Caribbean, 1992.

Vincent, Richard. "The Future of the Debate: Setting an Agenda for a New World Information and Communication Order, Ten Proposals." *Beyond Cultural Imperialism: Globalization, Communication, and the New International Order*. Ed. Peter Golding and Phil Harris. London: Sage, 1997. 175–207.

Walcott, Derek. "A Letter to Chamoiseau." *What the Twilight Says: Essays*. New York: Farrar, Strauss and Giroux, 1998. 213–232.

——. "The Figure of Crusoe." *Critical Perspectives on Derek Walcott*. Ed. Robert D. Hammer. Washington, DC: Three Continents Press, 1993. 33–40.

——. "The Caribbean: Culture or Mimicry." *Critical Perspectives on Derek Walcott*. Ed. Robert D. Hammer. Washington, DC: Three Continents Press, 1993. 51–57.

Walcott, Derek. *The Antilles: Fragments of Epic Memory*. New York: Farrar, Strauss and Giroux, 1992.

——. "What the Twilight Says: An Overture." *Dream on Monkey Mountain and Other Plays*. New York: Noonday Press, 1988. 4–40.

——. "Pantomime." *Remembrance and Pantomime*. New York: Farrar, Strauss and Giroux, 1980. 89–170.

——. *"The Joker of Seville" and "O Babylon!": Two Plays*. London: J. Cape, 1978.

——. "A Far Cry from Africa." *Collected Poems, 1948–1984*. New York: Noonday press, 1987. 17–18.

Walker-Johnson, Joyce. "*Myal*: Text and Context." *Journal of West Indian Literature* 5.1–2 (1992): 48–64.

Wallerstein, Immanuel. *The Modern World System*. New York: Academic Press, 1974.

Warner, Keith Q. "Ethnicity and the Contemporary Calypso." *Social and Occupational Stratification in Contemporary Trinidad and Tobago*. Ed. Selwyn Ryan. St. Augustine, Trinidad: Institute of Social and Economic Research, University of the West Indies, 1991. 275–291.

Watts, Julia. "An Interview with Raphaël Confiant." *Plantation Society in the Americas* 5.1 (Spring 1998) (Special issue on "Who/What is Creole?"): 41–59.

Watts, Richard. "The Rock of Identity: Figuring the Local and the Global in Chamoiseau and Glissant." Paper presented at the Caribbean Literary Studies Conference "Contextualing the Caribbean: Redefining Approaches in an Era of Globalization." University of Miami at Coral Gables. September 28–30, 2000.

Werbner, Pnina and Tariq Madood, eds. *Debating Cultural Hybridity: Multi-Cultural Identities and the Politics of Anti-Racism*. London and New Jersey: Zed, 1997.

West, Lois, ed. *Feminist Nationalism*. New York and London: Routledge, 1997.

Whitman, Walt. "Song of Myself." *Walt Whitman: Poetry and Prose*. Ed. Justin Kaplan. New York: The Library of America, 1982. 27–88.

Williams, Eric. *History of the People of Trinidad and Tobago*. Port of Spain, Trinidad: PNM Publishing Co., 1962.

Williams, Raymond. *Culture and Society*, 1780–1950. London: Chatto and Windus, 1958.

——. *Problems in Materialism and Culture: Selected Essays*. Verso Classics 6. London: Verso, 1997.

Wilson, Peter. *Crab Antics: The Social Anthropology of English-Speaking Negro Societies of the Caribbean*. New Haven and London: Yale University Press, 1973.

Wynter, Sylvia. "Beyond Miranda's Meanings. Un/Silencing the 'Demonic Ground' of Caliban's 'Woman.'" *Out of the Kumbla: Caribbean Women and Literature*. Ed. Carol Boyce Davies and Elaine Savory Fido. Trenton, New Jersey: Africa World Press, 1990. 355–372.

Yadav, Alok. "Nationalism and Contemporaneity: Political Economy of a Discourse." *Cultural Critique* 26 (Winter 1993–94): 191–229.

Yelvington, Kevin. *Producing Power: Ethnicity, Gender, and Class in a Caribbean Workplace.* Philadelphia: Temple University Press, 1995.

——. "Introduction." *Trinidad Ethnicity.* Ed. Kevin A. Yelvington. Knoxville, Tennessee: University of Tennessee Press, 1993. 1–32.

Yelvington, Kevin, ed. *Trinidad Ethnicity.* Knoxville, Tennessee: University of Tennessee Press, 1993.

Young, Lola. "Hybridity's Discontents: Re-reading Science and 'Race.'" *Hybridity and Its Discontents: Politics, Science, and Culture.* Ed. Avtar Brah and Annie Coombes. London and New York: Routledge, 2000. 154–170.

Young, Robert. *Colonial Desire: Hybridity in Theory, Culture, and Race.* London and New York: Routledge, 1995.

——. *White Mythologies: Writing History and the West.* London and New York: Routledge, 1990.

——. "Back to Bakhtin." *Cultural Critique* 3 (1985–86): 71–92.

Yúdice, George. "Translator's Introduction" to Néstor García-Canclini's *Consumers and Citizens: Globalization and Multicultural Conflicts.* Minneapolis: University of Minnesota Press, 2001. ix–xxxviii.

Yul-Davis, Nira. "Ethnicity, Gender Relations and Multiculturalism." *Debating Cultural Hybridity.* Ed. Pnina Werbner and Tariq Madood. Debating Cultural Hybridity: Multi-Cultural Identities and the Politics of Anti-Racism. London and New Jersey: Zed, 1997. 193–208.

Zamora, Lois Parkinson and Wendy B. Faris, eds. *Magical Realism: Theory, History, Community.* Durham and London: Duke, 1995.

Zavala, Iris and Rafael Rodriguez, eds. *The Intellectual Roots of Independence: An Anthology of Puerto Rican Political Essays.* New York and London: Monthly Review Press, 1980.

Index

12767132R00181

Made in the USA
Lexington, KY
27 December 2011